Advanced Praise for
THE HUMAN-ANIMAL CONNECTION

I have had the privilege of being a part of The Human Animal Connection's high school class, Canines Teach Compassion. I am always delighted to see how much joy the Therapy Animals bring to the students, how they help lower their stress levels, and to feel better about themselves. I heartily recommend this program and the methods described in The Human-Animal Connection book. *-Brigadier General Ken Johnson, USAF (Ret.)*

Please accept my sincere gratitude for the TREMENDOUS work you are doing through your program, Act Resilient, and its work with Therapy Animals. It is grass roots programs like this that are making the most difference in the lives of our Soldiers and their families...I applaud all that you are doing and continue to do... you are making a difference. *-General Peter Chiarelli, Vice Chief of Staff, US Army (Ret.)*

Non-human animals can reach people in ways that are deeper than ideas and thoughts. Love, authentic connection, and peaceful comfort are gifts of being sincerely present with an animal. The Human-Animal Connection methods provide a significant and profound contribution to trauma healing beyond words. *-Richard I. Ries, Psy.D., M.S.Ed. Chairperson of the Hawai'i State Council on Mental Health*

The truth is that it is humankind that needs rescuing! The Human Animal Connection is a tremendously valuable and friendly guide for learning to truly see, listen to and relate with our animal teachers. When we follow their wisdom, we receive the gift of returning home to love, wholeness, peacefulness, and joy. We remember our belonging, our true nature and can begin to heal our world. *-Dr. Patricia Billard, Psychologist, New York, NY*

Genie Joseph has captured the essence and mystique that surrounds the ability to communicate with animals, to hear their voices, and to connect to them on a deep emotional level. When I began transforming my non-profit equine rescue to being a voice for animals and to foster connections between humans and animals, I reached out to Genie and she guided me onto the path that I am on today as an advocate for animals. Genie teaches us that the animals are trying to communicate with us, we just have to be still and listen. Thank you, Genie, for being a voice for the animals and for letting us know that we have the ability to communicate with all life. *-Afton Whitmer, President, Wild Horse Haven Rescue, Safford, Arizona*

The Human-Animal Connection is a philosophy of transformation. These principles changed how I relate to my dog and gave me tools in my work with others based upon the wisdom of the senses and how we can listen to our own bodies for true guidance in our own lives. *-Peter Farrow, Somatic Experiencing Therapist, Tucson, Arizona*

As a facilitator of the Human-Animal Connection's therapy dog program, I was humbled to witness the healing powers of dogs interacting with high school students. Results showed over 50% decrease in stress levels, and a noticeable increase in social skills. I highly recommend using Dr. Joseph's approaches to therapy dog work in classrooms, as stress can have a dramatic and lasting impact on academic performance. *-Chantal Boshuizen, Psychologist, The Netherlands*

The Human-Animal Connection offers a manifesto for change that will profoundly alter our relationships with the animals in our lives.

It has the potential to revolutionize the way animals are treated in our society. *-Julie Sloane, NYU Film Professor, New York, NY*

I have always loved animals, but I have not always understood what they were thinking or feeling. This book gave me an understanding and a way to unlock the mystery. It has very much deepened my relationship with my cats. *-Matthew Gray, Entrepreneur, Honolulu, Hawaii*

Ms. Joseph's beautiful legacy is a tribute to our animals and to the animal within to teach us about ourselves. I wish animals could read, they would all say to Genie, Good girl! And thank you. *-Ginia Desmond, Film Producer, Tucson, Arizona*

The Human-Animal Connection draws parallels between the actions of other species and our own, giving us permission to view motive without judgement or reproach. It helps us view problem behaviors as the solutions they were meant to be, relief from fear or pain. This book gives us a safe way to observe, acknowledge and explore behavior. Every living thing needs choice to thrive, and this book gives you an easy map to follow. Read this book. *-Lynne Stott CPDT-KA Top Dogs Trainer, Pima Animal Care Center, Tucson, Arizona*

If you love animals…READ THIS BOOK! I've always enjoyed connection with animals, but the concepts and practical guidance found in "The Human-Animal Connection" have shown me ways of relating and depths of connection and communication with animals I never imagined possible. Using these techniques has forever changed how I relate to animals, myself, and fellow humans too. These teachings have started me on a profound journey. I can't wait to see where it takes me next! *-Nathan Bush, USAF Veteran, Boulder, Colorado*

The Human-Animal Connection by Genie Joseph is a must read in order to reconnect with the Goodness that surrounds us and that we often neglect to see or feel. Once you open your mind and your heart to see our interconnectedness with animals, you no longer can act without compassion and love. -*Marie Selarque, CPDT-KA Dog Trainer, Honolulu, Hawaii*

What Dr. Joseph has done here is to take concepts that until now were either intuitive or theoretical, and made them *practical*. Her ideas, approaches, techniques, and methods for interacting with and relating to our animal friends will benefit everyone who values those relationships. -*Curt Cressler, Screenwriter, Los Angeles, California*

A blessed book that can help us move beyond the boundaries of humancentric thinking to a truer self-understanding, as creatures living in mutuality with all life. -*Cesar Bujosa, Minister, Milford, Pennsylvania*

In reading about these 33 Principles, I am intrigued by Genie's work and research. I especially enjoyed the "Inner Compass to your True North", having had many like experiences. Also, the message that you can't fool animals, I know to be true of horses! They generally understand our emotional state better than we do! I enjoyed hearing and seeing Genie communicate with our horses, and look forward to further collaboration! -*Jeanie Shepherd, Horse Trainer, EASE Facilitator Equanimity Ranch, Tucson, Arizona*

I hope more veterans will be able to participate in The Human-Animal Connection's Therapy dog program. It is as healing for me as it is for the kids in the classroom. It inspires me to imagine a more peaceful world – for people and animals – based on better understanding and clearer communication. We owe it to animals to respect their unique wisdom. *-Sergeant Jim Filipiak, Vietnam Veteran, Tucson, Arizona*

After working with Genie with my beloved Oso for the last year, she has taught me the importance of recognizing we are in relationship with our animals, and on a journey of mutual learning that will last a lifetime. I have fundamentally changed how I view, appreciate, interact with, and love my animals. I value the wisdom I now get from my animals more than ever. Genie's 33 Principles are a practical guide to help us gain the insights and perspective necessary to incorporate a deeper human-animal connection into our daily lives, which helps us love, learn, and heal throughout life. *-Sara Shorin, Medical Advocate, Tahoe, Nevada*

Genie Joseph has written a comprehensive book on The Human-Animal Connection that goes far beyond most books to consider all the ways that we can create remarkable relationships with our animals. If you are an animal lover you will appreciate the care and love that she shares in her process to describe ways to effectively heal trauma, anxiety and stress in both humans and animals. She shows what resilience can look like for everyone including the animals and special groups like veterans, active-duty military, children and teens in a practical and understandable way. Her strong message is that "animals bring unconditional love and comfort in a way that is beyond words. *-Dr. Mitzi Gold, Psychologist, Honolulu, Hawaii*

The Human-Animal Connection presents a pathway to a more equitable, enlightened, and loving partnership with animals. Before this book, I had no idea how to communicate with my cat. Now I am learning to communicate with animals to improve the quality of their lives and ours. *-Jean Parker, Educator, Tucson, Arizona*

The Human-Animal Connection's program for active-duty service members, *Morale Dogs* and the veteran program *Heroes4Animals* provide a highly effective healing pathway for people experiencing high-stress and trauma. Animals provide comfort, relief, and a sense of connection to the good feelings that can jump start positive morale, readiness, and well-being. *-Lt. Colonel Dana Allmond, RET. US Army*

As one of our first public practitioners of the Trust Technique in the USA, Genie Joseph has a wide range of skills, one of which is her ability to write and share education with the many, via the platform of the written word. We congratulate Genie on the launch of her new book- The Human-Animal Connection. As the Trust Technique is for both humans and animals with its unique skill of identifying and reducing the shared feelings of stress between them as well as increasing the potential for peace. Genie's book is a wonderful intro-duction to the human/animal relationship. *-James French The Trust Technique - England*

Dr. Joseph does a great job highlighting the emotional, psycholog-ical, and physical effects animals can have on our lives. By creating a safe environment, people and animals can begin establishing a relationship based on trust that allows them to live more present, happier, and more fruitful lives. Fantastic insight! *-Blake Hardin, DVM, MPH, MBA*

THE
HUMAN-ANIMAL
CONNECTION

DEEPENING RELATIONSHIPS
WITH ANIMALS AND OURSELVES

Genie Joseph, Ph.D.

THE HUMAN-ANIMAL CONNECTION:
DEEPENING RELATIONSHIPS WITH ANIMALS AND OURSELVES
Published by SPIRIT ANIMAL PRESS
Tucson, Arizona, U.S.A.

Library of Congress Control Number: 2022903581
JOSEPH, GENIE, Author
THE HUMAN-ANIMAL CONNECTION
GENIE JOSEPH, Ph.D.

ISBN: 979-8-9858026-2-7 (hardcover)
ISBN: 979-8-9858026-0-3, 979-8-9858026-3-4 (paperback)
ISBN: 979-8-9858026-1-0 (digital)

BODY, MIND & SPIRIT / Healing / Energy
PSYCHOLOGY / Animal & Comparative Psychology
MEDICAL / Mind-Body Medicine

Editor: Bonnie McDermid (Wordsmith.ink)
Book Design: Chris O'Byrne (JetLaunch.net)
Publishing Coach: Susie Schaefer (FinishTheBookPublishing.com)
Cover & Interior Illustrations: Elisabeth Geel (ElisabethGeel.com)
Author Photo: Molly Condit (GBearMedia.com)

QUANTITY PURCHASES: Schools, companies, professional groups, clubs, and other organizations may qualify for special terms when ordering quantities of this title. For information, email SpiritAnimalPress@gmail.com.

Dedication

*This book is dedicated to everyone
who has loved an animal and been loved in return.*

DISCLAIMER

While this book offers many natural and complementary approaches to improving the well-being of animals, we are not suggesting that all issues can be solved by our methods. Many behavioral issues in animals have an underlying physical imbalance or cause. This book does not give medical or veterinary advice and is not a replacement for professional advice or treatment. Responsible animal stewardship/ownership must include consultation with veterinary professionals.

CONTENTS

Part Two:
WHAT ANIMALS CAN TEACH US
ABOUT BEING A HAPPIER HUMAN

Part Three:
THE SPIRITUAL CONNECTION –
HOW HUMANS CAN BE OF SERVICE TO ANIMALS

Other books by Genie Joseph, Ph.D.

The Act Resilient Method
From Trauma to Transformation
A Seriously Playful Approach to Healing

Love Hawaii Time
(a novel)

INTRODUCTION

This is a book about relationships: relationships between humans and animals. It was written for people who love animals and seek to go deeper in their communication and connection with the animal world. All relationships benefit from greater understanding and purer, more authentic communication—including the relationship with the animals who share our lives. Being more peaceful, balanced, and empathic with animals changes who we are. And just as importantly, it changes the potential for how we relate to other humans.

We know that animals communicate. While the full extent of HOW they communicate may not be fully understood, the body of evidence supporting how rich and deeply emotional their communication is grows by the day. Thus, we can no longer deny that animals *do communicate*. They teach, learn, remember, make complex choices, are capable of empathy, and have a sense of self and other. Animals are communicating all the time, but it is up to us to listen. Listening helps us connect in deeper ways and opens the door to a more loving and profound relationship. Animals have much to teach us—if we are willing to accept their wisdom. And not only can they help heal us, but by truly understanding them, we can be of service and begin to repay humanity's debt to animals.

We are living in a time of tremendous breakthroughs in the scientific understanding of animal cognition and intelligence. Animals can no longer be viewed through unenlightened prejudice as if they are simple, mechanistic automatons powered only by instinctual responses. They have minds—emotions, thoughts, and desires—and they have strategies for solving problems. They laugh, they play, and they bond deeply. It is exciting how many scientists, who are on the vanguard of animal studies, are willing to explore the rich inner lives of animals, including a few who dare to contemplate the question of animal consciousness. Now is the time to embrace what unites us with the entire animal kingdom, as, after all, *we are all animals!*

Learning to communicate even more deeply with animals will expand your world in delightful ways. I am thrilled that you are ready to take the next step on your healing journey, and I wish you all the wild joy of a deeper connection with all living beings.

Genie

HOW TO USE THIS BOOK

This book explores the thirty-three principles of our method, The Human-Animal Connection (HAC). The potential for personal and spiritual growth as we engage deeply with our companion animals who share our lives is thrilling, but it does take patience. Our method explores the importance of human learning (we need lots of training!) to enable us to cross the invisible communication bridge between all the other animals and us. In the HAC, we believe that animals are communicating all the time, and we can learn to connect in deeper ways, which opens the door to a more loving and profound relationship.

This book was originally conceived as a companion guide for participants in The Human-Animal Connection classes and workshops. But it has grown to be a book for everyone who loves animals and wants to explore the adventure of connection. For those working on their own, each principle has journal questions. In the appendix at the end of the book you will find practice exercises to deepen your experience. You can also find many resources and blogs on our website, TheHumanAnimalConnection.org.

The thirty-three principles serve as a progressive guide on your journey to a deeper connection with animals. There is a lot here, so naturally you want to move through the lessons in this book at a pace that is right for you.

In this book, when I am talking about the animals who share your lives, I often use the word "dog," but just about everything I say also applies to cats, horses, llamas, pigs, goats, donkeys, birds, and so on. However, if I kept listing each species, the language would be too cumbersome, so please translate for the type of animal you are working with. Thank you for allowing me to use "dog" as the stand-in and ambassador for all animals who share their lives with humans.

If you are someone who enjoys journaling about your experiences, you may want to have an Animal Connection Journal for your study notes. Choose one or two questions to focus on for each principle. It is lovely to get a study buddy and explore these principles together.

I have strong ideas and opinions. Please consider this book a "thought buffet." Take what you want and leave what you don't. But at least please taste the offerings I present. These techniques have worked for over a thousand animals, even those in zoos and with animals who would not have made it out of the shelter or who would have ended up back at the shelter as owner surrenders. We invite and welcome you to share your experiences on our social media or website, TheHumanAnimalConnection.org

Knowing more about the minds and emotions of other animals may help us to do a better job of sharing the earth with our fellow creatures and may even open our minds to new ways of perceiving and thinking about our world.

Virginia Morell

HUMAN-ANIMAL
C O N N E C T I O N

PART ONE

How to Be a Better Human for Your Animal

Overview

We love our animals. But we don't always understand them or their needs. So-called "bad" behavior is often an animal's misguided attempt to feel safe and connected, but it often produces the opposite result.

In Part One of *The Human-Animal Connection*, we explore several ways we humans can connect to our animal nature in order to better understand what their behavior is trying to communicate to us. One important way we do this is by "coming to our senses." This is how we can open up the world of communication between us and our wise friends in the animal kingdom.

Compassion for animals is intimately associated with goodness of character, and it may be confidently asserted that he who is cruel to animals, cannot be a good man.

Arthur Schopenhauer

OSCAR'S STORY

There is a saying, "Saving one dog will not change the world, but for that one dog, the world will change forever." Oscar was that one dog. When I adopted him, he had been at the shelter in Hawaii a very long time. He had that slow, sad-sweetness I just found irresistible. I didn't care that he was missing teeth, that he had scars all over his brown body, or that he was mostly pit bull. I was told he had been forced to be a pig hunter and had escaped with his expensive GPS collar and was never claimed by his cruel owners.

When I first brought him home, all you had to do was reach for something and watch him cower to imagine what he had endured. But Oscar was pure love. He taught me that we do not need to be ruled by our past; we are who we choose to be in each new moment.

Oscar and I learned to become a therapy dog team, and we made regular visits to Tripler Army Medical Center in Honolulu. One day, Oscar stopped outside the door of a room of a wounded young man, letting me know this was someone he wanted to meet. We went inside and sat next to Hector, whose head was covered in bandages. Oscar didn't care. He nuzzled his bandaged hand. Hector gave a crooked smile and a croaky laugh as Oscar settled his old bones ever so gently next to Hector. Oscar looked him in the eye as Hector whispered a long story in Oscar's scarred ear. I didn't try to listen; I knew the story wasn't for me.

At the end, Hector sighed peacefully, and Oscar replied with his own breathy sound. When we finally left the room, the nurse had a stunned expression on her face. "Hector never talks," she said. "We thought he had lost his voice." And I was reminded that one dog, one visit, one whisper at a time might not change the world, but it can make the world a place I want to live in.

Oscar—my first rescue therapy dog. He had so much love to give he changed the course of my destiny.

Principle #1

GOOD MEDICINE
What Animals Can Teach Us about Goodness

Animals are born who they are, accept it, and that is that.
They live with greater peace than people do.

Gregory Maguire

Overview

The Human-Animal Connection Philosophy

The Human-Animal Connection is both a philosophy and a method for relating to animals through a deeper and more authentic communication. We begin with the premise that there is an innate connection between people and animals. This connection allows us to communicate with animals, and if we are listening, they will communicate with us. For those who wish to experience this awareness more deeply, there are systematic methods for strengthening, clarifying, and expanding this connection.

It all starts with building on and focusing your attention on the quality of *good.*

The Force of Goodness

If you have shared your life with a dog, I am sure you have looked him or her in the eyes and said in your sweetest voice, "Good doggie!" Maybe the sentiment was returned with a tail wag, a soft look, a cuddle, or some other sign that your message was received.

When you invoke the words "Good doggie" (or any animal) and really feel the truth of it, it deepens your connection. In addition, this appreciative communication is good medicine for the dog *and for you — because when you say it, you feel the goodness too*. What if goodness was not just an abstract idea? What if it was a tangible experience, a force, like gravity? The experience of shared goodness is a healing force. Immersing yourself in this experience of goodness is what I call "Good Medicine." It allows the healing power of connecting to goodness to work its way through your entire life.

Your Goodness Tank

Metaphorically speaking, you have a *Goodness Tank* inside you that you can refill with positive thoughts, words, experiences, and actions. For example, every time you pet your animal in a loving way, you are raising the goodness level between you. Another way to fill your goodness tank is by saying the words "Good doggie" (or good kitty, or good birdie, or good piggie, or good horsie) to the being who shares your life. The higher the level in your goodness tank, the more optimistic, capable, compassionate, and loving you'll feel.

"Good doggie" is the equivalent of saying the words "I love you," as they both activate happy brain chemistry. If there is a human in your life to whom you say "I love you" frequently, that is terrific. But for those who don't or have lost the habit of saying *I love you* on a regular basis, no worries. This is where animals can be our partners. They can help us experience the goodness of life.

Dogs and other animals enjoy your ongoing recognition and expression of their goodness. They see it in your eyes and hear it in your soft loving voice. When you express your love to them, it helps them feel good. I am not sure they *need* acknowledgment—animals don't doubt their self-worth as much as humans do—but animals clearly benefit from feeling they are pleasing you. Even cats (who usually have a very secure sense of self) enjoy seeing you find pleasure in their presence.

When I say, "Good doggie!" to my Sophia, her ears perk up, her mouth softens, and she wags her tail. At times, I simply notice her across the room, or if she just looks over at me, I take this as a *good* invitation. We make eye contact, and I take a moment to acknowledge her goodness. Moments like this add a little dose of sweetness to our day.

I can even look at Sophia and just think the words, *Good doggie,* and her mouth softens in a "smile." Even though I haven't said the words out loud she receives my nonverbal communication. Perhaps the memory of the spoken words reverberates in her mind. Since we do this often, she understands my intention. It is very delicious to share this silent connection.

The Neuroscience of Goodness

Saying words that elicit *a sense of goodness* affects your brain, igniting happy feelings. These happy feelings translate to those around you, which science calls "emotional contagion." This means that the feelings of one person can transfer to another, which is true for both positive and negative emotions.

Neuroscience and brain scans demonstrate that specific areas of the brain "light up" when certain positive feelings are felt. Our dominant emotions affect our brain chemistry, such as the feel-good hormone oxytocin, one of the biological markers of bonding. Oxytocin is released when we feel a loving connection. For example, oxytocin is triggered when women are breastfeeding. Research on the positive impacts of interactions with animals shows increased oxytocin, dopamine, and serotonin levels in both the person and the animal. It is even triggered by simply petting or engaging with an animal, which is just one reason why animal therapy is so effective and why it is one of the antidotes to feeling lonely.

Words can trigger positive or negative feelings, so what you say matters. Your words reflect how you feel and affect the chemical messages you are giving your brain. The animal who shares their life with you feels your moods, so it makes sense to say words that trigger good feelings. Of course, faking it by saying "I love you" when you don't mean it doesn't fool an animal who can tell the difference.

Ask any person trained in natural horsemanship methods, and they will confirm that you can't lie to a horse. If you are tense, anxious, or fearful, false statements to the contrary will not convince a horse. You cannot pretend you are in control if you are not. The horse will see your true emotional colors even if you don't recognize them. This is just one of the reasons why interacting with horses and other animals is so authentic and satisfying. We've all had enough frustration from humans' confusing mixed messages and are hungry for authentic encounters!

As veterinarian Linda Bender says in her book, *Animal Wisdom – Learning from the Spiritual Lives of Animals*, "When we love animals and form close bonds with them, some of their happiness rubs off on us. To watch them enjoying their lives makes us smile. Their good moods are infectious. Their affection for us has the power to reach the place in us that feels unworthy of being loved, and in feeling how they love us, we can feel how God loves us too."

Love at the Shelter

If you are looking for love, look no further than your local animal rescue or shelter. I am so happy I adopted Sophia from the shelter. If you are not in a position to share your life with a dog or another animal, please consider volunteering at a shelter or rescue or fostering an animal to help them get ready for adoption.

I volunteer at several shelters and enjoy lifting spirits in small but important ways. For example, I have a system for when I walk up and down the line of kennels that house anxious, confused, scared, and waiting dogs—who are barking their heads off! First, I take a moment to get peaceful and send them good vibes which begins to quiet things down. Then I give each one a treat, make eye contact, and tell them he or she is a good doggie. As I do this, I can see the dog soften and drop the edge of worry and distrust that is understandable in that unnatural and scary environment. What I find is that as I make my way down a line of frantic or defeated dogs, even the ones I haven't visited yet have begun to settle down almost as soon as I start. Shortly, the whole line is quiet. They respond to the shift in energy and a gentle presence in their midst. This shift to calmness all the way down the line of kennels tells me that the message I am sending has been received. That's how I know it is good for them, but honestly, *it feels pretty good to me too.* It always lifts my spirits to remind them they are not forgotten.

Resisting the Good

Why do some people resist feeling good? Even though good *feels good*, the exercise of saying "Good (and adding their own name)" is challenging for some. Feeling *bad* can be so familiar it becomes oddly comfortable, because at least it is predictable! And that can become a *bad* habit. Preparing for bad makes the world appear to be more predictable because uncertainty is hard. So, we try to compensate by grasping for a sense of safety through predictability – through assuming the worst -- to simulate a sense of control. But it does the reverse and leads to feeling powerless. Both humans and animals can resign themselves to feeling powerless, but it doesn't have to be this way. Helping a scared or traumatized animal to reorient their experience by coming more fully into the present moment is very healing. The way we shift an animal's awareness is by getting them to use their physical senses to bring them back to present time.

The facts of life are that there will be times when the dog with whom you share your life will do things you don't like. They will poop in the wrong place. They will bark when you don't want them to. They will devour something that you are attached to.

These are the times when we're tempted to call the dog *bad*. But these are behavioral issues, *bad doings,* not bad *beings.* While the behavior is not what you desire and is wrong in your eyes, it is important to separate the behavior from the being. This is not a *bad dog*! This is *bad behavior.*

At the same time, you do not have to live with bad behavior. Animals can be retrained through reeducation using gentle methods of redirecting, clear communication, and rewarding the behavior you want. Most behavior is changeable. You can learn how to correct and redirect your dog toward what you want by using methods that are not punishing or fear-creating. Fear-based aversive behavior correction methods have a very high cost because they undermine the bond between the two of you.

Good and Un-Good

Once we stop viewing animals as either good or bad, we can apply that same approach to ourselves. We all have parts of ourselves that we might rate as good and other parts that we label un-good (otherwise known as "bad"). We have aspects of ourselves we are proud of and admire, and other parts we feel ashamed of, and wish would go away. This is part of the human condition. Viewing this dichotomy through the lens of *separating behavior from beingness* is important for healing. To embrace (without self-condemnation) both your light side as well as *your shadow side* is the path to compassion and freedom. This is as true for you as it is for your animals.

There will be times when you have un-good or "bad" behavior—you may fail to take action, or you may take the wrong action, or you may not communicate effectively, or you may seek comfort in destructive ways. I am not suggesting that you ignore these flaws or pretend they are desirable. These actions (or inactions) could be considered *bad human doings,* but they do not mean you are an *un-good human being.*

You Are Good

The good news is that you don't have to *get to good.* Goodness is not something that must be acquired or arrived at; it is something you already have within. *You are good.* The only thing you need to do is *accept* your own goodness while simultaneously accepting your *un*-good aspects. When you realize that some un-good behavior doesn't negate an innate goodness, it is easier to accept the mix of goodness and un-good actions in animals and other people. Animals help us to accept that un-good moments of behavior do not negate their goodness, and this is perfect training to accept the same in ourselves.

When I am speaking of good here, I do not mean good in a moralistic or judgmental opinion of, say, good vs. evil. For me, good is the overarching animating life force, and it is the fuel for optimism. I am referring to the innate quality of good-ness, which transcends behavior. There is an essential goodness within you and the animals who share your life.

All Behavior Is an Attempt to Feel Connected and Safe

In The Human-Animal Connection (the HAC) we are always reminding ourselves that all behavior is an attempt to get something desired or to avoid something unwanted. Most animal behavior is done to connect them to whom or what they want. Or to separate them from something they perceive as negative or scary, to help them to feel safe.

Taking this perspective on behavior shifts the paradigm from judging ourselves and others through the lens of good and bad judgment. It is just too easy to label animals (and people) as bad, which creates excess stress, conflict, and judgment. But after teaching animals and humans for twenty years, I know we can reverse even lifelong *ungood habits*. It takes time and practice to reverse them, but that's okay. It takes patience to train a dog. And even more to train a human.

Over the years at The Human-Animal Connection, we have found that troublesome behavior in pets often has a corresponding reflection in their human's emotions. For example, a human who has trouble establishing healthy boundaries with people may see that same dynamic with the animal who shares their life and doesn't respect people's boundaries. These reflecting issues are usually unconscious, but as soon as the person sees them clearly, it is the first step to helping the animal change. In this way, the animal may become a source of truth for you, as he or she may be expressing what you are not seeing in your own heart.

Your personal growth accelerates when you embrace the idea that *behavior is just choices and actions.* Behavior is changeable, whereas goodness is fundamental, enduring, and essential.

The Good Doggie Practice

To expand the experience of goodness in your life, I invite you to embrace a goodness training meditation every day. To begin, get yourself calm and peaceful. Get present, which means to gather yourself and pay attention to just this moment. Choose to allow yourself to experience goodness as a visceral experience from head to toe.

Then, say the words (aloud or silently in your mind) "*Good doggie*" or "Good (use your own name)." Think of these words as spiritual medicine that flows through you and fills all the holes inside. Hold your focus on this good feeling as you repeat the words. Aim to sustain the sensation of goodness for ten to fifteen seconds. Let the sensation of goodness linger and wash over you like luxuriating in a warm shower of positive energy. Feel how it connects you and the animal you are communicating with.

Compare the way you feel after doing this exercise with the way you were feeling before saying the words. This practice gives your mind a shower of good hormones. So, say *Good doggie!* every day to elicit connection to our own good feelings. These words, said in a happy tone, get those tails wagging. And when we really mean it, *we feel better!*

After you feel comfortable working with the words "Good doggie" and Good (add your name)," you can do this as a walking meditation as you go about your day.

Filling Your Goodness Tank

If you practice this deliberate awareness of goodness every day, it will replenish your goodness reserves, which makes you more resilient and patient. This will begin to dissolve some of your self-judgments and chronic self-criticism and replace them with warmer, kinder feelings toward yourself. In our HAC high school class, *Canines Teach Compassion*, we find that many teens have an underlying feeling of being "bad" in some way they can't even define, but it surrounds them and everything they do like a dark cloud. Teaching them this goodness practice lifts this heavy curtain, and many behaviors improve.

We're all human. This means, like everybody else, we've got some good, some un-good, and some ugly behaviors. As Andy Rooney joked, "The average dog is a nicer person than the average person." That is why separating your choices and actions (your behaviors) from your innate goodness is beneficial. If you practice this Good Doggie/Good Person exercise on a regular basis it's like giving yourself a daily dose of vitamin G for goodness.

Our sense of goodness is an inner resource we were born with but diminishes as the events of our lives rob us of this awareness. Doing this awareness of goodness exercise regularly will fill your Goodness Tank creating an overflow that will cascade into other areas of your life and into the lives of the animals who share your world.

What Gets Your Tail Wagging?

When you say, "Good doggie," and it gets his or her tail wagging, doesn't it give you the same feeling? Think about what gets your tail wagging (if you had one). What gives you that same feeling of *happy all over*? What activities, thoughts, and words give you a feeling of wiggle-waggle-thump-thump?! Whatever that is, do more of it. These *good* activities will help remind you that you are a good person because you are!

Can you imagine a world where we silently recognized the goodness in all beings? What if instead of judging strangers, we acknowledged each other with the thought, "Good human!"

Journal Reflections on Goodness:

1) What gets your tail wagging? Could you do more of that each day?

2) How full (or empty) is your Goodness Tank?

3) What are three things (events/people/emotions) that cause your Goodness Tank to leak? And what are three things that cause your Goodness Tank to fill back up?

4) How do you feel about saying "Good (your name)" to yourself every day?

5) Are you ready to have more goodness in your life? If so, what would that look like?

Re-Minder: I am good.

Sophia, my rescue therapy dog, shares a sense of goodness wherever she goes.

Principle #2

CONNECTING TO YOUR ANIMAL NATURE
We Are All Animals

Everything in nature invites us constantly to be what we are.

Gretel Ehrlich

Overview

Somewhere along the line, we bought into the idea that, as humans, we were separate from and superior to all other animals. This was a huge fall from grace and from the truth, as we are all animals. Even worse, it resulted in us terribly mistreating animals. They were thought to be only acting on instinct, needing to be mastered, and at our service as beasts of burden. In addition to the horrific results this had for animals, it caused us to lose our connection with our own animal nature—our essential animality.

What Strongheart Knew

Animals have excellent instincts about whom to trust. Within seconds, they sense whether a stranger is friend or foe. J. Allen Boone talks about the time he took Strongheart, the German shepherd movie star, to an attorney's office. The dog was fine meeting the attorneys for the first time, but the clients with whom they were also meeting had been accused of some horrible crimes. Strongheart lunged at the criminals and barked ferociously. Someone watching this sudden wild outburst who didn't know Strongheart might have labeled him a "bad dog." It frightened the men who were on the receiving end of this display! But Boone knew how smart and accurate this dog's instincts were. These men were not innocent, as they had claimed. Boone had to leave immediately to calm the dog down, but he and the attorneys who knew him trusted Strongheart's animal instincts.

Welcome to Your Animality

*One benefit of accepting our animal
nature is that we feel more alive.*

In The Human-Animal Connection, I invite people to connect to their animality, their essential *animal-ness*. This is their truest, most authentic self. How do you feel about your animal nature? How do you define it? Are you comfortable with my statement that we are all animals? Do you celebrate your animal nature and all the gifts and skills that being connected to this aspect of yourself brings, such as being comfortable in your own skin, trusting your gut sense, and feeling like you belong? Or do you feel like your animal nature is something you need to control?

When I am talking about your animal nature, I am speaking not only of the so-called "primitive" instincts but also of your accurate intuition, your gut sense. And most importantly, your animal nature is your sensory world -- what you see, hear, feel, touch, taste, and smell, as well as what you perceive and know.

Connecting to your animality allows you to trust your visceral instincts, which fine tunes your intuition. It is the part of you that has a greater awareness of and connection to your environment. This sense of being at home in your own body is what helps you accurately sense the intentions of those around you.

Your animality helps you to feel grounded in your body and, at the same time, very aware of the space extending out from your body, also known as your energy field or aura. Science can now measure this bioelectromagnetic field. There is evidence for a field of energy that extends around every living thing. The healthier and more centered the being, the larger and stronger the field of energy or bio-field.

Animals use their connection to their energy fields to navigate their world. They can sense when something enters their field. They are in tune with their proprioceptive senses. Proprioceptive senses include the sense of position and movement of their body as well as the sense of force or heaviness and other details that helps them precisely orient to the world around them. Animals' excellent spatial awareness is one reason their reaction time is faster than humans' because their awareness extends far into the living bio-field around them. For example, a horse can instantly feel a fly settle on their back, even though it weighs 50 million times less.

Your animality, or animal nature, also includes your nurturing nature, your protective abilities and instincts, and your empathy and compassion. We will talk more in later chapters about the level of empathy animals have and how we humans can take a lesson from their kindness playbook. We also talk about the sociability of animals and their sense of connection. Animals literally sense their herd and can feel the emotions of those around them. This connection creates an experience of unity for which they are often willing to let go of minor squabbles in favor of the group harmony because this is the best way to ensure survival for social animals.

Richard Louv, author of over ten books, including *Last Child in the Woods*, talks about "nature-deficit disorder," which is his analogy for the cost of alienation from nature for both children and adults, which can lead to attention difficulties, diminished use of the senses, and a host of other mental and physical issues.

These are just some of my starting ideas about different aspects of our animal nature. What is your personal definition of your animality? I find it interesting to hear how people view their animal nature. Some see it as their more refined sensory nature. Others assume it is their lower nature, the worst part of themselves. I encourage you to do your own process of discovery.

In our Human-Animal Connection classes, some people are nervous at first about exploring their animal nature. In one class on a military base, students called out word associations for animal nature while I wrote them on the whiteboard. Words like bloodthirsty, ruthless, ravenous, aggressive, territorial, dominating, predatory, sexual maniacs all made the list. As we looked at our word list, one quiet airman observed, "That sounds more like a description of human civilization."

We have doomed the wolf not for what it is,
but for what we deliberately and mistakenly perceive it to be —
the mythologized epitome of a savage, ruthless killer —
which is, in reality, no more than a reflected image of ourself.

Farley Mowat

Nature Is Not All Rainbows, Roses, and Unicorns

Obviously, there is much brutality and killing in nature, generally for survival. Many species of animals kill for food for themselves or their families. Other species are territorial and will fight to protect resources. But in addition to food and survival needs, there are numerous examples of cruelty and dominance, such as bachelor gangs of parrots, chimpanzees, and penguins in South Africa who have been known to act like thugs at times. As Jane Goodall said in a *New York Times* interview, the chimpanzees she studied in Tanzania were capable of great acts of kindness, but she also observed occasional acts of violence and aggression. "Their behavior can be seen as cruel. But my definition of evil, it's when you can plan attacks on those who aren't there and then carry them out in cold blood. Chimps don't plan like that. They act on the spur of the moment. They're very territorial and dominance-oriented, but maybe because they haven't got language, they can't be evil."

Karl Berg, who has been studying wild parrotlet communities in Venezuela for more than a decade, has discovered evidence of these lovely little birds doing some very nasty things. As Virginia Morell reports on his work, parrotlet behaviors include "wife beating, infidelity, trickery and divorce, nesting box theft, murder and even infanticide."

You Are an Animal

Given that life in the wild isn't all cute and cuddly, can you accept the primitive forces living inside yourself? Embracing our animal nature is not as simple as the words *good* or *bad* might presume. A deeper understanding is needed to find the balance between the conflicting aspects within us. Then we can choose to tilt ourselves toward balance and harmony.

The great thing about being human is we can make choices about how we behave. We can choose the high road or the low road. We can face the allure of our "low" impulses and still choose a "higher" or more harmonious action. Accepting both our human and animal natures leads to more compassion and a more authentic sense of self.

Go Ahead—*Howl!*

One of our favorite workshops in the Human-Animal Connection is called Healing with Horses. In this class, we teach the humans how to dive into their animal senses to be able to share calmness with rescue horses, benefiting both. One of the horse rescue sanctuaries I worked with had some wide-open space, and there was plenty of sky to enjoy. We would do some full moon howling (the people, I mean) in the large corral. For some students the first time trying this —leaning their heads back, opening their mouths, and letting out howls—was a big stretch. But by the third howl, feeling the support of the group, it became a very freeing, joyous experience. Everyone looked forward to howling nights.

Accessing her primal senses was life-changing for one soft-spoken woman who attended our Saturday night howl. She told us she was having a very difficult time standing up to her coworkers. When she went back to work on Monday, she discovered that after claiming her freedom of expression through howling, she now had the voice to speak up in a department meeting for the first time. It silenced everyone. "My boss actually said he liked my ideas," she reported back at our next meeting. "It was a glorious sensation to feel heard by them." It is amazing how fast we can connect with our natural selves if we will just get out of our way.

Your Inner Compass Is Your True North

Your animal nature can help you tune your senses so that you can feel your True North, which is like having an inner compass. This is what helps you know what is best for you by connecting to your intuition, your gut sense, and to your natural "higher senses." These lead to hunches, or *immediate knowing,* which may not be logically explainable, but if you pay attention, it can lead you away from negative experiences and, in some cases, can be lifesaving. I call this awareness of the intuitive guidance of what is true and good for us our *Connection to our True North.*

Your *True North* inner compass, helps you make the best decisions, large or small. Maybe you get a sense to take a different route home and later learn that you avoided an accident. Or you sense a plan someone proposes is not going to lead to success. Perhaps you sense that someone you meet does not have your best interests at heart. By being connected to your animal nature and your animal senses, you will naturally be connected to your *True North,* allowing you to steer your life with greater ease and avoid unnecessary suffering. Imagine how your life would be if you routinely pay attention to your spiritual GPS, your TNGS—your True North Guidance System.

William J. Long, writer, naturalist, and minister, told a story about getting lost in the wilderness. After Long had exhausted all his methods to find the correct direction, he finally realized he was lost and turned the navigation over to Simmo, his Native American companion. It was Simmo who found their way in the dark and led them to safety. When Long asked him how he did it, Simmo replied, "When I was goin' right, I feel good; but when I was goin' wrong, I felt uneasy."

Connecting to your animal nature
helps you feel what is good for you.

We encourage our HAC students to learn to identify this sense of connecting to goodness in their own bodies and to recognize that sensation, just as Simmo used his senses to feel how going the right way felt good and going the wrong way felt uneasy. Your True North and gut sense may be a very subtle sensation at first, but the more you commit to listening to your body, the stronger this sense becomes.

Animals know so much more than we give them credit for because they are connected to their environment, to others, and to many levels of information we can only imagine. Thus, we can learn from them how we can access what Ruppert Sheldrake called the "unified morphogenic field," which is the spiritual dimension where all is known. Getting connected on a deeper level with animals is one way to help you connect to your own radar, your sense of truth. Tuning your senses to the animals' channel of awareness is one way to help you find your way.

Your Connection to Your True North

The veery bird is small enough to fit in the palm of your hand. One field researcher, an ornithologist named Christopher Heckscher, made a fascinating discovery about them. Veery birds' behaviors predicted the intensity of the coming season's hurricanes. How did he discover this? He observed that veery birds have very specific timing during their short lives; there is a season for mating, breeding, and migration. But some years, they adjust the timing of this entire cycle by beginning the entire sequence earlier. Heckscher, who published his two-decade study in *Scientific Reports*, discovered that this change to the timing by all the veery birds forecasted a severe hurricane season that year. In fact, veery birds were more accurate than the weather scientists in predicting the severity of the coming hurricane season. By carefully observing these birds, many human lives could be saved.

How do veery birds know about events that are several months in the future? Scientists don't have all the answers yet, but Heckscher's work proves that it would be wise to pay attention.

What we do know about veery birds and other animals is that they are connected with nature in a way we do not yet understand.

For example, veery birds have the ability to receive information as a species. This "group-knowing" or instant shared knowing allows them all to adjust their instinctual behaviors for their survival.

We see similar predictive behaviors in both domestic and wild animals. Many stories have been told of dogs running away from home just before an earthquake and wild animals who suddenly bolt for higher ground before a tsunami lands. Even though we don't yet understand how animals all get the message from nature, by paying attention to their animal wisdom and behavior, we will be wiser and safer ourselves.

In one of my favorite books, *How Animals Talk* by William J. Long, the author and naturalist observed many species giving signs that they were aware of upcoming weather events and earthquakes, such as a group of deer kneeling just before an earthquake tremor. Because he carefully watched the subtle behavior changes of birds, chickens, elk, deer, and others, he became aware that significant weather changes and geological shifts were on their way.

Long proposes that this awareness goes beyond the five senses. He says, "Such sensitiveness is not (the result) of any one organ, but rather of the whole body." He used the word "chumfo" to express what I might describe as *full-body perception,* a concept he learned from an African tribe living near Lake Mweru. He further describes this concept: "I think that besides our ordinary five senses, we have a finer faculty which I must call, for lack of a better term, the sense of presence."

Our Sense of Presence

Have you ever had a moment when you just *knew* something, when you listened to your gut sense, acted on it, and your gut turned out to be right even though you had no logical way of knowing this information? You can tune into the Sense of the Presence—of rightness or wrongness—about this situation or person. Or have you ever been given an opportunity that looked great on the surface, but something just didn't feel right? Whether you listened or not, in the end, did the result confirm your gut sense or intuition was right?

Like the tiny dung beetles who use the Milky Way to navigate, you will find reliable signs in your animal senses to help you navigate the twists and turns of life. Our animal nature connects us more fully to our deeper senses and can lead us all the way to the full-body perception or our Sense of Presence. By listening to our body and senses more deeply, our intuitive channel naturally turns on.

There have been many times when I have been busy with tasks at home and received a flash of intuition, a silent inner prompting, "Go to the shelter right now!" I know better than to ignore these messages, so I grab my treats, put on my shoes, and head out the door. I arrive just in time to meet a wonderful person who is adopting one of the dogs I have been working with. I get a chance to tell them how wonderful this dog is and to say a sweet, cuddly goodbye to a being I have been helping to release his fears, perhaps for days or weeks, preparing him for adoption. I don't always get the message, but when I do and follow the call of my True North, I am so grateful I listened.

> *Maybe it's animalness that will make the world right again:*
> *the wisdom of elephants, the enthusiasm of canines,*
> *the grace of snakes, the mildness of anteaters.*
> *Perhaps being human needs some diluting.*
>
> *Carol Emshwiller*

Animal Intelligence

In 1859, Charles Darwin published *On the Origin of Species.* He disagreed with the ideas held at the time that animals were just instinctual automatons. Darwin believed that animals used their senses to navigate their world, which he recognized as their specific *animal intelligence.*

Darwin's theories stated that all animals, including us humans, are evolving in response to natural pressures and changing conditions on Earth. He discussed how evolution shaped the mental lives of animals and proposed that all animals had rich and complex emotional lives. He also thought the difference between humans and animals was only a question of degree; we all shared the capacity for an inner life filled with emotions. In 1872, he published his third major book on evolutionary theory, *The Expression of the Emotions in Man and Animals.* He discovered how certain core emotions were expressed in similar ways across species, such as anger, fear, surprise, disgust, sadness, and happiness.

For many decades the belief that humans are superior because of their complex reasoning capabilities caused other animals to be devalued and often mistreated. Now science has helped us recognize that every species has impressive abilities and enviable sensory capacities leading to specific kinds of intelligence. Birds fly and land with amazing accuracy, pigeons can be trained to detect hairline fractures on x-rays, and dogs' sense of smell saves human lives in a variety of contexts.

Those at the forefront of animal science are beginning to explore the animal brain and emotions, but not from the prejudiced way humans have defined intelligence in the past. Today's animal researchers are beginning to uncover complex intelligence and social structures, empathy and reconciliation behaviors, tool use, planning, memory, communication, and a sense of self. Scientists are now providing evidence to support what animal lovers have known all along; they are beginning to recognize the genius in all animals. Thank goodness!

The Many Benefits of Connecting to Your Animal Nature

Thinking can be our best friend—or worst enemy— depending on how we steer it.

The irony of human history is that becoming divorced from our animal nature and from nature, in general, has not always helped us. Sometimes this separation has brought out the worst in us. It can lead to overthinking, which is not grounded in natural reality. Thoughts that spin on their own, without being tied to the natural senses, get us into all kinds of trouble—mental spinouts, anxiety, depression, and self-recrimination. If analytical thinking alone could solve all our problems, we would have done it by now. Instead, thinking *and* sensory intelligence need to be partners.

We can enlist our wonderful analytical thinking, and our executive brain function, to choose who we want to be in the world. We can use it to help us choose the high road, which has empathy and awareness of others. Often this is not the easiest path because the high road requires more than just our thinking mind; it requires the wisdom of the heart.

We always have the choice of living from our selfish or "lower" nature or choosing to take the high road in any situation. For example, while we can't control what others do or say, the benefit of being human is we always have a choice about how we will react and what actions we take.

One of the reasons the howling exercise is so effective (aside from being just fun!) is that it quickly connects us with our primal senses. For the most part, animals are in sync with their senses and thus their environment. They enjoy the simple pleasure of being alive and their connection with others. As modern humans, it is easy to feel disconnected. This creates a painful loneliness that we can't seem to chase away.

Embracing our animal nature brings us the priceless benefit of feeling like we belong and have a place in the larger world.

Unifying with our animal nature releases us from the tyrannical idea of hierarchy between species. Embracing your animal nature helps you to no longer perpetuate the false belief that one species is better than another. We are all worthy. We are all good. We all have our place in the grand scheme of life. And we all deserve the freedom to express our own nature—our human nature, our dog nature, our wolf nature, our cow nature.

Not all cultures view animals as separate or inferior. In India, for example, the cow is considered a sacred animal and is allowed to roam freely in many places. I read a story about one temple where they wouldn't begin the meditation service until the Temple Cow arrived. They recognized that the cow lived in harmony and peace and had a level of consciousness and divinity that they could only hope to aspire to after years of dedicated effort and practice.

There is a TED talk, "We Are All Connected with Nature," presented by Nixiwaka, a member of the Amazon Yawanawa tribe. He has learned English in order to communicate the need to protect the rainforest because it is not just the place they live. As he says, "The forest is our body." He speaks about how before the shaman pulls a medicinal plant from the ground, he asks for permission to take it and use it for healing. "If permission is not granted, the plant will not have the medicinal properties." This tribe lives in full connection with their human and animal natures.

While many indigenous tribes remain connected to their animal wisdom, modern culture has made a huge dividing line that separates human beings from animal beings. While there are significant differences between every species, we have more in common than we have differences. That unifying link is our animal nature. By learning to appreciate the inner lives of animals, we come to recognize our innate connection to them. They are not just dumb animals to be trained to do our bidding or to entertain us. Rather, they are teachers who can show us how to live, how to love, and how to embrace our animal nature.

Life Is for Living

In 1943 J. Allen Boone published a book titled *You Are the Adventure!* In one chapter, he presents what he called the Four Verities, the four truths about life as he came to understand them. I will mention just the first one here: *Life is for Living*. While this truth seems so obvious and simple at first, if you let it work its magic, it is spiritual medicine. Life is for Living is a good vision to muse upon. To what degree are you LIVING your life versus just existing or going through the motions?

Take a moment right now to breathe and silently repeat the phrase "Life is for Living." Can you feel it unfolding something deep and primal within? Something like an animal's wisdom? This spiritual medicine can awaken your senses. As Esther Hicks said, "Life will never be better than your willingness to be here right now."

The Circles of Connection

In The Human-Animal Connection program, we encourage people to consider several interlaced circles or spheres of connection. When you find the right balance among these circles of connection, you will feel a deeper layer of peace.

- Connection to self
- Connection to your animal nature
- Connection to another being
- Connection to family (and other close humans), groups, and society
- Connection to our Earth Self, and finally to our Universal Self

Feeling a strong anchor to your sense of self is what helps you navigate deeper connections across the other circles. This is because it is hard to relate with another being if you don't feel connected to all of yourself—your emotions, your desires, your intentions, *and* your animal nature.

If you would like to deepen your connection to others, a good place to start is by living in your own animal skin. Connecting to your animal nature helps you to care about what feels good to you. Paying attention to your animal nature allows you to engage with others more authentically. Being connected to yourself is a tremendous asset for having healthy relationships because it allows intimacy without feeling as if you lose yourself in the needs and desires of others.

All relationships benefit from this kind of healthy connection, where each is paying attention to their own needs. This connection to your self creates healthy boundaries, which is something you need to manage if you are going to engage with an animal.

Once you feel stable in these first two levels of connection, you can open your circles of connection to more members: family, coworkers, neighbors, friends, and a local community of like-minded folks. From there, you can widen your connection to larger groups, society, nature, and the earth. Balancing your needs for these various layers of connection helps you feel your sense of place in the world.

When you feel strong circles of connection across the various spheres, you will feel that elusive feeling of belonging. You will feel your connection to the All That Is, as horses do. William J. Long speaks about how horses are profoundly connected to everything around them, and this helps them "know" things that we humans don't: "…perhaps as a horse feels when he is holding the right direction through a blinding snowstorm, as he does hold it, steadily, surely, if you are wise enough not to bother him with the reins or your opinions."

Connecting to your animal nature will not lead you astray. In fact, it will help you find your way to your true purpose.

Journal Reflections on Connecting to Your Animal Nature:

1) How do you feel about your animal nature?

2) What species of animals do you admire and why? What do they teach you about living?

3) How would your life change if you embraced your animal nature?

4) Do you feel connected to your True North guidance system?

5) How would your life be if you had access to your natural Inner Knowing and were guided by intuition?

Re-Minder: I am a human animal.

Oso, you showed us the power
of the animal spirit. It was a
privilege to know you.

Principle #3

COMING TO YOUR SENSES
Awakening Your Sensory Intelligence

When someone says you can't attribute human sensations
to animals, they forget that human sensations
are animal sensations. Inherited sensations,
using inherited nervous systems.

Carl Safina

Overview

Animals rely on their senses to determine what is safe and what is not. They follow their senses to find food, mates, ease, and comfort. By paying attention to their sensory intelligence, they are not often led astray.

Many of us humans have shut down our senses and become numb to fit into the modern world. This can cause us to feel adrift or even lost. Animals can remind us that connecting with our sensory intelligence is a path to well-being. We too can learn to pay attention to and trust our human-animal sensory intelligence to help us find balance, safety, and pleasure in our own lives. If we are feeling adrift or lost, coming to our senses is the right path. Our natural human-animal senses will lead us home.

Finding Molly

The other day at the shelter, I was visiting with a marvelous dog named Molly. Her owners had surrendered her, and she was sad, confused and cowering in her kennel. Her eyes were so sweet and deep, as if she was asking me "Why?" I sat with her for about forty minutes, and she treated me to a sublime connection.

She sniffed my face as if memorizing me by my summer sweat, then she cuddled in my lap and rested her head on my leg. Her fur was silky, and I slowly let my hand wander until I found her favorite places. She was warm, and her breathing was a subtle massage against me. She settled into a soothing sleep.

As she blended with the dream world, I also had a break from words and worry. Our time together was a sensory vacation. It was as good for me as it was for her. I continued to work with her every day, and everyone at the shelter noticed that her trust in humans was coming back. Three days later, she was adopted by a nice older couple. I hope they know how lucky they are to have found Molly.

Trusting Your Senses

Animals navigate all encounters through their senses. Their sensory world is full and complete. There is nothing more to do than to experience what is present to their senses. It is satisfying to spend time with animals because we become aware of how completely grounded they are in their senses. This reminds us of our own primal connection to the natural world and how calming that can be.

Logic and analysis are essential and wonderful, but they are not always reliable. We need the balance that comes from including our sensory intelligence, which guides us to what feels good.

Do you feel connected to your senses and trust them? As you navigate through your world, do you allow your senses to guide you, to help you know what is best for you? Or do you dismiss them as a mere annoyance or afterthought, preferring to use your mind or logic as your primary guide?

We can relearn to live by and through our connection to our sensory capacities the way animals do. Even if our noses are not as wise as a search and rescue dog--who can find a body at the bottom of a river--we can still train our senses to lead us by orienting toward the good. This training begins with relearning to appreciate the power of sensory intelligence. In the domain of sensory intelligence, animals are our teachers.

Even though humans try so hard to fit into society's molds and can easily become disconnected from our inner core and sensory intelligence (particularly as adults), it is not too late to let our senses lead the way. Instead of doing a "should" override, we can once again pay attention to the truth of our senses. When we don't trust our sensory intelligence, we *don't feel very good.* If we become too disassociated and disconnected from our *sense-sations,* we feel out of touch with our truth, our purpose, and our Soul.

To function in this modern world in environments that are far removed from nature leads us to a pervasive feeling of discomfort. It takes a lot of effort to ignore our senses, which may be screaming, "Get outta here!" or, "Get away from that person!" Often, we shut off inconvenient warnings to comply with the way we think we *should* behave. On top of that, slavery to our electronics has hijacked our sensory receptors. Thus, without a reliable connection to our senses and our sensory intelligence we can become so confused about our true feelings that we can barely trust ourselves anymore.

As humans, it is best to have a balance of logic-intelligence and sensory-intelligence when making decisions. It is like listening to both sides of knowingness. But when we override our sensory intelligence, and we ignore our gut sense, then we can become confused about how we really feel, and we end up not trusting ourselves.

"The wind of heaven is that which
blows through a horse's mane."

Anonymous

One day at the shelter, I was working with a very shy stray dog who was afraid to be touched. Given the shelter name Buff, he would flinch with even the gentlest contact. I was also told that he wouldn't make eye contact. But by my third time working with him using our HAC methods, Buff put his paws on my chest and looked long and sweetly into my eyes. The sensation of his eyes deeply searching into mine was palpable. It was like we were melting into each other. He was showing me his willingness to trust. He then cuddled into my lap and slept for about fifteen minutes in spite of the normally high volume of noise in the shelter. The weight of his body against mine, his soft fur, and his gentle breathing filled my senses. We were both enveloped in a bubble of peace. I remember thinking, *this is what love feels like.*

Catching the Scent of Goodness

Sy Montgomery, the author of *The Good Good Pig*, quotes wildlife biologist Lynn Rogers who believes that bears "may be able to catch the scent of ripening hazelnuts forty miles away." Her research on Silvertip grizzly bears led her to state: "They have a sense of smell that's stronger than the bloodhound. Bears, in general, have more smell receptors than any other land animal."

Montgomery offers more examples of sensory intelligence when she says, "Pigs in the south of France can find buried truffles—the 'black diamonds' of Perigord which sell for up to $1,000 a pound." Horned toads, with two pinholes for ears, can hear an ant scurry from a foot away.

About the size of a small cat, African pouched rats can be trained to sniff and detect landmines. They can clear an area the size of a tennis court in twenty minutes. These rats are very effective and cost a fraction of the price of mine-sweeping technology. And they can also be trained to detect tuberculosis with greater accuracy than our current medical tests. Recognizing the value of a partnership with animals' refined senses is a great asset to humanity.

Sensations Connect Us to Our Animality

Accepting the wisdom of our senses is very healing. Our sensations lead us back to our core biological truth, our animality. We humans developed language and complex thinking, but the side effect was we learned to lie. Animals can remind us how to get our truth sensors back online. As soon as we reconnect to our bodies through our senses, it naturally leads to authentic experiences such as joy, simplicity, grace, harmony, peace, connection, empathy. This is the delight and beauty of full sensory awareness.

This is why our senses are *essential* partners in healing. With a connection to all our senses, we can prevent the endless spin in the domain of the mind. A quote attributed to Alfred Einstein is, "We can't solve our problems with the same thinking we used to create them." I am suggesting that *a mind connected to sensory awareness* is going to be more effective and will help you feel more fulfilled.

It seems that less and less of our time is devoted to feeling good. This is why in Principle #2, "Connecting to Your Animal Nature," we focus on using your senses as a doorway back to your true self.

When I ask our HAC students, "What percentage of your day is spent on the simple pleasure of the senses?" I get blank stares. Yet focusing on your senses is very pleasing. It's soothing and peaceful. It slows down the mind and connects you to your body's intelligence. Interestingly, some students are afraid that paying attention to their senses will cause them to feel *too* good. They are worried that they will surrender to hedonism or addictive behaviors. This fear is usually unwarranted as studies have shown that laboratory rats who have highly enriched lives rarely become addicted, even when given a lever to access cocaine. In contrast, rats raised without enrichment easily become addicted. Rats used to study addiction, can be trained to become addicted to drugs, but this is not normal behavior for them. Most animals fill their senses by laying in the sun, moving their bodies, eating what they need, sleeping as they need, and then they go on to the next nice thing.

To quote Mae West, "Too much of a good thing is wonderful." Go ahead and find out for yourself how much goodness you can stand by trying the following exercise.

Focus Fully on One Sense at a Time

To help our students reawaken their senses, we guide them through this multi-day awareness and journaling exercise: Start by devoting one day (or longer) to really focus on one core sense at a time. Each day, write down your impressions as you focus on that particular sense. Some questions you might explore are: What do you see around you? What do you hear? How does your body feel? What do your hands like to touch? Seek out sensory delights such as your toes in the sand, brushing your hands across the grass, the wind in your face, raindrops on your tongue. You don't have to go to a special place; use whatever you can find in your environment to reawaken your connection with your senses. Or use your powerful deliberate imagination, such as remembering how it feels to hold a rose petal between your fingers.

Being deliberate about sensory pleasure will change your life. The pathway back to a more balanced relationship with your senses is to enjoy simple pleasures *fully*. I believe that many obsessive pursuits of pleasure and self-defeating habits stem from our inability to experience the *simple* pleasures of being connected to our senses. This disconnection leads to feeling empty. Like a cup with a leak, it can never be filled, and the insatiable chase begins because it requires more and more of the object of obsession. Ironically, the more you chase, the more likely true satisfaction will elude you.

The Lessons of Simple Sensory Pleasure

The exercise above, where you learned to focus on and enjoy one sense at a time, will help you reconnect with simple pleasure. Once you fully experience the simple pleasure in small things, you will see the wisdom in stopping to smell those roses. Or really see the tree, or gaze at the sky. Or really enjoy nice textures. Or sigh slowly out loud. Or howl. Or giggle.

Immersing yourself in a sensory moment brings you into present time. It softens the mental chatter, the endless thoughts, the lack of real feeling.

Animals *live* in their bodies. We humans drag ours around, and we say terrible things about them like "I'm so fat, so old, so broken…" Our bodies don't deserve the abuse we heap upon them on so many levels.

Your senses are the pathway that leads you to who you truly are. We tune up our cars; how about tuning up the way we live? Start with the sensory exercise above. Even for one minute a day, dedicate yourself to the pleasure of fully experiencing the world around you—not through the mind, but through the body. *It's time to come to our senses.*

Go Ahead, Play with Your Food

When I invite students to come to their senses, they usually choose to focus on their visual and auditory senses. So, I invite them to reexperience sensory baby wisdom. When a baby is given a new object, they will often put it in their mouth first. Concerned about safety, the parent may interrupt this choice, and babies slowly learn this isn't the "right" way to behave. But think about how natural it is to explore the world through the mouth.

I suggest to students that they playfully rediscover their baby senses. After all, you are *how* you eat. For instance, try this at least once (maybe more often) at the dinner table: slow down while you are having a meal. Chew slower, really taste the food, and feel its texture. Act like you are in a slow-motion movie so you can experience each morsel. Be present during every bite. In the privacy of your own home, instead of using utensils, try using your hands and your fingers to "play with your food." Lick the plate like a kitten. Experience the food as a baby would, delighting in the textures and the pleasure of putting food in your mouth.

I know we have been programmed not to do this, and I don't suggest you do it in public! Just every once in a while, take a "baby break." Really smell, and look at your food, especially fruit. Squeeze it a little, roll it around, experience it as a baby would. How much pleasure can you add by involving all your senses?

Watch any animal to see how connected to their senses they are. They really see, they really hear, they look for comfortable spots to lay down, and they enjoy touch. Their level of sensory awareness can help show us how we can do the same. Connecting to our senses will help us step off the mental spinning wheel and to *feel* our way.

Learning Dog Sense

I mention J. Allen Boone (a descendent of Daniel Boone) again because he is one of my revered teachers. He was born in 1882, and may have been the first to study and write about nonverbal connection with animals. In 1954, he wrote one of my favorite books, *Kinship with All Life*. At that time, many humans trained dogs and other animals using fear and dominance methods. Boone knew there had to be a better way. He stepped out of that culture of inhumanity and turned the training model around. He submitted to instruction from an amazing German shepherd dog named Strongheart. Strongheart had been a military police dog before becoming a major movie star in Hollywood. Strongheart could be directed almost as well as a human and did amazing complex actions in his films, which were seen all over the world.

It all began when Strongheart's trainers needed to leave town suddenly on business. Boone casually suggested to his friends that he could take care of the dog. Even though he had no experience living with a dog, much less training one, they trusted him. What Boone thought would be a short assignment turned out to be a year spent living with Strongheart, and that year changed his life. He discovered he knew nothing about how to live with such an intelligent dog and recognized that not having preconceptions was a great advantage. So, rather than listen to the advice of "experts," he asked Strongheart to teach him, to help him understand what he *felt* and understood about the world. Boone used his human senses and his ability to open his mind and heart to become Strongheart's student.

As he relates in his book, sometime into his training by Strongheart, Boone was with a group of elite scientists who did not believe in animal wisdom or communication. Rather than argue, he asked them if they had ever had the experience of riding a horse and getting thoroughly lost. They all admitted that they had. He asked them how they had solved their problem. "Give the horse his head," they replied. "Drop the reins. He'll find the way home." Yes, indeed. Even when the human was lost, the horse always knew the way home; he could feel it. Some of them had to think about that for a while. A few were willing to acknowledge that animals had a kind of wisdom we can only dream of.

Earthing – Getting Connected to the Earth Again

J. Allen Boone liked to spend time in nature, specifically time where he could sleep on the ground or walk barefoot directly on the earth. Today, a movement called Earthing recommends that we humans need to spend some time with our feet or body in direct contact with the soil, grass, or sand—with the earth. Clint Ober and his research partners have discovered that grounding through direct skin contact with the earth has many health benefits, including reducing the health problems associated with inflammation. Over twenty published peer-reviewed studies of the benefits of grounding and earthing show how this process leads to balance in our cells. Ober's book *Earthing* explains this important discovery. Both humans and animals can benefit from some direct contact with the earth's natural electrical field for well-being. So, if possible, take off your shoes *and* let your animals romp around on grass, dirt, and natural surfaces. It's as essential for them as it is for us.

Touch is Communication – The Invisible Touching Exercise

Touch is a major channel of communication for animals who invite us to remember the power of the sense of touch. Although touch is such an important sense, many modern cultures give less and less time to it. Yet touch is vital to well-being. We know that just petting an animal feels good to our hands and our hearts.

Sometimes physical touch is not possible, yet connection can still be experienced. The other day at the shelter, a few of us were part of a team evaluating ten tiny dogs that had been confiscated from a hoarder. They had differing levels of terror of human hands. Clearly, touching them would not have been a friendly way to meet them. We had to gain their trust very slowly, over several hours of just sitting in the yard with them. We used our HAC method of "invisible touch" until they felt safe enough to approach. After one session using this invisible touch, eight of the ten were enjoying proximity and human touch. The other two would venture close, then veer away many times, as if they were "trying on the idea" of approaching. I was so grateful to have the tool of invisible touch, which is a way of connecting through calm energy without reaching toward them or using hands until they desire to be touched physically.

This is why the HAC workshops teach this technique of soothing "energy touch" not with hands but with your heart. Students imagine lovingly touching, but without using their hands.

Physical touch is wonderful. But for this specific training exercise, we temporarily put physical touch aside as a path to increase awareness of the subtler experience of "invisible energy touch." Some people find this method of "no touch" to be even more profound and delightful than physical touch. And the animals love it too.

You may want to do the invisible touch just for a moment or two because it can be intense if the animal is experiencing this focused energy-touch for the first time. Touching with intention and energy—with invisible touch—is a very good training exercise for humans. Invisible energy touch develops your awareness of the powerful yet subtle *sense of connecting* without the physical element of touch.

Coming to Your Senses Increases Communication

Another reason for humans to come to their senses is that it creates a doorway to enter the world of animals. It opens two-way communication between species. As we soften our thinking and increase our sensory experiencing, it helps us to move more into sync with all animals. From this tender place, it becomes easier to connect more deeply. Our senses are the pathway to communicate and to experience our Oneness or Kinship with All Life.

Journal Reflections on Coming to Your Senses:

1) Which is your favorite of the five senses? Which sense do you pay the least attention to? How about your sense of smell?

2) Do you spend any time barefoot on natural ground, like grass, soil, sand, or dirt?

3) Can you remember (or imagine) being a baby and the ways you experienced the world? Could you invite some of that innocent, pure experience back into your present-day adult life?

4) Do you trust your senses? How could you trust them more? What if your senses could lead you to more joy? What would your life be like with more of this joy?

5) What if your senses were the true experience? In what ways would that change how you live? What if what pleases you was more of a priority in your life?

Re-Minder: I come to my senses.

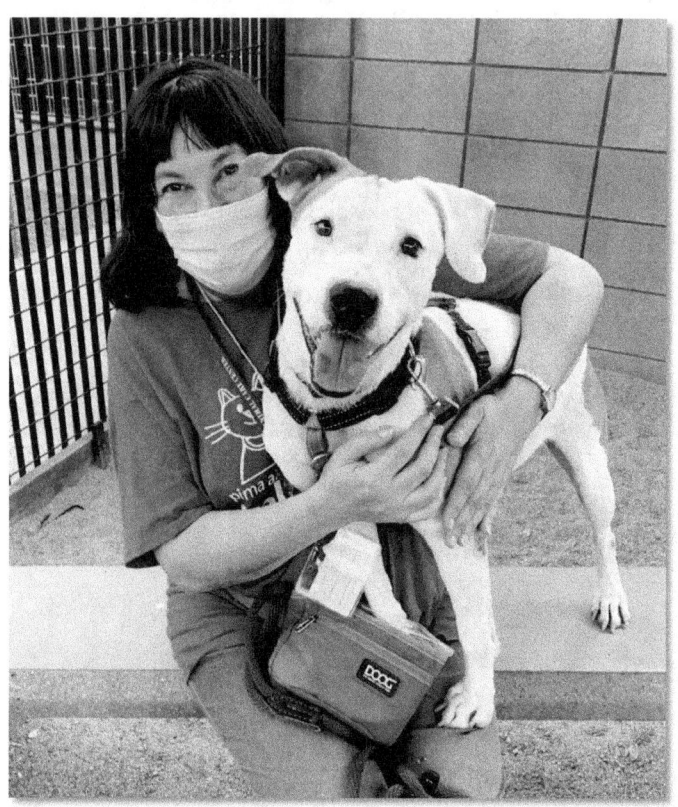

Buff went from being unable to be touched to loving being touched. In a class at the shelter, he became my demonstration dog in Soothing Touch for Animals.

Principle #4

SENSE-SATIONAL AWARENESS

Intuition is Your Path to the
Wisdom of the Senses

A cat can be trusted to purr when she is pleased,
which is more than can be said for human beings.

William Ralph Inge

Overview

If you would like a deeper connection with animals, intuition is your best friend. Intuition is an inner knowingness that helps you know what your animals are feeling and thinking. Logic is a valuable channel, intuition is a different channel, and each provides a certain kind of information. In the human world, we have come to rely on logic, but there are times when logic is not the best or most accurate way to connect with your animals. One way to increase your connection to your intuition is to pay more attention to what your body and your senses know to be true. This quiet world may seem mysterious at first, but it will not lead you astray.

"Be here now" is very good advice—if you can follow it.

"*How* do I be here now?" one veteran asked me. She felt as if a magnetic pull was dragging her backward to dwell in the past, even though she didn't want to be plagued by her memories any longer. This Army captain began her Human-Animal Connection program the day after she retired from the military, after serving eighteen years in a technical area that required her to use her brilliant mind. Now, I was inviting her to use her senses. "Honestly, you're asking me to speak a foreign language. I spent my whole career ignoring my senses."

Then I reminded her of a story she had told me about walking into a village in Afghanistan one day. "I don't know what it was, but something felt different." It wasn't something she could "see." It was what she didn't see. It was her "gut sense" that struck in an instant. Looking back, she realized what triggered her awareness was the absence of children and dogs running and playing. But in that moment, all she knew was something wasn't right.

She realized then that her senses had not abandoned her. They were her quiet angels, whispering that something was off. In a split second, she knew she had to change the plans, and she did. Moments later, a huge explosion occurred in one of the nearby buildings. Fortunately, due to her quick responses, everyone in her unit walked away with just a few minor scrapes.

Her keen situational awareness, as it is called in the military, saved lives.

Be Here Now – The Sensory Path

If you are feeling numb or disconnected from your senses, no worries. Like the Army captain, they are still there, just waiting for you to invite them into your awareness. Just by paying attention to your senses, you will begin to reconnect them to your experience and your conscious mind.

Dogs and other animals are masters at Sense-Sational Awareness. When a dog enters a new space, they will explore the perimeter, if they have the freedom to do so. While sniffing and walking around the boundaries, they are absorbing a lot of information about the energy and safety of the new space. This is a healthy process of orientation using the senses.

A dog who has not been traumatized will complete this reconnaissance process rather quickly, and after evaluating the area as safe, will then switch their focus to attending to people or other activities in the center of the space. They use their senses to gather the data they need first, and this allows them to then relax and enjoy the situation.

Using Your Sensory Awareness

We humans can harness the same orienting process as dogs in new situations to help us to *be here now*. Our senses bring us into the present moment. If our sensory antennae are working well, we can orient in seconds or less. We receive and process accurately what we need to know about persons, places, and events, then we can be present and alert for what is next.

Another term for this process is "resource orientation," meaning that you use your senses to get you out of a stuck place and bring you into present time. Somatic Experiencing Therapy utilizes resource orientation to counter the physiological stress response and to lead to a greater sense of stability and calm.

One way to experience the calming and stabilizing results of sensory orientation is to try an exercise that involves a few simple turns of the head. You have seen this familiar movement from dogs, as they do it when they are orienting.

First, look straight ahead. Really see what is in front of you. Breathe. Second, turn to the left and really see something—one specific thing—and focus on it completely. Breathe calmly. Third, turn to the right and see something else and really look at it. Breathe again. Finally, return to the starting position with your head and eyes facing straight ahead. When you take a moment to breathe and fully focus on what you are looking at, you will most likely feel more grounded, more peaceful, and lighter.

These movements of the head help reset the vagus nerve, calming the nervous system. By orienting to a sensory focus, you can quiet the mind. Concentrating your sense of sight on a specific focal point can help get you out of the mind chatter and into your body. This exercise takes only a minute or two and can be a good reset for your state of mind.

If you share your life with an animal, you have probably noticed that they have instant reactions to people. They either like them or not, trust them or not, all in a quick sensory assessment. If we used our intuition as successfully as they do and trusted our senses, we could avoid a lot of trouble.

Practice and enhance your own sense-sational awareness anytime you walk into a new environment, say an office, a restaurant, someone's house for the first time. Think of tuning your sensory antenna to "feel" the place. Maybe you can't pace the perimeter and sniff like a dog (which would be very effective but might get you kicked out), but you can tune in carefully to your senses. They will lead you to an overall impression or sensation of "what do you *feel* here?" What is your quick sense of the vibe of the place? What do you intuit about this place? Is it happy, sad, calm, chaotic? Places, as well as people, hold energy, especially if there is a lot of a particular emotion.

Treat this exercise as a game. If you get too serious, you will short-circuit your perceptions. Keep it light and fun. Just notice what you observe and don't judge your perceptions. It is not about whether you are right or wrong. It is just about tuning in to this channel of your perception so it is open and ready for a situation where you need to know something quickly, or a decision needs to be made. It will help you instantly know whether to move toward or away from a person or situation.

When you are first learning, it is best to practice this method when you are in a relaxed situation rather than a high-stress one. When you are first learning, high stress can throw off the correct reception of your senses. With more practice, you will be able to use it in more intense situations and still trust your sensory perceptions to be receiving clearly. For example, you will know instantly what feels good and what feels wrong.

Animals are masters at teaching us about the wisdom of moving toward what is good and away from what is bad (read more in Principle #21, "*Towards & Away*"). Those interested in further developing their ability to have two-way communication with all animals can begin by paying attention to their senses and opening this intuitive channel where all things are known.

The Sensory Focus of Anticipation

When I am opening a new bag of Sophia's favorite treats, she sits in front of me, the picture of total sensory focus, as I fumble trying to open the package. Her anticipatory drool falls in little puddles. She does the tippy-tap dance with her front feet. Her tail flies left and right. Her entire universe of senses is focused on the anticipation of the moment when I will present this delicious treat to her.

Anticipation is a powerful learning tool because it focuses the senses, tuning up the sensory mind. Of course, I am not talking about teasing, but a few seconds of delay (the amount of time it takes me to produce the goodie) is valuable because I have her sensory mind focused on a positive state of full alert.

As Victoria Stillwell puts it in her book *The Secret Language of Dogs*, "The anticipation of a reward is almost more powerful than the reward itself. When the dog anticipates a reward, the seeking system of its brain (the hypothalamus) is more active and sensitive to any stimuli that predict a reward." This is gold for teaching a new trick or behavior because it allows you to link a desired new behavior with the anticipation of pleasure from the reward.

Animals Predicting Natural Disasters

There are so many stories from every corner of the world of animals predicting natural disasters. While these may be anecdotal stories and difficult to test scientifically, the sheer volume of examples makes these events difficult to ignore. For example, just before the 2004 tsunami struck Indonesia, many people noticed that animals were acting strangely. As Linda Bender, DVM, tells the story, "Cicadas stopped rattling and birds stopped singing. Dogs refused to go outdoors. Elephants trumpeted in alarm and stampeded towards the hills. Relative to the human population, very few animals were drowned. They seemed to know what was coming, and what to do about it."

Animals are also good at predicting earthquakes and other natural events. In the 1970s, Chinese seismologists began training people to watch for and report signs from animals, saving many lives. During the World War II bombing raids over England, many Londoners reported their dogs gave them warnings a half hour *before* the air raids sounded. Clearly, we should consider animals part of our early warning system and pay more attention to dramatic changes in their behavior, especially among herd animals.

Your SENSE of Safety

Life presents many challenges to feeling safe. Worry about the future and the lure of the past both drastically deplete what I call your *Safety Tank*. Metaphorically speaking, your safety tank is an enduring sense of safety that allows you to feel stable even if you are facing challenges.

When your safety tank is full, you will feel more resilient no matter what comes your way. When your safety tank is low, even a minor event or squabble can be deeply upsetting.

No matter what happened in the past or could happen in the future, you can restore your *Sense of Safety* in this moment by using your senses to refill your safety tank. Switch your focus away from the past or the future and use your senses to bring you back to this present moment. Remind yourself that you are here right now, and you are safe, no matter what your mind is saying! To release the grip of anxious thoughts, focus on any one of your senses—sight, sound, touch, smell, or taste. Putting all your awareness on a single, simple sensory experience will help you to feel safe right now and help redirect your awareness away from what is pulling on you. When you orient or direct your focus toward what is sensorily pleasurable, it brings you into present time.

There is great power in focusing on our sensory awareness. Veterinarian Linda Bender offers a possible insight as to how animals trust their sensory knowingness. "Animals seem to be better at paying attention to whatever it is that they are sensing, better at interpreting it, and better at trusting it."

Journal Reflections on Sense-Sational Awareness:

1) How much time do you spend each day in the simple awareness of the moment?

2) What thought patterns keep you from being right here, right now, in the present moment?

3) Are you willing to have more pleasure in your life? Pleasure is something that you experience in the present moment. Even a memory of something pleasant or the anticipation of future pleasure is something you experience right now.

4) What would it take to add more pleasure to your life? What would you have to add or subtract?

5) Would you like to increase your Sense of Safety? Focus on one sense at a time and let that experience fill you.

Re-Minder: I sense what I need to know.

Donkeys are masters at sensing what is safe and will orient toward safety. And Charlotte, the donkey, loves the feeling of safety that comes from being loved.

Principle #5

ANIMAL PRESENCE
Animals Are Masters of the Present

The most important hour is always the present.
The most significant person is precisely the one sitting across
from you right now.
The most necessary work is always love.

Meister Eckhart

Overview

One of the reasons it is so enjoyable to be with animals is that they lure us into the present moment where they spend most of their time. In our HAC workshop with horses called *The Power of Presence*, we have systematic, body-based methods to lure people into the delicious experience of being fully present. The horses know the difference between when we are present, and when we are distracted, divided, or trapped in our heads. They respond to us very differently when we are present; they choose to engage and fully communicate. Horses provide us with the perfect partners to experience and develop presence. There is a certain feeling of authenticity when you are with a being who is not trying to be somewhere else or be someone else.

The presence of animals is powerful and healing, perhaps because it inspires you to feel love.

The Rabbit Test

There's a little hole at the bottom of the fence in my backyard. "Doncha wanna fix that?" a neighbor asked. Nope! It's a doorway into a whole new world where a small, wild rabbit lives. He is gray and very shy, and his ears are almost as big as he is. But don't underestimate his power to teach. He has taught me to tenderly save my celery scraps, romaine lettuce, and baby carrots and dutifully bring them to the doorway between our worlds every morning.

The first month after we met, he wouldn't come to my side of the fence unless I was in my house behind the sliding glass door. Then I moved closer, at a turtle's pace, and sat outside in the rocking chair in my yard. He would venture out only if I was physically *and mentally still*. If I even moved my eyes, he would dart away. Even if my thoughts were too noisy, he'd wait to eat until I went back inside. This was my daily Rabbit Test of how internally quiet I really was.

After a few months, I was able to sit outside, and he would come halfway through the fence. I could just barely see his eyes and his nose, and he would nibble, nibble, nibble. His mouth was moving so, so quickly. Watching me the whole time. And together, we would share something peaceful. Slowly and gently, he taught me to let the flurry of the world float away with the clouds. Just the sight of his munching and crunching softened time. This little rabbit showed me how much more I can hear when I am silent. Now we are at the stage where I can work out on my creaky, squeaky exerciser in the yard twenty feet away from the hole while he sits on *my side of the fence*. He just watches me while he nibbles on his carrot.

What has been very fun for me is the new rabbits I meet for the first time seem to have learned that my yard is a safe place. When they approach, they are less afraid and progress through the process of feeling safe enough to eat in front of me much faster.

How lucky I am to have a hole in my fence just big enough for a little rabbit. He is teaching me about the mysterious power of peace. I listen. Because in silence, all answers can be heard.

The quieter you become, the more you are able to hear.

Rumi

The Power of Presence

The poet Lucille Clifton once said, "In the bigger scheme of things, the universe is not asking us to do something, the universe is asking us to *be* something. And that's a whole different thing."

To *be here now,* you simply need to be present. Being in the present moment is relaxing. In contrast, dwelling in the past or worrying about the future produces sadness, regret, anxiety, and stress. We all do this, but you want to start flipping the balance so that you spend more time in the pleasure of the present. Animals can teach us how to be in the present moment if we let them. They are great partners in the practice of mindfulness and peace.

One day when I was observing the doggie playgroup at Pima Animal Care Center shelter, a very shy stray dog, who was given the shelter name Buff, was cowering in the corner by the fence. I began working with the Trust Technique to send him healing energy. Although I was about thirty feet away from him on the outside of the fence, he sensed there was some comfort in my direction. He slowly crept his way toward me. The other dogs were very interested in this brave voyage across the yard. They crowded him, and one mounted him. When they finally backed off, Buff crouched against the fence beside me. I sensed that he responded to my energy-greeting, the invisible touch, and stayed with me for about fifteen minutes. Buff could feel I was offering some silent comfort.

This was not a dog who would make eye contact, and he would flinch if anyone tried to touch him. But he made eye contact with me as if asking for safe haven. I surrounded him with invisible cozy energy. When he had soaked up enough to partially fill his safety tank, he ventured across the yard again. After about a week, he began to play in the doggie playgroup.

Even though I was told he was too scared to be touched, after our first Trust Technique session together, he was clearly a dog who loved to be touched. He would soak it up for several minutes before walking away to integrate the healing. A moment later, Buff was back at my side for more. During our third session, he crawled into my arms and went to sleep.

A month later, Buff was my demonstration dog in an animal massage class I gave to volunteers at the shelter. Everyone knew how scared he had once been and was moved by how brave he now was, greeting several people in a classroom full of people. It opened everyone's hearts to see him on the table and see how blissful he became as he received the soothing touch.

Peace Is Good for All Beings

The more peaceful you can be, the more you can share that calmness with animals. Removing stress is good for all animals, including sheep. Sheep raised without stress produce higher quality cashmere. The luxury brand Loro Piana pays its Mongolian sheep herders extra money to raise their standard of living, so they will be more peaceful when they interact with the well-pampered sheep. The Loro Piana sweaters cost between one and three thousand dollars. As Fabio d'Angelantonio, the chief executive of the company, says, "The wool of a happy sheep is a better wool than a very stressed sheep."

Miss Betsy – A Connoisseur of Peace

If you need a dose of quiet, sit with a horse. In The Human-Animal Connection Program, this is one of the exercises we do to tune up our own sense of peace. We bring a chair and just sit next to a horse. We don't talk or touch or engage at first because it is up to the horse if he or she wants to interact. (Horses are so often told what to do and when to do it, that just giving a horse a choice about whether or not they want to approach is a very kind thing to do.)

If your mind is busy, chances are the horse will just ignore you. But if you get peaceful, most horses can't resist and will approach. They recognize a soft, calm energy signal as a kindred spirit. If they have been traumatized, be prepared to sit for a while, maybe even come back a few times and just sit. In my experience, even traumatized horses come around to explore a peaceful person.

When I was volunteering at one horse sanctuary, I met a horse named Miss Betsy. Miss Betsy was a large quarter horse, over seventeen hands, and a lovely blond color, but she was so scared when she first arrived that she was dangerous. The barn guys fed her by throwing hay over her fence and darting away because she would kick with all four legs and with great speed.

The vet estimated Miss Betsy was in her thirties. She couldn't be ridden because of her injuries. She had a rough life. She had been forced to be a drug-runner, where they would tie the legs of all the horses together so they couldn't escape. When they were finished with her, they left her trapped in her stall to starve. She was a bag of bones when she came to the rescue sanctuary. She had a lot of reasons not to trust humans.

This is how I began to work with her: I just sat near her. Then I moved closer. Soon she was taking carrots from my hand. By being still and not asking her to do anything she didn't want to do, I began to gain her trust. I used the Trust Technique with Miss Betsy during six sessions when I was training for my Trust Technique Practitioner Certification. Soon, we could walk together very gently. With her altered gait, she was the lowest ranking in the herd. The other horses would bite her if she got close, but she kept trying. She so wanted to make horse friends.

I spent a lot of time with Miss Betsy, pampering her and walking her around the barn like a princess, parading her past the other horses. Finally, the other horses began to show her some respect—or at least stopped picking on her. Every day she became gentler, more trusting, and she opened like a flower that everybody wanted to sniff.

Miss Betsy became our best therapy horse. She was so calm that people felt healed just by being in her presence. She has since passed, but I thank her every day for how much she taught me about the power of healing. Of course, I loved her from the start, but it took her time to be able to receive love because of the heartbreaking amount of trauma from her past that she had been carrying.

Yes, animals can experience trauma—*and they can experience healing*. Perhaps they even heal more easily than we do because of their natural connection to their senses which keeps them linked to the present moment. But if they are severely traumatized, they may have temporarily forgotten how to return to a peaceful place. Once you remind them, they respond as if to say, "*Oh, yeah. I remember that. That feels better. I choose peace!*"

The Trust Technique is essentially this: we get peaceful ourselves, and the animal responds very quickly. As he or she relaxes and their nervous system begins to unwind, it awakens their good memories. Soon they find their way back to their natural state, which returns them to their natural behavior.

When I first started working with her, Miss Betsy was terrified of dogs. She would rear and bolt in a panic if a dog was nearby. Yet once Miss Betsy had released the bulk of her pain, she was able to give and receive love--and with dogs too. And she had a lot to give. Before we knew it, Miss Betsy was able to calmly munch on hay right next to my dog Sophia.

On one occasion, I was sitting next to Miss Betsy and letting her free feed on a bale of hay. She stopped eating, walked over, and stood right next to Sophia and me. She looked me right in the eye with such powerful gratitude that I almost fell off my chair. Miss Betsy reminded me that Love is a force that can wash away the past.

Journal Reflections on Animal Presence:

1) What is it about being in the presence of an animal that feels so good?

2) Can you remember the first time you felt the profound presence of an animal?

3) How present are you when you are with your animals?

4) Can you see how presence is a gift? From us to animals and from animals to us?

5) What is it you feel when you are present?

Re-Minder: My presence is my power.

Miss Betsy was a horse who at first had no trust of
humans, but by being present with her, she taught
me how trust can be regained.

Principle #6

LOVE BEYOND WORDS

How Sharing Love with an
Animal Changes Us Both

Many people will walk in and out of your life,
But only the true friends will leave footprints on your heart.

Eleanor Roosevelt

Overview

Sometimes we have an ache that only love can heal. The same is true for animals. When animals are hurt or wounded physically, they know to become very still and let their body do its healing magic. When animals have emotional wounds, our love can cross the divide between species and bring healing. And animals can love us back with profound purity. Sharing love with an animal heals us both.

Horses Heal with Love

Animal communicator Sandra Mendelson, writes in her book, *We Walk Beside You – Animal Messengers for an Awakening World*, about how her dog, Mr. T, suddenly had trouble walking. The veterinarians had no explanation for why one of his back legs wasn't able to bear weight. Shortly thereafter, Sandra was working at a therapy horse ranch with Mr. T by her side. One horse spontaneously took an interest in Mr. T and began vigorously licking him at the base of his spine; he licked intensely for about twenty minutes. It looked like a horse version of a chiropractic adjustment with its gentle manipulation of Mr. T's lower back.

The next day a different horse gave Mr. T the same treatment. And on the third day, yet another horse gave Mr. T his "adjustment." After that, her dog was as good as new. It is amazing that the horses knew what to do, and even more wonderful that they cared to do it! If this isn't love…

The Healing Power of Love

Dear Reader, you wouldn't be reading this book if you didn't believe in the healing power of love. You have witnessed it and have had your own undeniable experiences. You have read about it and watched videos on social media where animals in seemingly hopeless situations have been healed by the love of one person or a family or another animal who took them under their wing.

Yes, these are anecdotal stories, but biologist Marc Bekoff makes the point that discovery begins with the first observation, which may someday be proven. In his words, "The plural of anecdote is data." Fortunately, recent science has now proven what anyone who has spent loving time with animals knows: animals have emotions. And their most significant emotion is love.

I have spent thousands of hours volunteering in animal shelters and have worked with at least as many animals. It hasn't always been easy. When I began volunteering at the Hawaiian Humane Society, I cried my whole first year. Simply taking a dog out of their kennel and watching him or her roll on the grass touched me so deeply, that I fell in love with each one. There was so much joy in this simple moment and such a sense of hope and appreciation for those twenty minutes of connection with a human. And I felt the love from them to me.

Almost all my encounters have shown me that animals' capacity to experience and express love is so vast that it almost feels like we humans are beginners at love. I am convinced that animals love in a way that is both powerful and pure. Their love is beyond words.

Animals Love Beyond Words

One of the doorways to experiencing the powerful love of animals is inviting them to be your teachers, as J. Allen Boone did in his life-long journey of discovery. He learned it is possible to communicate with monkeys and even with a fly just as he did with Strongheart, the German shepherd movie star. His profound experiences led him to believe that animals are ambassadors of love. If we allow them to, animals can show us how to love more deeply and in more nuanced ways. Words are just one way to express love. There are so many other ways.

Animals offer a continuous invitation to broaden our under-standing and to experience more profound layers of love. Marc Bekoff, professor emeritus of Ecology and Evolutionary Biology at the University of Colorado and author of *The Emotional Lives of Animals*, has written much about how animals experience joy, empa-thy, grief, embarrassment, anger, and especially love. Their emotions are authentic, pure and trustworthy.

One person who learned a great deal about emotions and about love from observing animals was Sigmund Freud. Near the end of his life, he conducted therapy sessions with Jofi, his chow chow dog, at his side. According to BarkPost, Jofi had an impeccable sense of timing. Fifty minutes into a session, the dog would stand, stretch, and walk to the door, alerting Freud that it was time to wrap up. Freud also enlisted Jofi's help in assessing a patient's mental state. He thought dogs had the ability to accurately read people's emotional states, even if the patient was unaware of their own feelings. Jofi would lie relatively near a patient if the patient was calm but would keep her distance if the patient was anxious.

Freud also thought animals were great judges of character and was impressed with animals' emotional clarity: "Dogs love their friends and bite their enemies, quite unlike people, who are incapable of pure love and always have to mix their love and hate in their object relations."

In Jeffrey Moussaieff Mason's book *Dogs Never Lie About Love*, he states, "Dogs are without the ambivalence with which humans seem cursed. We love, we hate, often the same person, on the same day, maybe even at the same time. This is unthinkable in dogs, whether because, as some people believe, they lack the complexity or, as I believe, they are less confused about what they feel. It is as if once a dog loves you, he loves you always, no matter what you do, no matter what happens, no matter how much time goes by."

It's More Than Hot Dogs

There are still some folks who question whether or not dogs really love us or if they just love the food that we give them. Fortunately, there is now overwhelming evidence of animal emotions by researchers. Neuroscientist Gregory Berns, author of *What It's Like to Be a Dog*, presents strong evidence of love and other emotions in dogs. In his research, Berns taught awake dogs to go into fMRI machines to scan their brains and chart their emotional responses. He discovered that the brains of dogs light up with specific emotional responses in the same way human brains do. Bern's showed that dogs have specific "love responses" to the presence of their humans.

Admittedly, scientifically proving that love exists is challenging, but that doesn't mean it doesn't. Humans spend so much energy trying to prove to another person that they are loved. It is estimated that there are over 100 million love songs. Can you imagine if we just *knew* love was real? Would there be any songs left to sing?

In spite of the robust research, some scientists are still not ready to use the word love or acknowledge other "refined" emotions in animals. Their discipline requires them to use cautious language, so instead of saying animals *have* emotions, they will use phrases such as "emotion-like" experiences or "exhibiting emotions." As Carl Safina pointed out, "Why can't we say that a group of elephants caring for a baby are feeling love?" But at least it is progress to use the word emotion and animal in the same sentence without fear of an academic burning at the stake.

And it's not only dogs, dolphins, and chimpanzees who have emotions. Many species of animals who have been studied have been shown to have rich emotional lives that include both "positive" and "negative" emotions. Honeybees, for example, have been shown to experience happiness as well as both pessimism and optimism, as Melissa Bateson and Jeri Wright from Newcastle University in England discovered. They published their findings of the complex emotional experiences of bees in *Current Biology.* Their studies "suggest that honeybees could be regarded as exhibiting emotions."

Wired magazine reported, "Bateson and Wright tested their bees with a type of experiment designed to show whether animals are, as humans, capable of experiencing cognitive states in which ambiguous information is interpreted in a negative fashion." Thus, leading to cognitive and emotional states of pessimism. My question is, does this mean there are also optimistic bees? Perhaps in time, we can talk about love among bees. In the meantime, we humans can Bee Love.

Animals love beyond words. And we love them back. It's time to call it what it is: Love.

We Love Beyond Words

Readers of this book likely believe that love transcends species and we humans do not have a monopoly on this experience. Perhaps because other species love beyond thought, beyond words, their experience is purer. Love is more than an emotion. It is a state of consciousness. And I believe that everything alive has a degree of consciousness. And everything that is conscious is capable of experiencing the connection of love.

We humans can give love to all species, and many species can return this love. Why not expand your potential to experience different layers of love from many sources? If we are not the only species capable of great love, would you consider giving and receiving love to flowers and trees? Rivers and mountains, rocks and stars?

Every winter, according to Visit Tucson, about 65,000 rock-loving visitors descend on Tucson for the annual gem show that takes over the city. Rocks, crystals, gems, stones, and fossils from all over the world are on display. A few of these visitors, like one woman I met at the show a few years ago, understand that these gems are not just passive and pretty objects. She was holding a rock in the palm of her hand, eyes closed, swaying slightly. We struck up a conversation. "This rock is telling me this is not its home. It's also telling me that someone is lying to me about love." The owner of the booth, a tall man from Madagascar in a colorful tunic, suddenly appeared and popped a milky-pinkish stone in my outstretched hand. "This one rose quartz," he exclaimed. "Guaranteed to bring you love! Guaranteed!" The woman next to me nodded in agreement.

I can't say I was convinced by his guarantee. But I took it home. Just in case.

To Native Hawaiians, rocks are considered sacred ancestors. If you spend any time with native Hawaiians, as I did during the twenty-five years I lived there, you learn very quickly not to move a rock without asking it for permission to do so. Even though tourists are warned not to move or take any rocks, the Hawaii Post Office is filled with lava rocks that visitors took home and then mailed back. It seems that many visitors who took lava rocks and experienced great misfortune when they returned home sent the rocks back in desperation!

I knew one elderly woman, Kahuna (a wise healer), who would go to the post office, pick up the rock orphans, and take them home. She would sit with them around her in a love-rock ceremony. She explained to me that she would open her heart to each one and listen as she asked, *"Who are you? Who are you connected to? I did my best to hear where they needed to be returned."* She talked with as many as she could, but there were always many more than she could manage. Even with her massive love, it was not enough, as she said, to "win the battle of ignorance" of those who took rocks away from their island homes without considering the consequences.

Love Is Not ALL You Need

Love is essential for healing, but love alone may not be enough for some animals who have experienced significant trauma. It is a primary healing tool. But many other healing methods may be needed, including medical prescriptions for certain types of emotional wounding or extreme stress. We can't fix everything simply because we wish to or because we love our animals so much.

When you need help in a challenging healing situation, reach out for help from the Animal Kingdom in your prayers or meditation or inner work. Ask for understanding and wisdom. You will often receive guidance as well as the experience of gratitude from the Animal Kingdom.

Our job as humans is to use as many necessary options as needed from the vast healing toolbox. Love may be our most essential tool, but sometimes, we must be humble and recognize that other tools are also needed.

When Love Is Not Enough

While love is foundational to healing, there are some situations where love is not enough. People often struggle with guilt when their animal is sick, suffering, or in the process of leaving this physical realm. They believe if they *could just love enough* the animal would heal and stay with them. This is a very painful situation that puts pressure on the animal to live because they know how much they are loved. It also prolongs the person's grieving because on some level they feel guilty, believing that they didn't love enough.

Simply said, love can't "keep" an animal with you whose time has come to move on. It's not that your love is inadequate. Rather, it is that the Soul's timing and purpose can't be overturned. Knowing this allows you to continue to love while at the same time honoring the greater path that the animal is on.

Love's Rocky Road

Living in Hawaii, you learn that to love a rock is usually to leave it where you found it. Admiring it is not a good reason to move it. You don't try to take a mountain, or a river, or a tree, or a wild bird home. But we love animals so much, we want to keep them with us. Sometimes this is the right thing, as in a domesticated animal like a dog or cat who would do better with our protection. But listen very carefully before you take a healthy wild animal out of their natural environment.

One of the great experiences in this life is loving an animal and being loved in return. We love with everything we have, but there is a price because, at some point, they will be gone. The price of opening our hearts to this sublime love is losing, as all animals die. This is the hard lesson of loving both animals and people. Give yourself permission to take as much time as you need to heal from the loss of an animal who has shared their life with you.

When an animal has passed and I am asked to do an animal communication session with one who has crossed over, every animal I have spoken to has asked their family to love again. "Tell them to get another dog," was Romeo's response when I asked if he had a message for his grieving family, "even though he will not be as handsome as me." One departed cat named Figaro said, "Get another cat. But not one that is so loud." His owners laughed in recognition. It turns out Figaro had some very loud meows that got on the wife's nerves.

Even as we think we could never love as much as we have for the departed one, we are being asked to expand our hearts even more. These animals have made it clear they would like their human family (when they are ready) to expand their hearts beyond the grief of loss and to love again.

I believe that one of the main Soul purposes of dogs is to teach us about the importance of loving again. And again. And again.

Love of animals is a universal impulse,
a common ground on which all of us may meet.
By loving and understanding animals,
perhaps we humans shall come to understand each other.

Louis J. Camuti

Journal Reflections on Love Beyond Words:

1) What is it about animals that elicits love?

2) Reflect on your experiences of exchanging love between you and an animal. How has loving an animal changed you both?

3) Are you ready to deepen your experience in the realm of love with an animal?

4) If you couldn't use words, how would you express love to the animal in your life?

5) Are you ready to have your Soul touched by an animal's love?

Re-Minder: Loving animals heals us both.

Seraphina, my sweet therapy cat, helped me experience love beyond words.

Principle #7

THE LANGUAGE OF TOUCH AND CONNECTION
How Cuddles Can Combat Isolation

No matter how crappy your day is,
if you have a dog,
there is always a happy face waiting for you
to come home and cuddle.

Genie Joseph

Overview

The Power of Touch is something animals instinctively and intuitively know. From birth they begin exploring their sense of touch and learn to communicate through touch. We humans sometimes forget or underestimate the benefits of touch and how the *language of touch* helps us feel connected. Good touches are those that are mutually desired, that are delivered in ways that are as pleasant for the receiver as well as the sender. Thus, good touches set up a two-way flow of connection.

Touch Lowers Heart Rate

One Italian research study on animal stress found that when owners had to leave the house without their dog, if they took a moment to touch and give their dog affection, the dog's heart rate decreased by brief petting or affection. Further, the dogs' heart rates remained lower even after their humans left. Although the dogs' bloodwork still showed stress chemistry, this one factor of lower heart rate was significant to support the study's conclusion. Your touch matters because it is a form of communication your dog understands and benefits from.

Touch is Life

Touch is essential for the well-being of babies, children, adults, and animals. Without healthy touch from their parents, animals don't thrive.

Many dogs in shelters are surrendered because of behavior problems that originate from infancy. If puppies did not get enough time with their mothers or littermates or were not socialized with other dogs as puppies problems may surface later in life. Without the necessary developmental stages and sufficient tactile contact, these animals often show a host of behavioral problems such as not playing well with other members of their species, separation anxiety, more sensitive immune and nervous systems, and other issues. To find a remedy for this common problem, I have been exploring how these adult dogs can be "re-puppied" or, at the very least, "re-parented."

One method I use was inspired by the work of animal scientist Temple Grandin, author of several books, including *Animals in Translation: Using the Mysteries of Autism to Decode Animal Behavior*. Grandin is autistic and experimented with ways to manage her own stress levels when she was in college. One successful solution she created for herself was a "squeeze machine." She found that placing herself inside the device that gave her a full-body squeeze (like a firm hug) helped to lower her stress levels and reduce her reactivity.

We humans can help stressed animals relax by mimicking the types of touches they were deprived of as puppies, the same *light pressure touch* they felt from each other when they cuddled and slept in a pile or from their mother while nursing. A light touch, mimicking "puppy pressure," recreates the sensation of proximity. It is not a strong pressure. It is the kind of light, but firm, pressure you feel when a dog leans into you while cuddling or sleeping. I call this light-pressure touch the *human thunder shirt*. It may be used for a few seconds or a few minutes, but I have found this type of gentle and solid, nonmoving contact (not the petting kind of contact) can help stressed dogs calm down. I have also used it with horses who are head-shy or nervous about human contact. And I do see extended stress reduction lasting beyond the treatment itself, which is why I use this technique with many shelter dogs who respond well to it. It can be even more effective than petting.

Petting can be a wonderful thing, but it is not the only way to touch. As long as you and the animal enjoy it and you are sensitive to when the animal is full and has had enough, petting is a lovely way to connect. In the HAC program, we teach a variety of methods of contact. Some involve touch. Others do not require touch. You might call these healing methods the *Invisible Touch*. They can be quite effective, especially if you are working with animals in zoos and shelters or with animals who are not ready to be touched. Welcome to the wonderful world of invisible touching.

Giving Touch vs. Taking Touch

Sometimes when people are petting their animal, it is more for their own benefit than the animal's pleasure. In the moment, they are often not aware of their animal's feelings as they repetitively pet them as if on autopilot. In this mode, the human is not being present for the animal and is doing what I call "taking touch" rather than "*giving touch.*"

Giving touch is an exchange of good energy. However, if you are not emotionally present for the animal, you may not sense whether or not the animal is truly enjoying the touch. If you are thinking about a million things or stressing while you are petting him or her, this is taking touch and is barely beneficial for the animal. Taking touch is more about doing it for your own comfort.

The best touch is when you are present and aware, noticing when the animal is enjoying the touch as much as you are. Giving touch should feel as good to you as it does to the animal. It is the opposite of mindless or compulsive touching. The late, great actress Betty White was a tremendous champion of animals. She was a regular friend of Gita, an elephant at the Los Angeles Zoo who just loved to have Betty slap her tongue as hard as she could. "Gita just thought that was wonderful." Many elephants enjoy this from people they love and trust. Perhaps each species has their unique favorite touches.

Protactile Touch

A new language is emerging in the Deaf-Blind Community called Protactile communication. It uses touch to convey words and meaning amongst people who are both deaf and blind. They use touch-only cues with each other and to tell their dogs what they want them to do. This innovative language of touch-only communication has created many new nuances of understanding. One idiom of this language is instead of the text LOL – they use LOY – which means *laughing on you,* and is communicated tactilely. This powerful, rich language of touch and texture, reminds those of us who hear and see just how amazingly subtle and sophisticated touch is as a world of communication.

Touch is Communication

Author and expert horseman Mark Rashid, who is also an Aikido master, writes that a gentle touch of connection is the best way to achieve cooperation with an animal. And he is not just speaking of the moment of physical contact. Touch-connection encompasses the entire interaction—the approach, connection, and aftermath. In one of his books, *Journey to Softness – In Search of Feel and Connection with the Horse*, he states his belief that softness is a way of life. As he puts it, "There is strength in muscle, but there is power in softness."

Rashid speaks of giving up the struggle that many people inadvertently fall into with their horses when they are not communicating well together. He says, "I have come to realize that softness *begins* with one simple truth: it's not what we do that starts us on the path to softness, but rather, it's what we don't do. When talking specifically about working with horses, it is my belief that softness begins with learning how not to pull or push. In other words, we find a way to take the adversarial emotion out of a situation that pulling and pushing creates and replace it with one of neutrality."

Inviting Softness into Your World

When you are in a calm state of mind, this is the best time to touch an animal. *HeartMath* calls this state *coherence,* a unified mental state when your heart, mind, and spirit are aligned. Animals respond to our mental states. We can't hide or pretend we are peaceful when we are anything but coherent.

Some animals, like cats and horses, will walk away when they have had enough physical contact. This is a very valuable communication for you. It would be a mistake to pursue an animal who has had enough physical contact.

In our Human-Animal Connection Soothing Touch course, we present about a dozen different styles of healing touch and various massage methods such as Tellington T-Touch, Reiki, and Hawaiian Lomi-Lomi to name a few. One that a miniature horse and I invented I named *Contra-slide*, where I use a light-pressure moving massage and he moves in opposition, something which he loves and seeks out whenever he sees me, even if we haven't seen each other in months, he remembers and initiates this. We also employ variations of speed, depth of pressure, and using different parts of the hand. In every case, we are learning to put our full attention on the animal to gauge how the animal is receiving our touch.

If we are not sure about the animal's response, we will follow James French's advice, which is to stop touching for a moment and wait for the animal to move closer, turn their head toward us, gently nudge us, or give us another physical communication that they would like us to continue. This practice of only touching by "invitation" is very good training for the human and very pleasing for the animal. Each animal is unique and has preferences for where and when, and for how long they want to be touched.

Since each dog is an individual, their response to our "re-puppying" touch methods will vary. You wait for the dog to give you some sign that they desire touch. I like to have a dog, especially a shy or shelter dog, initiate contact before I touch him or her.

Treats are a wonderful way to test a dog's current stress level because they will not take a treat from you unless they feel safe enough to do so. So, acceptance of treats becomes an accurate calibration language to judge a dog's readiness and progress in a shelter context or when meeting a dog for the first time.

If you are working with a dog who has trust issues or who is very shy, gently toss a treat near them. (Do not throw it at them, but to the side.) Toss it near their feet, where they don't have to move from their safe zone to get it. If they don't take it, you want to look away and remain very still -- as still as a statue -- and don't look at them. Make sure you've given them a nice, stinky "high-value" treat that is hard to resist. If the dog eventually takes the treat, then toss another one just a bit further away from the dog and closer to you so that he or she must move just a bit to get it. They must make a choice: stay safe and stuck--or approach and get a treat. This movement is therapeutic because it starts to unwind the "frozen" stress response.

Hopefully, the dog will approach you for the treat soon. I never touch a dog who hasn't approached or touched me first; it is only polite to wait for an invitation.

I wrote several in-depth articles on working with very shy dogs which you can find on the HAC website. They go into greater detail and provide a touch-by-touch description of working with Smitty the Pitty, or Buff's story "Shelter Dog Who Was Afraid to Be Touched."

Once a dog shows they are interested in being closer, say in taking a treat from my open hand, then it is time to try a very brief touch. Perhaps on the chest or shoulder, never over-the-top-of-the-head for an initial touch. Then, I see how he or she responds to slight pressure on his body. When they are ready, a few minutes of light pressure touch will put them into a very relaxed state and often puts them to sleep. The next time I see them, they initiate this kind of touch by leaning against me.

Helping a shy shelter animal learn how to enjoy touch is so powerful it can change the outcome of their lives. Dogs who seek out and enjoy human touch and contact have much greater chances of adoption because they seek affection when they meet a new person.

Science Proves Touch Is Essential

There is a wide body of research on the critically important role of touch for human babies. It helps the child and parent to bond.

Skin-to-skin time during the first hour after birth helps regulate babies' temperature, heart rate, and breathing and helps them to cry less. It also increases the mother's relaxation hormones, such as oxytocin, the feel-good hormone, and leads to better nursing.

Many National Institute of Health (NIH) studies report how essential touch is for normal development. Infants raised in some Romanian orphanages and who did not receive touch failed to thrive physically and mentally. This study suggests that it was not simply the absence of the mother but *the absence of touch* that was critical in developmental issues.

We know that humans experience emotional issues such as attachment disorders from lack of touch. I believe animals can suffer the same if they do not receive the right kind of touch early in life or even later. They can also suffer if they are with a human who does not pay attention to them or respond to their signals and needs for loving touch.

In the 1950s and 1960s, Harry Harlow and other behavioralists studied infant monkeys, who they separated from their mothers. In one study, the infant monkeys were given a choice of a wire replica of a monkey who gave milk or simply a soft mound of terry cloth cotton to cling to. Although the cloth surrogate gave no milk, the infants chose the soft "mother" over the feeding "wire mother." They always chose the soft fabric mound to grab and hang on to for some semblance of comfort.

(These studies sound cruel and horrific to me, even though they did increase understanding of the importance of touch. I believe the infants, who look terrified in the pictures from these studies, suffered terribly in these experiments. Unfortunately, these kinds of studies continued for years by various researchers.)

Around the 1990s, researchers began to study the impact of the lack of touch using more humane methods. Touch seems to be decreasing in our society, as you can see when you are in a public place like a restaurant. When people are having dinner together, chances are they will spend part of the time on their phones. Even people clearly out on a date have their hands on their phones. The Covid-19 pandemic resulted in millions of deaths around the world, and the lockdown also resulted in severe emotional distress, partly due to the lack of contact and physical touch.

Tiffany Field, head of the Touch Research Institute at the University of Miami's Miller School of Medicine, talks about the significant decrease in touch in our modern world. Here is a quote from an article about her work on the website Greater Good, summarized by author Johnathan Jones.

"Aside from the Romanian (orphanage) case, which is an extreme example, we also compared kids in Paris with kids in Miami. We looked at preschoolers on playgrounds, and we also looked at adolescents in McDonald's restaurants. For the preschoolers, the kids in Paris were getting touched more by their parents on the playground than the kids in Miami. And the kids in Paris were less aggressive, verbally, and physically with each other than the kids in Miami."

In my research, I attended a wonderful workshop interacting with horses led by Karenne Koo, Sabrina Geoffrion, and Keita Tsutsumi. We would dance with the horses and one of the program activities was to touch the horses without using our hands. Since horses are so big, it was easy to use other parts of our bodies to gently lean into and make contact with them. Since horses don't have hands, perhaps this handless body contact was more reassuring than hand-petting. To me, it seemed more respectful to introduce ourselves with physical contact but without hands.

What You Can Do to Bring Touch to Others

If you are lucky enough to share your life with an animal, you are likely receiving many benefits from touch and physical contact (depending upon the animal). Here are a few ways you can help others enjoy those same benefits:

- If your animal is a good candidate for therapy work, consider getting certified as a therapy team and bringing your animal on therapy visits. You can work with kids, adults, veterans, healthcare providers, and others. For the elderly, in a variety of situations, it brightens their spirits. Animals make wonderful companions for anyone who could use more touch in their lives.

- Consider becoming a foster by taking an animal home temporarily to give them love and care so he or she can become more easily adoptable.

- If you are not able to care for an animal at your home, consider volunteering at a rescue or shelter.

- Never adopt from puppy mills or pet stores because you don't know where these dogs came from, if they have health or behavior problems, how they were treated, or if they have had severely compromised early life experiences. Rescue, rescue, rescue—the one being rescued will also be you!

Journal Reflections on Touch and Connection:

1) How have animals in your life helped you feel "touch-full" instead of "touch-empty"?
2) Are you ready for more loving touch in your life?
3) Animals have a love language that is based on touch. How is love without words different from love with words?
4) How do you feel about the level of touch in your life?
5) How could you add more touch in your life?

Re-Minder: I am willing to be touched.

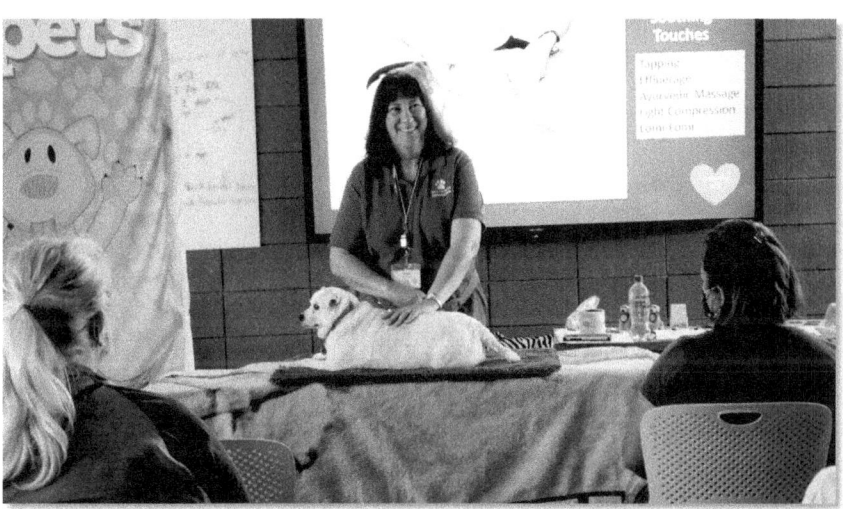

Soothing Touch Class demonstration at Pima Animal Care Center. Sophia loves to be my demonstration dog, and we demonstrate Soothing Touch with shy shelter dogs.

Principle #8

THE HEALING POWER OF PLAY

Play Restores the Spirit

All animals except for man
know that the principal purpose of life
is to enjoy it.

Samuel Butler

Overview

Play is an essential element of a balanced life. This is as true for humans as it is for animals. Spending time with animals helps us reconnect to the power of play which is like pressing the "reset button" on joy.

For young social animals, play is a critical element in brain development and learning how to behave as an adult. The play fights of kittens, puppies, cubs, and others teach appropriate social behaviors, the survival skills they will need as an adult, and the acceptable boundaries in all the rough and tumble. For example, puppies learn bite inhibition during play, which helps teach the soft mouth play-style that is essential to do well in a home with humans. For many species, play is a natural way to express their behavior, release energy, and of course, to have fun.

The Flirtatious Octopus

In *The Soul of an Octopus*, author Sy Montgomery tells the story of an octopus in captivity who enchanted her and an aquarium technician with gentle and tantalizing touches. The octopus played with the humans by touching their hands with gentle suction contact and a mesmerizing dance with her arms. While the octopus had captured their entire focus and attention, one of her other arms snuck around them and stole a bucket of fish at their feet. Moments later, the humans realized how easily she had outwitted them. This octopus understood that it was possible to distract the humans and even noted when they were sufficiently distracted so she could steal the treats. She was swallowing her bounty before the humans even knew she had them.

Play, Glorious Play

If you observe young children or young animals together, you will see lots of play behavior. Some animals have a sense of humor and continue to play their entire lives. As psychology professor John Pilley said, "I have seen how play frees the mind from tension and anxiety, thereby opening the mind to creative thinking." This observation applies to animals too. If you are training animals, your training will be most effective if it is fun because play opens the mind to learning. (Read the story of how Pilley taught his dog Chaser to understand over a thousand words by making sure it was always a fun game in Principle #14.)

Almost every animal that has been studied can be seen to play. Horses, rats, monkeys, dolphins, crows, and elephants all play. Beavers will juggle with rocks and keep their favorite stones their entire life. Bears sometimes hum when they are playing. Adult ravens have been videotaped sliding down snowbanks on their backs, then flying back up and doing it again and again.

Stuart Brown, MD, offers many examples of animals playing in his book, *Play – How it Shapes the Brain, Opens the Imagination, and Invigorates the Soul.* "One of the hallmarks of play is that it *appears* purposeless." Like a kitten endlessly playing with a ball of yarn, a dog with a squeaky toy, or an otter juggling a rock. "Bison will repeatedly run onto a frozen lake and slide on all fours while trumpeting exultantly." *The purpose is joy.*

Brown also makes it clear that play is anything but frivolous. As stated earlier, play is essential to brain development, emotional well-being, and the development of social skills. For animals in shelters, play can transform their quality of life as well as increase their chances of adoption. People like to adopt happy dogs and seeing them play is the best way to introduce them to potential adopters. If you need even more evidence for the power of play, I found it fascinating to discover that Brown made a study of murderers in Texas prisons and found that "the absence of play in their childhood was as important as any single factor in predicting their crimes."

The more we study animals, the more we understand the role of play in making their world a happy place. An excellent documentary, *My Octopus Teacher*, features an octopus playing with other fish and a human, using many sophisticated strategies to achieve her desires. Octopuses were once thought to be solitary creatures, and this documentary popularized the fact that octopuses play—and play with other creatures.

Brown's studies on the value of play also had an influence on hiring practices at NASA's jet propulsion laboratory (JPL), where innovation and the ability to think outside the box are mission-critical in certain positions. Hiring managers added questions to their standard interview process about an applicant's youthful play history and creative projects. JPL managers discovered, as Brown had, that "there is a kind of magic in play. What might seem like a frivolous or even childish pursuit, is ultimately beneficial. It's paradoxical that a little bit of 'unproductive' activity can make one enormously more productive and invigorated in other aspects of life… I don't think it is too much to say that play can save your life."

The Purpose of Play Is Joy

Play is not the opposite of work. Play resets the brain in a way that allows for more productivity. Play uniquely helps a tired brain perceive new possibilities. Shifting your focus to a softer, more fluid state, allows new ideas to come. Play leads to a more joyful state which makes everything easier. One is reminded that Einstein used to ride his bicycle in circles, and this "mindless" activity led to many inspirations. Similarly, observing animals is not only fun and playful, but it awakens the mind to new insights.

Famous examples abound: Nicola Tesla practiced a nearly obsessive study of pigeon habits and activities to understand the rules of nature, and Leonardo da Vinci dedicated himself to observing birds in flight as research for his flying machine.

Play Is Healthy for People and Animals

For animals, playing is a sign of well-being. Of course, there is tremendous variation in how much individual animals will play, but it is a good indication of their mental and physical health. Sick, injured, and traumatized animals do not play or do not play much. It is a sign that they are beginning to heal when they feel safe enough to let their playfulness emerge. When I adopted Sophia, a former street dog, it was about a year before she started to play with toys. Watching animal playgroups in shelters, you will see very shy or frightened animals, who won't play at all at first, begin to trust as they begin to play. It is a beautiful experience to witness this transformation.

A friend of mine had a feral cat she rescued from the streets of Jersey City. She named the cat Willow. Willow never played with toys in the seven years they lived together, and she felt her cat was missing out on the benefits of play. Her vet just said, "Some cats don't play." But my friend was still curious if there was something she could do to introduce play into her cat's life. She spoke with a pet psychic who said that Willow had a gut imbalance and needed probiotics. My friend doubted that the two things were related but decided to give it a try. When she made this one change in her cat's diet, Willow started playing with toys. They then had many delightful play sessions together and it deepened their bond.

Play as Medicine

For some animals, play is medicine. I have seen many dogs in shelters cowering or listlessly laying around. But pair them with the *right dog in a play yard*, and you would barely recognize the depressed or anxious dog you just took out of the kennel. These two dogs, who may have just met moments ago, are suddenly tumbling and cavorting like puppies. While not all dogs enjoy exuberant play, it can be a tremendously potent tool in their healing process for those who do.

Aimee Sadler, a dog trainer, and creator of *Dogs Playing for Life* (DPFL), has introduced her wonderful, lifesaving program to several hundred shelters. They set out to address the problem that many dogs languish in shelters far too long because they have been labeled *dog reactive*, meaning they get overstimulated and bark or lunge in the presence of other dogs. Of course, this behavior dramatically reduces their chances of finding a home, as many great potential adopters already have a dog and will be discouraged from meeting a dog labeled as *dog reactive*. In shelters that have high euthanasia rates, *reactive dogs* are often first on the death list.

The Dogs Playing for Life (DPFL) program affirms that dogs need to have playtime every day and evaluates dogs for their temperamental play style so that they can be matched with others with the same or similar energy. They identify four main play styles, from gentle play to rough and rowdy styles. They strongly recommend that dogs should be separated according to their playstyle for maximum safety, positive experience, and enjoyment.

Not all dogs enjoy playgroups, and those who don't should not be forced to engage, as that would have the opposite effect of the goal of enrichment. Even if they are a little shy at first, dogs should indicate that they can thrive in this experience. If they tire of playing, they should always have the choice to opt out to prevent any negative learning experiences. Careful dog interactions, in which behavior is closely observed to see how the dogs are reacting to each other is critical. *How dogs are introduced to each other* can have a huge impact on the success of the interaction.

DPFL-trained teams learn to identify *helper dogs*, those with excellent social skills and friendly playstyles. These special dogs help dogs with less developed play and social skills by providing comfort as well as helping them to learn appropriate social skills. Very little upsets a good helper dog. They give gentle corrections to dogs that are too rough and those not following good dog etiquette. A good helper dog can do more than a human to correct dogs appropriately and teach them how to get along with others. Pima Animal Care Center (PACC), where I volunteer, is one of the many shelters that has been DPFL trained in how to run effective playgroups. In time, even the shyest dogs can learn to thrive in playgroups if allowed to come out of their shells at their own pace.

Helper Dogs Can Burn Out

Lynne Stott of Top Dogs, the volunteer training team at PACC, cautions that helper dogs can't work every day. They can play this role for maybe three days a week and then need time to just play without the responsibility of helping, teaching, and correcting other dogs. Helper dogs are amazing in their ability to not take things personally, to be the peacemakers, and to encourage others to play fair. But, if they don't get enough breaks, they can burn out from having to be the *Doggie-Buddha* in the shelter. One day, if they are pushed too far, they can snap. For this reason, it is very important to rotate helper dogs and not put all the burden on a single dog.

PACC runs playgroups seven days a week, letting up to 100 or more dogs out of their kennels and into the play yard every day. Twenty minutes of engaged play has the same exercise benefits as a two-hour walk. But playgroups do more than exercise the body. They exercise the mind, the emotions, and, just as importantly, the sense of social connection. This play is healing for the dogs and for everyone, as the joy of watching dogs in playgroups is indescribable.

Playgroups can be particularly helpful to dogs who might have seemed to be too intense in the kennel and are doing poorly with kennel confinement, causing them to bark and lunge at people and dogs. These dogs often release their frustration and tension in playgroups and thus become much easier to handle. DPFL has excellent statistics that show a nearly 30 percent reduction in shelter bites as a result of dogs participating in their daily playgroups.

Not all dogs will play well together. Some dogs read each other's signals immediately and accurately. Other dogs, just like some people, miss the cues entirely and don't realize that a particular dog doesn't want to play. That's why it is essential to recognize dogs should be separated by energy level and playstyle.

I wish more rescues and shelter facilities were set up to have doggie playgroups, with the right pairing of dogs for compatible, supervised play. Many modern shelters in the United States don't have the behavioral staff resources to evaluate dogs carefully, don't have safe play areas with the right entrance configuration, or the right staff to supervise them. Shelters are often too afraid of dog fights to consider putting dogs together in playgroups. Rightfully, they are concerned about the dog reactivity they see in their shelter environment, where dogs growl, bark, or lunge at other dogs as if they were auditioning for a role in a horror film. While safety must be the top priority in these larger shelters, it would be wonderful if more effort could be directed toward resolving these issues with trained evaluators, proper matching, and careful observation of daily playgroups. If future shelters could be designed with different play areas for different play styles, it would greatly improve the humanity of these shelters.

On the other hand, some shelters have no choice but to have dogs living communally, which eliminates the problems caused by isolation. It is always amazing to see the grassroots shelters, ones in other countries, and sometimes smaller rescues that have groups of animals living together. Territorio de Zaguates, the street dog free-range rescue in Costa Rica, is a good example of communal living. This sanctuary simply has no choice but to put all the dogs together in one space. (Some free-range shelters are able to have some separation for large and small dogs.) While I am sure there are still occasional "problems" with enough food and space, these communal dogs tend to resolve squabbles on their own.

Of course, this type of free and natural interaction is impossible in every situation, such as in public shelters with liability concerns. But with more awareness of the importance of play for well-being, beyond the obvious physical needs, we could move the needle a little toward recognizing that *play is an essential need*. Shelters provide for crucial needs such as food and water, medical attention, and protection from the elements. But once these basics are handled, play and social connection are the next most important needs for quality of life.

Communal living works for cats, too, especially in a couple of innovative cat shelters in Tucson, Arizona. The Cat Hermitage No-Kill Rescue and Sanctuary and the Hope Rescue and Sanctuary are two that I have visited where cats are not stuck in cages but instead live together socially; I am sure there are more. These shelters provide smaller rooms, separate areas, and many little hidey-holes where loners can hang out, but it is nice to see the cats have the choice to move through the space and to choose whether or not to interact with others. (See our HAC podcast interview with the Cat Hermitage.)

People often think that cats don't get along in groups, but feral cats often work it out. Cats in communal environments such as the two mentioned above seem much less stressed and are happier and healthier. I hope that with more understanding of how important play is to express natural animal behaviors, more safe opportunities to play with members of their own species will be provided in more shelters in the future.

If you share your life with an animal, it is important to spend some regular, dedicated time engaged in play. Think of it as a play date. This is time you are spending together, when you are not distracted, and your full attention is on the animal. Even a few minutes of attentive play can go a long way in strengthening the bond between you and your friend. Every animal is unique in how they like to play and for how long. Sometimes the simplest things are the best, such as a crinkled-up ball of paper or a feather toy for a cat.

Your playdates will have the greatest benefits when your games are fair and balanced and combine some elements of unpredictability with other known and repeated elements. Remember, don't tease to cause frustration. The animal should feel some challenge but not feel defeated.

Play Is a State of Mind – The Act Resilient Method

Play is a powerful tool that restores balance to the body and mind of animals and people. Play is not just a silly activity. It is *a state of mind*. In 2010, I created The Act Resilient Method (and a book by the same name), which uses therapeutic play, therapy animals, improvisational comedy, laughter therapy, and the expressive arts to help people heal from the effects of trauma, including post-traumatic stress.

Act Resilient has been presented to over 4,000 U.S. military service members, veterans, and their families. My program taught me how powerful play is as a tool for individual, family, and community healing. Post-Traumatic Stress Disorder (PTSD) doesn't exist in an individual vacuum; thus, an effective healing program will focus on restoring healthy human connections and group cohesion. Participants in Act Resilient reported an over 80 percent reduction in the symptoms of PTSD.

We received letters of commendation from General Chiarelli (RET), former Vice-Chair of the Army. Our team at Tripler Army Medical Center in Honolulu was given a National Workplace Resilience Award from the American Psychological Association for this work, as well as for the animal therapy program that dovetailed with it. I was given President Obama's Volunteer Service Award for this program.

In the Act Resilient program, we teach the Power of Play as a potent tool to help people find themselves again. As Benny, a Vietnam vet, said after his first Act Resilient class, "That's the first time I laughed like that in thirty-eight years." Laughter is healing. Group and social play are often underestimated as a pathway to wellness.

Being silly is a reboot of our resilience. I wish more people understood that this inexpensive, all-natural method could be lifesaving, literally.

A few years into creating and presenting the Act Resilient program, I began bringing therapy animals to class. My first therapy animal was a rescue dog, who I named Oscar (whose story is in this book). Oscar had lived a rough life. He was forced to be a wild pig hunter, where owners would underfeed the dogs to make them more aggressive. Oscar had escaped from this terrible situation with missing teeth, scars all over his body, and a very expensive GPS collar. His abusive owners wouldn't even risk claiming him.

Oscar had been at the Hawaii shelter for a long time when I met him. With minimal training and a lot of healing touch, Oscar became one of the best therapy animals I have ever encountered. I could walk him with just one finger looped through his leash, and he would follow with the precision of a ballroom dancer.

Despite his past, Oscar was the sweetest dog in the world. He would enter a room full of tough soldiers suffering from PTSD. He would greet each soldier, avoiding those with a fear of dogs—without being told. Then Oscar would "select" the one person who needed the most attention at that moment. He would settle down with this soldier, who would invariably drop down to his belly to play with this large, gentle dog. Their hearts would open instantly. Perhaps they identified with the slower movements, missing teeth, and visible scars. Therapy dogs with missing limbs are often revered by service members. Many service members with PTSD have had to shut their hearts down to survive. A gentle therapy dog, without requiring any need for talk, helps them to open their hearts again, and this begins a process of healing. In the words of Pope John Paul II, "The worst prison would be a closed heart."

Oscar always knew who needed attention most at that moment and would be right there to help them. I saw him do this time and again. His instincts were impeccable, even when people were disguising their pain. One reason you can't hide feelings from a great therapy dog is they can "smell" emotional pain. You certainly couldn't fool Oscar.

He also worked with children who had emotional stress. When engaging with a group of children, Oscar would instantly detect which child had the greatest emotional need and attend to that child first. As a formerly abused animal and then a long-term resident at a shelter, my sweet Oscar seemed to have deep wisdom about the needs of wounded humans.

Good therapy dogs read human emotions well. They have a furry key that opens hearts. Even people who are reluctant to talk to therapists will often speak to a dog. Therapy dogs can be a tremendous asset to therapists; Army studies show that patients will talk 50 percent more if a dog is in the room. It was amazing to see these big tough guys who didn't want to talk about their pain—or anything else—get down on the floor to give Oscar a belly rub.

It is a foundational principle in The Human-Animal Connection that animals can heal people, who can then turn around and heal other animals in need. We encourage our military veterans to volunteer with the shelter dogs. If they have the desire, we train them how to work with shy, frightened, or traumatized dogs. And we teach them to encourage play. Our methods are quick and effective, as they must be in a shelter environment. Helping a dog come out of his shell, unlock the grip of the past, and become a dog that seeks human contact for safety and affection is life-changing for the dog and the person who helped them become adoptable.

Rats Love to Laugh

There was a time when it was thought that humans were the only species that laughed. Now, with new high-tech sound and brain analysis research tools, researcher Jaak Panksepp and others have discovered that several species laugh, including great apes, chimpanzees, bonobos, orangutans, dolphins, lions, dogs, and rats. Hopefully, as our research methods expand, we will find even more species that laugh.

Many dog owners swear to me that their dogs laugh while they are playing. To our human ear, a doggie laugh sounds like a little huffy pant. But when this *play pant* was analyzed with sophisticated sound analysis equipment, the *laughing* sound was distinctly different from a regular pant. It's also infectious: when you play the sound of a dog laughing to another dog, it soothes them, and sometimes they laugh along. Can you imagine using this "dog laugh-track" in shelters?

And rats laugh! Jaak Panksepp has published over 400 papers in his field of research, emotions in humans and animals. Virginia Morell reports that he has "pioneered the field of what he calls affective neuroscience—the zone where neurons, emotions, and cognition meet." Starting in the 1980s, and using sophisticated computer audio systems in his lab, Panksepp was able to record the sound of rats laughing, which is inaudible to the human ear. He discovered that when rats play, they laugh. They also laugh when you tickle them. And, when the tickler enters the room, they laugh in *anticipation of* being tickled.

As Panksepp said:

"Without laughter, there will not be much joy in life. It's a little shocking how little we know about how brains generate positive feelings. When we discovered laughter-type sounds in rats, I think people laughed at us a bit. But now we know more about the 'laughter' of rats than humans. And we have learned that a study of these happy sounds can illuminate human problems, even drug addictions, and depression. Even though we cannot do detailed research on these systems with humans, we have mapped out the brain networks in rats along with some of the controlling brain chemistries. Currently, it is one of our major measures of depressive feelings in animals. This allows us to focus on the feelings of rats rather than just their behavioral changes. Laughter and joy are aspects of both the brain and mind. We still have a science that respects animal behaviors and brain molecules more than mind functions they create. That should change as we learn to understand the minds of other animals."

Panksepp was a special scientist with an integrated vision. He understood the connections between play, social contact, cognition, and a healthy emotional life. He mapped the emotional systems in the brains of rats in the mammalian subcortex, very similar to what you would see in humans. He defined seven core emotional systems, clearly demonstrating that rats have a rich emotional life.

Panksepp's Core Emotions in Mammals

- SEEKING: Motivation, motor patterns, interest, frustration
- RAGE: Anger, irritability
- FEAR: Anxiety, phobias, panic, psychic trauma
- PANIC: Separation distress, sadness
- PLAY: Joy, glee, happy playfulness
- LUST: Erotic feelings
- CARE: Nurturance, attraction

For comparison, his control lab rats were never allowed to play with humans or other rats—ever. They slept a lot, curled in tight balls, and seemed depressed. Research showed clearly that the control group didn't develop as many neuronal connections as the rats allowed daily play. In other words, those who were play-deprived were cognitively impaired. In contrast, the rats who were given play time with other rats, and were tickled by humans showed enthusiastic, curious engagement, had better social skills with other rats, and could read each other's behavioral clues more accurately. In his words, "We argue that play—especially rough-and-tumble play—helps construct the social brain.... Laughter and play are evolutionarily so important for optimal social growth."

Play Builds Cognitive and Social Skills

The moral of the story is that *play is a natural need.* If you want to be happy, play more, laugh more. If you want the animals who share your life to be even happier, find ways that they like to play. Open your mind. A fun little game could be simpler than you think. Observe them and see if you can find the ways they naturally express this joyful side of themselves and then find ways to engage with them. It will do a lot of good for them and just as much for you.

No animal in your life? Volunteer at your local shelter. Or turn on the computer. There is a reason that kitties playing are some of the most popular videos online. We can all use more joy in our lives. And joy shared is one of the loveliest ways we can connect with others.

Journal Reflections on the Healing Power of Play:

1) Reflect on play in your life. What was play like for you as a child? Was it a solo activity, or did you play with others?

2) How much is play a part of your life today? Would you like to include more play in your life and in the lives of the animals in your life?

3) Reflecting on what was fun for you as a child, how could you reintegrate those activities into your current life? How could you play more as an adult?

4) Are there some groups of people playing in ways that you would enjoy? Can you do a little research to find out how you could join the fun?

5) Is there anything about letting more play into your life that makes you nervous? Do you have any negative judgments about play?

Re-Minder: I allow myself to play.

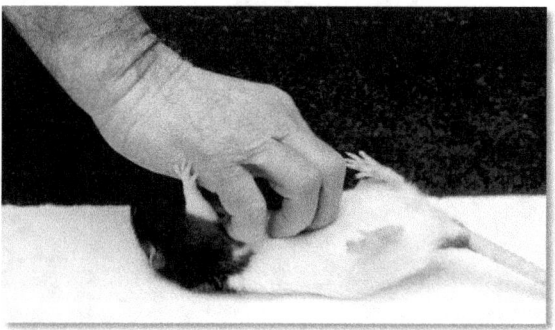

Panksepp tickles a rat who cuddles and laughs in response. Play led to happier and smarter lab rats than those who were never given the chance to play.

Principle #9

THE POWER OF FOCUS
Mastering Your Mind and Emotions

I have lived with several Zen masters—all of them cats.

Eckhart Tolle

Overview

The quality of your life is a direct reflection of your ability to manage your focus. What you focus on is what you get more of. So, if you are oriented toward goodness, you will experience more goodness. If you focus on anxiety-producing concerns, you will feel more anxious.

Learning how to focus on what is essential and to ignore what is not is a healing discipline that will transform every area of your life. A good life is created by choosing to focus on what serves you and spending less time on what causes stress and disturbance. This is as true for animals as it is for humans. We can assist animals to focus on what is calming, safe, and pleasurable.

Focus on Good

Focusing on what feels good can help shy animals get comfortable in their skin. I worked with a large white pit bull named Kayla, who had survived a terrible trauma as a puppy (I will spare you the details). She spent the next two years of her life in her crate. Even with the crate door open, she would only come out to do her business.

When I started working with Kayla, and her wonderful foster person, Sandy, Kayla would never make eye contact even when I used the Trust Technique to lower her stress level. Our next step was getting her to focus *outside herself* by using a slow process of redirecting her awareness to positive external stimulation. While she was not responsive to treats at first, the combination of treats and applying Tellington Touch (in this case, a specific circular massage under her chest) helped her shift her awareness. She learned to focus on the pleasure of the pairing of the treat with gentle touch.

Over the course of a few months and frequent repetition of these methods, Kayla began to feel more comfortable in her body. She had begun to lower her stress levels enough to come out of her crate. Soon after, she cuddled on the couch with her person for the first time. She even enjoyed and initiated brief moments of eye contact. Thankfully, Sandy, adopted Kayla. Although Kayla still preferred the safety of being at home, she had a wonderful life; they were even able to travel together in a van on a long road trip. It was an honor to work with such a sensitive dog.

Your Focus Is Your Power

If you want to know what an animal is thinking or feeling, notice where their focus is. What has their visual attention has their mind. For humans, our ability to direct our focus on what is positive in our life and the ability to redirect our focus away from what pulls us down is the secret to happiness because what we focus on, we get more of.

By directing our focus, outside influences and disturbances have less impact, and our life will be simpler, happier, and more productive. Animals are very skilled at focus, so if you want to learn about focus, spend some time with a dog with a favorite toy. Or a horse grazing in a pasture. Or a cat…being a cat. A cat's entire world is what is happening right now. The ability of a cat to give her full attention to whatever is most pleasing in the moment is a sublime power.

Mental, emotional, and sensory focus are pathways to mindfulness. Directing your focus allows you to "smell the roses," lovingly connect with animals, and enjoy your life. How the eyes are engaging (or not engaging) is a window into the brain. Eye movement (or its absence) can be a clue to a person's and an animal's emotional state. For healing, specific eye pattern movement can be a path to unwinding trauma, as is used in Thought Field Therapy and in Eye Movement Desensitization and Reprocessing (EMDR).

I use a version of these methods by inviting dogs to move their eyes in a therapeutic pattern to help them release trauma. When working with shelter dogs, it is important to pay attention to how they are using their eyes. Are their eye movements soft and fluid, or static and stuck? The way a dog looks at you can tell a lot about how they are feeling about you in that moment.

Playing with animals using the movement of toys to invite fluid eye movement can help soften their eyes, lower their stress levels, and lead to more emotional freedom.

Remember, while the dogs who share your life with you may love gazing into your eyes, not all dogs enjoy sustained eye contact. After all, a stare—especially a hard stare—can be a signal of dominance or aggression in nature. If you meet a silverback gorilla in the wild and stare him down, he will attack because *you started it!*

In most Western cultures, sustained eye contact is highly valued. But other cultures have very different social rules about eye contact.

In Japan, it is considered polite to avert your eyes, especially to show respect to an elder or higher-ranking person. If you were in a job interview in Germany and you didn't look your boss in the eye nearly 100 percent of the time, you might be considered weak, unconfident, or lying. The point: eye contact is culture and species-specific.

When it comes to shelter dogs, some are very excited to make eye contact, especially if they have previously lived with a human. Animals who share their lives with humans get very good at reading our faces to understand our emotions and intentions, and they expect the same kind of insight from us about what they are feeling. If a potential adopter approaches, and the dog puts their paws up and looks them in the eye with an irresistible "take me home" expression, many adopters will be instantly smitten. And off to their new home, this eye-contact-loving doggie goes.

I often ask people who have adopted dogs what convinced them that a certain dog was "the one." Why take this dog home among the hundred other dogs needing homes? The answer I most commonly hear is, "The way he looked at me. I couldn't leave him there."

This is the reason why we teach our HAC students who wish to volunteer in the shelter that our first dog training priority after "sit" is "focus." Some trainers use a different cue, such as "Watch me," or "Look at me." Continue using whatever words you have already taught your dog. We use the word *focus* because we also teach the humans this skill: managing. their mental focus.

To begin teaching a dog focus, hold a yummy treat up to your forehead, right between your eyes. The exact second the dog makes eye contact, say "Yes!" or "Good!" in a happy voice and immediately give them the treat. Most dogs learn focus in one short training session. A few minutes, and more than a few treats later, they will understand the association. What you are doing in this first stage of teaching focus is pairing the action of looking at you with an instant "Yes!" or "Good!" which must be immediately followed by delivering the treat.

Once they learn what you are asking for and follow your hand with the treat to your eyes, *then* you add the word *focus*. You only add the word after they have learned that the action of making eye contact results in a treat.

When you are first training this skill of focus, the instant the dog makes eye contact, they get a treat. But, as the dog learns the meaning of focus, I hold the treat just a little longer, making them sustain eye contact for two or three seconds or several seconds (but do not turn this into minutes of focus as that can lead to frustration). Only after they are succeeding at brief focus would you extend the duration by a few more seconds, so they learn to sustain their attention a bit longer.

This method of sustaining focus is not just about obedience; it is a positive training method for maintaining connection. It is a great tool to avoid potential problems, like if a trigger captures your dog's attention. The focus cue is an excellent method of regaining your dog's attention and nurturing a healthy relationship.

I like using the word "focus" over other words for several reasons. First, it is short, distinct, and it is not a word they hear in many other contexts. Second, the concept of focus connects to other elements in our HAC curriculum. The third reason I recommend "focus" is that "look" can be used to teach your dog to follow where someone points, which is great if you plan to have your dog read to children, as it will make the kids feel as through the dog is really following along with the story. "Look" is also a common que for other fields that work with animals such as on film sets where "look" is used to tell a dog to turn their head. And finally, as mentioned above, you can use "Look" to get the dog to follow healing eye movement patterns, which helps to unlock a stressed nervous system.

It is important to utilize the focus cue *before* your dog becomes highly reactive, such as barking intensely at another dog. Asking for a sit and focus before the situation gets out of control is one way to allow you to manage the dog's nervous system activation without having to get into harsh corrections and stressed states. The last thing you want to do is add stress once the dog has already reacted and is barking intensely at another dog.

The earlier you catch their rising excitement, the more effective the focus intervention will be. The secret is to be observant and *anticipate* a potential trigger. This is a key principle in the Trust Technique, as well as in other positive training methods. Being ahead of the trigger reaction gives you a chance to deescalate a situation. Once the dog is barking and pulling, it can cause the human to get more stressed. Now we have two stressed beings!

FOCUS Builds Positive Connection

The focus cue is a way to maintain a positive connection without getting overly agitated by a stressful situation. Practice it daily, away from situations that have any stress. I do this process of "sit, focus, stay" every day and every night before Sophia gets her food dish. This slows down her excitement and keeps the feeding sequence calm. Then I say, "okay," to signal that she is released, and then I put the bowl down. This creates a positive association between the focus cue and food. Further, this practice provides regular reinforcement of the focus cue, which is helpful when I need to manage her behavior easily and gently out in the world.

Focus is a pivotal concept in the human aspect of our training. We teach humans to be able to *switch their focus* to what is desired instead of what is troubling them. This is empowering because you realize you don't have to be victimized by negative focus.

Another reason being able to direct your focus is one of the keys to happiness is that it protects you from being at the mercy of other people's energy. You don't want others' thoughts, moods, agendas, opinions, and judgments to take up any more of your mental space. You want a "clear headspace" so you can focus on what is good, what is present, and the animal right in front of you.

We also encourage people to put their full focus and attention on the animal with whom they are working. Animals sense when you have split focus, and it can be confusing, even uncomfortable, for them. I can tell you from personal experience that horses don't want anything to do with you if your mind is running a mile a minute.

Balancing *Soft Focus* with *Laser Focus*

Soft focus is the opposite of a stare. Soft eyes have a diffused focus. This is the kind of interaction you want to use with your own animals and with shelter dogs in particular. Spending time in soft focus while connecting with animals will relax you both and keep your hearts open.

Soft focus is important for your own well-being, too. I recommend that you spend some time each day working with soft focus because it helps to balance out an overabundance of *directed focus,* as cognitive scientists call it, such as staring at a screen for hours or any activity that requires intense laser-like focus and mental concentration. Alternating between directed focus on a task and soft focus is one technique that will help prevent burnout.

One ancient way to train focus is to gaze at a candle flame in a softly lit room. Let your eyes soften, and your vision blur as you maintain visual connection with the flame. You will feel your eyes go into soft focus, and these *soft eyes* are powerful when working with animals. The ancient technique of focusing on a candle flame also helps open your intuition. If you don't want to work with a candle, you can do this with a tree, a mountain, a rose, or a body of water. Something you find beautiful that awakens a sense of peace, such as an image of a Japanese garden or a lovely nature photo on your wall, will also work as long as it is an image that truly pleases you.

The point is to switch to soft focus, even for a couple of minutes, to reset the mind. Keeping the eyes soft and still will slow down your nervous system and reduce the trauma response of freeze, fight, or flight, just as it does for your animal.

Balancing soft and direct focus is a valuable resilience tool. Your directed focus is a muscle. You can literally tire it out if you use it too much in a day. Markham Heid writes in the journal *Elemental*,

> "According to researchers at the University of Exeter Medical School in the U.K, your ability to effortfully focus your attention is finite. Just as an overworked muscle grows weak, overworking your attention seems to wear it out. When that happens, a lot can go wrong. For one thing, your ability to concentrate will plummet. Your willpower and decision-making abilities also take a hit. According to a 2019 study in the journal *Occupational Health Science*, attention fatigue may also contribute to stress and burnout."

Soft Focus is a resilience skill and can help you reset and rebalance your brain. In the Trust Technique, we work with the alternation between a meditative stillness and focused attention. This alternation increases the relaxation response and can be healing for both the human and the animal as they play or move about. This alternation of focused and unfocused states—stimulation and relaxation—is a key principle in The Act Resilient Method as it restores neuroplasticity.

Neuroplasticity allows the brain to restore a sense of balance. Trauma is all about the brain *getting stuck* in a trigger feedback loop.

It is like the alarm that goes off at a hair trigger. It is hard to bring the mind back to a peaceful state when it is screaming. Retraining the mind to be more flexible, slow down, and make a choice about where to focus, are all powerful tools to restore healthy responses to life.

Focus Is Healing Medicine

Having used The Act Resilient Method with thousands of traumatized people, I know that both animals and people can heal from trauma. Using soft-eye gaze, even for a few seconds or however long the animal prefers, can stimulate the feel-good chemical oxytocin.

As you master your own ability to focus, the quality of your "headspace" will improve. That is, you will not tolerate indulging negativity for as long because focusing on what is *good* feels so much better than wallowing in the bad. When you direct your mental focus, you are literally reorienting your thinking, which has enormous consequences across all areas of your life and relationships.

Journal Reflections on Focus:

1) Take an honest self-assessment. How much of your time is spent focusing on things that feel good versus things that cause stress?

2) Are you willing to take back the reins of your focus?

3) Focus on goodness is a discipline. And the more you use soft focus, the stronger the relaxation response gets. Remember to take breaks from too much directed focus. If your mind has been running wild, it will take some time before you feel YOU are back in control. As we say in the Trust Technique, be patient. Be persistent. Be peaceful. Switching to soft focus is one of your best tools to live in peace.

4) Take a self-inventory and see what the significant focus-stealers or focus-splitters (like electronic devices) are in your life. Who are the people who attempt to steal your focus?

5) Would you be willing to reduce or eliminate the major and chronic sources of split focus in your life?

Re-Minder: What you focus on is what you get.

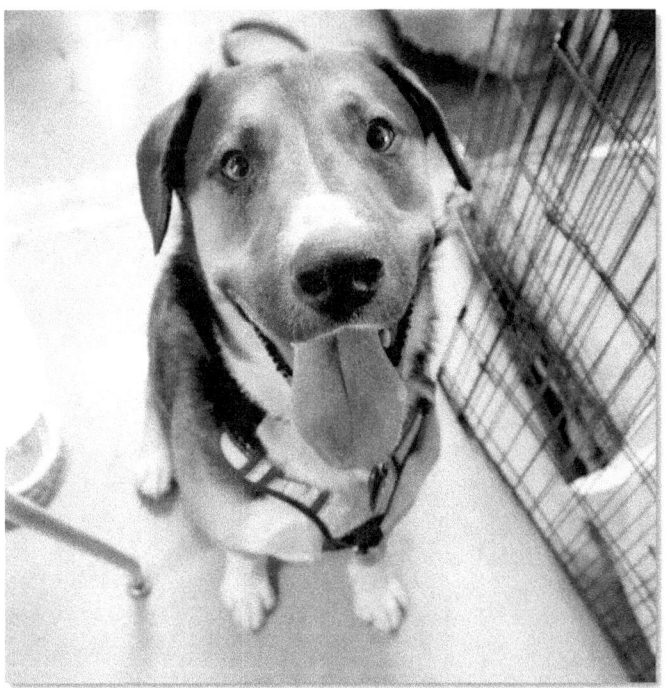

Milo, a former shelter dog in our HAC Therapy Dog Training program, learns focus. This skill helps him to learn to calm his brain and maintain connection with his people.

<h1>Principle #10</h1>

ANIMALS HAVE OPINIONS

What Does That Mean for
Sharing Our Lives Together?

*You cannot share your life with a dog or
cat and not know perfectly well that
animals have personality, and minds, and opinions.*

Jane Goodall

Overview

To say that animals have opinions is another way of saying they are sentient beings; they have thoughts, feelings, emotions, moods, desires—and opinions. They like what they like, and they don't like what they don't like.

If you share your life with an animal, it doesn't mean they will always get what they want. But it is important to recognize that they have preferences. They will be happier, and your bond will be deeper when you can listen to and, when possible, accommodate those preferences.

Listening to the Opinion of a Donkey

My friend Afton has a small animal rescue and mustang sanctuary on his ranch. He is in the habit of rescuing horses that are on their way to the glue factory. Afton also has donkeys, chickens, a goat, a huge pig, and a llama named Cuzco.

One of his elderly donkeys, Charlotte, was being picked on by the other donkeys, who were keeping her from getting her fair share of food. She was losing weight, so he knew he had to do something. He made arrangements to transfer Charlotte to a friend's ranch where other "last chance" horses were sheltered.

I was there with Afton that day and offered to help load Charlotte into the horse trailer. It seemed like the right thing to do, so we began luring Charlotte in with her favorite treats. She was willing to put one hoof into the trailer, and then she stopped. If you know donkeys, it is not easy to get them to do something they don't want to do.

Donkeys have been given a bad reputation because people think they are stubborn, but this is not necessarily the truth. Often, they are just being true to their desires. If something doesn't feel safe to them, they want no part of it. (If only humans had more "donkey sense.")

We tried a few tricks, but none of them worked, and Charlotte was about to bolt. Then I thought, *Oh, maybe I should ask her what she wants.* I asked, and she communicated back to me, "I don't want to leave my friends." Perhaps she knew the new rescue place had no donkeys! She also told me that "I want to stay with Cuzco." (Cuzco was a llama who was her friend). I want to be near the other donkeys but stay on the other side of the fence."

I told Afton what she had said, and fortunately, he trusted me and put Charlotte in with the llama. Charlotte could still see the other donkeys on the other side of the fence, but now she could eat her food in peace. She still had company, but no more struggles.

Charlotte became one of Afton's best "reading donkeys." When young children came to his ranch, they wanted to read to Charlotte. She would wait 'til the child sat down in the reading chair and opened their book.

Then Charlotte would slowly approach, look over the child's shoulder and follow along with the picture books. The children loved reading to her. One little girl begged her parents to let her come every day. She was so sure Charlotte was following every word and was determined to finish the story. The parents were amazed at Charlotte's gentle focus and presence. This inspired Afton to introduce more parents to the wonderful connection that is possible with animals.

Charlotte is such a sweet donkey girl, and I am so happy she was able to tell me what she wanted. She had a very harmonious plan that we might not have thought of without her telling us. Life is so much sweeter when you consider an animal's opinion.

"Of course we have opinions."

Miss Betsy (a horse, of course) said this to me.

Our most basic emotional reactions—liking or disliking, being drawn toward or away from something, preferring one thing over another, loving versus fearing—create opinions and preferences. Simply, we want more of what we like and less of what we don't.

In this principle, we explore the idea that animals have opinions. Further, if animals have opinions, this assumes that they have emotions, which implies that they may have a degree of consciousness. And finally, if animals have opinions, how does that change how we should relate to them?

There's a reason I believe animals have opinions: as soon as I started listening to animals, I got an earful. It is an art to consider an animal's opinion. It is a combination of neutral observation (meaning you don't insert your own wishes and judgments) and listening.

When I first adopted Sophia, I wanted to make sure she had a comfortable bed. And I learned the not-so-soft way that what *I* thought was the perfect bed and what *she* thought was the perfect bed weren't always the same. Fortunately, we could shop at Petco together. I love Petco because I could put two beds down on the floor and let her pick the one that she liked, which she indicated by promptly laying down on one and showing no interest in the other.

But then I would find another doggie bed online that I thought was wonderful. I loved the color, or it looked to me like a great bed, and I would order it. It would arrive in a big box, and I would proudly present it to Sophia like I was Mrs. Santa Clause. Her opinion? *Meh.* She would sniff it and then walk away as if it was a nuisance. Postscript: I gave away a lot of *meh* beds to shelters and friends whose dogs thought they were just fine. Sophia taught me how expensive it could be not to consider her opinion. Currently, she has seven different beds in our house, and each one is perfect, in her opinion.

You will have no doubt that animals have opinions if you choose to observe and listen to them. However, you may not always hear what you want to hear. Being willing to listen to their opinions deepens the relationship and increases connection. If animals are sharing their lives with humans, the animals are not always going to get what they want all the time. You wouldn't let a kid eat all the pretty things in a candy store. But with limits and boundaries that are gently and clearly communicated, we can collaborate on how to make life good for humans and animals who share each other's company.

Christina Hunger, a speech pathologist, learned a lot about her own dog's opinions when she taught Stella to communicate three-dozen words by stepping on talk buttons that spoke individual words. She noted, "We are not as separate from animals as many think we are. We all think, we all feel, we all have opinions, we all communicate, and we all want to connect."

A Puppy's First Opinion

A neighbor family adopted an eight-week-old beagle puppy from a breeder and invited me over for the puppy's first introduction to their three joyous young children, all under the age of ten. Of course, each child wanted to energetically play and cuddle with the puppy. When the puppy was finally put down on the ground, he lay like a log, legs spread in all four directions. It looked as if he had collapsed.

The mom turned to me to for help. I told her the puppy was overwhelmed. I gently explained that as much fun as this was for everyone, the puppy had just been taken from his mother and siblings, and this much activity and attention from the children was exhausting. I suggested that the family pay attention to the puppy's rhythms and desires for play and interaction. I recommended that they consider the puppy's opinion on when she had enough play.

As the puppy got a little older, she began to continually disappear, no matter how escape proof the family tried to make their house and yard. The puppy would get out and run to different neighbors' houses, crawling under cars and furniture to hide. Then she would take a nap in this quiet place and not respond to being called. This caused the family much stress as they couldn't find her for hours. It would have made all their lives easier if they had paid attention to the puppy's desires, her need for more balance, and her opinions. Then they might not have had a master escape artist on their hands.

The Power of Observation

One way to deepen your connection with the animal who shares your life and with all animals you meet is to strengthen your power of simple and neutral observation. This means to see, hear, and perceive what is right in front of you without judgment or preconceptions. To be in your senses instead of your mind will help you to simply observe, which leads to better listening. The more you practice neutral observation, like with a muscle, the stronger it gets. You begin to see and hear with greater accuracy and are better able to understand what the animal's opinion is.

This type of non-cerebral observation is very calming. Neutral does not mean detached; it is a very connected state of being. This is the world in which your animals live. And when you connect to your dog through your senses, you enter the dog's world. Notice how your dog enjoys it when you enter the "neutral observation zone."

As you observe your animals, you will come to understand their opinions about the routines of their lives. For example, notice what your dog is doing, what they might desire, and how they are trying to connect with you. Are they feeling safe at this moment? Are they moving towards or away? What is their favorite position in which to sleep? What would they say to you if they had words?

When you put your full attention on your dog and are simply present, you will feel a two-way flow of love and affection because it is nourishing for both of you to enter this state together. While it may last for just a minute, it will likely be the brightest, most fulfilling part of your day—and your dog's.

You Talking to Me?

Like people, some animals are easier to communicate with than others. Many have not been introduced to humans who are interested in talking to them. When I communicate with an animal for the first time, such as in a shelter, I sometimes see the equivalent of a shocked expression: *You talking to me??* They are not used to having their opinions recognized. But with patient practice, just about every animal is happy to be heard, just like we humans are.

Communicating with animals begins with reminding yourself that animals have opinions. This important step opens the door to allow you to be able to perceive them accurately. Even if you don't know what their opinions are, start by observing what they move toward and what they move away from. *Towards & Away* is such an important concept that we devote an entire chapter to it in Principle #21.

The second step to understanding the opinions of animals is to have an awareness of and connection to your own opinions. Sometimes we humans are not always sure about our own opinions; of course, we know the extremes, what we love and hate. But become more aware of the more subtle senses, what you feel drawn to—what you feel attracted to—versus what you feel repelled by.

Practice this subtle sensing in ordinary moments, such as when you are in line at the grocery store. Notice what you feel about a stranger. Are you drawn to their energy, or do you feel a desire to put distance between you and them? This is a great exercise to do with strangers because, hopefully, you have few preconceptions or at least nothing at stake because you will likely never see them again. This trains you to simply notice your own opinions in your casual encounters with others.

This practice is a quiet exercise where you cultivate trust in your initial instinctual response. It is not about taking any action or expressing words to another person. The purpose is to connect and *pay attention to your own antennae.* It is important to restore faith in your own instincts because our culture asks us to act a certain way in order to fit in, to play nice with others, or to be responsible for others' needs. But the consequence of continually ignoring our true impulses results in losing the subtle sense of awareness of our own opinions. Coming Back to our Senses (Principle #3) will help us stay connected to our opinions, our sense of truth, and our genuine desires.

Nonverbal Communication and Respect for Animals' Opinions

When I walk through the shelter, where a hundred or more dogs are barking and begging me for attention, I send a nonverbal signal to the dog I am scheduled to spend time with that day because it is polite to do so. If I am not coming to work with a specific dog, I will send out a silent greeting to all the animals and see who responds. I pay attention and wait for a return signal from the dog who is "the one" for that day. Almost all want attention, but I am looking for the one who wants, needs, and is ready for the specific kind of healing I can offer. I will often spend forty minutes with one dog, so I want to choose well—and be chosen in return. I want to work with the dog who has a positive opinion about the kind of work that I do, one that gives me a response like *Yes, please. I would very much like to have your attention.*

A Declaration of Consciousness

Once we accept that individual animals have opinions, the next step is to consider that they are conscious beings. In England, on July 7, 2012, a groundbreaking document was created that does just that: the Cambridge Declaration on Consciousness. A prominent group of international scientists signed their names to this document to declare that animals are conscious beings.

The document says in part, "Humans are not unique in possessing the neurological substrates that generate consciousness." These scientists are in the vanguard, and not all agree. As one scientist at a seminar explained his position to me, "I can't prove that you are conscious. How can I say that animals are conscious?" So just because animal consciousness is not yet provable doesn't mean it doesn't exist. Even if we have a way to go before there is scientific evidence of what animal lovers and many veterinarians already believe, sharing our lives with animals and seeing them as sentient beings improves the quality of their lives and ours. One way to make this a living principle is to pay attention to and consider their opinions.

In 2001, distinguished neuroscientist Rodolfo Llinas said, "Consciousness does not belong only to humans. It probably belongs to all forms of life that have a nervous system."

Jen Kotzmann, researcher and animal advocate, is not afraid to explore the question of animal sentience. In her words, "Sentient is an adjective that describes a capacity for feeling. The word sentient derives from the Latin verb *sentire,* which means 'to feel.' The first letters, 'sen,' match the beginnings of common English words, including sentiment, sensory, and sensation—all of which give hints as to the meaning of the term. Dictionaries define sentience as "able to experience feelings," "responsive to or conscious of sense impressions," and "capable of feeling things through physical senses"

Sentient beings experience both wanted emotions like happiness, joy, and gratitude, and unwanted emotions in the form of pain, anxiety, suffering, and grief. These emotions form opinions which direct behavioral choices.

It may be easy for you to think of a dog or a primate as sentient. How about other species? How about fish? Do fish have opinions? Do fish prefer comfort over pain? While fish lack facial expressions and communication methods that we can recognize, biologist Victoria Braithwaite has written a well-researched and groundbreaking book, *Do Fish Feel Pain?* She has proven that fish have pain receptors and has located twenty-two nociceptors, the nerve cells that detect pain, around their face, head, and other places.

Braithwaite also showed that fish have behaviors indicating they feel pain and this *suffering* (the cognitive aspect of pain) even interferes with their ability to navigate their environment and make the best choices. When the fish were given a choice, they chose to avoid pain. When forced to experience pain, they made poorer survival decisions from the vulnerability of being in this state of pain.

Darwin wrote of this a hundred years ago: Animals who were suffering greatly would become dispirited, depressed, or lethargic. The fact that animals prefer not to experience pain is one way of saying they have an opinion about what they want to experience.

I attended a conference with the bold title of *Animal Consciousness* at New York University and heard Braithwaite speak. She faced staunch opposition from some old-guard scientists who insisted that it is impossible that animals and fish feel pain, but they presented no evidence to support their opinion. I was shocked at the position of her opponents, which seemed very closed-minded and closed-hearted. It reminded me of the fact that only two hundred years ago, "researchers" performed major surgery on fully awake dogs (un-sedated) in front of audiences, insisting that they felt no pain.

However, Braithwaite's research offers substantial proof that fish feel stress when experiencing pain through their hormonal stress chemistry. She also provides ample evidence of their inner lives and different personalities and shows that some fish species have memories that last for a few days or even months.

If you have any doubts about the complex social structures of fish, I encourage you to explore the world of cleaner fish. Cleaner fish perform a vital function for other fish species by eating or removing harmful ectoparasites. Because they clean damaged tissue from the wounds of fish, it is generally assumed that their services improve the health of their "clients." (The fish they serve are referred to as clients in the literature.) They often have "repeat customers" that remember specifically who are the best at giving the desired cleaner services. The clients are discriminating and make decisions about which fish to return to. They will either come back to the same "shop" or choose a better proprietor to do their cleaning. This is another example of fish having an opinion.

As further evidence of fish intelligence, wrasse cleaner fish have been shown in one study to pass the MSR, mirror self-recognition test, at the high rate of 94 percent. Braithwaite is one of the bolder scientists who is daring to explore the opinions of fish as evidenced through their behavioral choices and their chemical indicators of stress.

The Truth of Opinions

Those who are not up to date on the recent tidal wave of animal studies and who have no counter-research upon which to base their objections to this illuminating new data may try to maintain the status quo, but fortunately, the truth is marching on.

Frans De Waal has done much research on animal emotions, and he states, "Animals experience love, hate, fear, shame, guilt, joy, disgust, and empathy. These emotions form opinions and drive behavior. In scientific terms, we are just beginning to see the tip of the iceberg of the inner lives of animals." But for those people who care and observe deeply, there is no question about the rich emotional complexity of animals.

Harvard professor Donald Griffin is a pioneering scientist and animal physiologist who discovered that bats navigate and hunt prey via echolocation. He began arguing in the 1970s that just because we can't prove that consciousness exists in animals is no reason to insist that it doesn't. And he says animal consciousness is a subject worth exploring. His brilliant book with the brave title, *Animal Minds – Beyond Cognition to Consciousness*, was first published in 1992, and his ideas are still on the cutting edge of thinking.

Virginia Morell, a science writer, wrote a wonderful book titled *Animal Wise – The Thoughts and Emotions of Our Fellow Creatures*. In the first words of her introduction, she writes, "Animals have minds. They have brains, and use them, as we do: for experiencing the world, for thinking and feeling, and for solving the problems of life every creature faces. Like us, they have personalities, moods, and emotions; they laugh, and they play. Some show grief and empathy and are self-aware and very likely are conscious of their actions and intents."

In short, animals have opinions about what they experience. Darwin explored this inner world of animals in his 1872 book *The Expression of Emotions in Man and Animals.* Darwin believed that many species had emotions, including lizards, birds, cats, dogs, horses, monkeys, and apes, and acknowledged their rich inner lives.

Beyond Words

Evidence of the emotional lives of animals supports my premise that they have opinions about what they like and don't like. In Carl Safina's *New York Times* best seller *Beyond Words – What Animals Think and Feel,* he makes a compelling case for animal emotions and how ridiculous it is to assume otherwise.

He asserts that humans must find another reason to feel "special" because we are not the only species who have rich emotional lives. In his words, "When someone says you can't attribute human sensations to animals, they forget that human sensations *are* animal sensations. Inherited sensations, using inherited nervous systems. Simply deciding that humans [are the only ones who] feel is a cheap way to get a monopoly on all the world's feelings and motivations...

"We never seem to doubt that an animal acting hungry *feels* hungry. What reason is there to disbelieve that an elephant who seems happy *is happy?* We recognize hunger and thirst while animals are eating and drinking, exhaustion when they tire, but deny them joy and happiness as they're playing with their children and their families. The science of animal behavior has long operated on that bias—and that is unscientific. In science, the simplest interpretation of the evidence is often the best. When elephants seem joyous in joyful contexts, joy is the simplest interpretation of the evidence. Their brains are similar to ours; they make the same hormones involved in human emotions—and that's evidence, too."

He notes that humans and animals share many emotions due to our similar brain structures and chemistry that originated in our shared ancestry. He lists a few of these emotions: fear, aggression, well-being, anxiety, and pleasure. Then he adds, "I am not suggesting that humans and elephants have *all* the same emotions. Self-loathing seems uniquely human."

> *We will never have to tell our horse that we are sad,*
> *happy, confident, angry, or relaxed.*
> *He already knows—long before we do.*
>
> *Marijke de Jong*

Jealous Dogs

Ask any dog person, and they will swear they have seen their dog show jealousy. The intensity and cause will vary among individual dogs, but recent studies demonstrate more precise evidence for this complex emotion in animals. One study used realistic stuffed dogs that the owner petted and talked to in front of their own dog, versus the control, where the owner petted and talked to a padded shelf. The researchers noticed that the dogs reacted with more stress when they determined a rival was getting good attention. The dogs had an opinion about their person giving attention to another dog.

David Nield reported on this in his study published in *Psychological Science*: "Research has supported what many dog owners firmly believe—dogs exhibit jealous behavior when their human companion interacts with a potential rival." Psychologist Amalia Bastos from the

University of Auckland in New Zealand stated, "We wanted to study this behavior more fully to determine if dogs could, like humans, mentally represent a situation that evoked jealousy. In humans, jealousy is thought to be closely linked to self-awareness. Hence, the research also has something to say about whether or not dogs are actually aware of themselves—and the mental processes that might be behind the jealous behavior that so many owners see."

Gregory Berns's fMRI studies have exploded our understanding of the canine brain. He demonstrated this by scanning the brains of awake dogs to show how specific areas were activated from the experience of different emotional states. What was also striking was how precisely similar the canine brain is to a human brain, and the same regions light up with the same emotions.

Safina says, "How might we discern an elephant or a mouse's sense of the world? Elephants and mice might not tell us what they are thinking. But their brains can. Brain scans show that core emotions of sadness, happiness, rage, or fear, and motivational feelings of hunger and thirst, are generated in deep and very ancient circuits of the brain (as Jaak Panksepp discovered). Rage, for example, gets produced in the *same parts* of the brain of a cat and a human." It is exciting to see the cumulative evidence proving animals experience complex emotional states.

All beings—human and nonhuman animals--have emotions which means we all have opinions and preferences. We all enjoy having our emotions acknowledged. Recognizing the emotional lives and the opinions of animals makes their lives better—and makes us better humans.

Journal Reflection on Animals Have Opinions:

1) Do you consider the opinions of the animals who share their life with you?

2) When you consider the idea that animals have opinions, how does that make you feel? How does this awareness change how you coexist with the animals in your life?

3) How do you feel when you ignore an animal's clear opinion?

4) If animals have opinions, what does that mean from an ethical point of view? What changes need to be made as a society? Or to situations where animals are in captivity?

5) What is one small step you could take to include the idea that animals have opinions?

Re-Minder: Animals have opinions.

Listening to Charlotte's opinion about where she wanted to live and who she wanted to live with (she wanted to live in the same stall as Cuzco, the llama) allowed us to make the best decision for her future, and she soon became Afton's best reading donkey.

STORY

Beautiful Jim Key – The World's Most Educated Horse

Dr. William Key was born a slave (most likely in 1833), and even as a child, he had the ability to heal and tame all animals. As a free man, he led a successful entrepreneurial life developing his own product line and promoting his liniment in traveling medicine shows. There were many times he had to use his wits and poker skills to escape death at the hands of others, especially during the Civil War.

As an adult, he rescued Lauretta, a formerly prized Arabian horse who had been badly abused by multiple circuses. Lauretta was rumored to have been stolen from an Arabian prince and then sold to a circus for $50,000. Doc Key bought that "broken down" horse for $40 and nursed her back to health. She gave birth to Jim Key, a colt with crooked, spindly legs who could barely walk. Everyone told him he should put the young horse out of his misery. But as a self-trained veterinarian, Doc Key believed he could heal him using natural methods, including the Keystone liniment he had created. To nurse him back to health, he let the crippled horse sleep next to him in his house. Jim Key healed into a very strong and elegant horse. The bond and the love between them were very strong, and Jim Key followed the doc around like a dog.

The horse became so attached to Doc Key that he couldn't be left alone, so Doc took him on his traveling medicine show as he sold his "miracle cure" liniment. When people saw the horse perform, they would try to bid hundreds of dollars to buy him. As soon as the Doc pronounced "Sold!" Jim Key would put on a display of illness, lameness, and appear to be at death's door. The sale was immediately canceled. Then the doc would treat Jim with Keystone liniment, and the horse would immediately come back to life. Jim Key was a consummate entertainer!

Doc Key began to realize that Jim Key was beginning to outsmart him, finding apples hidden in a drawer and closing it after the horse finished helping himself. He seemed to understand so much that Doc Key decided to educate him. The horse would answer yes or no to questions about what he wanted. For their entire life together, Doc Key would always ask his horse's opinions on important decisions that affected their future as well as a variety of daily subjects. Using teaching methods of kindness, patience, and persistence, Doc Key eventually taught his horse to read the alphabet and spell. The horse could count to thirty to add and subtract and recognize the value of coins. Jim Key won spelling contests with children and answered questions with a nod or a shake for "no." He even expressed his opinions on politics, claiming to be a Democrat, even though Doc Key always claimed to be a Republican.

They were a huge hit on the performance circuit. It is estimated that at various world fairs and other events that ten million people, including President McKinley, saw Doc and Jim Key perform where the horse would correctly answer questions, do math, and file letters alphabetically.

There were many accusations of it all being a hoax, but no one was ever able to prove that. A team of Harvard professors tested him and couldn't find any evidence of the horse being cued (as another performing horse named Clever Hans had inadvertently been shown to do). Jim Key was "highly educated" and could perform the same tasks for reporters even without Doc Key's presence.

Doc Key was happy to have the reporters test Jim Key without him being present but asked them to have an apple in their pocket. One reporter, who was at first convinced that the horse was hypnotized by the doctor, came to interview Jim Key. The reporter tested him, and the horse spelled out all the correct answers with his letter board. The reporter exited but without giving Jim Key the apple he was expecting. The reporter left a believer, but when Doc Key asked his horse how it went, Jim Key spelled out the word "fruitless."

At a time when 25,000 horses died each year in the streets of New York City from abuse and overwork, this was just the beginning of the humane movement that would educate the public that animals needed better care. Jim Key became an ambassador for the cause. His intelligence was proof of an animal's potential inner life and the need to treat animals humanely. As a result of seeing a horse trained by kindness, over two million children signed a pledge to be kind to animals.

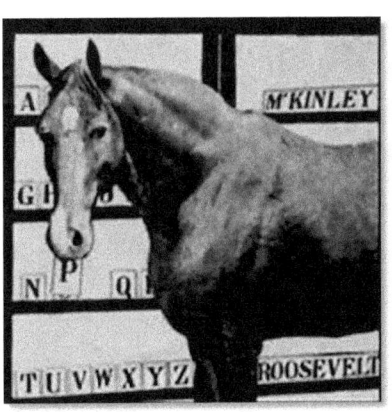

THE PLEDGE
of the Jim Key Band of Mercy.
"I will try to be kind to all harmless living creatures, and try to protect them from cruel usage."

Beautiful Jim Key at his letter board. He could spell the names of presidents, make predictions that turned out to be true, expressed his strong opinions, flirted with ladies in the audience, and often showed a sophisticated sense of humor.

Jim Key Pledge:
"I will try to be kind to all harmless living creatures, and try to protect them from cruel usage."

CANINES TEACH COMPASSION

Empathy for Animals Makes Us Kinder People

When we learn to respect all life,
we learn to love all life.

Anthony Douglas Williams

Overview

Animals can teach us much about empathy, which was once considered to be an "elevated" emotion that only humans were capable of expressing. We have so many examples of animals showing compassion as they recognize pain, suffering, stress, and loneliness in others, including members of other species, and come to their aid. It is no longer possible to ignore that many species are truly empathetic and act with compassion. Examples of one species caring for an orphan of another species, as well as cross-species friendships, show us that animals can recognize the emotional state of others and can choose to take actions to comfort those in need.

Empathy Leads to a Better World

Frans de Waal, the Dutch primatologist, was named by *Time* magazine as one of the Top 100 Most Influential People. He is also the author of several wonderful books, my favorite of which is *Mama's Last Hug – Animal Emotions and What They Tell Us About Ourselves*. He has researched animal emotions for decades and has contributed significantly to the study of emotions, empathy, and a sense of fairness in animals.

He did a TED Talk about his research on empathy with capuchin monkeys. In his study, two monkeys in side-by-side cages were trained to hand the researcher a rock, and in exchange, they were given a small piece of cucumber to eat. The monkeys gladly repeated this activity over and over until the second monkey was given a higher-value treat—a *grape*—while the first monkey only got the same cucumber treat. This inequality angered the cucumber-receiving monkey, who rattled his cage and threw his rock at the researcher in frustration.

These monkeys had a sense of fairness that had been intentionally violated by the experiment procedure. The rule, "Give a rock, get a treat," was being applied unfairly. Ultimately, both monkeys refused to play the game until both were given the same treat.

Canines Teach Compassion

My decades of working with traumatized soldiers and animals has deeply influenced my belief that the world has an urgent need for more empathy and compassion and, more importantly, that each of us can shift the scale in that direction. Becoming aware that others are experiencing something other than what we are, that they may be suffering, and that there is some kind of caring action we can take to alleviate that suffering will surely lead to a kinder world. But I can't just wish the world into being a nicer place for people and animals.

One thing I can do to shift the culture is to teach compassion to high school students. Or even better, let the dogs teach it. Our HAC high school program is called *Canines Teach Compassion*. We bring trained and certified therapy dogs into the classroom to teach a curriculum that combines learning social skills and kindness through the process of interacting with cuddly dogs. Students who were withdrawn and depressed open like flowers. Anxious and angry students learn to regulate their nervous systems by being enveloped with the calming presence of trained therapy dogs.

Acts of compassion change both the giver and receiver and cultivate a culture of empathy. Our therapy dogs model kindness and acceptance because they love all the kids without judgment. They don't care how the students look; they look at their essence. The dogs lovingly connect with the students and exude joy because they recognize that the students are good people. They are treated kindly by the students, and the dogs respond with kindness in return.

The program begins with this teaching point: *This is a good doggie, and because you are loving to this animal, you are a good person too.* This is a foundational point because before we can expect kids to behave compassionately toward others, kids need to learn to be kind to themselves. You have to be kind to yourself before you have a reservoir of compassion for others. Young teens are often very self-critical, comparing themselves unrealistically to those they admire. Canines Teach Compassion offers tools to intervene in the students' negative self-talk and helps quiet their inner critics.

In one session called Same & Different, we line up five very different dog breeds in a range of sizes—a black Labrador, a white Chihuahua mix, an English bullmastiff, a standard poodle, and a sheepdog. We ask the teens to make a list of what the dogs have in common and what is different about each one. We point out that little Sophia (the Chihuahua mix) is not trying to be Shadow (the bullmastiff), nor is Shadow trying to be Sophia. Shadow and Sophia are role models for accepting themselves as who they are. We discuss how there is often a lot of pressure to be the same – but that isn't always right for us. We need to support our desire to be different. Just as there are times we want to feel different, there are times we want to feel our sameness with others. We need to honor our own truth, no matter how others choose to be.

Another exercise helps the students experience the dynamics of leading and being led on a leash. With one teen on each end of the leash, they walk together around the obstacles in the room to experience what it feels like to be led. They get to experience the difference between the ease of being in sync with each other and the disruptive feelings when the leader yanks on the leash, disregarding the other person's rhythm, timing, or desire.

We also teach them the neutral observation of body language and how to distinguish between the dog's *come towards me* signal and a *please don't touch me* signal. We then help them relate this experience to the way they feel when they don't want people to come too close. Teens can experience much more success in social situations if they are correctly reading nonverbal communication signals from peers. Success in social interactions is a strong predictor of resilience and leads to better academic outcomes.

Compassion Is an Antidote to Stress

It is easy to feel compassionate toward a loving dog, and our program uses this experience as a gentle way to explore how to expand compassion to oneself and then to others. The teenage years, especially the early teens, are a minefield of self-rejection. Loving dogs interrupt that cycle, just long enough to challenge the relentless cycle of isolation and inner turmoil.

At the beginning of each Canine's Teach Compassion class session, we ask the students to rate their current stress level, with zero being the complete absence of stress and ten being the worst stress ever. At the end of each session, after they have interacted with the dogs and experienced our other exercises, we ask them to rate their stress level again. We total the stress level of the group and then the total drop in stress levels. I am currently working on a book for teens about this program. On TheHumanAnimalConnection.org website you can see videos from Canines Teach Compassion classes and this chart demonstrates the significant drop in stress levels after one hour of interaction.

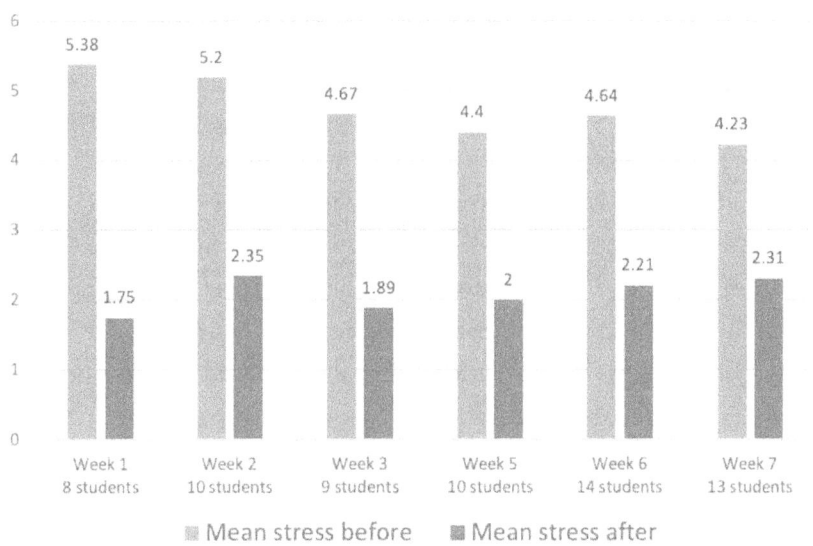

Mean stress before   Mean stress after

Animals' Sense of Fairness and Empathy

In a shelter, dogs will assume that if you give one dog a treat, you should give a treat to the dog in the next kennel too. I have observed their innate sense of fairness many times, so now I know to be prepared to treat all of them if I treat one of them. And if you have any doubt that dogs can count, put two treats in your pocket and give a dog one of them. They will accept the first treat and then eye your pocket while patiently waiting for the other.

De Waal's sense of fairness study with capuchin monkeys has been replicated by various researchers with other species. In one study, rats were faced with the choice of getting a coveted treat or stopping to rescue a neighbor who was experiencing pain or the threat of drowning. Between 50–80 percent of the time, the rats would choose to help the other rat rather than take the high-value treat.

The ability to accurately *read the feelings* of others is a critical component of empathy. Similarly, a dog's ability to instantly decode body language correctly is crucial to social success in a shelter or group environment. We do find some dogs who don't read each other's body language correctly and misunderstand each other's signals, like those indicating whether he or she wants to play and how intensely. Unfortunately, in many shelters, a dog who doesn't understand the social cues correctly gets a bad rap and is not allowed to play with other dogs.

De Waal discovered that the chimpanzees he studied were experts at reading facial expressions, especially those of their own species. The chimpanzees could tell the difference between a smile and a frown, a threatening expression, a friendly eyebrow flash, or a friendly lip smack. As De Waal states, "Facial expressions stir up emotions and empathy." He explains it is hard to have empathy without the ability to accurately read facial expressions.

Species, like dogs, who are typically excellent at reading emotions, are skilled at empathy. They read our faces, body language, tone of voice, posture, fluidity or rigidity of movement, our mood, and our energy. (Chimpanzees, by the way, are also keen observers. On photo tests of recognition, chimpanzees can recognize individual members of their social group by simply seeing a close-up of their rear ends.)

Emotional Contagion

John Warzluff at the University of Washington has done extensive research and demonstrated that crows have emotional states and emotional memory. Other researchers at the University of Austria in Vienna discovered that not only do crows hold grudges, but they also remember those humans who have done them wrong. Crows also experience "emotional contagion," which means that if a happy crow is close to a depressed crow, both can experience the other's emotion.

Every person who shares their life with an animal and feels a deep bond with them will tell you that their dog, or cat, or horse will notice their human's emotions and distress. If I start to cry, my dog, Sophia, will often stop playing and will come over and rest her paw on me or lick my hand to try to comfort me. De Waal notes that several species will show comforting behavior to each other and sometimes to other species. "Many animals, from dogs to rodents, and from dolphins to elephants, exhibit comforting behavior, even though each species uses its own gestures."

Kindness in Animals

We see many examples of same species kindness, such as rattlesnakes babysitting for their gal pals and bonobos (a species of great ape) sharing food and acting as midwives during difficult births, or vampire bats who share their nightly feast with others who were not successful in their hunt. Even wild adolescent male chimpanzees have been observed by Jane Goodall to adopt and care for orphaned infants. Elephants who comfort friends, dolphins who do favors for each other, and rats who would rather rescue a fellow rat than take a delicious treat are all examples of evidence that animals can be kind.

But what about animals helping those of other species? Many species are trainable to help others, such as wolverines taught to rescue human survivors of avalanches, and they will dig quickly and determinedly to rescue a person. But there are also many examples of animals acting compassionately without any human training or intervention.

Anjana is a chimpanzee in a rescue sanctuary who has twice mothered helpless Siberian tiger cub orphans who would not have survived without her constant care. She held a bottle to feed them, cuddled and comforted them, and put up with their exploring sharp claws. There is no biological imperative for assisting a helpless member of another species, and yet Anjana filled the role of a surrogate mother without having any human training to do this.

Empathy was once thought to be a strictly human capability. But with so much evidence of animals exhibiting empathic behavior, we could benefit from following their lead. We have all seen the videos on social media of one species of animal caring for an orphan or vulnerable animal of another species, even though there is no biological imperative to do so. The only explanation is that animals can sense the pain or need of another and can choose to take action to bring comfort and safety to one who needs it.

On social media, you can watch all kinds of unexpected and unlikely friendships and compassionate connections between species. Dogs and chicks, orangutans and dogs, dogs and baby lambs, baby chicks and cats, and on and on. If only humans had as much tolerance and appreciation for differences! We can learn a lot about empathy, compassion, and cooperation from our animal friends.

Trees Nurture Each Other

Empathy is woven into the fabric of nature and ensures the success of many species. Scientists are now showing evidence that "mother trees" help other trees (even other tree species) to thrive through a vast system of underground support with an intricately interconnected network of mycorrhizal fungi that colonize trees' roots. And acacia trees will "communicate" danger to other trees by releasing a chemical warning if there is a leaf-eating predator in the vicinity.

Animal communicator Anna Breytenbach tells a story about how she was brought in to work with some oak trees, some of which were dying of a disease. When she spoke to them, they were unconcerned about the disease but very concerned about the wild rabbits that no longer came around. They accepted that some of the trees would die in order to strengthen the remaining trees' immunology. They wanted to know from Anna if the rabbits would be alright.

Males and females of all species have the capacity for empathy. Perhaps the hormonal incentives of oxytocin (the feel-good hormone) illuminate our understanding of empathy because when men and women are given a dose of oxytocin spray into the nose, we see increased behavioral expressions of empathy.

While both genders are capable of empathy, there are some biological factors that lend themselves to social skills. Simon Baron-Cohen states, "At birth, girl babies look longer at faces than do boy babies, who look longer at mechanical toys. Later in life, girls are more pro-social than boys, better readers of facial expressions, more attuned to voices, more remorseful after having hurt someone, and better at taking another's perspective."

Not every animal is Mother Theresa in fur. There is certainly plenty of evidence of animal aggression. However, the research on animal empathy does show that humans do not have an exclusive hold on this refined emotional state. Some argue that animals can't experience empathy because they can't make a cognitive analysis of a situation. However, if empathy is defined as the ability of one animal to recognize that another is suffering and can choose to take compassionate action to relieve that suffering, this is empathy. In this situation, animals have shown that they can:

1) Recognize that another animal is having a different experience from themselves.

2) Recognize that another animal is suffering.

3) Recognize that something can be done (an action taken to comfort or relieve this suffering).

4) Choose to take an action to comfort or relieve this suffering, in some cases with novel strategies to intervene.

Given these cognitive choices, it would seem impossible to deny that animals *experience* empathy.

Ever wonder how your animal sees you? We humans need to accept that we do not have a monopoly on refined emotions like compassion and empathy and, in fact, need to practice it more often with animals. As Victoria Stillwell comments, "The more we understand the emotional experiences of dogs, the more we can help them live successfully in our human world, because the similarities are undeniable—dogs have the same brain structures that produce emotions in humans, produce the same hormones, and experience the same chemical changes that humans go through during emotional states."

Understanding these "higher-mind" emotions of compassion and empathy in animals will hopefully encourage us to respect and treat them with the appreciation they deserve. Empathy for animals and respecting animal wisdom can help make us kinder to people, thus leading to a better world for all.

Our task must be to free ourselves...
by widening our circle of compassion
to embrace all living creatures
and the whole of nature and its beauty.

Albert Einstein

Journal Reflections on Compassion and Empathy:

1) What situations or events cause you to feel empathy and act in a compassionate way? When has compassion been shown to you?

2) What kind of score would you give yourself on an empathy scale with 1 as no empathy and 10 as high empathy?

3) How does your level of empathy, or the lack of it, affect your social interactions?

4) Have you seen an example of an animal showing compassion or empathy? If so, how did that make you feel?

5) Are you willing to increase the level of compassion in your life and your behavior? How can you do that? How would you benefit from more empathy toward others?

Re-Minder: Compassionate connections
make the world a better place.

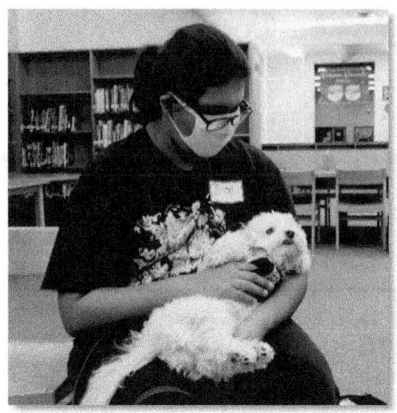

Walter is a three-legged dog with Sunshine Therapy Animals and inspires compassion. The love he shares in our Canines Teach Compassion class is contagious!

Our HAC Therapy Dog Team and students.

A moment of joy and connection makes the whole day better.

STORY

Odin Sidewinder: The Equine Ambassador of Peace

Could a horse be an Ambassador of Peace? Could he communicate to a whole herd of rescue horses that they are safe? Such a being could communicate without words, in the "Language of Horse" across vast distances. One horse can: a mustang named Odin Sidewinder.

Odin Sidewinder was born in South Dakota, right below the bluff where the Lakota and many Plains Indians celebrate the Sun Dance, where the Cheyenne River runs north, south, east, and west. He was part of a wild mustang herd at the Black Hills Wild Horse Sanctuary, which was started in 1988 and covers about 11,000 acres.

The sanctuary owners quickly realized that Sidewinder had the unique talent of helping younger and anxious horses to settle down and feel safe in the sanctuary. They also knew that Sidewinder had a special empathy and a destiny—and that he needed to help others.

That's when Afton Whitmer from Wild Horse Haven Rescue got the call: "We want to give you this horse." Small problem: Afton lived in Arizona and couldn't leave his ranch and his horses behind. It would take a miracle. Fortunately, one was on its way. But first, Odin Sidewinder would make the twenty-eight-hour journey from South Dakota to Valley View Equine Rescue in King City, California, where he stayed for a few months and was the confident and gentle peacemaker in the new herd.

Afton had also been on a long personal journey. After ten years as a military contractor, he returned from Iraq and Afghanistan to the ranch where he grew up. "All I wanted was to live the rest of my life in peace," he said. But Afton had read some articles about wild mustangs being slaughtered that opened his mind and his heart. He began to hear them in his head in a way he couldn't ignore, "Save me! Give me a home! I could hear the wild horses talking to me. This feeling would be so intense it would wake me up in the middle of the night with the sound of horses' screams of anguish, pain, and loneliness."

Afton got to work. He started rebuilding the old corrals on his ranch. He wasn't sure what would happen next, but horses just started coming. First one, then another, and another. He would get calls about mustangs that just couldn't be gentled or were injured and could never be ridden; they needed a home, or they would go to slaughter.

The next thing he knew, he was caring for twenty horses on his ranch. Injured ones, very elderly ones, wild ones, some with such severe fear of humans they couldn't be touched. He gave them all a home. "I love them all, no matter what they do. My travels around the world and the horses have changed my life, turning my focus to compassion for animals. That's why I call my place the Wild Horse Haven Rescue."

I recently went to visit Afton at his ranch. We talked about the ways horses can heal people with PTSD, anxiety, and depression. I assured him he wasn't crazy for listening to horses and letting them *lead him*. I know from my own work with horses and people that if you open your heart deeply to a horse, the horse will lead you to heal. Afton knew it was time to turn his rescue work with animals into healing work with people. He could feel he was being led to something big. A horse with a huge spirit, Odin Sidewinder.

Although Afton had never met anyone from the Black Hills Wild Horse Sanctuary, they knew he was meant to be Afton's horse. Six months after this horse was first offered to Afton, a miracle happened. Marlene Dodge from Valley View Equine Rescue, was asked to pick up four horses in Arizona. Although she almost never travels near Safford, Arizona, where Afton's ranch is, she said she would drive Sidewinder the thirteen hours to his ranch. The timing of Sidewinder's arrival was also a miracle, as a recent family tragedy made Afton realize it was time to do more. It was time to open his ranch and the horses to people who needed to heal their Souls. The arrival of Sidewinder was the perfect sign that he had made the right decision to go in this direction. Sidewinder would be the perfect partner for this new step in the healing journey.

"Although I feel all twenty horses at Wild Horse Haven Rescue are family, I don't feel they are *my* personal horses. They are their own spirits," Afton said. A few of the wild mustangs are free to come and go and roam the mountains during the day. They leave after breakfast and return to the ranch for dinner.

When Sidewinder first arrived, it was as if he knew he was home. Even after the two-day drive, he just calmly walked out of the trailer. He knew exactly that Wild Horse Haven Rescue was where his destiny lay. "Most of my experience with mustangs when they get here is they either stay in the trailer and take their time getting out, or they burst out of the trailer. Either way, it is because they are confused and scared. I never force or prod them out of a trailer. I let it be their choice. They have had their ability to choose taken away from them so many times, and I try to give some of that back to them here. It was pretty amazing to watch how confident and peaceful Sidewinder was."

Afton wasn't the only one watching. All of the other horses came up to the corral to meet Odin Sidewinder that first day, with nickers and nuzzles and lots of curiosity from the herd. After letting him settle in for two days, Sidewinder was turned out with two of Afton's other horses, Sirocco and Rowdy. Sirroco and Sidewinder met and connected, nuzzled, and he knew they were good.

Rowdy, on the other hand, lived up to his name and postured and reared up, but Sidewinder stood his ground with him. He didn't run away but held his space as if to say, "I'm not scared of you, and we are going to live together in peace." And that is how they worked it out.

One of Afton's other horses, a small mare named Tuffy, was a mustang who was born with hip deformities and crooked back legs. "She let me know how she felt—she had been watching Odin Sidewinder over the fence. She wanted to know him." Tuffy seemed to instantly know they were about to become best friends, so he turned Tuffy out with Sidewinder. The care and love that Sidewinder showed his new friend are healing just to watch. They will remain together for the rest of their lives.

Odin Sidewinder's story is a great reminder that every animal is unique, and each has their own destiny. Our job is to pay attention to that. As Afton said, "I knew right away that not only was Odin Sidewinder going to be my partner in peace, but he was going to be a great therapy horse. He is terrific with kids, vets, and anyone who wants to calm their Soul."

Since being at Afton's ranch, everyone who visits is drawn to Odin Sidewinder. He has shown many examples of empathy toward people and other animals.

One woman came to visit the ranch who recently had brain surgery and wasn't able to speak. Sidewinder gently approached. She hugged him, and the tears she hadn't let fall for months finally came. After just a few minutes of receiving Sidewinder's love, her face erupted in a smile her family hadn't seen for a very long time.

As Marlene said, "Sidewinder is a great representative for what a wild mustang can be if given a chance. His presence lends itself to peace, gentleness, and forgiveness."

Odin Sidewinder gets lots of love and grooming every day. And Afton talks to him. "He is a very good listener!" Sidewinder seems to know that he has a special mission—being an ambassador of peace. The world needs to know that there are more Sidewinders out there. We just need to recognize them.

Odin Sidewinder comforted Tuffy (the disabled horse) and brought peace to the entire herd.

RELATIONSHIP TRAINING
The Secret to Better Behavior

*Those who teach the most about humanity
aren't always human.*

Donald L. Hicks

Overview

In many cultures around the world, humans and animals still live and work in partnership. Some cultures treat animals as sacred, such as in Bhutan and Mongolia. But modern culture has seen a tremendous dissolution of balanced relationships between people and animals.

An enduring belief that humans must dominate animals has resulted in misinformed training methods that use punishment and fear as the primary method and motivators. The old thinking was you had to "break" a wild animal's spirit to make them compliant. Now that we understand more about animal intelligence and emotions, we need to use respectful methods and can work *with* them instead of *against* them.

Positive methods are a better approach to animal training. The HAC believes that the healthiest way to share your life with an animal is not just to focus on obedience as an end goal. Rather, we view training in the context of building and sustaining a healthy connection. We call this approach based on mutual understanding and respect *Relationship Training*.

A Place for Love

If you are in a bonded relationship with an animal and need to understand a particular behavior the animal is showing, it's important to also consider what is going on inside of you. Does this animal's behavior reflect some fear or anxiety that you both share? Conscious or otherwise, the animal may be reflecting your unresolved issues.

I once consulted with a client, Barbara, who had two rescue greyhounds and a potbelly pig. One of Barbara's greyhounds, Brie, had a troublesome habit of relieving herself on the living room rug even after being taken outside for a potty break. Barbara is a very clean person and was at her wits' end with these "accidents" that often happened just when she was about to go to work. They were causing her enough distress that she wondered if she should re-home Brie.

Brie was new to the family; Barbara had adopted her to keep her first dog company after his mate passed away. Her current dog had suffered a significant depression when his mate died, and she knew he needed companionship.

Barbara asked me to do a communication session with Brie to see if we could understand her behavior. When I connected with Brie, I asked her why she was doing this upsetting behavior. Brie told me that her new owner hadn't fully opened her heart to her. She felt like *I have no place in this home.*

When I told this to Barbara, she recognized immediately that this was, in fact, the dynamic between her and Brie. The reason? Barbara was still grieving the loss of her first greyhound and didn't want to be disloyal to that love. She didn't realize she was hesitating to open her heart and love the new dog completely. Once she understood this dynamic, she was able to open her heart to let Brie *in*. And the accidents *in* the house stopped. When I checked in a few months later, Barbara felt her heart was now fully open to Brie, and they were a family. And there had been no more house accidents.

Training for Love

There are probably as many approaches to dog training as there are people who have tried to train a dog, and every dog is unique, so one size is not going to fit all. As a dog trainer myself, I have learned which methods are most successful and which are not. Since this is not a traditional book on dog training, I want to just briefly introduce you to our basic training principles, and you can discover for yourself which you think will work best for the animals in your life. But let's start by dividing the numerous training methods into two categories:

1) Dominance and coercive methods
2) Positive methods

In the dominance model, the human seeks to subordinate the animal's will to his own; the trainer may use aversive techniques such as fear and the threat of punishment or pain to ensure compliance. The animal learns that to avoid a negative experience, he must do what the trainer is demanding. Although these methods may create compliance, they do not create true learning, except learning to avoid punishment.

Positive methods, which have been tested over the last forty years, are based on rewarding good behavior and redirecting undesired behavior. The emphasis is on teaching the animal the specific desired behavior. Through repetition, the animal learns what you desire and are asking for and *chooses to comply.* Many positive methods use rewards to communicate that the behavior produced is what was wanted. When an animal makes a choice to comply, the relationship is strengthened.

In the United States, there are about three million duck, pheasant, and migrating bird hunters who work with hunting dogs. Although positive training has been proven to be more effective, most hunters still use coercive methods like ear pinches, choke chains, prong collars, and electric shock collars. Robert Milner, the author of *Absolutely Positively Gundog Training,* provides his scientific studies showing how positive training is 300 percent more effective, even for novice trainers, than compulsion training. The new evidence of the effectiveness of positive training and force-free methods with search dogs, hunting dogs, agility training, and military working dogs show the dogs learning in a third of the time needed in compulsion methods, performing well, and retaining this knowledge over time.

Dominance and coercive methods tend to emphasize punishment or induce fear for not following the commands. The best positive methods are kinder, more humane, and more "animal friendly" because the trainer maintains awareness of an animal's opinion and emotional state.

Positive training is a form of communication. It preserves one of the essential needs of all sentient beings—the freedom of choice. We value choice in life, which is why Freedom of Choice (Principle #27) is one of the HAC's thirty-three principles for the well-being of humans and animals.

When I see an animal who has been traumatized and is shutting down (something I see far too often in shelters and rescues), I can only imagine what misinformed humans have done to get them to this level. It appears as if these animals have collapsed and retreated to an inner world in the hopes that no more harm will come to them. They want nothing, respond to nothing—except in fear—and do everything they can to avoid engaging.

One of my first steps with these emotionally wounded animals is to find a small pathway back to experiencing their ability to choose. It could be as simple as choosing to stretch out their neck to reach for and accept a treat I offer from my open hand.

Rewarding Desired Behavior

In positive training methods, the first step is to discover what motivates the animal to please you. Some dogs will do anything for a treat, others for love, others for a favorite toy. Some like it all. Since every animal is unique, you will need to observe and experiment to find out what motivates them. Once you understand how the animal prefers to be rewarded you have a communication method that helps the animal to understand what you are asking for. Then you can offer this--playtime with toys, or food, treats, affection, freedom, or positive reinforcement methods such as an enthusiastic tone of voice saying, "Good boy!" Training an animal becomes easier and fun once you understand what will motivate your animal to perform in the ways you desire.

One of the mottos positive dog trainers use is: "The amount of force required to train a dog is inversely proportional to the skill of the trainer. Those with more skill use less force." Positive training produces positive results and, at the same time, maintains the spirit of the dog. It also increases the bond between the human and the animal, thus leaving both in a better place of communication and connection. In the end, *we are all in training for love.*

The Training Toolbox

There is a huge range of techniques in the field of positive training, and each brings something of value. When possible, I take the opportunity to learn from other positive trainers who have some different methods than I do. Even when I don't completely agree, I always find something good to take away. That way, I expand my training toolbox because every dog is different, and you never know what might work best for a specific situation. When I was learning dog training, my mentor used 100 percent positive methods, which I totally appreciated. Later on, I also came to understand that there are some situations where stronger corrections have a place—especially to protect safety—as long as they are not cruel.

For example, I am volunteering in a shelter that has several hundred dogs, and I'm often meeting a large dog for the first time. Because I need to take him or her out of the kennel, past a row of leaping, barking dogs, I would do well to use a leash technique that gives me more control. In this case, it makes sense to use an additional leash called a British slip lead, which is worn high and reasonably tight around the top of the dog's head. If you have ever watched show dogs in the arena, their handlers typically use the British slip lead. Because this is our first meeting and we are not bonded, I need to create an immediate sense of being in the driver's seat. It is not just about controlling the dog; it is about being *in control of the situation.* This leash technique allows me more control over the dog's head in a stressful shelter environment by directing his focus away from other dogs. This gives me more ability to steer the dog toward the door without the dog being overly distracted or triggered by the other highly animated dogs or people moving through the shelter. In the context of getting a shelter dog in or out of a kennel, where the priority is safety, there is value in using a method that I wouldn't use in a bonded partnership. I wouldn't use a British slip lead on my own dog, Sophia. We can walk on a loose leash without the need for this more controlling method because the relationship between Sophia and me is what sustains the desired behavior.

When meeting a new dog in the shelter, I take a couple of minutes of "kennel contact" to build a bit of bonding and trust and to create as much calmness as I can so I don't have to "woman-handle" an overly excited dog. (You can read more on our HAC blogs if you would like to have more details about how to create better "kennel contact" quickly).

As mentioned, I seek opportunities to observe other positive trainers because there is always something to learn from each one. I remember observing one class led by a trainer who I admire very much. A client came to his class with a young and very exuberant, very barky, standard poodle. All the owner did was yell at his dog, "Sit! SIT!! SIT!!!" The man "barked" so much at his dog that it was hard for the rest of the class to concentrate. We all felt so bad for the dog and understood why he was barking back at his person. They were reinforcing each other's intensity. The *man* was out of control, so that's what he got in return—an out-of-control dog. Finally, he left class halfway through. It allowed the trainer to make the point that "barking" at a barking dog just makes more noise.

Let me summarize what my goal is in training an animal who shares his or her life with you: the most essential element is building and sustaining the quality of the relationship. This is why I call the type of positive training that we do in The Human-Animal Connection "Relationship Training." Our training is as much (or more) about training the human as it is about training the animal.

The Quality of Sacred Connection

In Relationship Training, the focus is on the *quality of the connection* between the human and the animal. That is our guiding principle.

Nothing is more important than that. If the dog is not behaving as I wish, I would rather be patient and wait a few extra seconds for the dog to choose to comply than allow myself to become triggered and angry or anxious because that just undermines our connection. What I have learned is that if my dog doesn't do as I wish, *I need to calm down!*

In my experience, training is perhaps 75 percent human skill and behavior and 25 percent dog skill and behavior. As Bob Bailey, former Director of the U.S. Navy Marine Mammal Program, says, "Training often fails because people expect way too much of the animal and way too little of themselves."

Compliance is not the primary objective of Relationship Training. Our primary goal is a connected, mutually respectful relationship where we understand each other's communication. When that primary objective is achieved, the second objective, obedience, comes naturally because the dog *chooses to obey* because the connection is important to him or her.

When this principle of harmony is pursued, mutual understanding occurs. There is always a reason for the dog's behavior, although it may not be obvious at first. This is where intuitive communication can help you reach across that invisible barrier and lead to a happier coexistence.

As dog trainer and behavior specialist Lisa Desatnik explains, "As living beings, we always have a reason for our behavior. Our behavior either helps us gain more of what we value or helps give us distance from what is negative to us. When it comes to behavior management, you can either motivate an animal with a behavior consequence that adds enrichment or with a bad consequence that is punishing. Which motivation do you think will create a love of learning in your pet?"

Relationship Training Builds Trust

Relationship Training builds trust. It builds rapport. It adds to the joy of living with an animal. When done right, it strengthens the relationship bond because when you both learn to work in sync, desired behaviors will be expressed. This synchronicity creates what James French of the Trust Technique calls "the invisible lead," where an animal seems to know just what you want or responds very quickly to a soft voice or a gentle gesture of invitation. It makes your life that much more fulfilling for you and your animal.

Some animals who have not been given effective training and are out of control are hard to include in activities outside the house. Unfamiliar people can react very negatively to these dogs, making the world smaller and smaller for that animal. Relationship Training is needed to create a common language and a chance to succeed for both of you. Once the animal understands what you are asking for, he or she can make better behavioral choices leading to better outcomes for everyone.

In dog training, as in any profession, there are examples of excellence, adequacy, and mediocrity. I hear horror stories from clients who were given training advice for their dog that induced fear and anxious behaviors. By way of illustration, if a mugger points a weapon at your head, you might give him your money, but you never want to see this person ever again. The mugger got what he wanted, but a positive connection with that person is never possible in the future.

Look for a trainer who has a positive approach, respects you and your animal, understands your animal's unique needs, and, ideally, someone your dog is delighted to see again. If you are working with a trainer, ask yourself, "Does this method, and this person, help me to have a deeper bond with my animal?" If the answer is yes, you have found a good one. If the answer is no, find another.

I have a friend who adopted a rescue horse named Daisy. My friend's goal was just to take nice rides in the woods, but it wasn't always going smoothly. At the barn where she boarded Daisy, people with more experience told her she needed to train her horse, who was sometimes compliant and sometimes very stubborn. So, my friend began training with the experts. Sometimes Daisy would "obey." At other times, she would seem to just shut down and refuse to do anything, even move forward. At the barn, this behavior got Daisy labeled "stubborn."

The trainers had harsh methods and yelled at them both, making my friend feel awful. "You gotta control your horse," they hammered, "or she'll walk all over you!" She left lessons in tears because the trainers made her feel three feet tall. Every lesson was a battle—that she often lost. Struggling to comply with the expert's instructions, my friend stopped listening to her own intuition about what Daisy wanted. Intuitively, she felt that Daisy was frightened, and that's why she would just freeze. It took her a while to realize she needed to listen to Daisy, not the experts. She gave up the lessons and went back to the simple joy of riding Daisy in the woods.

Over time, my friend learned more about animal communication, and she and Daisy were able to get on the same page. She began to understand that Daisy had her own sense of timing. When she tried to rush past something that was making Daisy nervous, this was when Daisy would dig in her hooves. My friend realized she needed to go slow and let Daisy work out her own fear. Soon their rides became calm and connected. Away from the training arena, she and Daisy had found their synchronicity, and the joy was back!

You and your animal should feel a little tired mentally and physically after a lesson, but always hopeful and joyful. If a trainer makes you feel bad about yourself or your animal, find another one.

I am constantly in awe of a dog's ability to develop deep bonds with their humans once we commit ourselves to nurture them with love, support, and compassionate guidance.

Comehereboy.com

Journal Reflections on Relationship Training:

1) How do you feel about your connection with the animal who shares your life? Or a previous animal in your life?

2) Is there some way you could improve this connection? What would you like to improve? What do you think you need to do to improve it?

3) Do you have any preconceptions about training that might be limiting the potential between you and your animal?

4) What is most precious to you about your relationship with the animal who shares your life?

5) Do you have any regrets that need to be healed, either in this relationship or in a relationship with an animal who has passed away?

Re-Minder: My relationship with
(your animal's name) is precious.

Zora learning focus, one of the tools we emphasize in our HAC classes to strengthen relationship building, trust, and connection. Focus is a wonderful tool to maintain eye connection, to help the dog "read" your desires, and choose to behave accordingly.

<h1 style="text-align:center">Principle #13</h1>

HONORING ANIMAL WISDOM
Makes Us More Loving People

I have studied many philosophers and many cats.
The wisdom of cats is infinitely superior.

Hippolyte A. Taine

Overview

In The Human-Animal Connection, we believe that all animals are sacred. Animals are connected to the earth in ways we barely comprehend. We humans likely would not have survived or thrived without our partnership with animals. It is time to acknowledge that animals have done a great service to humanity. And humanity thus has a debt to repay, starting with treating animals with greater respect.

Honoring animal wisdom is one way to show respect for our animal friends. Connecting with their wisdom makes us wiser and better people because animals have much to teach humans, and we have much we can learn from them. Humans can be spiritually elevated if we embrace this perspective. Recognizing the wisdom of animals is a critical step to treating them more ethically.

My Wise Wolfie

My cat, Wolfie, was wiser about relationships and had better intuition about the men in my life than I did. Wolfie was a stray cat in New York City who clawed his way into my life one bitterly cold winter night. I lived alone in a ground-floor apartment at the back of the building. I heard this noise, and at first, I thought he was a burglar trying to break into my bedroom window, which had happened before. I yelled to scare him off, only to be met with a tiny meow in response.

I thought to myself as I opened the back door of the building, *I'll just give him some milk, let him in out of the cold. Just for one night!* At the time, I was working in the movie business and didn't have time for myself, much less another creature. For sure, I wasn't planning to open my door—or my life—but he ignored the bowl I left outside my door and walked right inside my apartment and deep into my heart.

Soon into our life together, I discovered Wolfie's remarkable intuition when I had to choose between several film projects. I would lay the contending scripts down on the floor, walk away, and pretend I wasn't paying attention. Wolfie would briefly inspect the scripts one by one. Then he chose his favorite and would sit on it. I learned to give a lot of weight to his opinion because Wolfie's choice was invariably the best of the group.

And I discovered that I could rely on his strong "opinion" in other situations, too, including the men in my life. Some men he had no interest in. Others he would tolerate. And a very select few he adored. One day, I was having a business meeting at my house. Wolfie tramped across several laps, finally chose one man's lap to settle on, and proceeded to purr for the duration of the meeting. I wish I had learned to listen to Wolfie sooner. He could have saved me a lot of pain.

Wolfie Wisdom

If we take a moment for honest self-reflection, I think we would all agree that there have been some situations in our lives in which a little more wisdom would have gone a long way. We made decisions we thought were right but looking back, we might wish we had chosen differently. While we did the best we could at the time, we can't help but wonder why we didn't see the warning signs that silently screamed, "Don't go in there!" Perhaps if we had maintained better access to our own animal wisdom, like Wolfie, we would have steered a different course. Ever wonder how your life would have been different if you had full access to your animal wisdom?

We humans think we have cornered the market on making well-thought-out decisions. Assuming that humans are the more logical species, we go about training our "simple-minded" dogs. But when you think about what humans teach dogs *sit, stay, roll over* and various obedience tricks, maybe we are missing something. As Anthony Douglas Williams said, "We have more to learn from animals than animals have to learn from us."

For much of humanity's history, our lives have been intertwined with animals; they have helped us with hunting, farming, transportation, and protection. They have provided us with warmth and companionship. We might not have survived as a species if it wasn't for our relationship with animals.

There is a saying that "a dog may be man's best friend, but the horse wrote history." It is impossible to imagine geographical exploration or even war without horses to ride into battle. In his book *The Paw Prints of History*, Stanley Coren tells many stories of lives transformed by their contact with animals.

One story from his book is about Florence Nightingale, whose life direction was transformed because of a chance encounter with a wounded dog. She rescued this dog as his owner was trying to kill him and was able to nurse him back to life. The power of this experience shifted her life focus to healing.

Ancient Egyptians revered cats so much that they built temples dedicated to them. Nobility was often buried near or next to their cats. It is said that modern-day cats haven't forgotten their status in ancient Egypt.

Even though it has only been in the last few hundred years since humans have become increasingly separated from the land, that change has cost us much in terms of our connection with animals. Civilization brings many comforts—plumbing, temperature-controlled environments, and technology—but when we left the land, we lost our reverence for animals. Many of the indigenous cultures I have studied recognize that animals have a deep understanding of the natural world and much mastery over the environment. This wisdom warrants respect, not only for the animals which serve them daily but for all animals. Those people who are still connected to the land are usually very connected to the animals with whom they share it.

Burdened with the economic and other stressors of modern life, most people do not have a chance to spend much peaceful time in nature. There are hidden costs to our well-being when we don't have access to natural rejuvenation. Ted Andrews reminds us in his book *Animal-Wise – Understanding the Language of Animal Messengers and Companions* that "recent surveys indicate the average person in the U.S. spends less than an hour outdoors per week. Spending time outdoors is necessary for our physical, emotional, mental, and spiritual health. And we are not likely to have an actual animal encounter without spending some time outdoors."

Snakes As Brothers

This disconnect between humans and animals is a relatively new phenomenon in human history, taking a dark turn in just the last century or two. As an example of this cultural shift, naturalist J. Allen Boone observed that white people and Native Americans experienced rattlesnakes in completely different ways. White people considered rattlesnakes to be deadly enemies and would not hesitate to kill one on sight, and white men were frequently bitten. Native Americans viewed rattlesnakes as their *little brothers* and were rarely bitten. Boone suggested that the "murderous thoughts and energy" of the white men made them attractive and vulnerable to the snakes, who responded by defending themselves. In contrast, the natives spoke to them and treated rattlesnakes with respect. As a result, they were generally not bothered by them.

Many indigenous cultures consider animals to be sacred carriers of wisdom. They have long-standing practices and ceremonies of connecting with and communicating to power animals or spirit guides in the form of animals. In Hawaii, it is believed that a particular species is your protector or "Aumakua." Throughout their lives, many native Hawaiians remain receptive to mystical encounters and experiences with their Aumakua and communicate intuitively with these messengers. Important life decisions are made based upon guidance heard from these Aumakua.

Many people who share their lives with animals talk to them. Some even feel they can "hear" the animals speak to them. While not everyone believes this, a growing number of people will swear that animals do understand us, or at least our emotions. For our part, The Human-Animal Connection is committed to helping people better understand and appreciate the animals who share their lives. While communicating with animals may seem like a *new* concept to some, it is important to remember that shamans and wise men and women from all cultures have relied on animal wisdom to guide them since the dawn of civilization.

In Christopher Manes's book, *Other Creations – Rediscovering the Spirituality of Animals*, he states, "So important are animals to our spiritual lives that we do not merely use animal imagery to embody religious themes; rather, we discover spiritual values through animals." Animals can help us connect in ways that are beyond words, that illuminate the essence of life.

Dognition: Unique Canine Intelligence

Brian Hare coined the term *dognition* to refer to the unique nature of canine intelligence. He states in his book, *The Genius of Dogs – How Dogs Are Smarter Than You Think*, "In the last ten years, there has been something of a revolution in the study of canine intelligence. We have learned more about how dogs think in the past decade than we have in the previous century." (Remember, in the last century, "researchers" would operate on a living dog without anesthesia because they didn't believe the yelping meant the dog felt pain. The surgery was performed in front of live audiences.)

Having respect for animal intelligence helps us to see everything we do with animals in a new, more compassionate light. Even with the continued use of animals in research, there can be more humane treatment and methods, such as those employed by Professor Matsuzawa at the Kyoto University Primate Research Institute in Japan. He allows his chimpanzee research subjects to choose when to participate in the study and when they want to hang out and play with the other chimps. This one change is a revolution in kindness in a laboratory setting.

One of the chimps Professor Matsuzawa has been studying is named Ayuma. This intelligent chimp can recognize and remember ten number positions and their order after they are flashed for less than a second on a computer screen and does so with greater accuracy than any human. The average human can accurately remember three or four positions. Ayuma would take a *mental picture* of an entire screen of scrambled numbers and remember where each one was with a near 80 percent accuracy. In Mutsuzawa's words, "He has an actual picture memory in his mind, an eidetic memory and can hold it." Even when Ayuma is distracted and turns away from the screen, ten seconds later, he can still remember where each of the numbers was and assign them in the right order.

In addition to respecting animal intelligence, if we choose to, we can open our hearts and our minds to our *own animal wisdom.* It starts with an intention to do so. It is valuable to cultivate *respect* for animal wisdom and how well they navigate the world. For example, how is it that some animals separated from their humans can travel hundreds of miles to find them? There are so many stories of cats and dogs traveling great unfamiliar distances to find their way home or to their person. Are there times when this sense of direction could help us better navigate our own life decisions?

And finally, honoring animal wisdom helps us to recognize that animals can be our partners in healing. For example, enlisting dogs' amazing sense of smell to detect illnesses has been lifesaving. Dogs have been trained to detect the presence of cancer, tuberculosis, malaria, Parkinson's disease, and other illnesses. Trained Covid detection dogs can detect the presence of the virus with an accuracy rate equal to the medical test, and they can detect it five days before symptoms have even occurred. This is significant because 40 percent of people with the virus in their system have no symptoms. (You can read more about this on my blog Canine Covid Detectives.) Recognizing the power of partnership with animal wisdom can save our lives—and theirs.

"This Book Is for the Birds"

In Principle #2, I shared how the tiny veery birds have proven to be accurate predictors of hurricane intensity in the upcoming hurricane season. After studying these birds' habits over decades, Christopher Heckscher, ornithologist and associate professor at Delaware State University, found that the birds' prediction months in advance was more accurate than the forecast of the National Oceanic and Atmospheric Administration (NOAA). In 2018, the NOAA scientists predicted a mild hurricane season, but the veery birds didn't agree. According to the Audubon Society website, "The birds were saying *bad season*, and everyone else was saying *below-average season*…In the end, the birds were more accurate…. The birds appeared to sense what the season had in store *months before* most tropical storms form."

Connecting to animal wisdom is both spiritual and practical. In fact, spending time with some wild birds in my backyard inspired me to write this book. I spent time tuning in to the birds. And I "heard" the book's title and the format for our thirty-three principles. It pays to listen to birds.

One of the greatest gifts of opening oneself to innate animal wisdom is understanding the forces of life balance. Observing the balance inherent in animals' lives can teach us about being present in the moment, about harmony, strategy, and the unity of all life. We have paid a high price for leaving our connection with the land and our intuitive connection to animals. But that can change. We can reconnect. The animals are willing—if we are—to reconnect, re-engage, and once again become our active partners in the journey of a more balanced life.

Journal Reflections on Honoring Animal Wisdom:

1) Do you feel connected to your animal wisdom? What could you do to increase your receptivity to this universal knowingness?

2) Is your personal "wildness" calling to you? How would your life change if you connected to your innate animal wisdom?

3) When was the last time you were in the presence of a wild animal or wild birds?

4) Is there an animal in your life to whom you feel you need to apologize? Can you do that now?

5) Do you feel you might have an animal Aumakua? A spirit guide or protector? Maybe you are drawn to this animal or have received dreams in which this animal appears, or you have been given signs at important times. Maybe you collect images or figurines of this animal. What animal do you feel it is?

Re-Minder: I connect with my Animal Wisdom.

My friend Tom having a conversation with a cardinal in New York City's Central Park. This wild bird shared with him a feeling of peace amidst the Covid epidemic.

STORY

The Shelter Houdini

Big Red was given that shelter name because he had a beautiful silky red coat, and well, he was big—physically big and personality big! Big Red was also a Houdini. He could escape from any kennel because all he ever wanted was to be near a person. So, he would climb chain-link fences over six feet tall. We would find him wandering the shelter with his kennel lock firmly closed behind him. But he wasn't trying to escape the shelter, he was just looking for a person to love.

To keep him safe, Big Red was put in a special room that had a floor-to-ceiling closure. However, he could still body slam against the glass door to try to get it to open—*Bang! Bang! Bang!*—and he wouldn't give up, even after the door was blocked shut with drums filled with water and cement blocks. Visitors saw him leaping, flying, and flinging himself against the thick glass window—above their heads. Big Red was put on doggie Xanax. (In many shelters, a dog with this much energy and difficult to contain would have been euthanized.)

Big Red loved to chew his elk bone, loved his massages, and was easy to walk, but he was not easy to return to his kennel! It took two or three people to get him back inside his kennel, as he knew all the tricks and could outsmart us. And his reactions were always faster than ours. A lot of volunteers gave up trying to walk him, as it could take you twenty minutes to get him back inside afterward. One of his tricks was to wedge his head in the doorway so you couldn't close it, and leave him inside. Some of the larger men were able to overpower him and roughly force him back, but I wasn't willing to do that.

One day I took him out for a walk through a different door. He watched closely how I opened the door. I swear he was memorizing how the handle worked, and I knew he could open that door after seeing me do it just once. Some days, while on our walk, I could communicate with him and ask him to go back into his kennel nicely. And he would. But the next day, I would forget to ask him, and there we were struggling, me on my knees (this was during Covid, so I was sweating and panting in my mask), and Big Red's body was only halfway through the door. I had forgotten to get a buddy to help me with this human-tries-to-exit routine. So, I am pushing with all my weight against his, and he is pushing against me with all his amazing determination not to be left alone in his kennel.

Finally, out of fatigue, I just relaxed. The instant I did, he stopped pushing against me. Our bodies were still pressed against each other's, but the fight was gone. I was amazed that as soon as I changed my strategy, he changed his. We spent some time pressed close together, breathing together. I told him how much I loved him, and he went quietly back inside on his own.

Big Red was a great teacher.

You can see a video of this wonderful being on our Human-Animal Connection YouTube channel. It shows a visit where we went on an adoption adventure at the mall. Big Red had perfect instincts about people. He knew to be gentle and roll over for a belly rub for older women and then be spunky with young men. He was a very special Soul!

Thankfully, Big Red was adopted by a man in Sedona. A man with a big red truck and an even bigger heart.

Big Red was a shelter Houdini.
He taught me so much about
canine intention. All he wanted
was to be connected to a human.

HUMAN-ANIMAL
CONNECTION

PART TWO

What Animals Can Teach Us About Being a Happier Human

Animals in the wild are seldom depressed. They are not riddled with anxiety about the future. If they are a social species, they feel connected to their herd and have a sense of belonging to their world. They are a reminder of the deep healing feeling that comes from our sense of connection to others.

Animals have a balance of play and relaxation. We humans can learn about emotional well-being by letting animals teach us a thing or two about how to be happy and balanced. They have a rhythm that is tied to body wisdom that keeps them safe and healthy.

Animals can help us find peace in their presence. Practicing mindfulness with animals is a wonderful way to expand our spiritual connection.

Principle #14

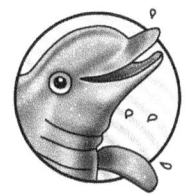

OPENING THE DOOR TO ANIMAL COMMUNICATION
Animals Are Always Communicating

Some people talk to animals.
Not many listen though.
That is the problem.

A.A. Milne

Overview

Animals are communicating all the time. The question is, are we listening? If we are, do we even know what they are saying? What would animals say to us if they knew we wanted to hear?

Animals communicate with each other and with us in ways we do not fully understand. It is possible to learn to communicate better with animals, and we can come to understand how they communicate with us. Animals and humans can communicate with or without words. Intuition is one doorway that allows us to enter the animals' world.

As Wallace Black Elk said, "There was a time when we communicated with all animals, and they communicated with us."

"Tell me something only you and your person knows."

James French tells a story about working with a client's daughter who had a horse, but she didn't believe in animal communication. James had a chat with the girl's horse and said, "You better tell me something that only you and she knows, or she won't believe any of this."

The horse told him that sometimes, rather than taking time to walk the long distance to the house, the girl would pee in the corner of the barn. The horse turned his head to indicate the spot. When James reported this secret, the girl was instantly convinced of his ability to communicate with animals.

Animals Are Always Communicating

Body language, movement, and facial expression are the primary nonverbal methods animals use to communicate. Sometimes an animal's body communication happens in a flash, sometimes over several seconds. It is usually a lot faster than words, so our brains must catch up. Emotionally balanced animals use these instantaneous communication styles to make friends, establish desired boundaries, and avoid conflict. If we humans improve our skills of neutral observation and learn to correctly interpret their signals, it will greatly improve our connection to animals. When we communicate better, the quality of our relationship improves, as well as the quality of our lives together.

When two dogs are on leashes, it can sometimes interfere with the animal's ability to send and receive clear signals because they aren't able to do their natural behaviors. For example, they need to circle each other, turn away, or sniff front and back. If the leash causes restriction of natural greeting behavior, it can lead to frustration, mixed or missed signals, and disruption of otherwise polite greetings. If we learn to be aware and respectful of the ways dogs communicate, we can adjust our behaviors in ways that allow them the freedom to "converse" as they wish to. This will lower their stress levels and help them have more fun together.

As Turid Rugaas says in her book, *On Talking Terms with Dogs: Calming Signals*, "Dogs being flock animals, have a language for communication with each other. Canine language in general consists of large variety of signals using body, face, ears, tail, sounds, movement, and expression. The dog's innate ability to signal is easily lost or reinforced through life experience. If we study the signals dogs use with each other and use themselves, we increase our ability to communicate with our dogs. Most noteworthy of all canine signals are the calming signals, which are used to maintain a healthy social hierarchy and resolution of conflict within the flock."

Good Communication Leads to Good Connection

Communication between humans and animals is a daily occurrence. In the Human-Animal Connection, we believe the quality of a relationship is reflected in the quality and depth of communication. Good communication leads to a sense of connection; conversely, poor communication results in poor connection. Because we want to have a good connection with our animals, it only stands to reason we would have a hunger to better communicate with animals.

Animals' Communication Is Truthful

We, as humans, use words, tone of voice, body language, facial expressions, and other nonverbal ways to communicate with each other. But we trust language the most. The problem is that humans can use words to tell the truth—or to lie. Thus, verbal language is not as reliable as body language, as body language often reveals the real truth. We've all had the experience of believing someone's words (especially if they were the words we wanted to hear) while our intuition or gut reaction told us that person's words concealed the truth.

While animals can play tricks and fool us, they don't generally lie about *how they feel about you*. If they want to interact with you, they do. If not, you can't make them trust you or want to interact. Humans have the unenviable ability to show themselves one way while feeling very different inside.

Obviously, over time, you can train an animal to respond the way you want, but their feelings will remain the same. If you share your life with an animal, you may have noticed that they form instant opinions about people; they like certain folks and dislike others, even on a first meeting. This is because to an animal, people reveal their truth, no matter what their words are saying.

These are a few reasons it is so pleasant to spend time with animals. They are genuinely who they are. This experience of authenticity is very loveable.

Each Animal Is an Individual and Communicates Uniquely

When first exploring animal communication, we need to remember that every horse, cat, pig, whale, or mouse will have unique ways to express themselves, just as humans do. Some animals are better communicators than others.

Some animals will "put their own spin" on communication, like the horse, Jacob, did when I practiced with him in my animal communication skills training. I was asked by his barn manager to talk with Jacob to find out why this previously very sweet horse had become very aggressive to the mini-horses around him, to the point where his owner isolated Jacob in his own stall and fenced-in corral. When I asked Jacob about his new behavior, he explained that in the old barn, they were all together, and he and his favorite mare, Millie, were always together. Jacob wanted to be with Millie and was angry about this new separation.

When I told the owner this, she laughed and said Jacob and Millie were together at night. I was embarrassed that Jacob left this fact out of our conversation. I went back to talk with him, and he explained that he wanted to be with her all the time. I then explained this to the owner, who was not really a believer in this "animal communication stuff" but agreed to put them together day and night. Well, Jacob's problem behaviors disappeared, and harmony on the ranch was restored. And I learned a good lesson: Ask more detailed questions!

Call Me by My Name

"I failed seven times," said a gentleman who had fostered twenty-three cats over eleven years for a local shelter. He explained that "foster-fail" is what fosters call themselves when they can't bring themselves to return a foster animal that they have been taking care of, back to the shelter. Thus, he now shares his big house with seven cats that entered his life as fosters but never left. Some were missing an eye, a foot, or had other issues that made them less likely to find homes.

He had taught three of his cats to be toilet trained, and one even knew how to flush, using a method Charles Mingus, the jazz musician, outlined in a pamphlet he wrote in 1954. Princess preferred the litter box, and "the other three came and went outside through the kitty door, except when it was raining."

"They can all be hanging out with me in the den while I am watching TV, and I call one of them, like you would a dog, 'Come here, Heidi!' And Heidi will completely ignore me, just flick her tail, and continue staring at the TV. But the other six will turn and look at Heidi."

When I asked what made him keep those seven, he said, "I choose the ones who love me the most. Which is not much when it comes to cats." Then he added with a smile, "Oh, they love me. They just expect me to know it."

Dolphins Outsmart their Trainers

A friend of mine was a dolphin trainer in Hawaii. The trainers routinely ran the dolphins through their dull daily drills where the dolphins had to perform simple behaviors they already knew well. It was a series of steps: *Put the red ball in the left net, take the green ball to the side of the pool.* All of these repetitive training routines were performed multiple times, with minor variations, and all of it was videotaped. One afternoon, it was as if the dolphins went on strike. They did all the instructions incorrectly, even though they knew what was being asked. Then, seeing the disappointment on the trainers' faces, they stopped entirely. The frustrated trainers kept trying—no balls, no nets, no luck. Later, they looked at the videotape and saw that when the trainers turned their backs, the dolphins did all the exercises perfectly. But when they turned around again, the dolphins swam lazily, with just the hint of a smile.

Communication Gestures

If we become very accurate observers of body language, we can gain many clues as to what animals might be feeling and can communicate more effectively with them. Scientist and professor Brian Hare has conducted innovative research to establish how well dogs can follow human gaze and gestures and understand our communication intentions. Hare's later research shows that even puppies with minimal human socialization can understand the meaning of pointing and other gestures. He also noted that dogs, who are very attuned to human gestures, are better at understanding the meaning of pointing than chimpanzees are. "Dogs are most likely to follow your gaze if you indicate your communicative intentions by calling their name and looking directly at them before indicating where they should look."

Cosmo, an African Gray Parrot, played many communication pranks. She would give the dog who lived with her commands in a human voice. With her owner, Betty Jean Craige, Cosmo would wait until Craige was in the shower, then would precisely imitate the sound of the phone ringing. When Cosmo was alone and did something that she knew she shouldn't, she could be heard saying, "bad birdie."

You may have heard about the famous gorilla, Koko, who was taught American Sign Language, and could use it to communicate her desires, values, and emotional states with the vocabulary of a three-year-old human. She was trained by Penny Paterson and the team at the Gorilla Foundation. Koko was often seen "signing to herself" to process her thoughts and feelings just as a human would talk to themselves.

One of my favorite Koko stories occurred when she was a youngster. Penny, her trainer, had to go on a business trip where she would be gone for two weeks. She knew that Koko understood the concept of one week but didn't think she would understand the idea of two weeks, so Penny told Koko she would be gone for one week.

When Penny returned, Koko was moody. She had ripped out her sink from the wall. Penny asked Koko if she did that; Koko signed *No*. Penny repeated the question, and Koko again signed *No*. Penny said, "You lied to me." And Koko replied, *You lied to me first.*

Interpreting Animal Body Language

There are many excellent resources on interpreting the body language of animals. One simple and informative book I recommend is *The Secret Language of Dogs* by Victoria Stillwell.

In the HAC, we believe that a particularly important aspect of physical communication is what we call "*Towards & Away*" (discussed in more detail in Principle #23). Simply put, animals generally move toward what they want and away from what they don't want. Fish are great examples to watch of *Towards & Away,* moving toward what they want and away from what might be dangerous or disturbing. In addition to this larger motion, an animal may turn their head toward what they want and look away from something they would prefer to avoid. When my dog, Sophia, wants something, she will stare at it and assume I should understand what this means. And I do, which means she has me well trained.

When I first adopted Sophia, I didn't have much skill with animal communication. Even though I would take her for a walk before I went to bed, she had frequent accidents in the house in the middle of the night. Clearly, we didn't have a reliable signal that I could understand.

Now, she will wake me up with a certain breathy sound, move in a circle, and put her paws up on the bed to let me know she wants to go out. I much prefer this to waking up to a mess. Since we are doing much better with sending and receiving each other's signals, we almost never have that problem. Good communication makes every aspect of sharing lives together easier.

Words, Glorious Words

What do animals communicate about? Everything. From their desires and emotional states to statements, as Koko did, expressing concerns about global warming.

There is a long history of finding ways to teach animals to communicate *in human terms* or in our world of language. This is one approach to animal communication. A dog named Rico opened this door by learning over 300 words. Then came Chaser, a border collie trained by psychology professor John Pilley who wrote the book *Chaser: Unlocking the Genius of the Dog Who Knows a Thousand Words*. Chaser could identify the names of several hundred toys and could distinguish verbs and actions such as retrieve, carry, touch. He could perform simple actions on a verbal cue, such as "Fetch the blue ball," "Carry squishy bear," "Roll tennis ball," and so on. Chaser also understood elements of grammar and understood references about time and sequence, such as the communication: "Not now, later."

Alex, an African Grey Parrot, was a remarkably good student who learned several hundred words, many concepts, and some basic math from Dr. Irene Pepperberg. Guided by Dr. Pepperberg's unique teaching methods of watching and imitation, Alex learned to identify many objects and say what texture they were, such as wood, metal, or plastic. Alex could add, subtract, and count up to seven objects. He could understand some abstract ideas and even understood the concept of zero. He would make requests for specific treats and would even reprimand his fellow parrot lab mates if they were being lazy with their lessons.

Alex, with a brain the size of a shelled walnut, could comprehend concepts like *same* and *different*. Pepperberg could show him several objects on a tray and ask him what was the same or different. He could identify "bigger or smaller," or different colors, shapes, and materials in answer to her question to him, "What matter?"

Pepperberg's "watch and learn" method is a key training tool we use in The Human-Animal Connection, especially in our Therapy Dog Training program, as dogs learn much faster if they see another dog perform a requested task. Claudia Fugazza has a related training method called "Do as I Do," which has the human demonstrate the desired behavior when teaching something new to a dog. Imitation is a powerful learning tool for animals and humans. Another example I love is the story of the horse, Beautiful Jim Key, who as a colt, first demonstrated to his person, William Key, how smart he was by imitating the family dog by doing all the same tricks the dog would do, including sit, lay down, and fetch. This demonstration of intelligence is what inspired William Key to teach his horse the alphabet.

Pepperberg's research with Alex the parrot led to a much greater understanding of the potential for avian learning and communication. Dr. Pepperberg explains her innovative and respectful training methods as follows:

"My plans for training Alex differed from the accepted standards of the time. Under the prevailing psychological dogma known as behaviorism, animals were seen as automatons, with little or no capacity for cognition, or thought. Biology was little better, dominated by theories claiming that much of animal behavior was innately programmed. Experimental conditions for working with animals were very tightly prescribed. Animal subjects were actually supposed to be starved to 80 percent of their body weight so they would be eager for the food given for a 'correct' response. They were also to be placed in a box so that the appropriate 'stimuli' could be very tightly controlled, and their responses precisely monitored. The technique was known as 'operant conditioning.' This was, to me, completely crazy, not to put too fine a point on it. It was contrary to all my gut instincts and commonsense understanding of nature."

While she struggled to find acceptance in the academic field at first, her research with Alex broke new ground in understanding both animal communication and cognition.

But what impressed me most was the fact that, at times, Alex seemed to be able to understand Dr. Pepperberg's thoughts. Once, she was reading a magazine ad for a car she was thinking about buying. Alex couldn't see the interior of the magazine, nor had she ever spoken of this vague desire, but he spoke up, "You want a new car."

Alex, always full of surprises beyond what he was trained to say and do, would say, "Good night, I love you!" whenever she would leave for the night. Dr. Pepperberg stated, "Clearly, animals know more than we think and think a great deal more than we know."

"Blue shirt small human walks slowly"

Animal behaviorist Con Slobodchikoff has been studying Gunnison prairie dogs for over thirty years and discovered that their communication between friends and family is quite complex. Analyzing their "danger calls," he identified and decoded over 100 yips, chirps, barks, and other vocalizations that he then cataloged into unique linguistic tools that fit our categories of nouns, verbs, adjectives, and even adverbs. In one experiment he demonstrated the sophistication of the prairie dogs' language. For this study, he hired assistants and had them all dress the same way except for different colored T-shirts (blue, green, yellow, or gray) and instructed them to walk among the prairie dogs at a different pace. Then he had each assistant change the color of their T-shirts and walk at a different speed. When he analyzed the prairie dog sounds, he was able to detect that the animals communicated to each other very specific information, such as *blue shirt small human walks slowly.*

According to Brenda Recio in her lovely book, *Inside Animal Hearts and Minds*, Con Slobodchikoff recorded prairie dog communications which appeared to include a specific call for *gun*, which they would use in combination with the call for *human.*

Squirrels have been known to eavesdrop on songbird conversations. If they hear a warning sign, they treat it with proper respect, understanding that a hawk, owl, or other predator is nearby. Some squirrel species will even pass the word by mimicking the birds' warning alarm.

Karl Berg's studies of wild parrotlets in Venezuela have shown a connection between recognizing each other's unique calls and the development of communication. Further, Berg's studies also show how this communication increases social skills, which lead to survival, evolution, and advancing intelligence. Parrotlets are lifelong learners, and they recognize their mates and friends from their unique *name signature* sounds. Parrotlets must send and receive each other's messages and greetings correctly or risk death from not recognizing the calls of competitors and predators who have been known to steal wives and infants.

Kanzi, a bonobo, was taught to use symbols called lexigrams on a special computer screen by researcher Sue Savage Rumbaugh and consequently knows several thousand words. In addition to her structured lexigram teaching method using computer graphics to stand for words, Dr. Rumbaugh talks to Kanzi as she would to a child.

Kanzi seems to understand so much more than the words on his computer screen. I've seen one video of Kanzi and Sue making dinner in the kitchen. Sue gives him very specific instructions, "Put water in the pot," which he follows precisely: Kanzi turns on the water and puts some in the pot. Sue looks over and says, "More water," and Kanzi adds more. Then she tells him to add the potatoes. He follows all these instructions as a young child might. I find their level of understanding and cooperation amazing.

Kanzi has also made up his own combined words and meanings, such as "big water" for a storm that came through and "slow lettuce" for kale, which he had to chew slowly.

Similarly, Koko, the gorilla, is famous for combining words to create new meanings, such as "finger-bracelet" for ring or "eye-hat" for mask.

Nim Chimsky, a chimpanzee, was raised just like a human baby with a human family and had been taught sign language. However, Nim was later sent away when he became an adolescent and began to bite. Although Nim had the ability to communicate some of his wants and needs, sadly he was discarded when his behavior wasn't manageable in a human setting. Bob Ingersoll, a graduate research student, later met Nim in a primate facility. Ingersoll saw that Nim was sad and depressed and wished he could do something to improve his quality of life. Ingersoll decided to try something that worked for him – so he offered Nim a puff from a marijuana cigarette. Nim was intrigued and took to it immediately, acting just like a happy, stoned human. Soon Nim was asking for more. He surprised Ingersoll by making up his own signs and communicating, *Stone smoke time now.* This story of a chimp who wanted to get stoned was reported in *High Times* in 1975.

Doggie Talk Buttons

In her delightful book, *How Stella Learned to Talk*, speech pathologist Christina Hunger tells her story about teaching Stella, her Catahoula/Blue Heeler mix, to communicate thoughts and desires by stepping on talk buttons on a homemade board. Each talk button spoke a single word when Stella stepped on it. Stella's training began with the word "outside" so she could communicate when nature was calling to avoid indoor accidents. Hunger slowly began adding words, and, by the end of the book, Stella knew about three dozen words on her board. But what was exciting was Stella began combining words on her own to communicate more complex ideas, quickly taking her communication abilities to new levels. Hunger added words like *help* when one of Stella's toys was stuck under the couch. When taught the word *no,* Hunger didn't anticipate that Stella would use it to comment on *their* behavior. When Daylight Savings Time began in the spring and delayed her dinnertime, Stella stomped on three of her talk buttons, *STELLA. NO. EAT. STELLA. NO. EAT.*

Christina taught Stella references to time, such as *later,* which was important because once they taught her to say *beach,* one of her favorite places to go, she wore out that button. Stella learned to request specific things like asking for her husband Jake to toss the ball: *Jake play!* Stella tapped. One day, Stella brightened their morning when she put together this sequence of words: "Good girl, Stella. Good Stella, love you."

Another day, when a group of friends came over and were fawning over Stella, and Christina called to her to come, Stella replied with two buttons: *Christina. Later.* Everyone burst out laughing. "I'm in constant amazement and shock," Hunger said. "Every day, she says something cooler than she said the day before."

Once you teach your dog how to communicate even simple desires, watch out! Dutch, a young man, taught Lola, a Siberian Husky mix puppy, to use talk buttons for *toy, outside, yes, no, hide-and-seek, bath, and treat.* Lola loved playing hide-and-seek and would often use that button. But Lola hated baths and would run like the house was on fire at the sound of that word button. She would, of course, hit the *treat* button repeatedly. In fact, she loved her treat button so much that she would wear out its batteries faster than any other button. And when Dutch would say "No" to her treat request, the look on Lola's face was tragic, like taking candy from a baby! So, you do have to consider if you are ready to have your dog make talk-button requests of you. Because if you don't deliver, are you ready to face "the look"?!

Not All Dogs Are Ready to Talk

Bo was an owner-surrender, an eight-month-old dog at the shelter who was so frightened that during the several months she was there, no one asked to see her. If you glanced at her in her kennel, she would run to her outside section. If you went to see her in the outside section, she would run inside. Of course, her adoption prospects were near zero because all anyone ever saw was her tail running away.

I began working with Bo, but she was so scared of me at first that I almost gave up. Then I brought Caleb, one of our HAC board members, to meet Bo at the shelter. He was her first visitor. It was love at first sight! (Read this happy-ending story on my blog, "Bo's Second Chance at Love.") Caleb took Bo home that day.

After several months of living together with Milo, his partner's dog, Caleb decided to see how Bo would respond to learning to use the talk buttons for *play, food,* and *go outside.* Interestingly, Bo was still so insecure she never made any requests for her needs and didn't use the buttons to communicate. But Milo, a more confident dog, understood when Bo needed something and would use the talk buttons to communicate *Bo's needs* to her humans!

Clever Hans – Even Smarter Than They Thought

Early in the 20th century, a horse named Clever Hans became a world-wide sensation. It seemed he could spell, count, and solve simple math problems by stomping his foot the correct number of times. People came from all over to watch these amazing demonstrations. And, of course, there were many who tried to discredit him. But no matter how they tried to vary the way the questions were asked, Hans just kept getting the answers right. Even when strangers posed the questions, Hans stomped out the correct answer.

Finally, Professor Oskar Pfungst discovered how Clever Hans was able to do it. The horse needed to see his owner, a mathematician, to read his very subtle body language cues. The owner was completely unaware that he was communicating to his horse through uncon-scious body language and was astonished that his horse was accurately reading it. This was a terrible scandal and a disappointment for his legions of fans, and the whole story became known with a derogatory connotation and went down in history as *The Clever Hans Effect.*

From my point of view, instead of being a disappointment, Clever Hans offers a stunning demonstration of the powerful communication potential between humans and animals. We should be wildly impressed that the horse was accurately reading such subtle cues. This horse had very high social intelligence; he could read his human better than the man could read himself.

Beautiful Jim Key – The Educated Horse

Before Clever Hans, self-taught veterinarian, and former slave, William Key taught his own horse, Jim Key, a variety of tricks. Jim Key knew the alphabet, could spell, count to thirty, tell time, could add and subtract, and express his opinions on a variety of subjects. (His story appears earlier in this book after Principle #10). When they performed for large crowds, the horse would flirt with certain women in the audience he was fond of, showering them with attention in a way that made everyone laugh and the women swoon. When President Roosevelt's daughter Alice attended the show, Jim Key "predicted" who she would marry by spelling out her name and adding the last name of the man she would marry—even though this partnership had not yet entered her mind. It is estimated that over ten million people saw these performances. Unlike Clever Hans, there was no evidence that Doc Key was cueing the horse because Jim Key could perform just as well in his absence.

An unparalleled, deep connection existed between Doc Key and Jim Key from the time the horse was born crippled and barely able to walk. Doc Key raised the horse in his house and nursed him back to life. Thereafter, the horse followed Doc Key everywhere and watched everything that he did. Using patient and kind training, which was not the norm in horse training at the time, Doc Key began to recognize that the horse displayed an amazing level of intelligence.

They had an invisible way of communicating that was based on mutual respect. They were inseparable, so when Doc Key would go on the road, he took Jim Key, who performed and even improvised with the skill of a great actor. Although many bits in the show were rehearsed, there were always inexplicable demonstrations of Jim Key's spontaneous intelligence.

In one bit, Jim Key would go to a trunk, open it, and retrieve a folded towel. The towel was for wiping his face after he performed a trick: retrieving a silver dollar from a large glass filled with water—and not drinking any of it. One time, the stagehand forgot to replace a fresh towel in the trunk. When Jim Key discovered the used towel, he unfurled it, made a disgusted face, and ceremoniously dropped it on the ground.

There were so many spontaneous, unexpected actions Jim Key did on stage in which he responded in ways that weren't planned it is impossible to say it was just training. There was a magical connection between Doc Key and his horse. Could there have been a telepathic communication between them?

The Question of Animal Telepathy

Beyond the exciting experiments in teaching animals to communicate on human terms, animal communicators also seek to communicate in *animal terms*—to use their intuition to "hear, feel, and know" what animals have to say in their own *language.*

Penelope Smith has been practicing telepathic communication with animals for over thirty years and is the author of *Animal Talk – Interspecies Telepathic Communication.* She believes that "everyone is born with the power to communicate with other species, and, although it is a long-lost skill for many people, it can be regained for the benefit of all beings on Earth."

Smith points out, "Most animals are willing to come into a closer relationship if they are understood as they are and approached from their level of awareness. In some cases, they are more perceptive or aware than the humans who attempt to understand them."

Penelope Smith also believes that, as a species, we can restore telepathic communication, which she defines as follows: "*Tele* – refers to distance, and *-pathy* refers to feeling. So, telepathic communication involves the ability to feel another across a distance.... More than anything else, telepathy is a connection, a direct link to the Soul of all beings.... Such contact is based on the recognition that all beings are intelligent and can understand, interrelate, and communicate. [Animal Telepathy] is the experience of receiving direct thought transmission, images, feelings, and concepts from individuals of other species, repeatedly confirmed by often drastic changes in behavior and enhancement of cooperation, peacefulness, and closeness." She also states that this type of communication is not restricted to animals who are physically in your presence. "It also appears that telepathic communication is not a matter of developing some new power through mental exercises. *It is more a matter of opening up to love.*"

There are many situations where I have found that love is the key that opens the door to telepathic communication with animals. One person I worked with, Jeanie, a lifelong horse expert, had taken into her ranch a former racehorse, once sold for $65,000, then later "discarded" when his injuries made him unrideable. His papers were gone, most of his history unknown, but somewhere along the line of being passed through various facilities, he had gained the name Ralph. When I met Ralph, who was "donated" by the last facility he was in, one of the first things he telepathically told me was that Ralph was not his real name. I called him by the name he preferred, *Romeo*.

He is happy at his new ranch, Equinimity Tucson, with Barbara Collier and Jeanie Shepherd. There he can move freely in the corral, but was facing some challenges integrating into the new herd. Ralph/Romeo began doing some harmless, but odd behaviors, which I was asked to interpret. One of which was he would pee on the fresh dung of a mustang horse, Epona, the alpha mare in the herd. Jeanie had never seen a horse do this and was confused and wanted me to ask Ralph/Romeo why he always did this. She wondered if it was an attempt to show dominance since Epona had kicked Ralph really hard, several times. Ralph telepathically told me that this behavior was his way of trying to connect with the mare. He explained he had been kept as a solo horse, always in a stall, and didn't have the best horse-social skills. But he did have a sense of humor and explained that some of his antics were to lovingly show Jeanie that she didn't know *everything* about horses.

Jeanie has been working with an expert intuitive farrier, who has been helping Ralph reduce the pain in his body. I have been working with Ralph/Romeo on healing and communication and he is becoming an excellent equine therapy horse who loves to communicate telepathically. When our students sit in a circle in our HAC class *The Power of Presence*, Ralph stands in the circle with us, enjoying and supporting the peaceful energy. Ralph/Romeo has told me that this work is his true purpose. The other day, two visitors came to the ranch to see him. One had asthma; the other was having pain in her foot. Ralph/Romeo put his head on the woman's chest, and her breathing cleared in minutes. He put his head on the other woman's foot, and she said the pain was gone. This once traumatized horse is transforming before our eyes and becoming quite the communicator!

Veterinarian Linda Bender tells the following story in her book, *Animal Wisdom – Learning from the Spiritual Lives of Animals*: "On the evening of April 14, 1865, President Lincoln's dog (Fido) went berserk (as Lincoln was about to leave). Though he normally accepted Lincoln's comings and goings with composure, that night he began howling, urgently and piteously when the President and Mrs. Lincoln left the White House to attend a play. Nothing would calm the dog, and no one could understand the reason for his extreme agitation. Fido was still howling when the report finally came that the President had been shot."

Can you imagine if Lincoln understood what his dog was trying to say?

Dogs Know When Their Owners Are Coming Home

Cambridge and Harvard-educated researcher Rupert Sheldrake, PhD, wrote *Dogs That Know When Their Owners Are Coming Home – and Other Unexplained Power of Animals*. While some have questioned whether his methods were conducted with sufficient scientific rigor, Sheldrake has conducted over 4,500 case studies which he believes show that dogs knew the moment when their owners *decided* to return home. His sample group included owners who were not on a regular time schedule or who could be identified by the sound of a specific car or the smell of imminent approach.

I have been told so many stories by members of our Special Forces who, for security reasons, would return to their families without any advance notice. But their dog would always know, sometimes hours before the arrival, and the dog would sit by the door or on the front porch, waiting. The spouses were grateful for their dog's early warning system so they could get themselves ready for the "surprise visit."

There is a group of scientists in the vanguard creating a revolution in the general public's understanding of the inner lives of animals. But there is still resistance from those invested in outdated views like behaviorism and the mechanistic misconceptions of animals just being instinctual automata. This old school still believes animals don't make choices, don't have emotions and intentions, and don't communicate in the ways we have discussed in this chapter.

Despite the controversy over his methods, Sheldrake's book is one I recommend to those who want to explore the possibility of animal prescience by means other than the five senses.

Sheldrake says he follows "an open-minded system of inquiry, paying attention to evidence and testing possible explanations by means of experiment. The path of investigation is more in the spirit of science than the path of denial. And it is certainly more fun."

Sheldrake's theory is that animals know many things about their human's actions and feelings through their connection to morphic fields, which are like *information-carrying fields of energy* that can be tapped into to perceive things beyond what the five senses can know. He explains in his book, "I suggest that telepathic communication depends on bonds between people and animals—bonds that are not mere metaphors but actual (energetic) connections. They are connected through morphic fields."

Sometimes I play with this possibility of telepathic communication with my dog, Sophia, by sending a silent "hello" communication along the morphic field. If she is in another room, usually, she will come trotting into the room where I am. Sometimes I send a silent signal when we are in the same room. It could be as simple as *I love you* or *good doggie,* and her tail will wag as if I said the words aloud. Sometimes, I send her a message about going on a therapy dog visit we are going to attend later. She will just watch me with soft eyes— not looking away, just gazing back, as if she doesn't want to miss a word. I will see little ear twitches or tail wags, and we just enjoy this moment of connection. It is very sweet. Try it. You and your animal might really enjoy it.

The Bogey-Man: Anthropomorphism

Every field of science has people who are willing to go where no man or woman has gone before—and those who are determined to sustain the status quo. For many years, forward-thinking scientists in animal studies lived in fear of being accused of being anthropomorphic, defined by Merriam Webster as giving "human form or human attributes to nonhuman things." Numerous exciting discoveries have been abandoned by the mere suggestion, "Aren't you being a tad anthropomorphic?" And the new idea would be hidden from public discourse for fear of banishment to academic purgatory. Even today, I meet scientists who will privately tell me they agree with many of the HAC principles but are not able to speak of this publicly for fear of retribution.

Just a few decades ago, if you declared that animals had emotions, intentions, memory, thoughts, planning, strategy, tool-use, and communication, you would be forced to wear the scarlet letter "A" for, you know, *that* word. It is exciting to observe current scientists using verifiable methods to provide proof of the inner lives of animals. I hope that the use of the A-word as a bludgeon against those on the vanguard of perception and discovery will fade away.

As Marc Bekoff says in the preface to *How Animals Talk: And other Pleasant Studies of the Birds and Beasts* by William J. Long, "There is no adequate substitute for being anthropomorphic, we can only communicate about animals with the language we use in all other aspects of our daily lives…The careful use of anthropomorphism, in which we always take into account the animal's point of view, can only make the study of animal behavior more rigorous and more interesting and more challenging."

So, dear reader, please do not be haunted by the fear of bringing your own perceptions to observing animals. We must start somewhere, and we start with what we know. From there, we can test our ideas to see how they hold up against the rigors of science.

Perhaps William J. Long, whose book is based on his own observations from his time spent in nature, anticipated the impact of the "A-word" that would come decades later. He confidently put more credence on field studies in the wild over the sometimes-absurd academic positions of his day when he said, "It is doubtless much easier to deny such a conclusion than to prove or disprove it, but denial is commonly the first refuge of ignorance and the last of dogmatism."

Bekoff and Jane Goodall co-founded the Ethologists for the Ethical Treatment of Animals. Bekoff wrote the preface of *Animal Talk*, one of the most precious books on animal telepathy, which was published in 1919 and is still groundbreaking. The top scientists today are just beginning to present evidence of what Long spoke of during his decades observing animals in the wild. Some of the animal thought leaders I admire greatly are *discovering* what William J. Long wrote over 100 years ago. Bekoff says, "In the arena of animal emotions and animal sentience, I have argued that we do know enough to make informed decisions about animal emotions and animal sentience and why they matter. And even if we might be 'wrong' some of the time, this does not mean we're wrong all the time. At least we won't be adding more cruelty to an already cruel world by granting that animals are emotional, sentient beings and accordingly treating them with respect."

There was a time just a few decades ago when animal cognition research was considered a career killer. As science writer Virginia Morell states, "Old-school skeptics and naysayers…may dismiss the latest findings on animal intelligence as so much sentimental, romantic, anthropomorphizing. But why is it romantic to acknowledge that animals are thinking and feeling beings? Considering the weight of the recent scientific evidence, I would argue that it's actually realistic to do so."

"How Do I Know I Am Not Making It Up?"

When people first begin to study the art of animal communication, one of the first hurdles is recognizing the difference between their own thoughts or opinions versus a communication that is coming from the animal. Self-doubt is the biggest obstacle to learning animal communication. Carol, one HAC student, said when she was first learning animal communication, "I look at my dog, and I think he is feeling sad. How do I know that is what he is feeling, or is it something I am projecting because I feel guilty for going to the shelter to work with other dogs?" It is honest to struggle with this question because it is very easy to assume we *know* what our animals are feeling because this is how *we* feel. Or this is how we feel when we interpret a certain look on their face. It is easy to imagine we know what they are feeling as we naturally filter our interpretations through our own emotions.

To communicate with animals, you need to be both peaceful and neutral. This means you learn how not to impose your own ideas but instead to listen to what they have to say. The more you cultivate a state of being in witness, meaning not attached to a specific outcome, you will strengthen your ability to hear what animals are saying. In time, and with the practice of your animal communication skills, you will begin to feel the difference between a thought or a feeling that is *generated from within* and a thought, feeling, impression, or information that *comes from without*. With observation and patience, you will feel the difference, just as we know the difference between initiating communication by starting a call and answering a ringing phone. Both can result in talking to another person, but there was a different step that got us into the conversation.

I know what my thoughts and feelings *feel like*. I know the sound or emotional quality of the thoughts I generate with my mind chatter. Listening to your animal is like tuning to a specific frequency on a radio. Further, with practice, I have learned that *receiving information feels different.* When you hear someone you know say "hello" on the phone, it feels like them, their voice, not yours.

Everyone hears, feels, and sees differently when animals communicate with them. For me, I often get the feeling of what I call a *data download.* In one flash, I receive a huge ton of information. It is not like English syntax, one word following another. It is as if I understand the totality of the communication in an instant. From there, I can ask questions, listen to answers, and it can become more of a dialogue, but it still feels like I get the whole answer in complete, instantaneous knowing. Sometimes this information is so unexpected and provides new details I couldn't know. It has a clear sense of coming from a specific *personality* or point of view that I know it couldn't have come from inside me.

If animal communication is new to you, this may sound wild. But if you are patient and dedicated, it will become second nature to *hear/perceive* what animals have to say. It all starts with a willingness to accept that animal communication is possible. From there, add a few principles and techniques for how to communicate, and then make sure to keep it light and fun (if it isn't easy and fun, you are working too hard).

Continue to keep an open mind. Just because it isn't easy today doesn't mean you won't develop confidence in time when you have proven it to yourself. Just like learning a new language, it takes patience, persistence, and practice.

Four Steps to Beginning Animal Communication

For those who are interested in exploring this domain of animal communication, you want to cultivate an *open channel* with your intuition and practice, practice, practice. Of course, you must be in a relaxed state. Stress sends and receives mixed messages, and too much effort will usually end the communication cycle, like a dropped call.

Here are four steps to get you started.

Step One:

Acknowledge that you are an intuitive person. It starts with accepting that you can "know" things you didn't consciously know. You can "know" across space and time, across the boundary between life and death, and across species. Remember, this was the Native Wisdom for thousands of years before we forgot it. It is never too late to remember.

Step Two:

Accept that your way is right for you. Don't waste time comparing yourself to others. Everyone's intuition works differently. Some people hear words. Some people see pictures. Some people feel body sensations. Some get full perceptions. Some people get all the above. In training, you will discover what is your natural intuitive style so that when you get messages from the animal, it will have a very specific feeling or what I call an "energetic signature."

Step Three:

Focus on the difference in sensation between sending and receiving. This helps you recognize the difference between intuitive communication and your own internal thought process. As I mentioned, my intuitive messages often come in what I call *instant downloads,* meaning I get an entire story dropped into my awareness in an instant. This is very different from my mental thinking or conventional grammatical syntax, where one word follows another. This is all-knowing in a flash. This helps me to distinguish between a message that is coming from an animal versus my own subjective thinking process.

Step Four:

Listen with your whole body, not just your physical ears. It is like listening from a place deeper inside than we usually use to hear words. For this to happen, your thoughts must be quiet so that you can hear ideas that are deeper than and quieter than a whisper. More about entering the language of silence in the next chapter.

Listen Deeper

There is an art to listening at a deeper level. But the more you practice, the stronger it gets and the more accurate. James French, creator of the Trust Technique, teaches Animal Communication Technique, a beautiful class that is available online. I highly recommend it. For our students who are practicing with us in the animal shelter and with their own animals, the idea of being able to listen to animals can feel like a mysterious process at first. I remind them that we are listening, but not just with our ears. Some call it *listening with the heart* or listening from a deeper place, a place beyond words. When I say *deeper,* some people get this look on their face, like they should put in more effort—as if *trying harder* will help them hear. I remind them, "Instead of trying harder, try softer." Listening deeper is a different channel; it is softer. You will just get static if you try too hard.

Sometimes animal communication is just for fun, but other times it is critical to get it right. When my beloved therapy cat, Wolfie, was in the process of leaving this world and was no longer eating or drinking, the veterinarian suggested it was time to euthanize. But I wasn't sure. Of course, it is so hard to make this decision. Why make it alone?

I asked Wolfie what I should do, what he would like. He told me that he would prefer to go on his own. He told me the day he was going to pass and that he would pass between three and five a.m. He passed that exact night at 3:30 a.m. I was prepared because I knew he was prepared. It was still very sad to lose him after seventeen years, but at least I knew he had told me what he wished, and I was able to honor that.

The Leopard Alert Call

Animals communicate with each other, of course. And just like with other species, sometimes communication is misunderstood. But usually, it is loud and clear. Klaus Zuberbuhler and his team were studying the warning calls of Diana monkeys in the Tai Forest in Cote d'Ivoire. He found they had one warning call that meant an eagle was nearby. This distress call was immediately understood by the entire pack. When one monkey saw an eagle, the call was sent out, and all the monkeys would scamper down from the trees to the ground.

They had a different warning call for a leopard. When this call was issued, they would all run up to the highest tree branches for safety. What was even more intriguing was *that other species understood* these Diana-language distress calls. Birds and several other species in the vicinity would make the correct interpretation of these sound signals and take the right action.

One night, after Zuberbuhler returned late to his camp, he began to hear the monkeys' calls as they gave the alert for a leopard nearby. At first, he thought this was interesting until his intuition correctly told him that *the leopard was stalking him.* Good thing he listened and lived to tell this tale.

I worked with Sara, an experienced German shepherd dog trainer. Sara had adopted a ten-month-old mistreated German shepherd puppy after her beloved shepherd had passed. She also had two cats that had gotten along very well with her previous dog. But Oso, her new dog, had spent his life chained up in a backyard, was very reactive and high-energy. Oso was completely untrained when she adopted him, and she was concerned about his prey drive. She had tried many methods to slowly introduce Oso to her cats, but she was still nervous, and for good reasons.

We began working with the Trust Technique and made a lot of progress in creating more calmness with Oso overall. But when we experimented with the boundaries of bringing the dog and cats together incrementally, such as having the cats in a protected tent and letting the dog approach, it was still way too intense.

Before we tried anything else, I suggested we talk to Mika, one of her cats. So, we did an animal communication session with Mika and asked her what would make this introduction process more comfortable. She explained that she would like things in the house to be fairer. She requested that instead of always requiring the cats to be contained to appease the dog, it should be balanced. Mika suggested that the dog should be in his kennel and let the cats sniff and explore him while he was inside. This was brilliant. And it worked. It eased the tension among the animals and thus the humans. She sent me a photo of Mika resting on a pillow outside of Oso's crate. It pays to ask a cat—*and to listen!*

Talk to Your Animals!

Talking to animals has many benefits. It strengthens connections and can be reassuring and soothing if you are using a gentle tone of voice. Animals not only recognize the voice of their person but can understand that various tones of voice have different meanings. Additionally, many animals respond to words. Talk to them about what is going to happen next that is relevant to them. I will say to Sophia, "Wanna go for a walkie?" or "Ready for dinner?" or on a therapy visit "Say hi!" and so on. It pays to talk to them, and they begin to recognize that some of your repeated words are meaningful and pay more attention. It strengthens your connection.

Some animals seem to know what we are saying through word recognition, such as the examples mentioned in this book of Chaser, Koko, and Kanzi. Other animals seem to *understand our intention* (what we mean in emotional terms) more than specific word recognition. Science is just beginning to understand the deeper layers of understanding that animals have and their potential for communication which is surely beyond words.

A few times, I had the privilege of walking Annie for an elderly neighbor. This eight-year-old giant schnauzer had no formal training at all, but I had worked with her a few times when I was learning the Trust Technique. I swear she could understand English, even without looking at me. When we would walk together, I could say "This way," and she would turn in the direction I was intending, even though she was walking on a leash ahead of me and couldn't see any body language cues I might have been giving. I could say, "Go in my car," and she would head to *my car*. Or "Let's go visit Doug and Maggie," and she would turn toward their house. I had not trained any of these specific meanings, but she always amazed me with how much she understood. When we talk to animals, they enjoy the sound of our voice and our desire to connect. So, it is worth doing for that reason alone. But you may be surprised. Give animals the benefit of the doubt; they might understand more than you think.

Quiet Communication

Words are just one way to communicate. There is a whole world of quiet or silent communication. Communication is a spectrum; you can have a lot or a little and everything in between. It can be high-quality (meaning the information the communicator sends is accurately received) or very *noisy* (meaning the communication is diluted or unclear by either the sender or the receiver). Learning how to communicate with animals accurately and objectively is a lifelong learning process of refinement, so if you are new to this journey, be prepared to be patient. If you are open and relaxed in your expectations, you may surprise yourself with how easy it can be to "hear" what animals are feeling. It is very important that you be in a quiet and receptive state. If your expectation level is too high, this self-imposed pressure will get in your way.

Always remember that language is just one way to communicate. As Linda Bender, Doctor of Veterinary Medicine (DVM), expressed, "Maybe animals don't use language because they don't need to. They communicate and understand perfectly well without it." They have ways of *knowing* things and communicating what they know that is beyond words.

I was recently asked by a social scientist to give her a demonstration of talking to her rescue cat, Jupiter. I wasn't sure if she would be open to this brave new world, but Jupiter had quite a bit to say and even talked about memories he had of a past life. She was amazed that in one session, she felt the door open, and she began talking to her cat on a regular basis. Soon behaviors of Jupiter's that had been really bothering her diminished. She mentioned her delight to a few friends who knew her well, and they asked, "Are you becoming a woo-woo?" This is a good reminder that while everyone is curious, not all your friends are ready to accept this possibility.

Everyone has their own opinion about the possibility of communication across species. Some people do not think such a thing is possible or that it is just your imagination if you hear the animals *talking*. Even those who believe it is possible to communicate may at first think they are making up the answers they hear to the questions they ask. This is because when you *tune your antenna* to the animal's communication channel, it is incredibly easy and fast. Sometimes the communication floodgates open. For others, the information comes slowly at first. It might take you a long time to get to the point of sufficient relaxation and receptivity. Please be patient with yourself because getting frustrated makes it harder to hear.

Even if you don't believe that animals can sense what we are feeling or can hear our messages, but you enjoy talking to them out loud, and this is enough for you, then that is fine. They do enjoy the sound of your voice and your desire to connect, even if you think the communication is only going in one direction. So, keep talking!

If you would like to explore the possibility that communication could be a two-way experience, I highly recommend J. Allen Boone's book, *Kinship with All Life*, which shows how he crossed the bridge and was able to communicate with all animals. And this book was published in 1954! In The Human-Animal Connection, we teach a basic introduction to developing your accurate intuition. My favorite teacher for Animal Communication Training is James French of the *Trust Technique*. I think his online class in Animal Communication is brilliant in that it reminds us that this is something that anyone with a strong desire can learn to do, and it changes everything between us and the animals who share our lives.

If you choose to take the journey of learning how to communicate with animals, it will open your heart to another world. Life is so much richer when we appreciate animal intelligence and are willing to understand them at a deeper level. I am almost always surprised by what I hear from animals. I often find them to be wiser than I expected, more whimsical, more engaged, and more playful. And they are always insightful about their world.

As Wallace Black Hawk says about the ability of humans and animals to communicate in *The Sacred Ways of a Lakota*, "At one time we could all talk to each other. No matter how many countless languages, forms and shapes, and symbols there were, the (elders) say we spoke the same mind.... The trees talk. They have a language all their own…And every creature has a song…. We are losing that silent communication."

I invite you to be brave, to move beyond limiting beliefs about what is possible. Animals are profound communicators and we can strive to rise to their level of authentic communication. We owe it to them to do our best.

If you talk to the animals, they will talk with you
and you will know each other.

Chief Dan George

Journal Reflections on Opening the Door of Animal Communication:

1) What are your beliefs about the possibility of animal communication? Do you believe it is possible to know what an animal is feeling? How do you know?

2) Would you be open to exploring and expanding your ability to communicate with animals?

3) What would your life be like if this human-animal communication channel opened for you? What would you most like to know?

4) Is there any part of you that is resistant? Afraid? Skeptical about animal communication? Why?

5) What would you most like to know from your animal? What would you say if you knew they could hear you?

Re-Minder: I can communicate with animals.

Bo with Caleb. Even though Bo was too shy to express her needs, his other dogs would use the talk buttons *to communicate Bo's feelings* to Caleb.

Principle #15

ENTERING THE LANGUAGE OF SILENCE

Where All Answers Can Be Heard

Some of my best friends never said a word to me.

Anonymous

Overview

Words are wonderful. Words are sacred. But they can be defiled. We should protect our words from those who seek to dilute their purity by co-opting them with false meanings.

While words are one of the many blessings of the human experience, they are not the *only* way to communicate. In The Human-Animal Connection, we know that many animals do respond to words and the intentions behind them; however, we want to expand our communication possibilities through the many ways that animals communicate.

If we want to enter the animal's world and communicate with them, we need to open the door to the realm of silence. In this realm, animals have much to teach us as they are carriers of vast knowledge. Their silent realm is a glorious adventure and too delicious to ignore. Begin the next step of your journey by entering the sacred Language of Silence.

Patience Opens Communication

I received a call from Ayama, a retired woman who had opened her home to a new dog named Sophy after her previous dog had passed. Sophy was part whippet, with soulful eyes, but it was a challenging adoption because she was so afraid of everything that she couldn't leave the house, even to potty. Consequently, Sophy spent many of her waking hours curled tightly in her bed and soft blanket. Ayama, a very kind and gentle woman, loved Sophy, and they had a tender connection. But she wondered if she could live her life with a dog who was terrified of leaving the house or having anyone enter it. Even a visiting vet couldn't get near her, as Sophy would shut down for days after any stranger attempted contact.

Sophy's behavior and lack of movement didn't appear to stem from a physical injury because when Ayama would go upstairs at night to go to sleep, she would hear Sophy prancing around the living room, jumping on the couch, and playing with her toys. This was greatly relieving to discover, as it meant that Sophy's lack of mobility issues did not stem from medical issues.

Since Ayama and Sophy lived out of state, we began working over video conferencing with the Trust Technique to lower Sophy's fear level. Before our first session, Sophy would only eat when she was alone in the kitchen. But after a couple of sessions, she became willing to accept treats from Ayama's hands. We had made significant progress, but we still had so much further to go that we didn't know if Sophy would ever get there. Frankly, I was wondering, along with Ayama, if they would ever have a normal life together.

We discovered that Sophy was so sensitive to Ayama's thoughts that when she had a passing thought about giving Sophy back to the shelter, Sophy's body would shake. Sophy was Ayama's mind reader! Ayama learned she had to be much more deliberate about her thought process in the presence of such a prescient being.

At this point, I had a chat with Sophy to get some insights. One of the first things she told me was, "I am not broken. I am not unhappy." She didn't want us to view her as a "problem dog." She was deeply content with her life with Ayama, no matter how it looked to others. This was so important for Ayama to hear, as she wondered if Sophy was having any quality of life.

After many sessions, Sophy took her first tentative steps out into the yard to potty! With new hope, I began teaching Ayama how to silently communicate with Sophy. One day, while Ayama was doing some cleaning, she heard Sophy's words burst into her mind, loud and clear, *Don't give up on me!* That was the moment Ayama understood that her dog had been reflecting some of her own life issues and recognized her need for patience and self-acceptance. And this was the moment she came to see Sophy as her teacher.

In Silence, All Answers Can Be Heard

Cultivating a love of silence is fertile ground for developing animal communication as they communicate in many ways besides words we can hear. As you strengthen your *silence muscle,* you are more likely to receive other channels of information. Blue, a forty-year-old horse I worked with at Equinimity Ranch Tucson, would only "speak" to me if I was supremely silent – meaning the temporary absence of thoughts. Naturally, this was not a state I could achieve all the time, or for very long, but I began to notice that he was *training me* by only rewarding me with learning from him when I was perfectly peaceful and energetically fully silent. Only then would he share something. And it was almost always truly profound.

Silence is not just the absence of noise. Silence is a receptive state of mind. It is the presence of the "hum" of the universe. When you tap into this neutral state where you are not indulging mind chatter, you become aware of the *all that is.* You will come to see, hear, and know beyond the human thinking mind. This is how and where we can connect with animal minds. It is as if they are inviting us to meet them beyond words.

In his books, J. Allen Boone recounts how he learned to communicate with animals by putting himself in the role of student in their presence. This attitude gave him access to a profound level of intelligence and wisdom with which he conducted his life.

In the forward to *Kinship with All Life,* he writes, "As you read these stories, you will see that whenever I was properly humble and willing to let something besides a human be my instructor, these various four-legged, six-legged, and no-legged fellows shared priceless wisdom with me. They taught me that perfect understanding and perfect cooperation between the human and all other forms of life is unfailing whenever the human really does his required part."

While Boone (who was born in 1882) used words—and heard words in return—it was his commitment to tuning into the *frequency* of animal communication and his willingness to go beyond human language that allowed him to experience a deep connection. He also learned a great deal from Native Americans and wise men across the globe. But his most rewarding and life-changing experiences came from his direct experience of silent communication. This domain allowed him to enter the world of animals and see things as they saw them.

Boone believed that anyone could learn this type of silent communication. He didn't waste even one moment thinking he was special or that he was doing something that couldn't be replicated. His message was never about tooting his own horn, but rather, it was always about inspiring others to follow in his quiet footsteps.

The Knowingness of Silence

In the domain of silence, you can hear more deeply and communicate beyond words. It takes a clear intention, dedication, and practice—especially if listening to the Knowingness of Silence is new to you.

Our species has a habit of mental chatter; that is part of the human experience. We are overthinking creatures. But for those interested in the path of animal communication, you want to find a balance between relentless thought generation and cultivating the peace and silence that is necessary to hear clearly.

Boone was able to have clear communication encounters with a fly he named Freddie. One thing he requested of Freddie, who spent time in close contact with him in his house, was not to land on his face or his skin. He could land on his shirt or clothes, but Boone asked for this one courtesy. Freddie never violated this request, even though the fly would perform great acrobatic displays nearby. And amazingly, every fly Boone met for the rest of his life, even in foreign jungles, understood this same rule. Boone could walk in any area of the world, and while all the flies would gather around others, they kept a respectful distance from him.

You may be wondering how a fly could understand human instructions and respond with specific behavior as requested. Boone recounts this story in great detail in his book. He explains how he believed there is a level of harmony and cooperation when two beings choose to meet each other with mutual respect and a desire to connect. These experiences and many others shaped the rest of Boone's life.

In the words of Frances Hodgson Burnett, "How it is that animals understand things I do not know, but it is certain that they do understand. Perhaps there is a language that is not made of words, and everything in the world understands it. Perhaps there is a soul hidden in everything, and it can always speak, without even making a sound, to another soul."

Can you imagine how lovely it would feel to be understood by an animal? Beyond observing and interpreting, would you like to understand behaviors and the emotions that an animal is experiencing? This is the adventure of animal communication and the deeply peaceful language of silence. It is a glorious vacation from daily life. It is like a rejuvenating shower of the mind. I invite you to enter this wonderful world of silence!

There is a huge silence inside each of us
that beckons us into itself.
And the recovery of our own silence
can begin to teach us the language of heaven.

Meister Eckhart

Journal Reflections on Entering the Language of Silence:

1) Imagine you could communicate with animals—without words. Are you ready to enter the rich world of wordless silence? How would that change your world? And theirs?

2) Do you believe it is possible to communicate in a realm beyond words?

3) Would you like to expand your "hearing" beyond words?

4) Can you imagine opening yourself to silent communication? What would it inspire?

5) Are you ready to become a student of deep silence in the presence of an animal?

Re-Minder: In silence, all answers can be heard.

Miss Betsy, the horse, used to be terrified of dogs. But here she is with my dog Sophia. We learned to peacefully connect through the language of silence.

Principle #16

ANIMALS: OUR PARTNERS IN HEALING
Therapy, Companion, and Service Animals

There are two types of guide dog:
one that helps us see when we can't, and another
that helps us see ourselves when we lose our way.

Sanjay Gupta

Overview

There are so many ways animals can be our partners in healing—from service dogs, companion, and emotional support dogs to therapy animals. Pet therapy teams, which consist of a human handler and a trained animal, can have a significant, positive impact in a variety of contexts. They can open hearts and minds, lower stress, ease anxiety, help people cope with trauma, injury, and illness, and help people find a reason to smile. Pet therapy teams visit children and adults in schools, hospitals, jails, hospices, courtrooms, libraries, and many therapeutic environments.

An Elephant Removes Pain

A friend of mine was recovering from breast cancer surgery and still was experiencing pain in her left breast. At the time, the Honolulu Zoo allowed elephant encounters where the person could stand behind a low fence and offer carrots and treats to the elephants. To keep her spirits up, she had made it a habit of going to see the elephants. One day, she went to see her favorite elephant, who ignored her treat but *nosed* her left breast with such thoroughness that the zookeeper was concerned. But she sensed that this was important, and waved away the man's help. The elephant was deliberate and gentle, even though that wasn't how the massage appeared to others. Later my friend told me, "After that elephant treatment, I never had any pain there ever again."

How a Service Animal is Defined

Service animals are trained to help an individual with a specific issue, like seeing eye guide dogs for the visually impaired or hearing dogs for hearing-impaired people. Brace and mobility support dogs help people regain their footing after a fall or loss of balance. Service animals can help with many tasks that their person can't manage. They can be taught to turn lights on and off, to open and close doors and cabinets, and retrieve dropped items. Some are trained to get help by alerting a human who lives with their person and even pressing a button to call 911.

Service dogs can also help people with anxiety and symptoms of PTSD. They can anticipate high anxiety and can help the person calm down with a lick and a nuzzle and a furry reminder to come back to the present moment. Diabetic and Seizure Alert dogs can anticipate medical events and warn their person or caretakers. Autism support dogs can help reduce arousal in children. These companion animals and service dogs make the difference between a life in retreat or nearly full participation in life.

(Note about public access for service dogs: It is important to understand the difference in access privileges. Service dogs have access to any public place and cannot be refused entrance; therapy and companion animals do not have the same legal privileges.)

Medical detection dogs are trained to detect the presence of various types of cancer from saliva or breath samples. Trained medical detection dogs can detect Covid-19, malaria, tuberculosis, and Parkinson's disease (although there is no definitive medical test for Parkinson's disease).

Some pets will alert their owners to illness, even though they haven't had any specific training. The challenge is whether the owner recognizes the animal's "alert signal." One woman in England had had several mammograms, which all came back negative. However, her dog kept nosing one breast and seemed insistent that something was wrong. At first, she didn't understand, and the dog became so lethargic and depressed that she thought he was ill. Finally, the owner got the message and had a biopsy. The dog was right. She had a cancerous breast tumor. Once she got treatment, the dog recovered completely.

Canine Covid Detection Dogs

Canine Covid Detection Dogs can be trained to detect the presence of Covid with an accuracy equal to the current medical tests. They can detect the virus through their excellent sense of smell by sniffing articles of clothing or a face mask, sweat, or breath samples or by sniffing a person directly. In addition to their high levels of accuracy, they can detect the presence of Covid five days before a person would even be experiencing symptoms. This is significant since 40 percent of infected people have no symptoms. While no one is suggesting dogs should replace medical tests, they could work as an early warning system because they give results within two seconds. They can be trained in a month or two and can work in large, heavily trafficked areas like airports, train stations, schools, prisons, and sporting events. (Honeybees have also been trained to detect the presence of this virus.)

Dogs, of course, have been sniffing to save lives for some time. They are very effective at IED bomb detection. They can find corpses and people still alive under rubble. They can even detect the scent of cash, arson substances, and many chemicals. Of course, they are of great assistance to law enforcement for drug detection, search and rescue, and many other tasks.

Dogs are not the only animals trained to be our partners in healing. Pigeons have also been trained to detect hairline fractures on x-rays and are said to be at least as accurate as trained medical professionals. Pigeons can also detect metastasized cancer cells on slides with a high degree of accuracy. The African pouch rat can detect tuberculosis with greater accuracy than current medical tests. They can also be trained to detect the presence of minefields and can clear an area the size of a tennis court in twenty minutes. Fortunately, they are light enough not to trip the explosions. (See our HAC blog "Hero Rat Saves Lives").

According to APOPO, the landmine-clearing NGO that trained him, Magawa, the "hero mine-sniffing rat," was awarded a medal for bravery and lifesaving work in detecting landmines in Cambodia. He was retired after a distinguished five-year career in which he "found 71 landmines and 38 items of unexploded ordnance during his service."

Therapy Animal Teams

Another way pet animals can help people is by becoming therapy animals. These animals, who live with a specific person, work as a team with their person and visit those who could benefit from their love, their joy, and willingness to cuddle and connect. The duo of person and animal is called an animal therapy team.

There are several national organizations that certify handler teams, such as the Alliance of Therapy Dogs, Therapy Dogs International, and Pet Partners, just to name a few. The AKC website has listed over 200 local organizations also doing this wonderful work.

The qualifying tests vary by organization, but they are rigorous and require specific obedience and social skills from both the human and the animal. While dogs are the most common animal to be certified as a visiting therapy team, horses, miniature horses, cats, rabbits, llamas, dolphins, pigs, goats, birds, monkeys, and "pocket animals" are also certified by some organizations.

I had a rescue cat, Wolfie, who became a perfect therapy cat. Without any training, he knew exactly how to help the clients I saw in my home office. His timing was impeccable. During an emotional point in the session, he knew exactly when to enter the room and cuddle with the client. Then, when the emotional cycle was complete, he would jump off their lap and walk away. Wolfie always anticipated breakthroughs before people did.

Reading Dog programs where therapy dogs help reluctant young readers develop confidence and improve their reading skills by reading to a trained dog are very effective. A trained reading dog will look at the book and then look at the child when the child looks at the dog. This increases engagement because the children are convinced the dog understands the story. Since dogs don't correct pronunciation or care about stumbles, children feel less stress and gain more confidence in reading aloud. The supportive connection between the child and the dog is palpable. ABC News reported one study that showed reading skills improved over 12 percent in a ten-week program. Other animals can become great learning assistants too. As mentioned earlier in the book, Charlotte is an excellent reading donkey!

Recent studies show how a specific social curriculum that includes working with therapy dogs can also help children improve their social and emotional skills. Our HAC program, Canines Teach Compassion (discussed in Principle #11), utilizes therapy dogs to teach high school students greater self-compassion, resilience, and social skills through structured interaction with dogs.

In other programs working with a mentor and a therapy dog, children who need to learn social skills politely introduce themselves and shake hands with the dog. Then they introduce themselves and the dog to strangers. This exercise builds confidence and teaches them how to accurately read other people's reactions. Therapy dogs help create low-stress and nonthreatening learning environments for children and, in addition to helping with social skills, by lowering stress levels and raising confidence, can help the children have more positive academic outcomes.

Animal Assisted Therapy and Activity

Therapy animals provide interaction and companionship and may assist in emotional, psychological, and physical interventions in a variety of therapeutic contexts. There are two main categories of Pet Therapy in which certified and registered handlers/owners might participate:

1) Animal-Assisted Therapy (AAT)
2) Animal-Assisted Activity (AAA)

Animal-Assisted Therapy involves the owner and animal working in tandem with a health professional. The Pet Partners Standards of Practice for Animal-Assisted Therapy defines AAT as follows:

"AAT is a goal-directed intervention in which an animal that meets specific criteria is an integral part of the treatment process. AAT is directed and/or delivered by a health/human service professional with specialized expertise and within the scope of practice of his/her profession. AAT is designed to promote improvement in human physical, social, emotional, and/or cognitive functioning. AAT is provided in a variety of settings and may be group or individual in nature. This process is documented and evaluated."

AAT has been shown to have multiple benefits for a variety of patients. One randomized control study with patients hospitalized with heart failure was investigated by US Army researchers and reported in the US Army Medical Department Journal. They discovered that those who had just eight minutes of AAT reported less anxiety but also had a "change from baseline that indicated a significant decrease in systolic pulmonary artery pressure and pulmonary capillary wedge pressure" (US Army Medical Department Journal, Canine Edition - USAMDJ).

Another benefit of AAT is that patients who are less willing to comply with treatment or hospital procedures due to pain, depression, fatigue, or other reasons, are more likely to be motivated to participate in their treatment if a trained dog is present and involved in their procedures. This increase in compliance has been seen across numerous areas. One notable example is Canine-Assisted Ambulation (CAA), in which dogs help motivate patients to move more.

Researchers Knisely and Barker report that cardiac patients who initially refused ambulation with human assistance were then presented with CAA. They state that with canine assistance, 18.9 percent of cardiac patients reversed their attitude of not wanting to move and voluntarily ambulated with the dog.

"Patients who engaged in the CAA walked 96% more. This study suggests that CAA may be motivational and an effective adjunct to existing ambulation and patient care routines. Furthermore, as early ambulation has been associated with decreased length of stay and thus reduced patient care costs among cardiac patients, the use of CAA may additionally improve [patient] outcomes" (USAMDJ).

Even Short Contact Is Beneficial

In a Japanese study on AAT and the effects on the prefrontal cortex, published in *The International Journal of Psychiatry and Clinical Practice* by Aoki et al., it is suggested that

"AAT possibly causes biological and physiological changes in the prefrontal cortex (PFC), and that AAT is useful for inducing the activity in the PFC. Using NIRS (near-infrared-spectroscopy), the measurement of cranial nerve activity was measured in real-time, showing numerous positive benefits on the brain from as little as 20 minutes of contact, including holding or petting a therapy dog. Many patients look forward to these interactions above all other therapeutic interventions. This increased PFC activity had a positive impact on depression, and other studies have shown positive impacts on issues such as anxiety, fear, blood pressure, heart rate, salivary cortisol, and salivary alpha-amylase."

Aoki's study further suggests that AAT allowed a large region of the prefrontal cortex to be strongly activated, perhaps due to the combination of the stimulation of the senses of touch, sight, hearing, and even smell through the interactions with animals. This is very important because many patients with depression will exhibit a low level of cerebral activity in the PFC. Aoki's study, showing the biological and physiological changes induced in the activity of the PFC, gives evidence that AAT can be a useful tool in treating depression.

Animal-Assisted Activity

The other main category, the therapeutic use of Animal-Assisted Activity (AAA), is less formal. There are no treatment plans or notes; there is no specific agenda. Interactions are spontaneous, often joyful, and can be as short as two minutes or last for an hour. In many cases, the pet therapy team consists of a human volunteer and their specially trained, certified animal. The focus is on the human-animal bond, uplifting connection, engagement, social interaction, healing the spirits, and even entertainment. Miniature horses are often used in AAA.

As Pet Partners states, "AAA provides opportunities for motivational, educational, recreational, and/or therapeutic benefits to enhance the quality of life." These visits are not just for patients! Therapy visits can help providers and staff reduce their stress levels and lift their spirits. Sweet dogs make almost everyone smile, and this can help reduce the effects of compassion fatigue in staff.

Obviously, not all dogs are suitable to become part of a healing team, just as not all humans are adept at such tasks. Each pet therapy organization has slightly different criteria for testing. But they all involve a specific set of skills for the dog and their human. Animal handler teams must pass a rigorous evaluation and testing process.

Many organizations require a candidate to be able to pass the CGC (Canine Good Citizenship) test, which evaluates about twelve basic obedience skills or an equivalent set of standards. Some organizations consider passing the CGC test a prerequisite for certification; others do not and have their own testing criteria. In addition, a therapy dog must be able to handle the specific stressors that will present themselves on therapy visits.

Therapy animal teams visit patients in a variety of settings. Although dog and human handler teams are the most common, a few very special horses, llamas, cats, pigs, and other animals have been certified by some organizations. On social media, you can find lovely videos of a horse named Peyo as he walks through the hospital with his handler. Peyo chooses who he wants to visit and also has the ability to detect cancer and tumors.

My dog Sophia is a therapy dog with the Alliance of Therapy Dogs and has served with hundreds of hours of visits. It is incredibly rewarding for me, and she loves it too! One nurse who had just lost a patient said, "You don't know how important to me seeing Sophia was today. She cuddled me back to safe ground."

Animals Help Patients Heal Faster

Orlandi et al. conducted a study and evaluated a one-hour AAA session with oncology patients while they were receiving chemotherapy in a day hospital. Various markers of stress were noticeably reduced in this often-quoted study published in the *Army Journal of Medicine.* "Self-report measures of anxiety, depression, somatic symptoms, were collected as well as heart rate, arterial oxygen saturation, and blood pressure...Unlike the controls, patients in the AAA group demonstrated a decrease in depression and an increase in arterial oxygen saturation. Significant reductions in anxiety, aggression and blood pressure were also reported..."

Beneficial results for heart patients interacting with animals for as little as twelve minutes have been reported by the American Heart Association. This study (November 2005) reported that "twelve-minute visits with therapy dogs improved heart and lung function, reduced blood pressure, diminished harmful hormones, and decreased anxiety in heart patients" (USAMDJ).

Skills a Therapy Animal Must Possess

Just a few of the skills a dog must exhibit in the therapy animal testing and evaluation are as follows: Positive interest in strangers and their attention, being able to recover quickly from sudden or loud noises, ability to pass other dogs without distraction, ability to ignore food or toys on the floor when given the "leave it" command, ability to stay still for children who may not know how to appropriately pet a dog, tolerate hugging and clumsy petting, be undisturbed by rolling medical equipment, and genuinely want to give and receive affection.

In addition to all these basic requirements, when I was a tester/observer for potential therapy teams for the Army's Human-Animal Bond Program, I was always looking to see an excellent bond between the person and the animal. It is very important that the animal enjoys this activity!

Any breed of dog can become a therapy dog if he or she has the right temperament and has an excellent response to their handler's commands. I have worked with excellent therapy dogs that were German shepherds, pit bulls, boxers, Chihuahuas, and Shih Tzus—in addition to the more common golden retrievers and Labrador mixes. Shelter and rescue dogs, even those that have survived difficult circumstances, like my Oscar, can become excellent therapy dogs if they have the right temperament.

One of the essential qualities in a great dog/handler team is excellent communication between dog and human, a desire to please, and a very calm nature. The human-animal bond must be strong so they can read each other's nonverbal cues instantly. Since dogs can pick up and take on human pain, it is extremely important that a handler be attentive to when the dog has had enough. This is especially critical for dogs working in disaster response. After the visit, it is important to make sure the dog has a way to release any unwanted energy he or she may have absorbed through interacting with people in physical and emotional pain.

If you have an interest in doing therapy animal work and have a great companion animal, I highly recommend this meaningful work which generates smiles and so much comfort.

(Please view our online class to help you evaluate whether this work is right for you—*Could My Dog Be a Therapy Dog?* at TheHumanAnimalConnection.org)

Note: On our website, TheHumanAnimalConnection.org, you can see a short film I made when I was in the Human-Animal Bond Program at Tripler Army Medical Center in Honolulu, Hawaii, called *Dogs Are Healers*.

Journal Reflections on Animals as Partners in Healing:

1) Do you have an interest in becoming a therapy animal team? Who would you like to work with? Children? Adults? People with specific needs? In what environments would you like to work?

2) If you are sharing your life with an animal, do you feel he or she would be a good candidate for therapy work? If so, what qualities do you think you see in this animal? What areas would you need to work on more so the animal could pass a certification test?

3) Can you remember a time or a situation when you could have benefited from the presence of a therapy animal? In what situations do you imagine yourself contributing to the well-being of others?

4) Do you have the patience to work with people in need? Do you have an interest in training for therapy animal work? How certain are you that your animal would enjoy interacting with strangers, some of whom may be in distress?

5) Are you ready to take the first steps? If so, research what resources there are in your area and how to get certified by one of the reputable organizations that do this work.

Re-Minder: Loving an animal heals us both.

Oscar - My First Therapy Dog. At Tripler Army Medical Center, he brought so much peace, love, and joy to doctors, nurses, patients, and soldiers. Thank you, my sweet Oscar, for starting me on this journey.

HEALING FROM TRAUMA

For People and Animals

For the person who has learned to let go and let be,
nothing can ever get in your way again.

Meister Eckhart

Overview

Animals experience trauma and suffer its physical, emotional, and mental effects just like people. Animals, especially in the wild, have many strategies for remaining resilient, including the support of their herd, access to the healing resources of nature, and the freedom to pursue natural healing movement. On the other hand, trauma in domesticated animals is exacerbated because they don't have access to the same natural healing resources. The good news is that trauma is reversible. Both people and animals can unwind the past and heal with the right methods. Animals can teach people a lot about healing, particularly the way animals naturally release the past and welcome a new future.

Cherry – A Pit Bull Ambassador

In New York City, I attended a screening of Darcy Dennett's documentary film *The Champions – More Forgiving of Our Species Than We Could Ever Be of Theirs*. It is an amazing film for anyone interested in resilience and emotional healing in animals.

At the screening, I had a chance to meet Cherry, one of the pit bulls rescued from Michael Vicks's dogfighting compound. Best Friends Sanctuary had welcomed Cherry into their wonderful rescue facility. At first, Cherry was terrified of everything and everybody and would only do the pancake walk (belly to the ground). Eventually, he was adopted by a loving family and revealed what a wonderful dog he was and became a true ambassador for healing.

When I met him at the screening, I was so moved by how calm, loving, and engaged Cherry was with the large group of fans that huddled over him and showered him with adoring attention. I said to myself, *Cherry is proof that no matter how horrific the trauma has been, healing is always possible!*

The Act Resilient Method

The Human-Animal Connection began with The Act Resilient Method, a program I created in 2010 to work with active-duty military who were experiencing high levels of stress. Act Resilient uses laughter, improvisational comedy, emotional flexibility skills, and the expressive arts to help people recover from the effects of stress and trauma.

One of the methods I teach in both Act Resilient and in the HAC classes is the deliberate use of the alternation of stimulation and relaxation to restore more fluid brain function. A traumatized brain is stuck in the fight/flight/freeze cycle. A person or animal can get stuck in what I call the Freeze Brain. Anything can trigger this nervous system cycle of freezing, and for healing to occur, you have to release this "stuck in trauma" brain. The good news is that the nervous system can be *thawed* or unfrozen. When it is restored to a more fluid state, learning and new behavioral choices can be made.

I presented Act Resilient workshops to over 4,000 U.S. service members from all branches, veterans, and their families, as well as healthcare providers at Tripler Army Medical Center in Honolulu, Hawaii.

Participants in The Act Resilient Method reported an over 80 percent reduction in their trauma symptoms over a ten-week period of once-a-week classes. But once I started bringing therapy dogs into the classroom, the success was even faster and more dramatic. The impact of The Act Resilient Method was so significant that we were given commendations from generals, and our team won a workplace resilience award from the American Psychological Association. The success of the program led to President Obama giving me the Red Cross Silver Volunteer Service Award.

My perspective on trauma is that it is not just a purely psychological issue. While the mind can certainly harbor the trauma, unless you also deal with the ways the body and nervous system store trauma, it is bound to stay stuck and keep recurring. Further, to see the desired results of freedom from pain, anxiety, anger, and terror, one must also heal the moral or spiritual wounds.

In my book, *The Act Resilient Method*, I explain in detail my unique approach to freeing the mind and the body to release the spirit from the captivity of trauma. This comprehensive approach is what it takes to allow the whole being to heal. My work with humans is what has informed my understanding and approach to animals who have experienced life-threatening and soul-crushing trauma.

Working with Shut-Down Dogs

I have worked with over 1,000 shy and frightened dogs in shelters to help them overcome trauma. But there is a segment of dogs, sometimes referred to as *shut-down dogs,* who are in a class by themselves. In response to trauma, these dogs have collapsed and retreated into their own worlds. They often cower in their kennels and make it clear that all they want is to be left alone. They are often not motivated by treats, touches, kind approaches, or human interaction. Because many shelters do not have the training or resources to respond to such cases, these frightened doggies are often put down.

It's very, very rare, but sometimes an angel in a human body chooses to adopt such a dog knowing this dog will not have a normal life, cannot go on walks, or interact with the public. Sometimes people adopt a shut-down dog like this with sympathy and good intentions because "he was so scared," not realizing the challenging journey ahead. Others give up and return the dog to the shelter when they find they can't handle a dog that is so "damaged." Thankfully, some choose to stick with it and find coping methods as they learn to work with a dog who is very traumatized.

Heroes4Animals – Healing Human PTSD By Helping Traumatized Animals

One very effective way to release the grip of trauma is to help another being heal. By combining The Act Resilient Method with the HAC dog training, The Human-Animal Connection has developed a program for active-duty military and veterans called Heroes4Animals.

In this program we bring a veteran to the shelter and train them how to work with shut-down dogs. These shy and traumatized dogs are often not able to make eye contact. Some people call the shut-down ones "pancake dogs" because they lie flat to the ground and cower in their kennels when potential adopters approach. Most potential adopters walk away because they can see the dog is frightened, and they don't want to make it worse. Thus, it becomes a sad cycle with frightened and emotionally hurting dogs. These are the dogs who most need our help.

Rosa, a cattle dog, had been in the shelter system and transferred from one to another for over two years. Her adoption profile said she was dog reactive and thus, had to be the only dog in a home. Dogs in kennels will often develop dog reactivity even if they didn't have it when they first came to the shelter because this environment is so unnatural and stressful. Soon barking, lunging, and intense reactivity to other dogs frequently occur in the shelter. And once they get this label of *dog reactive,* it significantly limits their potential adoption options. In the case of Rosa, she was so shy at the shelter that no one gave her more than a glance. But after we worked with her using our HAC methods and patiently and slowly walked through the dog introduction process, first in a foster home and then with her adopter, Rosa was able to share a home with another dog, and both dogs are doing beautifully.

We train our HAC volunteers to use our gentle methods of rebuilding trust to slowly bring these pancake dogs out of their shells. This takes a great deal of love and patience, as the dogs will often avoid contact by every means possible. Ultimately, our goal is to teach these dogs that humans can be a source of safety.

Resilient Pitties

Tia Torres had a show I loved titled *Pit Bulls and Parolees.* One thing Tia and her daughters used to say to shy and frightened dogs was, "*You're okay!*" They sang these words in a friendly, confident, musical tone of voice. *You're okay!* is a really important message for dogs who have to "un-learn" some of the lessons from their past and learn to trust again.

I love how this television show helped educate the public that pit bulls are wonderful dogs. They have been given a bad rap by misinformed people, but they are only dangerous when they are trained to be so by violent humans.

Saying *"You're okay"* in a loving tone of voice (say it the exact same way each time) becomes powerful medicine for your dog—*and for you.* Imagine saying this to yourself the next time you get startled or feel you are inadequate. Or you get hit with a wave of feeling that you don't belong in a social situation. When you become your own silent cheerleader, a new boldness finds you. It is not easy being human, and this little dose of self-acceptance will go a long way to support your well-being.

Generally, dogs are very resilient creatures. After all, they must be in order to coexist in the human world! Pit bulls used to be called nanny dogs because parents could leave them alone to protect young children because they were so gentle and reliable. In my personal experience, I have found pit bulls to be role models of resilience. They constantly impress me with their ability to forgive. Metaphorically speaking, it's as if they have an extra *"R" chromosome* for resilience.

Helping Shy Dogs Heal

When I volunteer in shelters, I see many dogs who have been surrendered by their owners. There are so many reasons: sometimes the owner is just unable to care for their dogs, or can't afford to, or doesn't know how to handle behavior issues, or they must relocate. The dogs don't know why, but suddenly, they have lost their home and their family and find themselves in a very noisy shelter. Often, their response is to shut down and cower in their kennels, barely moving, and these shut-down dogs will often not even take tempting treats.

For the painfully shut-down dogs, we use my Soul Retrieval process to help traumatized dogs regain trust in people and restore their sense of safety. The purpose of Soul Retrieval is to retrain their nervous system. It is possible to regain a sense of safety once they have lost it. My goal is to help them refill their safety tank, as I call it, so they can then generalize their sense of safety in my presence to other humans, animals, and the larger world.

To help animals restore their safety tank reserves, I begin by gently introducing them to my presence, going very slowly. I wait until they are feeling increasingly comfortable and safe and give me a signal that they are ready for more connection. I start this process by getting peaceful myself, being very still, and letting them sniff me. Unless I am invited to do so, I do not move close to them; I let them approach me. At each step, I wait for a cue from them indicating that I can go to the next step of contact. Then I might toss a treat close to their feet. If they accept that treat, I know we have opened the door of possibility. I toss another treat a little closer to me. This goes on for as many times as it takes for the animal to associate my presence with safety and with treats. After multiple high-value treats (stinky morsels), the dog will often slowly choose to approach and take a treat from my hand. Sometimes it takes several visits to begin to refill their safety tank and to get to this step.

When you're working to gain the trust of a dog who has lost all trust in humans, it is essential not to have an agenda. Even a *good* agenda like "I'm going to get this dog out of the kennel for a walk" can block progress or set up resistance. You can't be attuned to the animal's pace and needs when you are trying to *fix* them. Animals can sense when you have an agenda, and they may resist out of fear.

In the HAC, we use the Trust Technique, where one of the primary principles is to work at the animal's pace, not the human's pace. It is good to have a clear intention, but it needs to be an intention of service. For example, "My intention is to help this animal feel safe," or "My intention is to help this animal trust," or "to be peaceful." Having a clear, service-oriented intention will keep you from inserting your own agenda and timing, which will undoubtedly backfire because that is more about one's own ego than it is about being of service to an emotionally wounded animal.

While we tend to think of dogs as giant fur balls of unlimited love, when a dog has experienced trauma or adversity, they may not desire or be ready for contact. In the HAC, our job is to be able to accurately assess the level of stress an animal is feeling. We use the Trust Technique's evaluation system for doing that. This is to help us be objective and to pay attention to the dog's readiness for our presence, our contact, and our connection. Some dogs will quickly respond to yummy treat offerings, but treats may not be enough to entice shut-down dogs who may not be ready to accept them. These are the situations where patience and persistence are essential.

(You can read my step-by-step process of working with these dogs on the HAC website blogs. In these blogs I show how slowly I work with shut-down dogs like Smitty the Pitty and Bolt. Search: *Smitty the Pitty Emerges From Fear*; *A Bolt of Inspiration*; *A Shelter Dog Was Afraid to Be Touched*; *Bo's Second Chance at Love*, and others.)

Re-Puppying

After many years of working with rescue animals, it has become apparent to me that some dogs did not get everything they needed in terms of nurturing and a sense of safety as puppies. Perhaps they were taken away from their mothers and siblings before they were truly ready (many puppies need more than the eight weeks they usually get from people anxious to sell off their puppies). Sometimes, the puppies faced adversity during the developmental "fear stage" or experienced recurring dangers, not enough food, or a lack of maternal skill. The first developmental fear period tends to happen when a puppy is 8–11 weeks old, and a second one happens around 18–24 months of life. Even simple experiences that are fear-producing during these critical developmental stages can leave lasting emotional wounds. Thus, for a variety of reasons, some dogs did not get the full safety tank needed at this critical developmental stage to help them feel fully confident to move forward in life.

After further research, observation, and practice, I developed a theory that these dogs need some "re-puppying" and that it is possible for a person to compensate for some of the lost sense of security. Re-puppying is my term to say they need to fill in what is missing from their early experiences. While it may not be possible to entirely reverse a lack of maternal nurturing, understanding this need can help you devise a strategy to begin to meet it. It takes time to make up for a lack of positive interactions with other dogs and people at these critical learning stages. Still, we can imitate some of the needed elements as a method to "shore up" the animal's psyche and emotional well-being.

Bolt, the sweet but withdrawn pitty I mentioned earlier, had spent much of his early developmental life in the shelter. His fearful behaviors told me he didn't get enough of the light pressure body contact, such as he would have experienced with his mom and litter-mates as they all slept in a pile. So, I became Bolt's human "thunder shirt" by replicating this type of contact, which helped him feel more settled, safe, and happy. But this level of trust didn't happen overnight. Helping Bolt refill his safety tank and gain his trust took many training sessions.

Remember, the dog determines—and will communicate through his or her body language—how soon they desire physical closeness, how much contact they want, and for how long. Sometimes, they want a few minutes, sometimes much longer. When we are working with a shut-down dog, as soon as he or she gets up and moves towards us and initiates physical contact, we silently celebrate.

And we are also just as happy when the dog moves away and then returns. This is a sign for us that the dog's natural *Towards & Away* impulses are coming back online (see Principle #21 for further explanation).

Stillness and Movement

From the point of view of the HAC, we view the *alternation* of still-ness and movement, connection and separation, and calmness and play as important tools in rewiring the nervous system.

Alternation of brain states, such as stimulation and relaxation, is a key idea for humans and is outlined more thoroughly in *The Act Resilient Method.* The alternation between these states (e.g., calmness and play -- or contact and separation) at the right rate for the person and the animal leads to a more flexible brain. A traumatized brain is very inflexible and habitually revisits the same painful mental path-ways. Any trigger can thus lead to instant overstimulation, and the reaction can lead to the habitual trauma responses of fight, flight, freeze, and fiddle. I add the fourth F-word, fiddle, as some dogs will show this pattern of excess movement. I say habitual because the repetition of this cycle leads to neural pathways in the brain that perpetuate themselves. Working with traumatized dogs, you want to interrupt this cycle to support long-term healing and for new neuronal circuits to fire correctly, which allows for new behaviors.

Nurturing and contact, play and freedom, and choosing instead of being forced are some of the pathways to freedom from the tyr-anny of the past.

Has a bee ever landed on you and instead of getting scared, you appreciated the possibility that you got confused for a flower?

Raman Khosla

Journal Reflections on Healing from Trauma:

1) Do you believe that we can heal from trauma? Do you believe you can help an animal heal from trauma?

2) How has reading this chapter made you think about (or think differently about) your own life experiences?

3) What are your perceptions and opinions about pit bulls? Are these opinions based on your own experience or other people's opinions?

4) Do you have a desire to help shy or traumatized dogs? Why or why not?

5) Do you believe dogs can be "re-puppied" or can learn to trust even if they have lost trust for good reasons? What about yourself? In what ways do you need to be "re-nurtured?"

Re-Minder: My past does not dictate my future.

Bolt, a shut-down dog, had bitten three people in the shelter.
He had spent most of his young life in the shelter, but once he
learned to trust again, his sweet, joyous nature emerged, and
he was adopted.

Principle #18

REBUILDING A SENSE OF SAFETY
All Beings Deserve to Feel Safe

*Until he extends the circle of compassion to
all living things, man will not himself find peace.*

Albert Schweitzer

Overview

All animals deserve to live their lives with a reliable sense of peace that comes from a visceral experience of safety. Unfortunately, some animals have had experiences that cause them not to feel safe, which persists even in situations where there is no external danger. This lack of a foundational sense of safety makes it hard to trust people, places, things, and other animals. It leaves them with an empty or nearly empty *Safety Tank* which compromises the animal's ability to properly recognize and experience a sustainable sense of safety. The good news is an empty safety tank can be refilled.

Seraphina

When I lived in Hawaii, before I understood what I now do about animals and fear, I adopted a cat from the shelter. I didn't realize how scared she was when I met her at the shelter, but when I got her home, she was terrified. Nothing I tried to do helped her to feel safe, so she spent the first six weeks under the bed. It took six months before she would let me touch her. I wondered how I could have made such a *mistake* in choosing a cat who was so frightened and withdrawn.

She did not respond to her shelter name, *Fluffy,* so there was no way I could use her name as a point of connection. I knew we needed to establish a new relationship, starting with finding her true name. I hoped that finding her right name could begin to give her a sense of safety, starting with a new identity. I listened closely to my intuition to find her new name and heard *Seraphina.* The name Seraphina had no previous history attached, and I hoped this new start would help create a sense of our belonging together. (Later in the book, I discuss this principle, the importance of finding the right name to help an animal feel more like themself.) As my cat learned that this name meant her, it began our journey together of creating a sense of safety. Over time, Seraphina became a wonderful, peaceful therapy cat and brought so much joy to everyone who met her.

But had you asked me in the fifth month, I would have told you I had made a mistake bringing her home! Of course, I knew I wouldn't give up on her, but I had my moments of doubt. As she began to feel safe, she blossomed. The sense of safety had been the one thing she was missing. As soon as she began to feel it, she became my snuggly little angel. She really helped me understand how crucial the feeling of safety is. It is the foundation upon which healing can progress.

Trust and Safety

Trust and a Sense of Safety are like two sides of the same coin. They are connected and work well together in a healthy individual. The more you trust, the safer you feel. The safer you feel, the more you trust. Lucy was a shelter dog that appeared to some to be "out of control." She would leap and bark insanely whenever a person or dog passed by her kennel. As soon as I met her, I realized this was not an aggressive dog. In fact, Lucy loved to cuddle. Lucy was a dog with an empty safety tank, so everything triggered her. It took about six HAC sessions to get her to begin to feel safe. When she felt safe, she was a completely different dog and ready to go to a home.

When an animal has a strong sense of safety, it will be easy for him or her to trust unknown people and places, as well as new experiences and things. Dogs who have a strong sense of safety can evaluate a new person, animal, or place in seconds and decide whether this new experience is safe. But when an animal's core sense of safety is compromised, it will be harder for that animal to make an accurate assessment. Usually, he or she will assume the worst—that something unknown is not safe.

Think of this like the metaphor of wearing rose-colored glasses and how they color your perception. An animal with a strong sense of safety could be said to be wearing *safety glasses.* In contrast, the shy or traumatized animal is wearing glasses that make everything appear unsafe and automatically perceives new things as unsettling, which can trigger the trauma response.

If you are working with an animal who has a low sense of safety, be aware that even something small could trigger the animal's flight-or-fight response, leading to a potentially dangerous situation. His or her fight response could be turned on just because you are standing too close. That animal's triggered brain will not have the presence to think, *Oh, wait, that is my friend*. Rather, their brain will simply react with lightning speed and turn on the nearest living thing.

All Beings Deserve to Feel Safe

Thankfully, shelters provide the basic physiological needs—protection from the elements and predators—as well as the other primary needs in Abraham Maslow's hierarchy model; in this case, water, food, and medical attention. But due to the number of dogs, each of which would love to have their own person, the next level of need in Maslow's model, *Safety*, is not always achieved. That's where a loving home comes in!

When I rescued my dog, Sophia, from the shelter, she had been a stray, a tough street dog. I noticed that small white dogs would cause her to bark intensely. Unfortunately, she had been attacked by a light-colored pug, and she then generalized that fear to every small white dog she saw. I had to be vigilant and anticipate that if there was a small white dog coming her way, it was a trigger for her fear, and it was going to get loud. Fortunately, as her sense of safety level rose, over time, she was able to release that trigger response.

If you are sharing your life with an animal that has a low sense of safety, you want to become very observant to be able to notice what triggers could cause your animal to react. Consider the list below to see if you recognize any of these common triggers in your animal:

- Meeting new people or animals
- Certain categories of people (men/women, children, people in uniforms)
- Other animals (the same or different species, larger or smaller)
- Do new situations or environments raise stress levels? Closed or open spaces? Inside or outside environments? Wind or rain? Thunder or lightning?
- Movement of another animal (towards or away) may trigger the chase or prey drive

- Hands reaching toward them, even if they are about to be petted
- Sudden or loud or intermittent noise

It is important to become an acute observer so you can anticipate and intervene before the animal encounters a triggering situation. If possible, prevent an upset by walking away and removing your animal from the trigger. Prevention is better than trying to deescalate a situation where an animal is triggered beyond his or her ability to feel safe.

The easiest time to intervene and redirect is when the stress response is still low. The best way to intervene is by taking the dog away from what they see that is upsetting them. Once the animal is triggered and the stress level reaches a certain level of intensity, it will be hard for you to have any impact or control because their primal responses are driving their brains.

Filling the Safety Tank

We all need strong reserves of a Sense of Safety to withstand insecurity, uncertainty, the unknown—and even real threats. If our *Safety Tank,* just like a gas tank on a car, is full or reasonably full, we are resilient when life tosses stressors at us, and we can handle these events with greater ease. We are resilient because we have a basic Sense of Safety in the world and know we can handle what comes. When our safety tank is low, even a minor stressful event can trigger a negative cycle of response and feelings of helplessness.

We can help animals refill their empty safety tank by interacting with them at a pace that is right for them. This will help to instill a Sense of Safety in our presence. We do this through honoring their needs, responding to their cues with respect, paying attention to their timing and desire for proximity or distance, and adding gentle love. The good news is that we refill our own tank by supporting their *Sense of Safety* each day.

Seeing how these HAC methods of restoring a sense of safety have helped many animals that were *lost causes* has bolstered my faith and optimism that healing is possible. Even animals who have experienced tremendous trauma can have joyful lives once they have loving support to refill their safety tank. Building up their safety reserves leads to more and more trust and a growing connection with their human.

But as I often unfortunately see in shelters, if an animal has been significantly traumatized, just like a human, they may have a damaged sense of connection and may disconnect from their own body. It is as if a part of them is absent, leaving a dull, depressed, listless animal behind. They may go through the basic motions of eating and eliminating, but not much more. These animals appear not to be fully present. They are *ungrounded*, and thus it is hard to connect with them because they are avoiding connection with you. In human terms, this is called *attachment disorder*, which has been seen and studied in orphanages in Eastern Europe and in those dreadful primate experiments in which infant monkeys were deprived of contact with their mothers.

Animals Can Have Attachment Disorders

I believe animals can have attachment disorders just as humans do. Some animals have a secure attachment style. They bond easily and deeply, can form new bonds, and can withstand periods of separation. Conversely, those with a degree of attachment disorder can find bonding more challenging; it takes longer for them to build trust. But in time, with the right loving human and a safe and predictable environment, they can learn to form healthy bonds.

Attachment issues in humans and animals exist along a spectrum, and there is a wide range of related behaviors. Some animals are a little disconnected; some are a lot. These detached animals will not be inclined to connect with humans, games, toys, treats, or the routine of living because, at a core level, they have lost their sense of safety and don't know the way back. For them, the way to a jerry-rigged sense of safety is *withdrawal*. So, as humans, we need to respect that this is the best choice they can make with the resources they have. We can't rush them back to safety. We must build it brick by brick, breath by breath. Moment by moment, the safety tank can be refilled.

At one end of the spectrum there are *Velcro dogs,* who cling on to humans for dear life and are very insecure if left alone, even for short periods of time. This is a form of *insecure attachment.* These dogs need to learn self-soothing methods to experience more independence. Even aggression can be understood from the lens of attachment disorder as many cases that appear to be aggressive are at root fear-based attachment disorders.

When dogs are kept chained up, left in yards, and humans do not respond to their needs, they may give up trying to *signal* what they need. They give up on the idea that humans can provide for them in terms of a sense of safety, belonging, and worthiness. Their unfilled needs can create an attachment disorder, which we witness when these dogs end up in the shelter. Over time, when an animal's needs are consistently ignored, the dog will give up trying to connect to a human to have those needs fulfilled.

At this extreme end of the attachment spectrum are those dogs that do not feel safe in the presence of humans and are unable to feel comfort from them. They don't bond, or at least not quickly. It appears they have *checked out.* They can be somewhat disconnected from their bodies and their spirits, and thus, they have no *connection muscle* left. They have no resources that enable them to see a human and recognize, *Here is somebody to love, and someone who will love me in return.* That part of their spirit is broken. So, they self-soothe by retreating deep inside themselves, blocking off as much stimulation as they can in order to construct a sense of safety. Many of these shut-down animals have a hard time getting adopted because they don't connect or engage when people come by. Sadly, there are many shelters that put these dogs "out of their misery."

In the HAC, we believe that there is hope for these animals, even though some of the most severe cases I have seen will take months to heal, sometimes years. With love and patient understanding, healing is possible, but the timing of full recovery has many variables, including the degree of trauma and how well the human intervenes with suitable methods.

It is important to note that love, while a powerful healing force, will not be enough once an animal has gone to the shutdown stage. We believe these animals need encouragement to *come back into their bodies*. This is why it is important to encourage movement and play, hopefully also in playgroups with other dogs, even though these animals will appear to have little interest in doing so at first. In this case, we are happy to see even a little play-like interest because free movement is a healing tool. Self-directed movement and healing are entwined. Freedom of movement through play is very beneficial in helping these animals recover.

On the HAC healing journey, we seek to get into sync with the animal's slightest indication of interest in engaging and support this with the appropriate response. This helps the dog learn that a human can understand their signals, which creates a willingness to communicate and connect because, perhaps for the first time, somebody is listening. This is how, moment-by-moment, we build a positive feedback loop that encourages more contact and connection.

Animal Soul Retrieval

Getting an animal to come back to their body, to re-engage with life, is a form of Soul Retrieval, to use a Shamanistic term. In these cases,

I have a talk with their Soul and ask for assistance as the personality is too shut down to accept help. At first, some animals don't want to come back. They feel they have had enough. But I find that almost all animals whose Souls I connect with accept the invitation. They just need the light to shine in a gentle way to point them back to themselves.

The good thing about doing Soul retrieval work is that it takes the pressure off me. I am not healing the animal, as I can't. I can't force an animal to want to reconnect; I can only invite, guide, and encourage. The healing happens as a byproduct of the animal *reconnecting* with their Soul-self, which triggers the re-engagement with living. This begins a cycle of healing, of interest in the world and the people around them, and the desire to engage. It is like their *pilot light for life* is turned back on. It isn't instant, but if you are watching closely, you can see small visible steps of behavior toward connection.

Miss Betsy, the horse I told you about earlier in this book, is an example of a horse who, I believe, had been separated from her Soul. The sense of disconnection from her spirit was apparent and very detrimental to her well-being. It was as if the emotional life force was worn out. I worked with Miss Betsy using the Trust Technique. I spent hours walking next to her. I brushed her and gave her tons of carrots. I spoke to her and told her how much I loved her. I introduced this physical wreck of a horse to new people as if she were the winner of the Kentucky Derby. In my eyes, she was a champion. If you recall, she had been forced to be a drug runner and then left to starve in her stall, but she had the spirit of a survivor. Miss Betsy became the best therapy horse I had ever met, and everyone who met her felt healed simply being in her presence. You could feel her gentle wisdom, perhaps because she had taken *the walk of despair* and found her way back. We all need to find our way back in varying degrees, and Miss Betsy was a shining example that this is possible.

Just one of many reasons it is so wonderful to be around balanced animals (who are not traumatized) is they are very grounded. Their spirits are alive and well and fully inhabiting their bodies. We humans are hungry for this authentic experience, too. We recognize it even if we don't always feel it ourselves. It is why we can be mesmerized by watching fish swim, kittens and puppies play, pigs delight in slop, and any animal being true to themselves.

As humans, when our sense of safety is high, we are less stressed, we make better decisions, and our relationships are easier. We are better connected with our intuition, our *North Star,* which means knowing what is right for us as well as who is trustworthy and who is not.

All Behavior Is an Attempt to Feel Safe and Connected

As I have mentioned, a key concept in The Human-Animal Connection is the idea that *all behavior is an animal's attempt to feel safe and connected.* In that sense, it is neither good nor bad; it is simply that animal's attempt to cope with feelings of unsafety. Of course, some behaviors are more effective than others, as they are with humans. Remembering this will help you refrain from labeling them a *bad dog.*

Those of us who work with animals in the healing practices have a responsibility to help all animals find their innate sense of safety. And when we teach veterans and others our HAC methods, more than one life is saved. It is a beautiful feeling, particularly when you help those who have no hope and little chance of a happy life. But there is hope with the right tools. Every being deserves to live with a sense of safety.

Journal Reflections on Rebuilding a Sense of Safety:

1) How is your personal sense of safety doing? Is your tank mostly full? Half-full? Half-empty? Less than a quarter full? Of course, this is a changeable situation. Your safety levels go up and down according to your internal thoughts and external circumstances. But in general, across the course of your life, where do you see yourself?

2) Pay attention to the gauge on your Safety Tank. Let's use a scale of 0–100. One hundred is a full tank, like a Zen Master. Nothing rattles you for more than a few seconds. If I could paraphrase Meister Eckhart's advice, "Let it Be, Let it Go, and Be Free" is a nice way to live. A zero level in your safety tank would be losing all hope. Notice how your levels fluctuate as they are influenced by your internal thinking as well as by outside events and interactions.

3) When was a time in your life, even for an afternoon, that you felt totally safe? What was it about that time that made you feel safe? Use this memory as a kind of "jumper cable" to mentally help you get back in the safe zone.

4) When do you feel unsafe? Notice patterns that trigger unsafety, such as: *When I am criticized. When I feel like a failure. When my bank account is dangerously low. When I am hungry, lonely, and isolated.* If you can identify the patterns that cause your safety tank to leak, you can anticipate drops in your sense of safety, and over time, work towards avoiding those situations that undermine your well-being.

5) Make a list of "quick refills" to your safety tank. These are things you can do or say to yourself to lift your spirits enough to get to the next step. It could be talking to

someone you love or trust, spending time with animals, getting out in nature, or doing anything you love. If you are an introvert, this may be a solo activity. If you are an extrovert, it will likely be something that involves connecting with other people.

Re-Minder: I am safe.

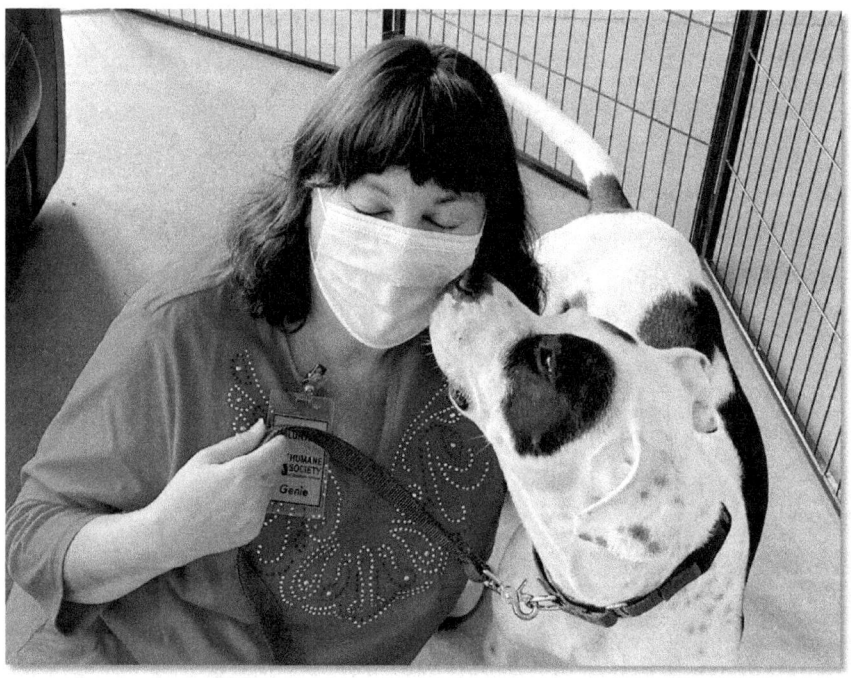

Lucy was a shelter dog who needed to have her Sense of Safety built back up. Knowing that a human was really listening helped her feel safe. This is her saying goodbye to me on the day she was adopted by a young man who loved her completely.

Principle #19

TRUST: THE FOUNDATION OF HEALING

The Formula of Healthy Relating

A dog may destroy your shoes,
but he will never destroy your heart.

Anonymous

Overview

When we feel safe, it is so much easier to trust. And when we are trusting, we feel safer. These two principles work together and support each other, leading to greater well-being. All of us have had many experiences that caused us to lose trust—in ourselves, in others, in the world. This is as true for animals as for people.

The good news is that trust lost can be regained. There are methods to rebuild trust! If we know we can rebuild trust, it means we are not at the mercy of our past experiences and histories. In this way, the past no longer needs to define us. Thus, the moment we regain trust, we can rewrite our future.

Mr. Mouser and the Circle of Trust

One day while volunteering at the shelter, a small white mouse in a cage enticed me to visit him. I was on my way to work with a dog when Mr. Mouser ran towards the window, stood on his hind legs, and looked at me earnestly with a look that said, *You're a human. You could do something for me.* Hard to resist a little mouse with such a big intention.

When I turned around and went in to see him, the other mice cowered in their cages. But Mr. Mouser ran to my side of his cage, again standing on two legs, front paws on the bars, and made complete and trusting eye contact with me, a stranger. Then he gave me that, *You look like you could have a treat in that pouch that I might enjoy* look. It worked. I produced a bit of string cheese I had been saving for a special dog.

Mr. Mouser watched me intensely as I struggled to open the packaging around the coveted treat, his nose and whiskers twitching in anticipation, still holding me in that eye contact. I fed him a piece, and he acted like it was the most delicious thing known to mouse.

I marveled at how much he trusted me, even though we were meeting for the first time. Trust is contagious, and I could feel the *circle of trust* flowing between us. Of course, by giving me the mouse equivalent of goo-goo eyes, he got me to feed him more little pieces. I was smitten.

I love how contagious trust is. When he had finished off my cheese supply, he gave me this look of absolute trust as if saying, *You will be back tomorrow with more, right?* Right he was—I could barely stay away a whole day! Two days later, he was adopted. I was happy for him, but I *still* miss my little pink-nosed teacher of the Power of Trust.

Trust Is the Foundation of Every Good Relationship

All good relationships are based on trust. Mutual trust leads to satisfying co-living and happier times together. Trust leads to everything good between people and animals.

What is trust? Trust means you feel you can rely on a person or animal to act within certain predictable boundaries. You feel safe and that you can count on them not to eat you or hurt or betray you intentionally. Trust implies a commitment to good and kind behavior.

Animals have a *sixth sense* of who trustworthy people are. Dogs form instant opinions of who they can trust; it is as if they can smell goodness and kindness. We humans often struggle with this instant knowing because trust requires a shared understanding of what truth is. If we don't share a common understanding of the truth, there will be no trust.

Trust is the foundation that makes all connections with animals better. Positive training is much more effective when there is a high level of trust. Trust leads to animals wanting to please their person, which results in satisfying behavior, which in turn leads to growing trust from the person. Mutual trust builds upon itself and creates more.

Trust is precious. It is also fragile in the sense that it can be easily bruised. One day at the shelter, a kennel worker accidentally lost control of the water hose and sprayed a dog named Bogo, who had been his buddy the day before. After that, Bogo cowered whenever that man approached. Feeling awful, the kennel worker approached the next day offering a cheeseburger, but Bogo wouldn't accept it or even look at him.

I felt sad about this episode and taught the shelter worker some methods to regain Bogo's trust. It took about eight days, but with some healing and another cheeseburger, they were back to being buddies. Bogo's story is just one demonstration that animals have memories. They remember the good, the bad, and the ugly. Some very resilient animals, such as pit bulls, are like saints when it comes to forgiveness and willingness to let go of the past when presented with a new, loving, and compelling present. Some dogs, even those rescued from dogfighting rings, are able to love again as if they had never been abused. My sweet therapy dog, Oscar, was my hero when it came to letting go of his horrific past and viewing each human being with an entirely clean slate. This is not a lack of memory; it is a willingness to love and trust again.

Feeling Safe Is the First Step to Building Trust

If I look back on all the dogs in shelters that I have been able to help in some way, it all began with paying attention to what would help them feel safe. Safety is the foundation on which trust is rebuilt. Restoring trust leads to deep peace, which leads to deep healing.

I use the Trust Technique and other methods such as Reiki, Energy Healing, Light Work, and Shamanic Soul Retrieval—each of which rebuilds safety and trust in a unique way. I also use several physical touch methods, such as Lomi Lomi (Hawaiian massage), Effleurage, Tapping, and Tellington Touch.

These are just a few of the many good healing methods we can use to help traumatized animals. I am always learning new skills and encourage you to do the same. It makes sense to have several healing methods in your toolbox because every animal is a unique individual, and you never know which key will open the lock and allow trust to emerge.

There are so many wonderful healing methods out there, and the Trust Technique is my favorite. In the Trust Technique, we learn to always work at the animal's pace. We learn how to get peaceful and then how to share that peaceful feeling with animals. In this way, we help them let go of their stress, their past, and their fears.

For those inspired to learn more details about the Trust Technique, information can be found on their website.

While I have my favorites, I do want to say thank you to all the good people doing great work in all healing methods!

Trust Starts with You

Given that trust is the foundation of every good relationship, where should you start when working with animals who have lost trust? It is always advisable to become aware of and deal with any conscious or unconscious *un-trusting* feelings you may be carrying. Your unresolved trust issues can create energetic baggage that can prevent you from being as present as possible with a sensitive animal-being. The more you can resolve your own personal trust issues, the more effective you will be working with animals.

However, this doesn't mean you have to be a saint or someone with amnesia about every trespass against you. It just means you recognize your own issues and are dedicated to healing them over time. I have had plenty of experiences that broke my heart and consequently have my own trust issues, just like the next person. Goodness, I was in the movie business, which is like experiencing nuclear-powered rejection every day. Knowing I need to be able to objectively observe how the animal is doing without my personal issues clouding my perception, I must discipline myself not to haul my mistrust history into the interactions I have with an animal.

I am sure that if I asked you to make a list of all the incidents in your life that broke your trust, you would be busy writing for quite some time. And if I asked you if an animal ever broke your trust, you would have to think long and hard. This doesn't mean that your animal hasn't misbehaved. However, he or she probably hasn't committed a heart-crushing trespass like some person has done.

Despite our histories, we must make a deep choice to rebuild trust. It's the only way we can be free of the past. To help you repair, remember what Meister Eckhart said, and the Beatles repeated, "Let it Be."

Bomb-Proof Dogs Are Trustworthy

In therapy dog training, we talk about certain dogs we absolutely trust as being "bomb-proof." What this means is not only are they calm and adaptable to new people and situations, but they are predictable. We trust them because we know how they will respond in novel situations. There is a high level of trust between these dogs and their handlers because they are so tuned in to each other's cues that a misstep is very rare.

When you are training a dog or animal, you need to be predictable too. You must be consistent in your cues and signals because absolute consistency builds trust. If you are vague or give mixed signals, the animal will be confused and unable to comply because the trust in the meaning of your communication is compromised. When we evaluate therapy dog teams in the HAC, we look for relationships with high levels of mutual attention, responsiveness to each other's cues, and ultimately trust.

What Animals Can Teach Us About Balance and Neutrality

Animals have a natural sense of balance and neutrality. They are much better equipped than we humans are to not judge as we move through the up-and-down moments of life. They are better at accepting circumstances for what they are and letting them be. Instead of analyzing every event, they just flow into the next moment. This is one reason why it is peaceful to be with animals.

When Distinctions and Judgments Are Needed

Of course, there are many situations in which we need to make judgments of "good/bad" or "right/wrong" or decide to move towards or away from a person or situation. Sometimes, these decisions must be made instantly.

Being able to make rapid, accurate assessments of people and situations is an important life skill, but if we are *always* in this critical decision zone, we can burn out. To prevent burnout, one way to recharge is to switch to the state of neutral observation. That means we simply observe what is without trying to change it. We need to find the peace in saying, "And so it is."

"All events are neutral" is the mantra Bob, a spiritual teacher and my friend, teaches to all his students. I remember being in his class when he taught this and watching everyone squirm. "But what about...?" (and they list all the bad things happening in their lives and the worst atrocities perpetrated by the human race). In response, Bob calmly repeats, "*All* events are neutral." This statement will either drive you crazy or drive you to freedom.

Similarly, the Serenity Prayer wisely advises us to separate the things we can change from those things we cannot. We should make any changes we can to improve our lives and the lives of other beings. And when faced with the things we cannot change, it is time to surrender the struggle and accept what is.

When one is in the grip of strong emotions or opinions, it is easy to get very attached to a specific interpretation of a particular situation as good or bad, true or false, right or wrong. Of course, all humans and nonhuman animals are entitled to their opinions. The issue here is getting ferociously attached to a specific outcome because we want to avoid feeling negative emotions, and *we believe only our desired outcome* will prevent us from feeling pain. This attachment to "our" outcome leads to biased judgment, and the intensity of these emotions interferes with our sense of peace.

In addition to the value of loosening *the grip of strong opinion-driven emotions* for your own well-being, turbulent emotions will make it difficult to have clear communication with animals. Brad Laughlin, a collaborator with animal communicator Anna Breytenbach, recommends cultivating a sense of calm. He calls this equanimity the Witness. He suggests you seek to find the balance or the neutral central position when you feel yourself being pulled one way or the other. And there is great peace in this. When we cultivate our Witness, as Eckart Tolle suggests, we move into the grand "*Satisfaction of the Is-ness of Now.*"

Neutrality Is Acceptance of *What Is…Is.*

Nature is an excellent teacher in helping you to accept what is. One of the pleasures of being in nature is the sense of neutrality or balance. We don't take nature's actions personally the way we do our human interactions. A tree is a tree. It is not mad at you or judging you. We don't think its branches curve a certain way because of something we said. We don't think a bird takes flight because we forgot to do something. We know she is flying for her own reason. The wind blows the leaves because that's what wind does. It has nothing to do with us.

The Zen of non-personalness—or *what is, is*—is a relief. You're not responsible for any of it, and none of it is responsible to you. You simply coexist. This perspective allows you to let go of thinking that everything is about you or responding to you. Nature brings us to experience neutrality. It invites us to be connected to our Witness.

Spending time in nature and with animals centers us because we can get out of our heads and into the spirit of the moment. Neutrality has power because it diminishes the tyrannical thinking process of overanalyzing *cause and effect*. It interrupts the spell of thinking. The experience that things just "are" takes us into human-being-ness.

One reason animals can heal more easily from trauma is they don't dwell on the events or the reasons for their role in it. That doesn't mean they don't experience trauma; it just means the pathway to healing is more visceral. The animal's ability to accept what is instead of ruminating over the past is a tremendous asset. It is a powerful "present intelligence" that we can learn from.

Animals Have *Present Intelligence*

Neutrality brings you into the present moment. If events *cause* trauma, we are at the mercy of events outside ourselves. But if it is *how we view events that determine their impact*, then we have power over how they affect us. If events are viewed as neutral, then we can begin to take back control over how experiences linger in our minds. We can learn how to process those events in a way that leads us to recognize we have a choice about how we store the memories. If a traumatic event occurs, and we make a decision about it, such as *the world is not safe*, or *I should have done something to stop it*, or *this (event) will happen again*. These *schemas* or stuck beliefs can be very destructive to our well-being. The way we process an event determines the level of trauma we continue to experience. Just like us, animals can experience trauma, but without the mental rumination, their pathway to healing is simpler. Therefore, we teach this important concept of neutrality in our Act Resilient course.

We see this play out in combat situations where multiple people experience the same event, but it settles differently in each of their lives. One psychological theory that postulates why a recent event can become traumatic is linked to the person's level of Adverse Childhood Experiences (ACEs), such as trauma in early life. While I believe ACEs are a factor, I do not believe it is an inevitable predictor of the enduring impact of trauma. I believe the greater factor is the way events are remembered and processed.

In the Act Resilient training, I discuss a distinction between memories in the *Active File* versus those stored in the *Inactive File*. Memories in the inactive file are like a movie you saw and enjoyed some time ago. You can remember it if you need to and may still have good feelings triggered by the memory, but you tend to remember the larger elements and delete details of lesser importance. You remember the emotional themes and important plot elements. Minor elements are forgotten because you have "sorted" this file for what you liked the best about the experience.

Memories stored in the Active File, on the other hand, are intrusive. They erupt whether or not you want them to, triggered by even unrelated stimuli. With intrusive memories, *the tiniest details loom large,* taking up more RAM storage space in your mind than even the larger event. These are the memories that taunt you and haunt you, replaying over and over. However, by using The Act Resilient Method, you can learn to reprocess those memories so they can begin to be stored differently, literally in a larger context.

The Medicine of Trust

Please consider the statement that *all events are neutral* as a possibility. I call this Conceptual Spirit Medicine. It can be a very useful healing tool because it frees you from labeling any event as *absolutely* positive or *totally* negative. Use neutrality as a strong mental condiment, sprinkle a little as needed, or use it often. Maybe the idea that *all events are neutral* rattles your cage, but it is also the doorway to tremendous freedom.

If all events are truly neutral, then no one can hurt you unless you process that action and permanently store it in the *Hurtful Event File.* If I look back on all the disappointments, rejections, and betrayals in my life that were earth-shatteringly painful to me at the time, they almost always led to better opportunities and experiences. These difficult events eventually had a positive purpose as they led me to make new choices or to accept new options. This perspective takes trust in life to a new level.

With this approach, you are not trusting an individual; you are trusting that all events have a meaning, purpose, or place in your journey of growth. This operating principle doesn't mean we don't have preferences, as do all animals. It means that we don't have to carry the yoke of un-trust, and baggage of endless betrayals, bringing them to every new situation.

Is it possible that many animals naturally live from this wise perspective? Get to know a pit bull and ask him or her.

Let's make a deal: Try on this idea of neutrality of events as if it were simply one possibility, like an item on a spiritual buffet you have yet to try. All day long, whenever you find yourself getting upset about something or someone, just repeat to yourself,

"All events are neutral, including this one."

Try on this perspective the next time you want to change something or find you are resisting someone or some event. Consider this as a possibility. You don't have to be certain it is true. You can change your mind later. Think of it as Trust Medicine. It will reveal a deeper order at work.

Recognize the impact this practice has on your well-being. Experiment and see if this mantra about all events being neutral brings you more peace.

In addition to the personal benefits of this peaceful practice, this is how you want to engage with an animal. It allows you to see all behavior as neutral; the animal is doing what it needs to do to feel safe. The behavior may not be your preference, but if you are in a state of calm and peace, animals will often respond in kind and be more willing to try something different that you offer. Trust is a tangible force of healing. It is a quiet, exquisite bridge that allows a terrified animal to take the first steps toward the treat in your open hand. And this trust is worth everything.

Journal Reflections on Trust:

1) If you are feeling brave, make a list of the big life events that caused you to lose trust in people. How many of these events still haunt you? Looking back, although these events may have been quite painful and heartbreaking at the time, how does the perspective that comes from the passage of time change how you look at these events?

2) What reactions come up in you as you read the words, "All events are neutral"? After you argue and struggle, can you find the potential key to peace within them?

3) Would you like to have more trust in your life? Who or what do you need to trust more, with the innocence of a child AND the wisdom of an adult?

4) Do your animals trust you? How does that feel? Do you trust your animals?

5) What do you need to do to experience more trust in your life?

Re-Minder: I trust what is.

Barbra attending an HAC class and practicing building trust with animals. It was as good for them as it was for her.

Principle #20

CONNECTIVITY AND BELONGING
The Healing Power of Connection

All things share the same breath,
the beast, the tree, the man.
The air shares its spirit with all that it supports.

Chief Seattle

Overview

Some species of animals are very social and gregarious, living in packs or herds or small communities of the same species. But even social animals exhibit a huge range of individuality in terms of the desire to cooperate, engage, and make friends. In pack species, such as chimps, wolves, dolphins and others, those with the best social skills have the most success. Other species, like the octopus and jaguar, are loners. Some domesticated animals prefer the company of humans. For many animals it is important they have the opportunity to play and be with members of their own kind to experience a sense of connection and belonging, which leads to well-being.

A Bonobo Says Goodbye

Evolutionary anthropologist, Brian Hare was a scientific adviser who worked with Claudine Andre on a project to release captive and orphaned bonobos back into the wild of the Congo. The following story of working with them and their bonobo matriarch, Etumbe, must have made a life-changing impression on him.

In his book, *The Genius of Dogs*, he writes, "We stayed for a week and watched the bonobos each day. Everyone had worked hard to get them back into the forest, so it was an incredibly fulfilling experience. On our final day, we did not want to leave. When it was time, and we started heading from the forest to our canoe, Etumbe (the matriarch) walked toward us in a determined manner. Knowing she was stronger than all of us, I was a little alarmed at her pace.

As each of us passed her to board the canoe, she looked deep into our eyes, took each of our hands, held it in her own, and shook it in a gentle goodbye. As a scientist, I have no idea what she was thinking, but as a person, it was the most heartfelt thank-you I have ever received."

We Are Social Animals

Aristotle said, "Man is a social animal." While we know that to be true in general, there is a huge variation between individual humans in their desire or need for social connection. The same can be said for individual animals within a species, as demonstrated at Chimp Haven, a wonderful sanctuary for former laboratory chimps. These primates, who have spent virtually their entire lives in cages and isolated from their peers, almost always form friendships or group alliances once they are rescued. However, even amongst chimps that came from the same research lab, there is a range of sociability among the individuals once they arrive at this more humane environment.

In some species, the parent's role is of short duration, just long enough for the offspring to become independent. Other more social species, like wolves, have lifelong communal living, including sleeping together, hunting, and foraging in extended family structures. On the other hand, I believe that domestic animals are often taken away from their mothers too soon, which results in a variety of behavior and attachment issues later in life.

Social Healing

In The Act Resilient Method, our approach is to treat PTSD as both an individual and social issue. People with PTSD suffer double because they are typically beset by feelings of failure, shame, survivor guilt, or other negative self-perceptions, plus they feel isolated and often feel they have lost their standing or connection with others. They don't feel like they belong anywhere. The disruption of social connections and the unspeakable sense of isolation are one reason PTSD is so challenging to heal. Thus, the best healing methods will involve good social reconnection and a community of support.

For humans, humor and improv comedy are two very effective methods we use in Act Resilient to quickly generate healing and "group cohesion," which is the connective power of positive group energy. While some people can heal through solo processes, most healing happens in a social context, as indigenous people understood. For example, in Polynesian cultures, healing is viewed as the task of the village, not the individual. So, when warriors returned from major battles, they took time together to decompress before returning to home and family.

I believe animals can also experience PTSD. A good pairing with a healthy animal friend of the same species or a "helper" animal of another species can do much to promote healing from trauma. Not just any animal will do; what's needed is one who connects well with the traumatized animal and encourages them to feel safe through connection.

What humor does for humans; playgroups do for dogs. A good playgroup is like a night out with your favorite comedian. The Doggie playgroups, which support re-socialization, are one of the great achievements at the Pima Animal Care Center (PACC), a municipal shelter where I volunteer. It is the largest government-run facility in Tucson and takes in *75–100 dogs each day*. With a dedicated army of volunteers, they ensure almost every dog gets out of the kennel and into playgroup every day. To make this program work, the first step is to identify "helper dogs." These are gentle dogs with excellent social skills who communicate clearly with other dogs. In playgroups, where dogs are meeting for the first time, well-balanced helper dogs with great dog etiquette will often show other dogs how to behave and will be the peacemakers in the group.

What one of these helper dogs can teach another dog in seconds or minutes is incredibly impressive. They can teach new dogs to respect boundaries, help them correctly read body language cues, help them feel safe in a group, and understand acceptable levels of energy for mutual play. Dog-to-dog instruction is like getting lessons from a master when compared to humans trying to teach their animals desired behaviors, which is like kindergarten. The helper dogs are so much more effective.

Most dogs are not helper dogs, but when you find one, they are like gold in a playgroup in a shelter environment because they can calm the other animals down. Animals who calm others can be seen in other species, as the story in this book shows about the wild mustang, Odin Sidewinder, in a horse rescue, who was an ambassador of peace in the herd.

This doesn't mean every dog needs a canine partner. In their home environment, some dogs do just fine being the only dog and prefer to be the *only child*. Don't assume every dog or cat needs a roommate. But some dogs do much better with a dog companion. How do you know what is best for your dog? You will have to experiment, and you may have to experiment many times by introducing different dogs. Some dogs, like some people, will like just about anybody and any dog. Other dogs are not as adaptable or have strong opinions about who they like. Remember Principle #10, "Animals Have Opinions"?

A Proper and Good Dog Introduction

The way dogs are introduced can make or break a connection. Unfortunately, I have seen many humans make mistakes with dog introductions. At some shelters, potential adopters bring their dog in for a meet and greet, which may or may not go well. If the introduction goes wrong, the shelter may incorrectly assume the shelter dog will not get along with another dog. But that may not be the right conclusion. Many factors can impact success -- the speed of the approach, the lack of proper pacing and distance, the lack of a sense of safety in the environment, leash restrictions, or too much stimulation are just some of the factors that can make an introduction go all wrong too quickly.

What often happens is the humans miss early-warning signs of discomfort with the method of introduction or stress signals from one or both of the dogs being introduced. The dog was signaling, perhaps subtly, indicating through body language that there was a lack of comfort with the method of introduction. Because those signals are ignored, and the introduction proceeds without adjusting, pace, distance, or other elements, the stressed dog escalates by barking, growling, lunging, or other display behavior. The humans are startled because this *sudden* outburst seems to "come from nowhere." But had the human paid attention to their dog's *early warning system* of body language, they could have had a much more positive outcome.

Of course, in a shelter context, safety is the priority. But when unfortunate mistakes during adoption introductions are made, the stressed shelter dog may get labeled "dog reactive," which reduces their chances of adoption. Further, a great adopter may be rejected because they already have a dog at home. Many wonderful adopters who already have a dog at home understand what it means to provide a dog with a good life. So, we don't want them to be turned away because of a poor introduction.

Dogs in shelters can easily become very dog reactive because that environment is extremely stressful. They are confined to small spaces, and their natural behaviors are restricted. They are being walked by unfamiliar people, have little choice or control, and almost no freedom.

And when they meet a new dog, they are on a leash, which can create challenges to a good introduction. When a dog is deprived of the ability to adjust their spacing and distance, it can lead to aggressive displays. Deprived of *flight,* they may choose *fight.* This is how many dogs in shelters get labeled "dog reactive" that could have done very well if they had had a proper, slow, appropriate introduction or by simply meeting outside the shelter environment, or at least not in the busiest, most fragrant areas in the shelter. I have worked with many such dogs who were given that label. Those same dogs were absolutely fine in a neutral environment with a slow and properly paced introduction.

I am always amazed at communal shelters with such limited resources that they must house all the dogs together. I have seen videos from shelters where a hundred or more dogs and other animals live in the same area, eating, sleeping, playing together. The animals manage hierarchy issues themselves. The dogs find their friends and know who to avoid. There are minor squabbles, but they work it out amongst themselves.

The Cat Hermitage No-Kill Rescue and Sanctuary in Tucson, Arizona, is a beautiful example of cats who live together socially in big and small rooms, according to age or physical conditions. These social cats are so much less stressed and present themselves better to potential adopters. (Please see our video podcast about the Cat Hermitage on our website.)

Tips for Positive Introductions

In the HAC, we are always in learning mode when it comes to making good animal introductions because a good introduction can make the difference between a happy life and (literally, in the case of some shelter dogs) no life.

There are many great resources that will help you learn how to do an effective animal introduction. And you should always adjust my advice to the specific needs and temperament of your dog. So, I will share just a few critical considerations that will help make your introductions go well.

1) Go slow! Very slow. Progress at a pace that is slower than necessary. Or at least move at a pace that is comfortable for the dog. This means letting the dog lead the pace of moving forward to the next step. (Cue: If the dog is showing happy, playful, wiggly, *and calm energy,* the dog is likely ready to go to the next level of interaction.)

2) If needed, arrange for the dogs to sniff each other through a barrier, such as a chain-link fence. Let them smell and see each other (front and back), but with a physical separation

between them to reduce stress. This separation can create a sense of safety and comfort better than putting them in a confined area together. Also, in this way, you can observe how they are interacting and their level of stimulation to determine if this could be a calm meeting. Having this initial barrier slows down everyone's reactions, including yours.

3) In shelters, dogs will have to be on leashes. Remember that leashes boost reactivity, as dogs feel more stressed when meeting on leashes.

4) If there is no fence barrier, avoid nose-to-nose contact. Avoid letting one dog stare at the other. Dogs in a "freeze" mode, with rigid body posture, are signaling their fear or agitation. We want to see waggy, soft body language. Look to see that both dogs seem calm before putting them in physical proximity with each other.

5) Be as calm as you can be, as your dog will pick up your stress levels. If you are nervous, your dog will sense that and may act protectively, which will not help the introduction to go well. Keep your focus on your dog to recognize signs of how it is going.

6) If the meeting with the fence barrier has gone well and the dogs seem friendly, you might be ready to let them move into the same space, where they are free to approach each other. If you are in a contained environment, you may be able to drop the leash, letting it drag (in case you need to pick it up). Of course, you need to be completely attentive in case you must intervene and separate them.

7) Remember, dogs are animals. They are unpredictable, especially when meeting another dog they do not know. The introduction may seem calm at first, but it can quickly

go in the other direction, so have your plan ready for how you will redirect them if needed.

8) Observe, observe, observe. Do not be chatting with another human or on your cell phone during a dog introduction. Your full attention needs to be on the animals so you can *anticipate* their moods.

9) Evaluate! Is it friendly? Is it safe? Is it fun? Does it appear respectful? Do they both get to sniff front and back? Is one dog overly dominant, or does the greeting seem fair, balanced, and compatible?

10) Remember that an introduction in a shelter may be more stressful than one in a neutral environment. It is always best to introduce dogs in a neutral environment rather than in one dog's home, as this may trigger territorial feelings.

These are just the basics; there is much more that may need to be considered in your specific situation.

Social Needs

The feeling of belonging is the third element in Maslow's hierarchy model of needs, after physiological needs and safety, which are the first two. People and social animals both have a need to feel we belong, but not all of us have our needs met. Some of us have effective social skills that lead to an easy, organic sense of belonging, while others lack these skills, leading to poor connectivity. This can lead to a chronic aching feeling of not belonging—*anywhere*. This lack of a feeling of belonging and connection causes much isolation and loneliness. Humans with poor social skills sometimes also have attachment issues, making it very hard to find their tribe and feeling like they don't belong in any group! Animals can be our role models for "finding our pack" and connecting with others to experience that elusive and delicious feeling of belonging.

If you put a bunch of chickens who don't know each other together, within a minute or so, they will have figured out the new pecking order, and every chicken knows where she fits in the hierarchy. This is usually accomplished peacefully and without bloodshed because somehow, they all know where they fit and accept it. Imagine if humans could understand how they fit with others in a group so smoothly!

The sense of belonging is not just a psychological issue; it has a significant economic impact on society. Deloitte, a management consulting firm, reports on a study of the impact of the sense of belonging in the workplace: "A 2019 study by BetterUp found that workplace belonging can lead to an estimated 56 percent increase in job performance, a 50 percent reduction in turnover risk, and a 75 percent decrease in employee sick days. The study found that a single incidence of 'micro-exclusion' can lead to an immediate 25 percent decline in an individual's performance on a team project."

Dogs Are Social Geniuses

Dogs and humans do so well together, not because we are so smart, but because they are! They are so good at reading our moods and understanding our intentions. They figure out how to please us and what behaviors annoy us.

For dogs, being connected to humans and being so good at reading our emotions and intentions has meant that they have been very successful in sharing lives with us. As Director of the Duke Canine Cognition Center at Duke University, Brian Hare, states, "The dog is arguably the most successful mammal on the planet, besides us. Dogs have spread to all corners of the world, including inside our homes, and in some cases onto our beds." And he concludes that this has been a great benefit for both species.

Perhaps, he suggests, because it has challenged our species and theirs to increase social skills and to become near-social geniuses. "Just about everyone thinks that domestication makes animals somehow weaker or less noble or just plain dumber since our assumption is that humans created domestic animals for our own needs. People think of wild animals as noble and natural and domesticated animals as artificial and engineered. It turns out the truth is more nuanced...." Domestication is here to stay, and our job now is to make these relationships beneficial and successful for all through a better understanding of each other's social cues and connection styles.

While every animal is a unique individual, their needs for social connection fall along a spectrum of needs—from very little to a lot. It is your job as the human partner to be attuned to their level of need, understanding that it may change across the course of the animal's lifespan.

Consider the possibility that the animals who share your life may benefit from contact with animals of their own species or other species. This is going to be a discovery process. You might think they need something they don't or miss the opportunity to become aware of how they could benefit from increased social connections. There is no one-size-fits-all approach when it comes to the need for social connection.

Shelters rely on volunteers to create a human connection with animals waiting to be adopted. It is a wonderful thing to do—to spend time with shelter animals to socialize them, take them for walks, and play in the yard if there is one available. But many shelters don't have the staff to provide safe playgroups with other dogs. It is a fundamental need for animals, as it is for people, to express themselves naturally, to play, and engage with others. It is our hope at the HAC that more shelters will be able to provide opportunities for animals to get their social needs met in the future.

Bonobos – Masters of Social Connection

Bonobos are our closest genetic relatives. We share a 98.7 percent DNA match with bonobos. Unlike chimpanzees, bonobos are peaceful creatures who would rather make love than war. If two groups of bonobos run into each other, it's Woodstock! Love, peace, sex, and happy camaraderie. Bonobos are a matriarchal society and place a high value on cooperation, affiliation, and reconciliation. One of their favorite ways to resolve conflict or squabbles is to have sex.

Bonobos show us that mastering the skills of successful social connection can lead to harmony in the community, satisfaction amongst individuals, and a great sense of belonging. The sense of belonging in a group leads to mental and emotional stability as well as physical survival. We can learn a great deal from animals about the value of social connections as a tool for healing trauma as well as for how to sustain healthy societies.

Journal Reflections on Connectivity and Belonging:

1) What is your need for social connection with humans? Low, very low, medium, fairly high, very high? How much are your needs for social connection with humans being met? Take an honest look at your needs to belong—or reluctance to belong.

2) What is your need for connection with animals? How are those needs being met? What could you do to increase the level of contact if you desire that?

3) If you share your life with animals, how are they meeting your needs for connection?

4) Do the animals in your life have a chance to connect with others? What could you do to safely increase the positive connection of your animals with others?

5) Do you prefer the connection with animals over connecting with people?

Re-Minder: I belong.

Animals help us feel connected—to them, to each other, and soothe the pain of the feeling of not belonging.

Principle #21

TOWARDS & AWAY

Your Natural Impulses Will Lead You Where You Need to Go

*Keep your eyes open, your feet and
your ideas moving forward.
You will find what you need.*

The HAC

Overview

Healthy animals naturally move towards what they like, want, and need and away from what they don't like or need. This *Towards & Away* movement is a healthy impulse for both animals and humans. But when trauma is experienced, this healthy impulse gets interrupted.

A key element of the HAC program is to help people and animals restore a healthy connection to the core sense of what is right and wrong for themselves. To understand each individual animal better, we pay close attention to the obvious and subtle indicators that an animal communicates through their body language of *Towards & Away*. Simply stated, they will move toward you if they want more contact. And if they are not ready to engage, they may show subtle movements such as turning their eyes, head, or body away.

Sophia Gets Loud

My therapy dog, Sophia, often accompanied me when I taught Act Resilient classes at Davis Monthan Air Force Base. She would always sit calmly on her dog bed. One day, class was already underway when an airman burst through the door and rushed to his seat. Sophia got up from her bed and barked at him as if she was trying to scare a bear away. I was embarrassed; this is not acceptable therapy dog behavior. But fortunately, everyone had a chuckle watching this twenty-five-pound dog, who they knew had always been completely silent in class, acting as if she was auditioning for Top Dog. First, she moved towards the airman, but when she saw she couldn't bark him away, she backed off, still watching him.

This was very unusual behavior for Sophia. She had been to countless classes before, and earlier in this session, she barely looked up when people came and went on Air Force business. She had never done this in any classroom situation, so I knew she was responding to something specific and was communicating her thoughts loudly!

After class, the airman approached me to apologize for being late. Again, Sophia backed away from him. This signaled to me that he was experiencing some intense stress. When I shared the meaning of Sophia's unusual behavior, he realized he was a lot more stressed about a situation at work than he had admitted to himself. It really helped him to recognize that. You could see the weight drop off him as he realized that he needed to take action to address the issue.

As soon as he got calm, Sophia *changed her mind* and became interested in meeting him. Maybe this human might have a treat? I gave him one to give to her, and they became instant friends.

How Towards & Away Are Connected

The movement of towards or away is a form of communication. We can learn much about how a being is feeling by watching this choice of movement. At first glance, it might appear that *Towards & Away*, which are opposite directions, are opposed to each other. But a closer look reveals how connected these opposites are. We only know *towards* because we know *away*. It is like a yin and yang dance of unified polarity. In any given moment, a being may appear to be moving only one way, such as away, but another glance might reveal how they are moving toward something else, such as *away* from something stressful, *towards* a sense of safety.

Animals have natural wisdom that tells them what to move towards and what to move away from. Humans can benefit from reclaiming this intuitive wisdom for themselves. Many of us feel we have lost touch with our natural *Towards & Away Guidance System* through the process of squishing ourselves to fit into society's norms. Even the requirements of social politeness can cause us to stay longer in a conversation we are tired of or remain in a situation we would prefer to leave.

Our body sends us "move away" signals, but if we think we must stay, we manually override our physiological impulse by ignoring it. If we spend a lot of energy trying to please others, in so doing, we may have frequently overridden our own body's wisdom. Over time, this manual override can erode our natural impulses, and we lose connection with our basic sense of *Towards & Away*.

On the other hand, listening to our natural impulses of attraction and repulsion, *Towards & Away* will help us make the best choices in challenging situations or when an important choice needs to be made. *Our Towards & Away signals are part of our Wisdom-Communication Channel.*

If this communication channel becomes too distorted because we are ignoring, overriding, or not listening to it, it can become weak and unreliable. Weak signals can cause you to move toward the "wrong" things" and people and away from "good" things and people. We see this happen in adolescence when people have lost touch with some of their innate childhood wisdom and sense of truth and seek the approval of others and new experiences. This blind-following behavior often has a high cost.

The good news is it is entirely possible to reconnect with this important guidance system that we in the HAC call *Towards & Away*. One way to help awaken this natural awareness is to carefully observe how your animals follow their own guidance. Unless they have been traumatized, they trust their own desires to move *Towards & Away*. This assessment can change quickly, such as when they are nervous about approaching someone or something new, and they step back, pause, sniff, decide the situation is safe, and reapproach. When you see how animals trust their *Towards & Away* senses, it can inspire you to connect with that wisdom in yourself.

If you observe animals interacting together, you will see a dance of *Towards & Away* behaviors. They approach, pause, turn away, approach again. In a healthy or well-matched playgroup situation, there is a constant motion of *Towards & Away*. Connecting and disconnecting. Engaging and disengaging. Many conflicts are avoided if the animals are watching and listening to each other's *Towards & Away* signals. If animals are not well socialized or have issues that impact their correct reading of body language, they may miss these vital cues, and that is when tension can temporarily erupt. But most times, the animals immediately receive the *Towards & Away* correction, and harmony is restored.

Observe Animals Towards & Away Communication

By correctly observing *Towards & Away* behaviors in the animals we work with, we can be of great service to them. James French tells a story of working with some injured wild mustang horses in a rescue. He had made some natural teas from herbs in the area, but because he wasn't sure which was the best one for a particular horse, he simply presented both. The horse chose the one he needed and looked away from the one he didn't need.

For annual migration, many species use magnetoreception which is the ability to use the earth's magnetic field to orient themselves and help them plot their course. Whales, dolphins, sea turtles, and birds use magnetoreception, but new studies show that some dogs will also use the Earth's north-south axis to orient themselves to choose which direction to find their way home. Some dogs will first orient on the north-south axis to choose where to pee.

If you feel your *Towards & Away* needs a tune-up, begin by simply recognizing that fact. Next, commit to listening to your inner silence and the subtle sensation of attraction or repulsion. This will lead you to pay attention to a body sensation that tells you what to move towards and what to move away from. The *Towards & Away* sensation is your inner knowing. Some people feel it, some hear it. It is often subtle at first, and with practice, it will become loud and clear—even difficult to ignore.

Practice with small decisions such as what color shirt to wear today, what piece of fruit to select in the produce aisle, or what direction to choose on a walk. It is good to begin with minor decisions because you are warming up your *Chooser Muscle,* as we call it in Act Resilient. (More on that in Principle #27, "Freedom of Choice.")

What is important in this exercise is to take a moment to FEEL into a given choice or direction. Then notice how it felt to follow your gut sense—or test the water by *not following it.* Let's say you get the guidance to wear the red shirt because you feel you need more vitality or *Fire Medicine* that day. This is what you heard, felt, or saw. Then put on the blue shirt to invoke *Cool Water Energy* and feel the difference. Does the blue shirt feel as good as your first impulse? On another day, your blue shirt may be the perfect choice if you need more harmony in relationships. Sometimes by feeling into the "wrong choice," you can refine your listening to your "*Good Antenna.*"

A good choice will feel better.

Even if the "good choice" is harder, like taking the high road when someone has taken the low road and you are tempted to match their energy. As you orient your *Towards impulse* to what is good, it will become a stronger pull, and it will feel satisfying at a deeper level.

Feeling Into a Choice

I mention the example of what shirt to wear to make the point that neither choice is good or bad, but one may be better for a specific intention or mood. This perspective helps us to soften the attachment to absolute right and wrong, as the next day, the blue shirt may be just what you need. It is less about *thinking* and more about *feeling into which choice feels better for this moment.*

Practice with minor decisions until you feel you have a strong sense of connection to your *Towards* decisions and an equally strong sense of how your *Away* decisions feel. Once you are connected to your inner guidance system, you can trust it with bigger life decisions.

When working with animals in the HAC, we are constantly perfecting our ability to understand their *Towards & Away* communication. When I spend a few minutes in the morning watching the wild birds in my backyard, I am often observing their *Towards & Away communication.* If there is a potential territorial conflict, usually over the pursuit of food, one bird will turn his head away or move a few inches away from the upset one to let him know there is no need for a battle. And that is it. Communication received. Of course, sometimes it escalates to a second warning, and the offending bird will then flap away a few branches, and harmony is restored.

Obviously, some animals, like horses, if they have the freedom to move, will be clear and direct in their *Towards & Away Communication*. I remember one reporter for the *New York Times* who wrote a story about her (lousy) experience with some people who claimed to be doing equine therapy. She was unconvinced of the value of the experience when she stepped into the corral. The horse took one look at her, turned, and walked away and never returned. The horse likely sensed the reporter's state of mind and clearly mirrored her reluctance. This was not the reporter's fault; she was not given instruction on how to approach and connect with the horse in a way that the horse would prefer. So, the horse responded authentically and moved away.

In a shelter environment, an animal may not have as much freedom of movement as this honest horse did. You may have to watch for more subtle communication signals, such as the dog turning his eyes, face, or body away. In that case, I would advise you to get very still and avert your eyes. Do not look at the dog's eyes or approach until you have more trust. Then with this new calm equanimity, the animal may choose to engage. It is very important not to take it personally if an animal turns away from you. It simply means he or she is not feeling safe enough to connect. This is a very honest and valuable communication, a gift from the animal because he or she is telling you that you need to slow your pace of *Toward* and either be still or move *Away* slightly yourself.

Curving Towards Calmness

If you observe animals meeting each other and interacting, you will see a flow of *Towards & Away* as a form of communication. You might see a slight head turning away, averting eyes, in a polite greeting that signals *I'm good, you're good, all is good.* When two dogs are meeting each other and they use these slight head turns, they are reassuring each other that all is well. You will also see a lot of curving movements, like circling and sniffing front and back. These slow, respectful movements reassure each other that they have friendly intentions and desire a calm connection.

When you are interacting with your own dog when you are a bit stressed, your dog may respond with ambiguous body language. For example, she may move away from you or show some curving motions as you approach with a leash as if to say *Okay, going out is good, but I want YOU to be calm.* When I have too much energy about leaving the house, Sophia will literally curve away from me, which is a reminder that I need to breathe and get calmer. Then she is happy to sit for her leash.

It is important not to misinterpret her action of fiddling around and moving away as disobedience or stubbornness. It is a sign that I am too amped up and need to get centered.

Humans – *Towards & Away*

There's a proverb: "When a man says he loves you, watch his feet." Regardless of the nice words, pay attention to whether he is coming closer or moving away. Words can lie, but body language is a more reliable indicator of how a person is feeling (except for people trained in the art of deception). Becoming an astute observer of how the body communicates the truth will help you better understand people and animals.

In human relationships, *Towards & Away* is a tremendously valuable skill because it leads to more balance in your life. We all have times and moods when we desire to move towards another. And there are other times when we need some away—or maybe even *a lot* of away. Understanding this in yourself will help you establish healthy boundaries. Understanding it in another person will help you not to take it personally when their moods, actions, or words are designed to create distance. Understanding the language of *Towards & Away* leads to more wisdom in all interactions between beings.

Begin to notice in your everyday interactions with people their subtle (or not-so-subtle) indicators of *Towards & Away*. People may not walk away in the middle of your sentence as that horse did to the *New York Times* reporter, but there will be other slight or less obvious indicators to which you can become attuned.

Are their words making a promise while their body is looking away, fidgeting, turning away slightly, or taking a step back? Get good at observing signals of *Towards & Away* in people and animals, and you will save yourself a lot of disappointment in the future.

And with yourself, are you agreeing to do something you really don't want to do? Notice if this internal conflict causes a body sensation or tension. Does a part of you want to retreat or avoid the commitment you just agreed to? Listen and be honest with yourself about how your body feels. Not listening to your true sensations is disempowering as you lose touch with your true needs. Awareness will help you to feel your power coming back as you stay true to yourself and your true impulses. By honoring your personal *Towards & Away* guidance system, you will have a smoother ride in life.

Journal Reflections on *Towards & Away*:

1) How do you feel your connection to awareness of your *Towards & Away* impulses are doing? Do you feel it is working and clear and its messages understandable? Do you feel you need to tune up your *Towards & Away* connection?

2) How could your *Towards & Away* Guidance System help you make better decisions? In what area of your life is this important to you?

3) What were some of the factors that caused you to feel separated from your true instincts about *Towards & Away*?

4) What are some of the ways that you observe healthy *Towards & Away* behavior in the animals who share your life?

5) Are you ready to get your *Towards & Away* system back online? Are you ready to listen to your inner guidance?

Re-Minder: I choose to move toward—
and I choose to move away.

Genie and Nathan, an Air Force veteran and HAC co-founder,
getting ready to do a session with Velvet. We wait for the horse
to choose to come towards us to let us know she is ready.

Principle #22

SHAKING WISDOM

How Animals *Let It Go*

In our worldview, First Creation is still present,
always ready to breathe its shaking
and changing into the stuck world of language.

Hearts of the Spears, Kalahari Bushman

Overview

In the wild, when a prey animal has been chased by a predator and escapes, one of the first things they do when the coast is clear is "shake it off." This looks similar to a dog shaking off the water after a bath, but this type of shaking does more than just dry off the fur. These animals are shaking off the interior cascade of stress chemistry of adrenalin and cortisol. Literally, they are helping to dissipate this energy through their body by shaking it out. This keeps it from becoming "stuck energy," which has long-term effects. Humans could greatly benefit from this wise practice as stress is not just in the head, but it is also in the body's chemistry.

Street Dog Shelter

In Costa Rica, a rescue dog sanctuary, Territorio de Zaguates, creates shelter for abandoned and homeless street dogs. Situated on two hundred acres, the huge-hearted owners planned to shelter 200 dogs, but so many people begged them to take suffering homeless dogs off the street that they ended up with 1,200. While their financial situation is precarious, as they endure only by donations, many elements of their operation work well.

They certainly didn't anticipate this challenge but have managed, and the result is that 1,200 dogs live, sleep, eat, and play together—with minimal fights and upsets. These dogs live a free-range lifestyle simply because there is no possibility of keeping that many dogs in cages. The staff knows how important daily exercise is for the dogs: "If they don't move, they get crazy."

Every day, several hundred dogs follow the humans and go for a run—off leash, of course. It is amazing to see the power of the pack as large and small, they race with joy.

Shake it Off!

The wisdom of shaking as a tool for healing is one of the great gifts that animals give to humans. Have you noticed your dog do a quick shake, or three very fast little shakes after a minor or stressful event? Animals wisely use the self-soothing technique of shaking to dissipate the cascade of stress chemistry, regain their emotional equilibrium, and reset their circuits.

Maybe you have also noticed when your dog is bursting with happiness, perhaps in anticipation of a treat or when you first come home, that they do this little tippy-tap dance with their front feet as if they can barely contain their excitement? Their joy must be expressed physically. And such joy is contagious!

Essentially, animals experience, express, process, and communicate emotions through physical movement and expression. One way they express and release minor stress is through shaking. And the wisdom of moving stress out of the body through shaking is a natural mental and physical healing method that we humans could benefit from practicing.

Many indigenous cultures recognize the beneficial and healing power of shaking. In Indonesia, Ratu Bagus has an ashram where he presents the practice of shaking as a form of healing meditation, which he calls Bio-Energy Meditation. A friend of mine, Richard Schiffman, a freelance reporter for the *New York Times* and a long-time meditator, said that studying with Ratu Bagus not only deepened his spiritual awareness but led to a greater sense of physical and mental well-being. Richard now hosts a shaking group in his New York City skyrise apartment every Saturday morning to energetic music such as Bhangra, Celtic, and meditative drum rhythms. Whenever I was back in New York City, I would go to these sessions, and I always felt better afterward than when I walked in the door.

NASA astronauts use shaking technology to improve their cardiac health and bone density after a mission, which helps their bodies readjust to Earth's gravity. I have tried their vibration platform, which is like the human equivalent of the paint shaker in the hardware store. It is a bit too intense for my taste, but I do have a consumer-level "shaker" vibration plate that I stand on every now and then. It is very good for stress relief, circulation, and a full body tune-up. But mostly, I prefer gently shaking on my own steam and rhythm, usually in the morning. I frequently shake gently to music for about twenty minutes, making natural sounds as I exhale. It does what you hope coffee will do, but better, and this starts my day on a much better track.

In Act Resilient, we shake as a warm-up or cool-down from an intense play session. We shake to a favorite song, allowing our silly, breathy noises to accompany us. It makes people laugh, and it moves stuck energy. After people get over the hurdle of looking goofy, shaking is one of the students' favorite quick tools for stress-busting.

I always remind students not to shake in public because some people get very nervous when they see others shake! (I got in trouble when hospitalized soldiers were horsing around and started shaking in the elevator at Tripler Army Medical Center.) As we observe in our animal friends, shaking is one of the best and most natural methods for releasing stuck trauma in the body.

Shaking is nothing new! Many cultures practice variations of shaking for spiritual connection and healing. Bradford Keeney says, in his book *Shaking Medicine – The Healing Power of Ecstatic Movement*, "Shaking bodies and vibrating touch have been known throughout the world as powerful forms of healing expression. Yet the value of trembling, vibrating, quaking, and shaking as a medicine for the body, mind, and Soul has been all but lost in recent times, particularly among the more literate and technologically developed cultures." He says the purpose of his book is "to reintroduce the oldest medicine on Earth—the shake."

The Alternation of Arousal and Relaxation

I was excited to learn that Keeney supports another method we use in Act Resilient, the alternation of arousal and relaxation for healing. We alternate energized movement with stillness or relaxation because I have observed that alternation of brain states is a key strategy in restoring neuroplasticity and undoing the effects of a traumatized brain on "lockdown." It helps shake out the cobwebs, the habitual thinking, and the mental stuckness of trauma.

When we want to provide the best quality of life for animals in captivity in shelters or other situations, as well as for the animals who share our lives, we want to understand the power of alternation of joyful movement (stimulation) and calming relaxation. It is as important for animals as it is for humans and is thoroughly discussed by Keeney. He has studied this oldest form of healing—which perhaps our ancestors "discovered" by observing animals—and has documented the power of movement as a core practice for spiritual, physical, and mental well-being. His investigations included the Shakers and Quakers of New England, Native Americans, as well as shaking medicine practices in Japan, India, the Caribbean, the Kalahari Desert, and elsewhere.

Indigenous wisdom knows that 'to live is to move.'
To awaken from a deep slumber means our bones will be
rattled, and we'll be shaken to the core. In this invitation
into very ancient medicine, we hear the voices of the elders
issuing a timely wake-up call.

Malidoma Some

Dr. Herbert Benson of Harvard Medical School coined the term "relaxation response" and did much to educate modern people about the power of stillness. So much benefit has come from Westerners adopting meditation. But there is more! Keeney adds to the relaxation response its essential opposite: "What we await is the other half of the picture. The complement to relaxation is arousal. This side of the healing process can be called the "arousal response." What we are ready to learn is that heightened arousal, whether through wild dancing, spontaneous jumping up and down, or body shaking, is as valuable a healing and transformational practice as sitting quietly in a lotus position… Heightened arousal serves to reset the organization of our whole being."

Shaking creates a specific kind of healing movement. Just like with a cat's purr, we may not fully understand why it is so effective, but we know it's good! As mentioned in Principle #8, "The Healing Power of Play," movement and play often go together. Watch an animal playing, and you will see a lot of body motion. This stimulates the body *and* the brain and is essential for animals and humans. Ask any young child, and they will agree! Or any dog with the zoomies—they gotta move!

Many early missionaries who met cultures where shaking was a common part of their healing or celebratory practice were confused, disturbed, and frightened by this kind of trance movement. Assuming it was sexual, primitive, or evil in some way, they wanted to stamp it out. But they couldn't stamp out the joyful nature of this very physical movement. Despite attempts to suppress it by dominant cultures, shaking has survived.

Perhaps we should look to the guidance of the Kalahari Bushman, who have been shaking for as long as they have walked the earth. Keeney talks about the joy in the lives of these Kalahari Bushman "whose prayer and practice is a shake and a song, whose conversations mention few outside spiritual ideas, and whose entire material possessions can be carried on his or her back."

Observing when your animal does a quick shake will give you insight as to what might be stressing him or her. This is one way we can better understand what is going on inside them. Shaking is a healthy self-care practice for the animal, and it can be for humans as well. It is time to invite shaking back into ordinary lives. More and more individuals are recognizing the power of this kind of movement for well-being. It is certainly time to release the old taboos against this type of free movement that has no leader, no choreography, and no price tag. Just the pure joy of expression and connection with the All That Is. Even if we can't spend decades learning from Shamans, we can introduce the beneficial experience of shaking into our world. This freedom is healing. Keeney describes this ecstatic movement that can lead to sacred experiences when he states, "Shaking and the holiest of experiences are inseparable. In these realms of experience, we are attuned, calibrated, freshly inspired, converted to a mission, infused with spirit, and reborn anew. It is that which we most deeply seek when we feel that something is missing in our lives."

Yet, some people have a fear of letting go using this freestyle movement. Something as pure and primal as this kind of free movement threatens our concepts of being "civilized." But since dogs, cats, hummingbirds, bears, and so many animals do it, we can't avoid its wisdom.

Keeney points out, "Most people's worst fear is losing control—of their circumstances, of their emotions, and especially of their bodies. Yet in order to experience deep healing, we must surrender control."

This is just one reason why the use of therapeutic shaking is so beneficial in healing from trauma. Just watch the animals. They will show you.

Movement Is Life

The key idea here is that movement is life—and movement is healing. This is just one reason why it is so tragic to see pigs, who are as smart as dogs, on industrial farms, raised in crates, barely able to move, spending their lives on concrete floors. Unless they are injured and unable to move freely, animals and human animals need to move to stay well. Any wellness program for people and animals needs to include a lifestyle of appropriate moving and contact with the earth itself.

For humans, shaking is an all-natural process that helps bring many of the body's systems into balance. And you don't need any special equipment, although it is nice to have music to help induce the full-body experience. Some people find that shaking can lead to a mesmerizing trancelike state which promotes mental and emotional healing. You can do it alone or, even better, in a group. You don't need a teacher, and it is free. How is that for good?

Dr. Peter Levine developed somatic experiencing, a body-based therapy, which sometimes includes shaking, as a way to unlock trauma. In his groundbreaking book *Waking the Tiger: Healing Trauma*, he sees this as a pivotal method to release stress and trauma and the grip of the fight/flight/freeze response.

Shaking Frees Up Energy

Students in Act Resilient regularly reported that shaking helped their "stuck emotions to unwind." This was done without words, without having to recall specific memories, or even to be aware of what specific issues were being released. It was a gentle process of releasing without the need to relive anything that you wouldn't want to experience more than once.

When we work with the Trust Technique, we often see twitching and involuntary body movements, such as in REM sleep when the animal gets into a deeper healing state. This is a sign to us that the animal is letting go of past trauma. We often see significant change after a session that has this depth and unconscious movement.

Shaking at the Shelter

Of course, there are many reasons for shaking. An animal might shake from the cold, for example, but we often see animals in the shelter shaking from fear. When potential adopters see the shaking, they often quickly walk by to the next kennel. Perhaps they don't want to cause the animal any more fear, or perhaps it is too unsettling to see an animal shivering and cowering. It really triggers something deep within us to see an animal shaking from fear. When I work with a shelter animal who is shaking, the first thing I want to do is make sure I don't make any assumptions about the shaking. It is not something I need to stop. But I can make an offer.

If the animal is shaking from stress or fear but shows they want contact by moving toward me, then I would meet that animal with touch, perhaps holding or cuddling, if the dog responds to that offer. These dogs immediately stop shaking with loving contact.

But I start from the premise that the shaking is serving a function. First, it is a communication to let me know the animal may be feeling a high level of unsafety, distrust, or fear. I must honor that before I move any further. Also, there is a difference between an animal who is shaking for hours or days, as some do when they first arrive at the shelter, and a brief shake to quickly release stress chemistry. Usually, the dogs that want comfort will stop chronic shaking after one or two sessions of healing connection and the Trust Technique or energy work.

Healing Vibrating Touch

There is another level of shaking that involves vibrating healing touch. For those students in the Human-Animal Connection who want to learn this technique, we encourage a variety of soothing touches such as rocking, subtle shaking, and other methods when we work with animals who show they desire this more motion-inducing kind of contact. We start with the lowest level of touch, such as light pressure or tapping, and proceed to these more active styles with animals who are responding to and expressing a desire to be given this lovely treatment.

Shaking is the skeleton key that opens the doors to the wild.

Bradford Keeney

Keeney observed vibrating touch in Shaman shakers in a state of pure divine union, as they used this specific kind of contact for healing others. He was privileged to learn this work over the course of a decade from the Kalahari Bushmen and writes about it in his book.

"The world's oldest living culture, that of the Kalahari Bushmen, most likely holds the oldest healing practice on Earth. It is based upon a disciplined way of arousing and orchestrating ecstatic body experience. Bushman shamans are masters of spirited expression. They know how to initiate body shaking and use it as a medicine when they touch others. Arguably more than any other culture, the Bushman cultures have explored and fine-tuned this kind of healing."

Well, even if you are not ready to spend a decade or more learning this ancient healing art, even just a few minutes a day of shaking in your own home can bring many benefits. You can do it in any way that feels good to your body. It can be slow or fast, subtle or big, energized or soothing, rhythmic or nonrhythmic. Shake off your troubles! If it feels good, you are doing it right. Find some music that makes you feel like shaking and go for it! My dog Sophia gets so excited when I do my morning shaking session that she sometimes gets the zoomies. We shake and zoomie together.

Shake it off, baby!

"It is now time for you to shake everything that is essential about and within you. As you tremble and shake, imagine that all your ideas, feelings, hopes, and aspirations, along with their opposites, are being shaken. A great mixing and stirring, and reorganization are being set in motion. You

may begin to wonder whether everything that you have learned and everything that has happened to you has simply happened so that someday you'd have something to shake up. You cannot become who you were born to be unless all the parts are shaken into place. Consider believing this and acting upon it."

Bradford Keeney

Journal Reflections on Shaking Wisdom:

1) How do *you* feel about shaking? Does it excite you or scare you to think about it? Although several religions practice shaking, there are still old taboos against this form of physical freedom. Cultures that practice it have been very harshly criticized by "civilized" outsiders. Many missionaries were frightened because it looked too sexual to them, and they tried to forbid it.

2) How do you feel about letting in some of this natural and primal energy in your modern life? Given that you can practice in the privacy of your own home or in the presence of others who are open to exploring this sacred energy, would you give it a go?

3) Do you have an intuitive curiosity or understanding that shaking could be good for you? Be gentle with yourself if this feels outside your comfort zone.

4) What music would you use? Find a private place where you don't have to worry about how you look. If you are first starting, maybe just do it for a few minutes, then increase the duration. You can start with just shaking your hands or one leg. Let the motion involve your whole body. Keep your knees soft, let your arms move, and flop—let everything shake. At first, you will just choose to start by using your mind to turn on the *permission-to-shake switch*. But as you surrender to it, you will feel that the force is SHAKING YOU. That's when it really gets good, when *you allow the shaking force to move you.*

5) Are you ready to add sound? Let a natural sound emerge from your breath and body movements. You don't have to "make" sound, just allow sound to emerge.

Re-Minder: I can shake it off.

Ti'hara and Sweetfire, two rescue horses I worked with, showed me the power of movement as a valuable component of the healing strategy.

THE ORDER OF THE SENSES
Leading with the Nose

I go to nature to be soothed and healed,
and to have my senses put in order.

John Burroughs

Overview

All of our senses work together, and each contributes to a balance of how we receive stimuli from the world. When the senses are in balance, this leads to feeling calm and safe. However, when one sense is working overtime, dominating and compensating for the others, it leads to what I call having the senses "out of order." In this case, one sense is overstimulated, which can cause stress levels to rise, which can have a negative impact on immunity and psychological well-being. This weakens the balancing, neutralizing effect of having all the senses working together and can cause more stress to the animal's system keeping him or her in a heightened state of arousal.

Simply, when one sense is working too hard, at the expense of the balance of the others, it creates overarousal. This creates more energy and intensity in one sense which leads to overstimulation at the slightest trigger.

313

When working with frightened or shy dogs in the shelter, I observe that some dogs are very sensitive to sound and easily become agitated and overstimulated by what they are hearing. Some are overstimulated by sights, and any movement outside their kennel can set off a fit of barking.

More secure and balanced dogs rely on their noses and their sense of smell to get the first sensory data—and then attune to secondary data from their eyes and ears. When dogs lead with their noses, they are calmer, less stressed, and better able to cope with the stressful shelter environment.

Stop and Sniff

I had one client who was a very experienced owner of several Basenjis. But walks were always stressful because he had been taught by a trainer who told him that he needed to dominate his dogs on the walk and not allow them to stop and sniff. Once I explained to him how important sniffing is to a dog, how it resets their nervous system, and how beneficial these "stop and sniff" moments are to a dog's mental and emotional well-being, he realized he didn't need to always be in "total control" on the walk. Sometimes it was good to let his dogs set the pace, to stop and investigate the scents along the way. He started to relax and let his dogs have this personal time, and this took all the stress out of walks for both of them. He felt much more in sync with his dogs now that the struggle to "keep walking" was over. "Letting them sniff brought the joy back to walking together," he said.

The Value of Stop and Sniff

Most people who live with dogs know how important physical exercise is to their well-being. Without the right amount of physical exercise, a dog's physical and mental health declines, the dog might become listless and depressed, and "bad" behaviors may emerge. It is essential that dogs move their bodies and get some exercise every day; some dogs need an extensive physical workout daily.

A dog's senses also need daily exercise. Yes, a dog's nose needs daily exercise; sniffing is one way a dog resets their nervous system. Many of my clients are surprised to learn that their dog's desire to stop and sniff during a walk is not bad behavior or defiance because it is a dog's way of orienting themself through "nose intelligence."

When I invite clients to allow their dogs some "sniff time" during their walks—instead of always tugging on their leashes to get them going again—many behavioral issues begin to dissipate. This is just one step, of course, but it is a pivotal one when the human responds positively: *Oh, we're stopping to sniff. How nice.* Instead of viewing their dog's behavior as difficult or annoying, they recognize the dog is doing something that is essential to their well-being. This "stop-and-sniff" routine is a good thing!

Of course, there are times when I am out with Sophia when I have my own agenda or need to get to the car or whatever crazy human stuff is driving me. But I try to make sure that during at least one of our daily walks, she gets some time to lead the pace and sniff to her heart's content. I recognize this as my moment too, when I need to pause and "smell the roses" myself. Sniff-time is the right time to take a deep breath, look around, and really see what is in front of me. If Sophia needs a moment of sensory presence, so do I. Letting her lead at least part of the walk is what humane partnership is all about.

Sniffing brings the animal's entire focus to what is in front of their nose. It puts the sense of smell first, which creates the healthiest order for their other senses. Just as humans can benefit from conscious focusing, which organizes the brain and brings us into present time, when your dog stops to sniff, it is a good invitation to get into agreement and alignment with this purposeful moment. Inhale deeply, look around, and focus on the one thing your eyes settle on. Focus your visual sense (or another preferred sense), bringing you into the here and now. A few deep breaths, and you and your dog are reset and ready to keep walking.

Making room for stop-and-sniff takes a lot of conflict out of walks, especially if the human thinks that the only value is when you are moving. Exercise and movement, as we said in Principle #22, are vital for well-being, but the dog understands the importance of the rhythm of alternation, too. So, stop, sniff, and reset.

Sniffing "pee-mail" also allows a dog to gather data about others in the neighborhood. All animals get a tremendous amount of data from sniffing the eliminations of other animals. According to Janet Jones, PhD, author of *Horse Brain, Human Brain: The Neuroscience of Horsemanship*, "Horses learn from manure and can determine a lot of information about even an unfamiliar horse such as the horse's sex, state of health, social rank, how long ago the horse left the area. They can determine if it is a mare and if she is in season and can follow her scent trail leading to find her. If a horse is sniffing a familiar horse's manure, they can additionally determine this information: which horse it is, the horse's state of mind or aggression levels, how calm or frightened they are feeling at the time of manuring."

Sharing the Lead

I know many trainers drill into people the idea that they must be in total control on the walk, that they must dominate the dog, and never let him or her lead. This approach leads to a lot of frustration and power struggles that leave humans feeling defeated and dogs feeling overcontrolled. I consider this domination approach an old-fashioned belief that has caused much damage to the human-animal connection.

What works best is a partnership; sometimes, you will be leading, and sometimes, you'll give the dog a chance to set the pace and the rhythm and decide when to stop and sniff. There are certainly times when I want Sophia to walk in the heel position. But there are other times when I enjoy following her lead. With this balance, walks are relaxing for both of us.

The Nose Leads the Way

My working theory after years of observation is that many shelter dogs have their senses out of order. In that environment, because they are subject to so much visual, auditory, and olfactory "continuous noise," it overstimulates their nervous system. Like an overloaded circuit breaker, their noses get blown out, or at least over-amped, so the brain tries to protect the nose, which is no longer in first position for sensory receiving.

At the HAC, we have learned how to quickly intervene and help these dogs relax and get "nose-focused" to help them get reoriented to the pleasure of sniffing. A hot dog or another yummy treat in front of their nose is compelling enough to gather and focus the olfactory center of the brain. If their brain is fully focused on smelling something desirable, they calm down quickly. (A dog's olfactory receptors are around forty times more effective than a human's, and this is a powerful way to regain balance in the brain and calm their mind.) As the dog devotes more of their energy to focused and pleasurable sniffing, less energy is directed toward distracting sounds and excess visual stimuli. In the shelter environment with overstimulated dogs, getting the senses in order reduces reactivity to every movement and noise outside their kennel. It is not good for their immune systems to remain in a heightened state of arousal, which makes them more susceptible to kennel cough and other bugs that naturally happen in shelters. This is why we need to get these dogs back to leading with their noses.

To help a dog who has their senses out of order, I increase stimulation from an enticing scent. At the same time, I reduce stimulation from the other senses by reducing my motion, eliminating eye contact, and either not talking or only speaking in a soothing voice. This helps to keep the dog's senses focused on the scent of the treat. I might get low to the ground and remain very still. Using stillness is a foundational principle in the Trust Technique. I sit to the side of the animal, which is more polite than sitting head-on, and remain as still as a statue and breathe slowly and evenly. Soon they become interested in me. Because I'm calm, I am irresistible, and they will want to approach and sniff!

It is very exciting when a shy dog *chooses to approach.* It is the first sign that they want to connect. Of course, I am armed with stinky treats like hot-dog slices and cheese or chicken. When I open my treat pouch, their nose is right with me, following my hand. I offer a treat, tossing it at the dog's feet if they are very shy. Soon, they are eating out of my hand. (Read the step-by-step details of this process on my blog "Smitty the Pitty.")

Shut-down dogs will not likely take treats right away. They will need the Trust Technique and other healing methods before they will be ready to engage.

It is important when working with shut-down dogs not to take it personally if they ignore you or cower from you at first. It is not about you! It simply means that their stress level is too high to engage right away. These dogs take a lot of patience, but all the shut-down dogs I have worked with made significant progress and were adopted.

For those dogs who are willing to give me the "sniff-over," I know we can make rapid progress in one visit. From sniffing to hand-feeding tiny morsels (so I can repeat this many times), we are building a calm connection and a foundation of trust. From there, I devise a plan to help this animal go to the next step. Once the animal feels calm enough to thoroughly sniff me, I know I have been accepted, and we have crossed the threshold. The healing journey has begun.

To Change a Dog's Emotional State – Go to the Nose

Dogs experience the world through their sensitive noses, and input from the sense of smell dominates their brain. By intelligently eliciting their sense of smell, we can use this pathway to teach, create changes, and improve emotional states in dogs. We can comfort them when they are stressed, engage them when they are distracted, and help them overcome fears by creating new associations. As Victoria Stillwell says, "A dog's sense of smell is so closely linked to their emotional memory, a dog's emotional experience is likely to be even greater than ours…This is one reason why I use food, not just to motivate dogs to learn, but to change the way they feel. Even if your dog is stressed or anxious, a positive emotional experience can occur with the anticipation of and presentation of food with its enticing, evocative aroma."

Prozac Dog-Nation

Dogs who share lives with loving humans get many wonderful benefits. However, on the negative side of the ledger, many share our sedentary lifestyle and eat highly processed dog foods. Some are confined to crates all day or all night, and unfortunately, some absorb the mental stress that plagues modern human life. By living with us in our world, they increase their share of fear, anxiety, and stress.

As a result of having to live by our rules and routines, many animals develop behavioral and physical problems. One of the more common reasons dogs are surrendered to shelters and sometimes euthanized is because humans do not know how to handle unwanted behaviors. Veterinarians usually have little or no education on the training methods we describe in this book. Further, they may underestimate the connection between human stress and an animal's stress. If they do have a sense of it, they don't know how to help. So, out comes the prescription pad. While some dogs can greatly benefit from medication for behavior issues, and it is a better alternative than being surrendered to a shelter, I fear we have gone too far in that direction. One study discovered that 83 percent of small animal veterinarians have prescribed dog formulations of Prozac and Xanax and other mood-altering medications for pet owners who are at their wit's end.

Are there other more holistic methods that could help? In a *Washington Post* article, Nathanial Morris writes, "Whether pets really need these mood-altering drugs remains controversial. Nicholas Dodman, a professor emeritus at the Tufts University Cummings School of Veterinary Medicine and author of the book *Pets on the Couch*, has written that animals experience behavioral disorders similar to those of humans, and pets may need medications to alleviate their suffering. Treating these conditions, Dodman says, might also prevent some pets with behavioral issues from being sent to shelters or from being euthanized. Thus, there are situations where this treatment may be a good choice.

"On the basis of a 2017 national survey, the market research firm Packaged Facts concluded that eight percent of dog owners and six percent of cat owners gave medications to their pets for anxiety, calming, or mood purposes within the previous twelve months. Because about 60 million American households own dogs and 47 million own cats, according to one estimate, these figures (83% of veterinarians prescribing mood-altering pills) suggest that millions of animals in the United States are taking medications for behavioral issues."

In some shelters, a huge percentage of dogs are medicated for everything from high energy, fear, anxiety, and aggression. And in zoos, many animals are on mood medications.

Nathanial Morris's article in the *Washington Post*, "Does Your Pooch Really Need Prozac?" writes, "Giving these kinds of drugs to pets isn't risk-free. Just as with humans, psychiatric medications for pets can carry plenty of side effects, including gastrointestinal upset, weight changes, and irregular heartbeats."

Pill-Popping Pets was the headline of a *New York Times* article by James Vlahos, who writes, "The practice of prescribing medications designed for humans to animals has grown substantially over the past decade and a half, and pharmaceutical companies have recently begun experimenting with a more direct strategy: marketing behavior-modification and 'lifestyle' drugs specifically for pets.

"America's animals, it seems, have very American health problems. More than 20 percent of our dogs are overweight; Pfizer's Slentrol was approved by the F.D.A. (Food and Drug Administration) last year as the country's first canine anti-obesity medication. Dogs live 13 years on average, considerably longer than they did in the past; Pfizer's Anipryl treats cognitive dysfunction so that absentminded pets can remember the location of their supper bowl or doggy door. For lonely dogs with separation anxiety, last year Eli Lilly brought to market its own drug, Reconcile. The only difference between it and Prozac is that Reconcile is chewable and tastes like beef."

While some behavior modification medications do some dogs a lot of good—and, importantly, allow them to continue to live with their families—it can't be the ONLY method we offer to our best friends.

One alternative to the risks of potentially overmedicating domestic animals is to recognize the needs of dogs to express their natural behaviors. We need to understand how their sense of smell needs positive stimulation as well as how to "turn down the noise" on other senses that have been overactivated. While we are not against the right medication for some dogs, our mission at The Human-Animal Connection is to teach people there are also natural alternatives that are based on the dog's true desires and needs.

The Nose is the Animal's Path to the Vagus Nerve

In the work of Peter Levine and somatic experiencing (SE) to reverse trauma in humans, much attention is paid to both how the body stores emotional pain as well as how the body can be used to release pain. There are gentle, natural ways to create changes in how the nervous system functions, which leads to changes in behavior. One of the most exciting developments in understanding how to resolve trauma is the latest scientific understanding of the importance of the vagus nerve.

According to Dr. Navaz Habib, author of *Activate Your Vagus Nerve*, "The vagus nerve system is the longest nerve in the body. The neurons that form the vagus nerve begin in the brainstem at the medulla oblongata. It senses, processes, and regulates the vast majority of the automatic functions of the body. It sends information to and from the brain to all the other systems in the body."

The vagus nerve system is the antidote to stress because it triggers the parasympathetic nervous system, which is the opposite of the fight/flight/freeze response.

Why is it called the vagus nerve? Vagus is derived from a Latin word meaning "wandering, rambling, strolling," which kind of reminds me of the value of letting your dog lead, at least some of the time. This strolling is like a "vagus reset." When you are not directing the entire walk, you get to experience being led by Animal Wisdom—and Vagus Wisdom. When the dog appears to want to wander, stroll, sniff and stop, this is your opportunity to feel the wonderful vague and uncertain nature of the vagus nerve. *Strolling resets our nervous system too.*

Resource Orientation

Healthy animals experience balanced senses. People can benefit by applying some animal-brain balancing methods in our daily life, too. The following simple exercise will stimulate your vagus nerve, help you reset your nervous system, and lead to a more harmonious state of mind.

In somatic experiencing, this exercise is called "Resource Orientation." Using the eyes and our visual sense in a deliberate way can have as much benefit to people as a dog using their nose to become oriented or grounded. Resource orientation is an easy method of focusing carefully on one visual element at a time and then consciously redirecting your attention in the opposite direction. This simple technique, combined with single-point focus, reduces spinning thoughts.

To begin, turn your head slowly to the left. The motion of slowly turning the head activates the vagus nerve. Focus your eyes on a single object. Really see it. Then turn your head slowly to the right and find something new and appealing to focus on. What calls to you? Really look at this object. If you enjoy what you are seeing, this also adds beneficial hormonal balancing qualities. This intentional focus brings your senses into a coherent state or order. Then turn to the left again and find something else to really let in visually. This turning of the head three times, coupled with the laser focus on something visually pleasing, becomes a resource or a reset that you can use to calm your nervous system.

Watch how animals use head turns as a way to orient and settle. When a dog is let into a new space, such as a new yard or room, one of the first things he or she will do if she has the freedom to do so is to explore the perimeter. The dog will literally case the outer boundary, sniffing, walking, observing. This is a very healthy process and should not be interrupted. It is the dog's way of using resource orienting to feel like, "Okay, that's what this place is all about. I can relax." If you allow your dog to have this moment of private exploration, he or she will feel much calmer in a new space. This is one way a dog resets and gets ready for something new without stress.

> *"One of the most neglected areas in the philosophy of perception concerns animal senses. It is surprising how many philosophers write about perception in the apparent belief that humans are the only perceivers in the world. Human senses evolved through the natural process as other animal senses, so there is no reason to regard human senses as special, or better than other animal senses."*
>
> *Rochelle Forrester*

Sense Perception and Reality: A Theory of Perceptual Relativity, Quantum Mechanics, and the Observer Dependent Universe.

Journal Reflections on the Order of the Senses:

1) Are your senses out of order? Do you get stressed by too much noise? Too many fast-changing visuals? Too much touch or tactile contact? Too many scents or varied tastes?

2) You may find that one sense quickly calms you down more than the others. Focusing on that sense will bring you into immediate balance. Other senses may become easily overloaded and cause you to feel spacey, irritated, or fatigued. Which sense do you need to decrease when you are feeling overstimulated? For example, if you discover too much visual information can tax your nervous system, spending even ten minutes in a dark room or with an eye mask will help you reset. If your auditory system gets overloaded with too much volume or too many competing sounds, wearing ear plugs or listening to your own music on headphones will soothe you quickly. Finding which senses to increase or decrease when you feel stressed will allow you to better manage your own brain.

3) Have you noticed that your dog is triggered by sights or sounds? Even the reminder of your scent can help to calm the dog down. Let them sniff your hand or put your hand under your armpit and then let them smell your hand. Get them using their nose, and they will start to settle down.

4) While each human and nonhuman animal is an individual, you can learn to recognize the patterns that both trigger stress and relieve it—through redirecting the senses. What sensory patterns do you notice?

5) Can you imagine having a more harmonious balance of your senses? What would that be like for you? How can you make that more a part of your daily life?

Re-Minder: My senses will lead me where I need to be.

Arlene and Peter learned to let Benny lead part of the walk, to stop and sniff, and walks became joyful again.

Principle #24

CHANGING YOUR RELATIONSHIP TO TIME

The Wisdom of Patience

Nature does not hurry,
yet everything is accomplished.

Lao Tzu

Overview

From work with Koko, the gorilla who was taught sign language, we know she has memories of the past as well as a sense of future time. Fortunately, for most animals, their mental resources are not hijacked by excessive dwelling on the past or the future. This seems to be a very human problem.

Animals are blessed with the *wisdom of ease* that comes from a predominant focus on and experience of the present moment. Although they can anticipate pleasure, they spend less time ruminating about the past. Generally, the present moment fills their senses. Being filled with the Now leads to a sense of calm and presence. Fortunately for humans, presence is a learnable skill, and one way to do this is to understand your own relationship to time.

Enjoying Time

Olivia was a gorgeous twelve-year-old white Great Pyrenees who came to the shelter after her owner died suddenly. She had been in medical holding for two months before she was put up for adoption. Olivia had a very calm and friendly nature, but at her age, her adoption prospects were slim. Still, she was a volunteer favorite; you couldn't walk by without saying hello, and she would look up and give a doggie smile. She walked very slowly, but the medical team said this was age, not injury.

When I first met her, I loved her immediately. I spent time brushing her thick coat, and we had a nice chat. I asked her why she walked slowly (I wanted to make sure for myself that she was not in pain). She replied, "I walk slowly so I can enjoy my time."

All the Time in the World

How do you relate to time? Do you view time as your friend or your enemy? Are you racing against the dripping sands of time? Do you feel like you are running out of time—or do you feel like you have all the time in the world? Our thoughts and thinking habits affect our relationship to time. For most of human history, our sense of time was tied to the sunrise, the moonrise, and the seasons. We didn't have the concept of minutes or seconds, and it wasn't until the fourteenth century that we had mechanical clocks. According to Guinness World Records, the first wristwatch appeared in 1868, and the race against time was on!

In Act Resilient, we talk about the value of becoming more flexible in our relationship with time. If you always feel like you "have no time," you will feel a lot of stress and dissatisfaction in your life because, in your mind, there is a "finish line" that you never cross. With that mindset, even minor daily tasks will feel like an interruption. Walking the dog will feel like an obligatory experience instead of an opportunity to accompany a Buddha on a stroll.

As I explain to our HAC students, there are different ways of relating to time. Each way serves a purpose, so one is not better than the other. But each mode has its optimal value for certain aspects of your life. My names for these two styles are *Now Time* and *Linear Time*. (Read more about how changing your relationship to time helps in trauma recovery in my book, *The Act Resilient Method.*)

Let me explain the difference. If you are having a *Now Time* experience, you are *here* physically, mentally, and spiritually. Whatever is happening in this moment fills your awareness and your experience. You are neither sucked into the past nor dragged into an imagined future. You feel whole and present. There is a sense of not being divided, but instead, you feel united. One student described this practice: "For the first time since childhood I feel like I have all the time in the world." This experience of *Now Time* is the opposite of stress and struggle.

Babies are in *Now Time*. So are animals, which is one reason it is so lovely to be with them. They invite us into the rich fullness of their world.

Being in *Now Time* can be either relaxing or fully energized. These are the moments of creativity, exploration, adventure, peak performance, and epiphany. Doing anything you love will put you in *Now Time*. When you love what you are doing, all your senses are engaged, and you can simultaneously feel peaceful, grounded, and fully enraptured.

On the other side of the coin is *Linear Time*. In Linear Time, you have a sense of yourself as if on a timeline. You know exactly where you are, and you also have a full sense of what has come before and what will come after. You are fully aware of how long regular tasks take or how long it will take to get to the next location. If I ask a Linear Time person what time it is, even if they aren't wearing a watch and can't see a clock, they will know what time it is. Ask a *Now Time* person that same question, and they won't know. And it will surprise them when you tell them what time it is.

Animals Have a Sense of Time

Animals have a sense of time, but it is different from ours. They are much more skilled at being in the present moment, so we can be inspired by this state of grace. Their sense of time is tied to their bodily senses. Catherine Raven, PhD and biologist, wrote a book called *Fox and I*. She had a cabin in the Montana wilderness and a wild red fox would visit her every day at 4:15 p.m. She never touched him, but he would sit near her chair as she read to him. Even though her routines varied, he always knew when it was 4:15 and it was time to visit.

I have a friend who feeds wild deer every morning in his yard, which borders wildlands in California. He slices apples and carrots and brings them out to the deer. They have come to expect these treats at a specific time. If he is late getting started, they line up outside his kitchen window and look in, watching his every move. They know precisely when it is deer feeding time!

As discussed in Principle #2, the veery birds change the timing of their migration in anticipation of the severity of the upcoming hurricane season. While they have an instinctual sense of timing, they adjust their actions according to *future* weather conditions.

One reason animals' sense of time works differently from ours may be because their memory is more sensory based than analytical.

As we come to understand more about how animals store memory, we may understand more about how they relate to time.

Many studies have shown how birds and other animals plan ahead by storing food for the winter. The wonder is how they are able to remember where their food is hidden. For example, squirrels who bury hundreds of nuts can retrieve many of them months later. Researcher Pizza Ka Yee Chow demonstrated long-term memory in squirrels—and even quality control. The squirrels knew which nuts were the most nutritious and would be able to survive buried under months of snow.

She also observed a fascinating skill: squirrels have an awareness of other squirrels' *future* intentions. To thwart thievery of their food stores, sometimes they will meticulously rearrange leaves over disturbed soil to hide where they have buried their nuts. "Commonly, they also pretend to bury nuts when other squirrels are watching and then scurry off to a secret location where they actually hide their edible treasures." This indicates that their present time experience includes a sense of the future and the idea that voyeur squirrels might attempt to steal their nuts in the future.

Balancing Now Time and Linear Time

Now Time and *Linear Time* exist on a spectrum of experience. You can be a little bit of a *Now Time* person or totally in *Now Time*. However, some people function better in one time perception but not well in the other. For example, people in *Now Time* can literally "lose time" or at least their sense-perception of time. They can become so completely immersed in an experience of the moment that they forget a future time commitment or how long it will take to get to the next appointment. Linear people can become so obsessed with what is next and with their "to-do lists" that their ability to enjoy what is happening in the moment is diminished.

The ideal is to move flexibly between *Linear Time* and *Now Time* so that you can have a more balanced relationship with time. That way, if you are with someone and want to be present for them, you can choose to be in *Now Time.* Most of us have likely had the opposite experience, usually with a Linear Time person who is operating on a strict timeline. For example, when you are with a doctor or other professional who is required to be with you, you may sense that they are only "partly" with you. They are very focused on a specific goal, and once that is achieved, they leave mentally, even if they are still physically in the room with you.

On the other hand, if you have a friend who is a total Now Time person, you have probably been kept waiting (maybe more than once) as they "lost themselves in time." These differences in time styles can result in a lot of tension and conflict for both people.

Animals can sense if you are in *Now Time* when you are with them. They may also sense the stress when you are in *Linear Time* and only perfunctorily engaging with them while tossing out their dinner, but your mind has spun ahead to what is next on your busy schedule. That time when you are serving them dinner is an opportunity for you to say a blessing and to be fully present and in *Now Time.* Being present is good for them and for your own calmness.

Donkey Time

When my geologist friend, Margaret Winslow, adopted a large, white donkey named Caleb, she had no idea she was in the presence of a *Master of Now Time.* Margie now says that if you want to learn patience, get a donkey because donkeys do things in their own time. She wrote a delightful book called *Smart Ass – How a Donkey Challenged Me to Accept His True Nature & Rediscover My Own.*

She was struggling to get Caleb to do what she wanted. She enlisted some expert trainers, but despite their best efforts, Caleb was not about to be rushed. As Margie said to me, "Caleb did what he wanted 95 percent of the time, and 5 percent of the time he did what I wanted." In working with the trainers, she suffered much humiliation in the training ring, riding alongside aspiring teenage champions on pedigreed horses. They would ask her questions like, "How come you didn't get a real horse?"

At first it was a contest of wills with Caleb, but over time, Margie had a change of heart and mind. She came to understand that Caleb was not designed to fit the mold, and it was time to stop trying to get him to conform. Caleb responded to her new understanding, and the dynamic of their relationship changed. Finally, she accepted what he wanted all along. "As soon as I realized that he expected an equal partnership, mutual respect developed. From then on, we were able to work as a team. We attended horse and donkey shows. True to himself, sometimes Caleb behaved like a champ, putting the other contestants to shame. Other times he did exactly what he wanted. Life with Caleb was always about accepting the unexpected. Usually with hilarious results."

Donkey time is healing time. "Caleb puts all of the hustle and bustle of my life in perspective. All he wanted was love, closeness, understanding, friendship, and...carrots." Yes, Margie learned a lot about *Now Time* from Caleb, who was 100 percent true to his own desires.

A Flexible Relationship with Time

One of the secrets to a happy life is to have a flexible relationship with time. It starts with recognizing what your natural time style is. You might find that your *natural time style* is more linear. (If you were part of the military or other structured system, you have been trained to always be on linear time.) The military could not function without strict, universal adherence to *Linear Time*.

Now Time folks who struggle with *Linear Time* are continually late, always running behind. It is as if they have "lost" time. If you are a *Now Time* person having to function in a *Linear Time* structure, you will often find yourself out of sync and suffer from either overt criticism or subtle messages that you are screwing up!

What happens when two people marry who have opposite time styles? There can be a lot of conflict over time, priorities, and numerous efforts to control each other. Both sides feel disrespected when the other tries to get their partner to comply with their preferred time style. Arguments about how money is spent – with a focus on the present or the future -- what time is the right time to leave, what priorities should get immediate attention, sexual styles—just about everything in their lifestyle can become a flashpoint of conflict. These often have underlying issues about different styles of relating to time. For people functioning in *Now Time,* whatever is happening "right now" is the most important thing and shouldn't be interrupted for something that is scheduled for later. For *Linear Time* people, whatever the next commitment is looms just as large (or larger) than the present moment.

Because differing time styles were such a source of conflict for so many military couples that I worked with (where they didn't understand each other's relationship to time), I wrote a fictional love story titled *Love Hawaii Time.* It's about two people who have opposite relationships to time. A Hawaiian man, an artist, and a businesswoman from New York City meet in Hawaii for her work assignment. She has to learn to let go of her rigid ideas about time and what she thinks is most important in life. The book reflects the indigenous Hawaiian wisdom of *Now Time.*

You can be both a *Linear Time* person when you have obligations and responsibilities with work and with others, then you can switch to *Now Time* to enjoy the weekend. If you allow the unexpected, the spontaneous, the magic of *Now Time* will unfold. The happiest people are those who can switch modes according to what best serves them in the moment. Sharing your life with an animal is the best teacher for being in Now Time if you will allow yourself to follow their rhythm.

The Bliss of *Now Time*

In the HAC training, we teach our volunteers how to quickly switch into *Now Time* to work more successfully with animals. *Now Time* is where the animals live—unless they are traumatized, in which case our job is to assist them in getting back into the present moment. As discussed in Principle #23, one way we do this is through engaging and focusing their senses on what is happening "right here, right now," as James French calls it.

Being in *Now Time* is essential for people who wish to open their channels to animal communication. I describe *Now Time* as a kind of rich, spherical awareness where you are at the center, and you expand your awareness to include another being even if they are thousands of miles away. It is an expansive awareness and very delicious. For this, you need to be relaxed, aware, and present-focused. Animals love it when you drop into *Now Time,* and you can see them respond within seconds, even in a shelter environment.

Linear Time is wonderful for getting things done, honoring commitments with others, and working in teams. *Now Time* is perfect for feeling the Bliss of Being.

You can have both!

Journal Reflections on Changing Your Relationship to Time:

1) How do you feel about *Linear Time*? How has *Linear Time* served you in life?

2) How do you feel about *Now Time*? Think about the times when you were most in *Now Time*. How did that feel?

3) How flexible are you? If you are making love, can you surrender to *Now Time*? If you need to meet your responsibilities with work or others, are you able to get Linear?

4) Would you like to experience more spherical awareness, to expand *Now Time* to include another being? What would you like to experience and why?

5) Have you judged others who have a very different relationship with time than you have? Can you shine the light of the awareness and understanding of time styles on those chronic conflicts you have had in your life?

Re-Minder: I have all the time in the world.

Reading with Charlotte in Donkey Time. The calm is irresistible.
Donkeys can teach us we have all the time in the world.

Principle #25

RHYTHM, TIMING, AND DISTANCE

Feeling In Sync with Life

*In their innocence and wisdom, in their connection to the
earth and its most ancient rhythms, animals show us
a way back to a home they have never left.*

Susan Chernak McElroy

Overview

All of nature moves to a rhythm we don't always comprehend. Animals
have rhythms for everything they do, seasonal rhythms, mating
rhythms, day and night rhythms, sleep rhythms, and many more
we don't see. Human society has become disassociated from many
natural rhythms, hence our culture's sleep crises. Connecting with
animals is one way we can become reattuned to our natural rhythms.

Animals also have a tremendous sense of timing. They are never
"out of time," as humans often feel. Rather, they mostly live in *Now
Time.*

Animals also have a perfect sense of distance for every encounter.
With their finely tuned proprioceptive senses, they have an excellent

awareness of their body in a spatial context. In other words, how close or far they want to be from others. They *feel space* as a form of communication. It leads to a sense of balance, and the *right space feels good.*

Sheep Wisdom

One of my most profound communication experiences happened as a student of the Trust Technique at Omega Institute in Upstate New York. As a training exercise, we were working with a herd of sheep. I had taken a break and was returning to the class when I became aware of one sheep who was about fifty feet away from me.

I wasn't planning to have a conversation with her, but I felt her eyes totally focused on me. And then the sheep gave me an important spiritual message that I really needed to hear. It wasn't a response to a question I had asked or an issue I was thinking about. The message was like a bolt of lightning in my mind. I "heard" three words that summarized a solution to one of my deep wounds in this lifetime, a wound that had caused me to make many bad decisions. The message I heard was the key that unlocked my path to letting go of my outdated belief systems.

For me, it was a sacred communication. The message had a gentle but earth-shaking clarity, the kind you might expect if you had a conversation with a Buddha. It was entirely unexpected, and it almost knocked me over. Those words continue to be a source of inspiration every time I think about them.

The sheep also taught me an important lesson about "perfect distance for any interaction." The distance between us, about fifty feet, was the perfect distance for our communication. I might not have heard the message had I been standing right next to this sheep. In the Trust Technique, we pay a lot of attention to the right distance for the animal we are working with. Too close may reduce our effectiveness. And the perfect distance is continually changing. Our job is to pay attention to the perfect distance for every interaction. Honoring the right distance is a form of respectful animal communication.

Sheep Dreams

According to the Centers for Disease Control (CDC), one in three Americans does not get enough sleep. If you are having trouble with your sleep rhythms and you don't have a herd of sheep to count, consider inviting a dog to sleep near you. They are role models for sleep hygiene. When it is time to sleep, they circle around a few times, flop down, and are out for the night. If they hear a surprising noise, they check it out, and if it is not a concern, they trot back, circle around a few times, flop down, and promptly return to dreamland.

Yes, animals dream. Science has shown active dream states in multiple species, including rats. Stanley Coren, Professor of Psychology at the University of British Columbia, said in a *Psychology Today* article, "At the structural level, the brains of dogs are similar to those of humans. Also, during sleep, the brain wave patterns of dogs resemble those of humans and go through the same stages of electrical activity observed in humans, all of which are consistent with the idea that dogs are dreaming." Typically, a dog will start dreaming after about twenty minutes of sleep. You might notice some body twitches or signs that they are dreaming, perhaps about running. Their breathing will become shallower and a little more irregular. In their dream states, they are often processing events of the day, just as we do. We can only wonder what else they are doing in the land of nocturnal adventures.

James French reminds us that domestic animals can also become sleep deprived, which can turn into anxiety, anxiousness, and other behavioral issues. He has seen many horses who were sleep deprived, in some cases these were elderly horses who were afraid they couldn't get up, and were afraid to let themselves lay down for a deep sleep. He recommends that owners who are seeing mysterious behavior challenges pay attention to make sure the horses are getting quality sleep that comes from being able to lay down.

The Wisdom of Animal Rhythm

The list of abilities we once thought were exclusively in the human domain has become significantly smaller as researchers discover more about animal capabilities.

It was once thought that only humans had a sense of rhythm, as in musical rhythm. This was one of those false dividing lines that have fallen in the face of new research. We also thought only humans make and use tools, and then we saw almost every species does. Even an octopus has been known to carry coconut shells around to hide under while they sneak up on dinner.

We once thought only humans could be left or right-handed. Now we have discovered that kangaroos prefer using their left-hand 95 percent of the time. Dogs have been discovered to prefer left or right hands. Sophia, my dog, salutes with her left paw. She shakes her tail to the left more often than to the right.

We also thought communication was uniquely human. While humans use verbal language, we now know that animals use sounds and other nonverbal methods to communicate very clearly. For example, prairie dogs communicate to their clan in remarkable detail, such as, "Look out for the man in the blue shirt, he's dangerous!"

It was also once thought that only humans laughed or had a sense of humor. Jane Goodall showed many examples of chimps playing tricks and using humor – which implied that not only did they understand their own intentions, but they understood that others might want something different. And it is not only humans who laugh. Remember Panksepp's discovery that rats laugh when tickled?

Animals clearly have memory. Crows will remember the face of a mean person—and communicate this to the other crows! Some species have self-awareness, which we have identified in primates, dolphins, elephants, and others who recognize themselves in the mirror. While most dogs don't recognize themselves in the mirror because visual is not their primary sense of identification, they can recognize the scent of their own pee and distinguish it from other dogs' deposits, indicating through smell their awareness of self-recognition. Can you imagine how poorly humans would do in a lab test if they had to identify their own urine from a series of samples? Yes, we wouldn't conclude that humans are not self-aware based on their poor sense of urine identification. And any horse could pass this test!

Remember those squirrels disguising where they hid their nuts when others were watching, and finding them months later? Well, now, we have crumbled the idea of animals not having musical rhythm. On social media, you can find wonderful videos of otters juggling stones with incredible precision and fluidity. Or sea lions bopping to the beat, belugas responding to a mariachi band, elephants who love ragtime, tuba-loving cows, and cockatiels dancing to music with many unique and specific moves.

Frankly, giving up the idea that humans own musical rhythm is long overdue. People who train their dogs to learn routines for doggie-dance competitions will tell you that their pooches have very strong opinions about which songs they prefer. It is always easier to train a dog to do a dance routine to a song they like versus one that leaves them cold. If you share your life with animals, experiment with their interests in specific kinds of music and specific rhythms. You may be surprised at the styles they prefer!

"He could tell by the way animals walked that they were keeping time to some kind of music. Maybe it was the song in their own hearts that they walked to."

Laura Adams Armer

The Language of Distance

In addition to the five senses—sight, sound, taste, touch, smell—human and nonhuman animals have a proprioceptive sense. This is a body awareness system, like radar, that lets your brain know about movement and your body's position in relation to your environment (e.g., which direction you are facing, how close you are to obstacles). Animals have an instantaneous awareness of how near or far they are from other animals, humans, and objects. A less obvious aspect of this sense is that humans and animals can tell when someone is staring at them, even when the starer is not in their sightline.

A group of marine researchers in Antarctica were on the final day of their project and were out on their Zodiac inflatable boat when they were surrounded by three forty-ton humpback whales. Perhaps the whales wanted to leave them with a final impression. They gently circled beneath and around the boat for about an hour. Swimming close enough for eye contact, they just barely grazed the boat, so gently that it barely moved the small boat. The researchers noted how strong the whale's sense of body awareness was and how careful they were not to disturb the boat with their swimming movements. The boats could have easily been capsized with an accidental touch, but the whales' performance was flawless. As they surfaced and made eye contact, the researchers waved and were greeted in return with a pectoral fin wave in a rhythm that matched the humans.

In non-traumatized animals, this proprioceptive sense works well. It gives them information about how close is a safe distance to be from another animal or person, or when they need more distance.

In traumatized or frightened animals, this system doesn't function as well. Everything and everyone can feel too close, and any movement towards them can trigger a fear response.

Spending time with horses, a prey animal, is a great way to observe how pervasive and instant their proprioceptive sense is. The slightest unexpected movement, such as a flag or object flapping in the wind, can trigger their desire to escape and move away. They will react to the distraction faster than your brain registers it. For this reason, if you are riding a sensitive horse, you need to be *ahead of time* and anticipate potential triggers.

Being in the presence of prey animals, since they are so precise in their awareness, will help you to become more receptive to sensory events, just as they are. Watch a horse's ears swivel in response to very subtle sounds to which they might need to attend. Allan Hamilton, M.D., author of *Zen Mind, Zen Horse – The Science and Spirituality of Working with Horses*, describes how horses also understand and respond to the flow of vital energy around them. "They use this energy, called *chi*, to communicate with their herd, express dominance, and sense predators."

Horses can sense your energy, your mood, and your intentions even before your body gets close to theirs. It is as if their "radar" extends very far. For their safety, they must be smarter about our emotions, our moods, and our energy than we are about our own. Thus, they can reflect our emotions, whether or not we are conscious of them. As Hamilton says, "I call my horses 'Divine Mirrors.' They reflect back the emotions you put in. If you put in love and respect and kindness and curiosity, the horse will return that."

In the HAC Power of Presence workshop with horses we help humans understand that distance and timing are a form of language—or, more precisely, a method of communicating—which is one of the ways we deepen our connection to animals. How you use distance and timing can communicate that you are a safe person, someone who intends to bring comfort—or someone who is not aware, perhaps dangerous, or at least clueless!

As we engage with the horses, we communicate through the speed we move, the direction of our movement (Principle #21, "*Towards & Away*"), the fluidity or abruptness of our moves, and if we are increasing or reducing the distance between ourselves and them. All these communications, the language of proximity and motion, the horse instantly receives, interprets, and responds to. Thus, they are, to repeat Dr. Hamilton's words, "Divine Mirrors," and the perfect teachers for increasing our awareness of how we present to them.

In the shelters some volunteers have a "natural" desire to get close to a shy or shaking dog. They want to close the distance gap, assuming this will comfort the dog. Closeness and cuddling may bring comfort for some, but not for all animals. Some may perceive your moving too fast or too close as an aggressive signal to them, and they may respond defensively.

The Perfect Distance

A key principle in the HAC is that humans need to observe and consider an individual animal's "perfect distance." As stated earlier, the perfect distance is not a fixed amount in feet or inches. It is a constantly changing distance that depends on specific environmental factors, as well as the degree of stress the animal is feeling. For example, one dog who is reactive to other dogs may become stressed if they are closer to another dog than, say, ten feet. At thirty feet, the dog can walk by without much more than a look, but once they cross that line (closer than ten feet), the dog may have a reaction, especially if they are on a leash.

Remember, what might have been fine on Monday may not be fine on Tuesday. This is because environmental or other factors change, and your dog may be responding to multiple stressors that stacked up, things that are scary, some of which you may not have specifically identified yet.

It is also important to remember "trigger stackers," meaning that the dog may be able to process one trigger, but if several more occur in rapid succession, faster than the dog can recover from, this can lead to the dog being *over-threshold* for how much they can manage. So "the perfect distance" is a dynamic "flow element."

The job of the human is to be observant and respectful of the animal's "perfect distance" at that exact moment. Five minutes later, a shy dog may be ready to engage at a closer distance after another stressor is removed. Or they may be calmer because you intervened with a treat, a distraction, or a counterconditioning technique. If we are aware of the rising reactivity in a particular context, we can anticipate the distance that is peaceful versus the distance that will be disturbing.

This awareness of the perfect distance for any interaction helps the animal feel you respect their invisible boundary, and this respect helps build trust. In the human world, there is a lot of bumping into, even crashing into, each other's boundaries. It is so commonplace that we ignore the fact that it doesn't feel good.

Having strong boundaries for humans and other animals leads to less stress and more freedom. We need strong emotional and physical boundaries to have healthy relationships. One way to strengthen your psychological and emotional boundaries is to increase your awareness of your physical boundaries. As you increase your awareness or sense of what feels physically good in any given moment, you build your "boundary muscles." What feels safe will change depending upon your trust in the other person, your current stress or peace levels, and other social and environmental factors. So *spacial comfort* is a dynamic experience. Paying attention to what feels right to you fills your safety tank and helps you to feel more grounded.

When you are working with an animal that is afraid of people or other animals, understanding proper distance is your priority. For example, you need to know at what distance the fear response may be triggered. Your understanding of the "safe distance" and the "unsafe distance" is essential to help the animal overcome fear.

In classical conditioning, we pair desired behavior with a reward. When we are working with a fearful animal, we might use counter-conditioning to dismantle the fear. In this case, we introduce the animal to something that evokes *a very low level of fear*, then we immediately give them a reward, beginning to pair the scary thing with a reward. For this to work, you must give the animal a treat when the scary thing is still at a safe distance BEFORE the fear rises to a level that the animal can't easily manage. If the fear level is too high, the treat will be useless.

With repetition and over time, the association of what is scary is paired with the experience of getting something delicious. This is a slow counterconditioning process, teaching the animal to see a trigger and, instead of reacting to it, to immediately anticipate getting a treat. The anticipation function in the brain will be the antidote to the fear-cycle reaction. It is all about the human getting the right timing and correctly understanding the language of distance.

Humans Have Distance Preferences Too

Human relationships also have a "right distance" zone for every relationship, although we are often not aware of this sense of perfect distance. We love some people, but we couldn't live with them. Some friends we like to see often and others we are fine to see occasionally, then there are those we sense we need to keep at a distance.

Success in social relationships comes from correctly reading your own and the other's dynamic preferences for the "perfect distance." Too much or too little distance in a specific case can weaken the desire to connect.

Earlier in this book, I related my profound experience with a sheep initiating communication with me during a Trust Technique workshop. That experience happened when the sheep and I were about fifty feet away from each other. Later that day, we had a chance to be in the pens with the sheep as a group. While this was very precious, that first sheep taught me a powerful lesson about distance. *There is a perfect distance for any interaction.* And it may be very different from what you might expect. I realized I had a mental construct of "close = more intimacy," but the sheep taught me that is not necessarily true. My job is to pay attention to what is the right distance for each situation.

If you want more training in what is the perfect distance, spend time with a cat! Because…

"Time spent with cats is never wasted."

Sigmund Freud

Journal Reflections on Rhythm, Timing, and Distance:

1) How do you feel about the fluidity and sense of rhythm in your life? Is there a sense of various rhythms, or do you feel there is too much automation and monotony?

2) If you have lost your sense of rhythm, how is that affecting the quality of your life?

3) In what way would you like to bring back natural rhythms into your day? Into your life?

4) How do you feel about Timing across your life? How much time in your life is spent feeling rushed? Do you feel in sync with yourself? Or feel you are often *out of time*?

5) How are your proprioceptive senses doing? Are you alert to when people are too close or too far? Can you begin to honor that sensitivity and fine-tune your preferences for "the perfect distance for any interaction"? What would that be like? How does your body feel when you even think about the words "perfect distance"? Do you feel like it expands your sense of safety because you are honoring your own boundaries?

Re-Minder: I have perfect timing.

Bolt was the dog I mentioned earlier in the book who had bit three shelter workers. I spent many hours doing calming methods, re-puppying, and the Trust Technique. I let him choose the timing, the distance, and the pacing of all our interactions. Several weeks later, he was adopted.

Principle #26

THE SECRET OF BALANCE
The Goldilocks Solution

To have a balanced life,
you need a dog to adore you,
and a cat to ignore you.

Anonymous

Overview

The secret to well-being is balance. Too much or too little of anything important can create stress. We need air to breathe, but I don't know too many people who enjoy hurricanes. Water is essential to life, but a flood can destroy. Fire is a wonderful thing, except when it is an out-of-control inferno. Health is always about balance. Physically we need activity and rest. Mentally we need arousal, and we need relaxation and peace. We need company, but we also need time spent in contemplation and solitude. In nature, animals usually find balance. When animals share their lives with humans, we need to be aware of their need for balance and seek to recreate the potential for natural healing in the home environment through what I call "The Goldilocks Solution."

A Gentle Dog Named Bear

Afton, my friend from the Wild Horse Haven Rescue, has a 180-pound dog named Bear, a Great Pyrenees and lab cross. As a puppy, Bear was raised with rabbits and still retains his gentle nature. His role now is to protect the ranch and the horse herd. He has the freedom to come and go as he pleases, the choice to go inside or out, and has the run of the ranch.

It is lovely to be in the presence of an animal who has so much freedom of choice; he just radiates contentment. A very calm soul, Bear is a beautiful example of the joy that freedom brings. He is what is referred to by some as a balanced dog, and he helps other animals regain a sense of their own inner equilibrium. Veterans come by just to sit with him.

He can bark **ferociously** to warn off predators, then turn right around and cuddle with those who need his gentle power. He is capable of complete relaxation as well as complete arousal when needed. He can switch quickly between states, but because these opposites are so fully exercised, he rarely, if ever, gets one or the other out of balance.

The Sublime Joy of Balance

We owe it to the animals who share our lives to seek to understand what elements of balance would help them have more satisfying lives. Animals need a balance of freedom and structure. They appreciate a balance of routine and having some choice about how they spend their time. In nature, they wouldn't need any help from humans to find this balance, as their senses would lead them to do what they need. It is amazing to realize that 70 percent of dogs worldwide live as strays, in the streets, or in the wild, according to author Alexandria

Horowitz. But in the context of coexisting with humans, especially those living imbalanced modern lives, we need to look for ways to help them regain their state of balance and harmony.

When It Feels Just Right, It Is Right

Each animal has unique needs for balance, so there is no one-size-fits-all solution. I look for *the Goldilocks Solution* because when it feels *just right,* it is right. To apply this principle, start by recognizing which elements there are a lot of and what might be missing as a result. For example, if a dog spends nine hours a day at home alone, what might he or she need when you return? If a law enforcement working dog spends most of the day on duty, what might she need at the end of the day? If a comfort dog spends two hours with victims of a mass shooting, what might that dog need to release that energy and decompress?

Of course, people get imbalanced, too. Have a look at your life circumstances and ask yourself which elements are out of balance and could benefit from compensation with the opposite activity.

The Six Zones of Balance

We invite students in the HAC program to consider six areas of exploration in the following zones of balance. This helps them bring awareness to their relationships with their animals and with the shelter animals we work with in the HAC program. We ask them to consider the zones of balance in their own life as you can't offer balance to an animal if you are not experiencing the same freedom.

The Balance of:

1) Stimulation & Relaxation
2) Connection & Independence

3) Predictability & Newness

4) Touch & Non-Touch

5) Freedom & Structure

6) Choice & Following the Lead

1) BALANCE OF STIMULATION & RELAXATION

A foundational principle in the HAC is that we all benefit from a balance of stimulation and arousal, fun and excitement, pleasure and challenge—with times of relaxation, peace, contentment, contemplation, prayer, or meditation.

It is a challenge to provide a balance of stimulation and relaxation to dogs in shelter environments. But just having this awareness will inspire your creativity to find ways to bring more balance. The question to begin with is: Does this dog present as overstimulated or under-stimulated? Once you determine the answer, then find ways to provide the opposite experience. Even five or ten minutes of peace for a highly stimulated dog can help reset their nervous system.

Dogs, like people, can become addicted to the stress chemistry caused by persistently chaotic shelter environments, and they need to be reminded how to relax. Dogs that are depressed need to get moving but preferably where they make the choice to move. One easy way to start them moving is to toss a treat where they must move their head and then their feet to get it. Then toss a treat in the other direction. Slowly increase the range of movement you are asking the dog to make through this game of alternating patterns and directions. The same can be accomplished with dogs who will play with balls or toys. Remember to refrain from expectation or judgment and allow the dog to progress at a pace that is right for them, especially if you are dealing with shy dogs.

2) BALANCE OF CONNECTION & INDEPENDENCE

Humans and animals greatly benefit from positive connections. And we also benefit from having some solo or internal time. Each person and each animal have a different ratio, their personal Goldilocks Solution for how much they need of each. Bella, one dog I worked with, needed 70 percent connection with her person and her dog-mate and 30 percent laying in the sun, playing by herself, and napping. Her older dog-mate, Ruffie, had the opposite desires.

The point is although all beings have a need for balance, this doesn't mean 50-50 equal time for every dog. There is a unique formula of balance for the individual that creates well-being. If Bella gets close to her ideal of 70 percent connection time, she is going to feel happy and will really enjoy her private time. Ruffie needs less interaction, which, thankfully, Bella seems to intuitively understand. She can get him to play, but after a while, he is done. Bella knows that is the time to let him be and drag her soggy, stuffed squeaky frog to her human to continue the game.

3) BALANCE OF PREDICTABILITY & NEWNESS

Dogs need a balance of predictability with the experience of newness, such as new people, places, things to do, or new tasty things to eat. They like routines for life's basics: what time they will get their meals and potty breaks, where, when, how they sleep, and when their humans will be home. They enjoy predictability when it comes to things that pertain to survival, safety, physiological well-being, and emotional comfort.

Once these routines are solid and predictable, then they want some exploration, some *unpredictability*. This could be playtime, new treats, and, depending upon the dog's temperament, going to new places, seeing and smelling new things, and getting attention and affection from new people. Naturally, every dog is different in terms of how much enjoyment and benefit they get from "newness." You want to pay close attention to your dog to observe what their perfect formula is for balancing these opposite desires for newness and predictability.

It will be interesting for you to observe if your personal needs and your dog's needs are the same or different. Be objective; don't assume what is right for you is right for your dog, even if your dog has fallen into your routines and has acclimated to your style. Experiment! Try something new. More than once.

4) BALANCE OF TOUCH & NON-TOUCH

All living beings benefit from touch, physical proximity, and connection. But every being has a different "Goldilocks Touch Point," meaning how much is too little, how much is too much, and how much is just right?

You yourself may or may not be getting the right amount or the right kind of human touch. Studies show that touch is diminishing in western cultures (see Principle #7). Collectivist cultures tend to get a lot more touch than we get in the under-touching individualistic cultures. Indigenous cultures value many kinds of touch, not just romantic touch, but holding other people's babies and animals, touching the earth, feeling the earth beneath their feet, and feeling the sun, wind, and rain on their skin.

Animals can fill some of our needs for touch. And they touch us in very deep ways. Most people would not consider animal touch a complete replacement for human touch, but it can *add* sublime levels of touch experience because animals can so fully receive our touch. They show us with their body language, facial expressions, and sounds how much they enjoy our loving touch. We have no doubt that what we are doing is appreciated. We get *the pleasure of giving pleasure.*

Become aware of your own needs and desires for touch or for not having it. Then become aware of the preferences of the animals who share your life. Their preference formula may match yours (sometimes they want touch and connection), and then enough is enough—especially if you share your life with a cat! If you continue beyond their full-of-touch-point, the cat might just jump off your lap and move beyond the range of your hands, or you might get nipped.

Experiment to find the *Goldilocks Touch Point* for your animals. And of course, not every day is the same for you or for them. If you are feeling stressed, they may want less contact until your energy is calmer. Animals are a good barometer for your stress level.

Experiment with different degrees of pressure (never hard, but variations on light, medium-light, etc.) Experiment with different speeds of hand movement. Experiment with different parts of the hand. Sometimes the back of the hand is better for a sensitive animal.

Touch the animal with different parts of your body. In the Dancing with Horses workshop I attended, we did exercises where we danced with the shadow of the horse, touching the shadow, not the horse's physical body. This is also an effective way to approach shy dogs at the shelter. Touch their aura or the energy field around their body without any movement and without making physical contact. The more peaceful you are when you do this, the more effective it will be. Notice how lovely it feels to you to touch without contact.

About half of the healing techniques that we do in the HAC utilize nonphysical methods of contact, especially for deeper healing work with shy or traumatized animals.

Nonphysical Touch

Physical touch is just one way we can connect with another being. Why limit pleasure to just one mode? We can also connect with a being through our voices, our faces, our thoughts, our mood, our consciousness, and our proximity. Animals are open to a wide range of connection experiences beyond just physical touch. They can feel your moods and your love for them at any distance. They can be warmed by your smile and your pleasure in them, whether or not that is accompanied by a physical touch.

If you are working with very shy animals in a shelter or even animals in a zoo, you may not have physical touch as an option. Sophia, who is both a therapy dog and my service dog, went with me to the Tucson Zoo. We watched the tiger pacing continually in the large outdoor pen with a glass window separating the tiger from the public. The tiger was fascinated by Sophia, so I sat on the ground, with Sophia on my lap, and I began doing the Trust Technique. The tiger leaned against the glass and watched us for twenty minutes. He was enthralled with the experience and stayed calm for a very long time, even after others came over to see him. This is an example where lack of physical touch was not an obstacle to profound connection.

5) BALANCE OF FREEDOM & STRUCTURE

Remember when you were a young kid in school, and the bell rang at the end of the school day or the school year? Remember that feeling of being released? Like being shot out of the "joy cannon"? Even if you didn't have anything great to do, the exuberance of being free felt so good. We need more of this powerful feeling in our lives!

One way to provide structure for dogs is short daily training sessions—five to ten minutes—where you are stimulating their minds and bodies by teaching simple tricks or reviewing cues they already know. From the HAC point of view, this time is an investment in your relationship and your connection, not just about obedience. It is also about improving the clarity of your communication, what you are asking for, and how well they understand and respond. And of course, they get treats, or motivating rewards, and affection for pleasing you! Training sessions should feel 100 percent like a fun game to them, physically and mentally stimulating. This is one way to add healthy doses of structure into an animal's day, especially if they have a sedentary lifestyle.

Individual animals vary in how much freedom they need versus how much confinement and structure. And for some beings, structure is liberating—it liberates them from the fear of freedom! Take an honest look at your own *Goldilocks Freedom Formula*. To what degree does your life accurately reflect your needs and preferences? If there is a good match between your needs for freedom and structure in your lived experiences, you will feel happy and satisfied. On the other hand, if your life doesn't at least somewhat match your true nature and needs for the right balance of freedom and structure, you will feel restless, frustrated, irritable, and lost. Your life will dramatically improve if you can make even minor daily adjustments to rebalance your ideal *Goldilocks Freedom Formula*.

Once you take an honest look at your own life, observe the animals who share your life. Do you feel they are getting their needs met with a satisfying balance of freedom and structure? Do they need more of one or the other? If you live in a city or suburban environment, you can't let your dog run free. But it is interesting to note that, especially in small towns or rural environments, up until about the 1950s, many dogs enjoyed this kind of freedom and just came home for scraps.

Even a small amount of appropriate freedom is powerful medicine. I live in a small city, but I have a very long gravel and dirt driveway between my house and the street, so I can allow Sophia to be off leash for this long walk. Because she knows the routine, she stops on her own when she sees the street and waits for me to catch up and attach the leash. We do this both coming and going back to the house. She gets to choose how fast she walks, and she chooses the point where she stops and waits.

We both love this little dose of freedom. It does a lot to reset our relationship. I get so much joy watching her trot at her own pace and then wait for me to catch up to her. She looks back at me if I am taking too long. When we are doing the leashed part of the walk, I also make sure she gets to lead some of the time. She chooses when she wants to stop and to sniff and for how long. These little doses of freedom of choice mean a lot to her. If I get busy writing and forget it is walk time, she will let me know it is time for this joyful event, even if she has just pottied in the backyard. The moral of the story is to find the right balance of freedom that works with your circumstances and considers your needs as well as those of the animals.

6) BALANCE OF CHOICE & FOLLOWING THE LEAD

Freedom and choice are twins. The sense of choice is closely connected to the sense of freedom. In Act Resilient, I talk about a part of brain function I call "the Chooser." As far as I know, the Chooser is not a literal location in the brain, but it is a cognitive process. In a healthy person, the Chooser is alive and well and enjoys making good choices. In a person or animal under extreme stress or with a history of trauma, the Chooser gets clogs in the gears. It can then become stressful to make even minor decisions. I call this "Chooser Burnout." When this happens, *having to make a choice* becomes stressful rather than joyful. This can happen if a being has had to make too many critical decisions and choices.

I remember one combat medic who was in my Act Resilient class. He had spent several tours in Afghanistan as a triage nurse and talked about getting flooded by multiple casualties arriving all at once, and he had to look them in the eye and make a flash decision as to who he could save and who was too far gone. It was a terrible burden of choice, but one that he had to do. Otherwise, no one would have survived. When I explained the concept of Chooser Burnout, it really helped him understand why he was feeling paralyzed in civilian life.

People with Chooser Burnout can benefit from a benevolent structure, which is like an agreed-upon time-out during which they don't have to make basic decisions—someone or some structure is helping them until they are ready to take back the reins of their life. It is agreed that this burned-out person will not make any major decisions without sounding it out with a designated neutral person. Otherwise, if they are in deep Chooser Burnout, they may bounce between being *unable to make decisions* to *leaping to poor decisions* just to get rid of the pressure of having to choose.

Another reason "the Chooser" can go offline is if someone has been making all the decisions for you for a long time. In combat operations, where so many decisions are made for you, you can get a flabby Chooser muscle. You don't have to think about what to wear; you have a uniform. Your schedule is always filled by the unit command. What you eat, when you sleep, where you go, who you work with, and a million other details are not in your control. Then, when the person is separated from the military, all of these small and large decisions can seem daunting.

Sometimes animals arrive at the shelter with adverse histories where they have been deprived of all, or almost all, choices. They typically present as depressed, listless, and helpless. They don't initiate any contact or want to play. They may be experiencing a lack of will to make choices, even good ones. They don't want to go for a walk, take a treat, or receive affection. They are locked down in a kind of depression of the will.

One way to help these dogs is to offer them the tiniest choice possible just to get them to start using this part of their heart and brain again. For example, I will put two delicious morsels on the ground at the same time. They can have both, but they have to choose which one to eat first, the one on the right or the left. Find tiny variations of choice options, the one closer or the one an inch further from their nose. In all cases, they get both, but they must choose which one is first. This gets the Chooser to come back online quickly. Keep it light and fun and stop when the animal has had enough.

To make good choices, you have to be in touch with your own needs and desires. An animal who is a long-term resident in a shelter or one who has not had his or her desires attended to will give up even knowing what they want as a result of this kind of neglectful abuse. It is a slow process to get them to trust you and themselves, to pay attention to what feels good, and to remember that making choices is empowering. It is a joy to watch an animal's Chooser come back online. Once it starts, it happens fast, and they quickly start acting "like a dog" and want to explore the yard, get treats, and connect. Provide lots of opportunities that invite them to experience the freedom of making their own choices.

Balance of Human-Being and Human-Doing

For animals, the balance of their beingness and doingness are perfectly interwoven and indivisible, which is another reason it is so pleasing to be in their presence. When they are busy doing, they don't lose their connection to their beingness. As humans with busy lives, and multiple responsibilities to others, it is easy for us to get out of balance when we invest more time and energy on "doing" at the risk of just being. This can lead us to feel burned out because we are literally putting out too much energy. When we extend ourselves in so many ways, we become human over-doers and under-beings. To balance this, we need to invoke *the Goldilocks Solution* and spend some time and focus on just being. *Being ourselves.* Being quiet and peaceful, contemplative. This will restore the sense of connection to being peaceful—and to human *being*.

The balance of being and doing is a valuable resilience tool and finding the right formula for yourself is essential. There is not a one-size-fits-all formula. Remember, it is not a simple 50/50 split between being and doing. Some people can do a lot of doing and still feel connected to their human-beingness. Others need more time in quiet reflection to feel like themselves. So, the secret to sustained well-*being* is finding your personal balance between being and doing.

Balancing Freedom and Safety

In Maslow's hierarchy of needs, safety takes precedence over freedom. Applied to animals, this means we would not put an animal in an unsafe situation in order to provide them freedom. Freedom and safety must be weighed against each other, and a proper balance found that allows the animal to have a high certainty of safety and freedom in the context they are in. If you live in the city and work away from home, it will not do to let your dog roam the streets until you get home. If you live on a farm or in a rural area, it may be possible to allow your dog a high level of freedom. But if an animal is sharing their life with you, your first responsibility is to make sure that the animal is in as safe a structure, circumstance, and environment as you can manage. Once safety is reasonably secured, then you want to ADD levels and moments of freedom, as leash laws will allow.

In the wild, animals thrive on freedom from human constraints. But once the animals share their lives with us, we have the responsibility to secure their circumstances and keep them safe from possible dangers.

It is important to *balance your needs* for safety and the security of the animal with doses of freedom for them. It is not about giving up your job or where you live so your animal can have total freedom; that might create an imbalance and unnecessary difficulty in your life. The goal is to find ways that allow you to maintain balance and stability in your own life and *add moments of freedom* to the best of your ability.

Leading is Structure

Animals also enjoy having you lead and create a structure. This is not about you dominating every moment; it is about allowing them to relax and trust because you are in charge and watching out for them. You certainly want to give them some freedom to express themselves. Like a young child who wants to explore, knowing that a parent is watching provides a balance of self-expression and comfort.

Having at least some time each day or each week to spend off-leash, to move at their own pace, to sniff what they want, to explore and choose direction and distance is very balancing for a dog who shares their life with a human. Even playing in a yard off leash will feel like freedom for most dogs. If you don't have a yard, can you make friends with someone who does? Can you find ways to allow your dog some tastes of freedom at least once a week?

When my dog Sophia and I visit my friend Afton's horse rescue, she gets to go off-leash completely. She loves the wild freedom for a while, and then after a bit, she comes bounding back, looking for attention and connection. After we connect, then she is ready to go lay down someplace safe. So, she has a rhythm of how much freedom she wants, and when that experience bucket is full, she is ready for connection and feeling the comfort of a safe space.

Animals want connection when they want it. And sometimes they don't want it or don't need it. Animals have complex social structures and relationships, just as we do. Mood factors in; how well they are feeling or if they have been stressed by something in the environment. All of these can create variables of desire, so don't take it personally if your love bug is not in the mood for a cuddle-wuddle. It is our job to read their signals accurately; otherwise, we could be unwittingly leading them into Chooser fatigue.

The best way to begin to approach balance with an animal is to become aware of your own needs for balance. If your life is out of balance, it may be hard to recognize how this is affecting your animals. This is one of those *put your mask on first* deals. But even a baby step of progress toward balance goes a long way toward well-being for both of you.

Living the Goldilocks Solution leads to more joy.

I close this chapter with the words of Wallace Black Elk from *The Sacred Ways of a Lakota:*

"The old people say that we used to have that balance. Like we say, we want to walk the earth in balance. We want to live in harmony. We want our Mother Earth to heal. But these creatures, like the bird-people and four-legged, they still have that balance. It's like a carpenter's level. You tilt it, and the bubble goes this way or that way to balance it. To balance it, you have to get that bubble right in the middle. It's the same with that magnetic balance in the brain, but man lost it. If it tilts this way, the bird has enough sense to go this way. If it tilts the other way, they bounce back. That's how come they go back and forth (migrate). But man lost it. Man lost his navigation in this world. So, he ended up not knowing which way was top or bottom or sideways."

Journal Reflections on Balance:

1) As you reflect on the Six Zones of Balance, what insights do you have about yourself and your life? What areas do you feel need some attention or adjustment to bring greater balance?

2) As you look at the animals in your life, where do you see the value of adding more balance?

3) Are you and your animals experiencing some similar issues regarding the need for more balance? Are you reflecting imbalance in each other?

4) How would your life be different if you had more balance in one area or another? What areas of your life could benefit from the *Principle of Balance – The Goldilocks Solution?*

5) What are you willing to change or let go of to have more of the balance you desire?

Re-Minder: I can balance my world.

Although we couldn't have physical contact with the tiger, we were able to have energetic contact. The tiger chose to sit with us, to participate with us in the Trust Technique. It was a very profound experience of balance and connection.

Principle #27

FREEDOM OF CHOICE
A Sacred Right

I believe animals should be respected as citizens of this earth.
They should have the right to their own freedom,
their own families, and their own life.

John Feldmann

Overview

Freedom is an archetypal value in American society, and many people have died to protect it. The most important freedom is the choice to live, and yet too many animals have been denied life out of a disregard for this fundamental right. Who are we as a species if we continue to deprive so many animals of this basic moral imperative?

Surely humans need to do better, or we may not survive. We need to do what we can to protect the physical lives of animals as well as to protect their freedom to live life expressing themselves naturally. For those animals who share our lives, we need to increase our understanding and respect for the balance of freedom they need while living in our care. When we respect animals' need for freedom, the quality of their lives and ours improve.

Precious Moon Bears

Moon Bears are small, sweet, lovely brown and black bears with a crescent-shaped necklace of yellow fur coloring at the top of their chest. They have been held in captivity in many countries in Asia so that their bile can be extracted, as it is falsely believed to give men more sexual potency. These bears are kept in small cages their entire lives, never get medical attention, or have the freedom to move or feel the sun on their faces.

Animals Asia Foundation has rescued nearly a thousand moon bears and taken them to their sanctuary for healing and much-needed medical attention. They have done much to get laws changed to make bear bile farming illegal in Vietnam and to rescue the bears held their whole lives in torturous captivity. One bear they named Uno, after eighteen years of unimaginable boredom and complete physical restriction, was able to learn to walk again and to play with his own kind for the first time in his life.

Animals Asia veterinarian Heide Quine talks about how wonderful it was to see Uno make a beautiful recovery and to find the freedom at the sanctuary "to simply be a bear. And to watch him the first time he felt grass and the sun on his face." On the *Animals Asia* website, you can see these adorable bears climbing, playing together, and splashing in their pool. They are proof that healing is possible, that resilience is natural, and that humans can begin to right some of the wrongs that have been done.

Finding Freedom

In this Principle of Freedom of Choice, we explore the issues of animals in our care or in captivity and how we can maintain some elements of freedom of choice to maintain their physical, mental, and emotional well-being. An animal who can make some basic choices—such as to go outside or inside, play or rest, eat or sleep, engage with others or not—will be happier and healthier. Exercising their *Chooser-brain* helps them feel free and healthy.

Obviously, the most essential freedom is the right to choose to live. Given that humans are one of the most dangerous deliberate predators on Earth, this is no small issue. While there is a normal or natural extinction rate for animals, our plundering of the earth has resulted in much destruction and loss of life for many species. The World Wildlife Fund estimates, "The rapid loss of species we are seeing today is estimated by experts to be between 1,000 and 10,000 times higher than the *natural extinction rate*." Please support those reputable organizations around the world who are doing heroic work to try to save animals.

Pima Animal Care Center, one of the shelters where I volunteer, has a wonderful program that allows us to take a dog out for a taste of freedom. Volunteers can take a dog out for a hamburger, an ice cream, a hike, or even to their home for the day. Buff was a former stray and longtime resident at the shelter because he was such a shy dog and was afraid to be touched (I tell his story in Principle #5). The first time I took him home for an afternoon at my house, the joy of watching him express his freedom was as entertaining as anything on TV. In the first hour he was here, I counted twenty-seven choices he made. He got to choose whether to come inside or explore the yard, sniff my dog, wander by himself, have a drink of water, engage with me or my elderly mother, cuddle on the couch, or sleep at my feet as I write this, and so on. Finally, he was ready to receive some deeper healing and take a much-needed nap in a quiet space. We cuddled and slept together on the rug. I was impressed that simply a few hours of freedom of choice helped him gain some much-needed balance and calm. When animals get to experience some freedom of choice, it goes a long way to restoring their well-being.

In Principle #26, I wrote about the balance of freedom and structure and about a more flexible approach to the twin dynamics of leading and being led. Sometimes we humans should lead, and sometimes, we would be wise to let the animal lead. There is great value in being the leader. And there is great value in allowing yourself to be led by a being who is following the call of ancient wisdom. If you share your life with an animal, this is an invitation to choose the balance that is right for you and the animal who shares your life.

Having respect for animals making choices for themselves turns our relationship from one of ownership to one of partnership.

There are so many benefits to being in partnership with animals. Ted Andrews, author of several books, including *Animal-Speak – The Spiritual & Magical Powers of Creatures Great and Small*, has dedicated his life to living in partnership with animals and respecting their freedom. In his book, he talks about a time when he was seriously lost in the woods. He spoke to his friends, the ravens, and told them he was lost. They immediately turned around and flew in the other direction, leading him to safety.

Three Domains of Animal Welfare

I took a course called the Human-Animal Bond presented by the NAVC, the North American Veterinary Community. In this course, the NAVC cites the work of Duncan Fraser, who defined the Three Domains of Animal Welfare as:

1) Physical Conditions
2) Natural Behaviors
3) Affective States

In this model, we see that the shelters do a wonderful job of addressing the first domain. Animals are safe from danger, and they are fed and given medical attention as needed.

In the second domain, volunteers fill the animals' essential needs for socialization, exercise, playtime, and connection.

The third domain is the focus of The Human-Animal Connection—the emotional health of animals. Affective states are the realm of paying attention to *what animals are feeling* and their emotional needs. In this third domain, we are focused on increasing their psychological well-being. Knowing that most shelters do not have the staff, time, or resources to devote to this important need—the *emotional healing and well-being* of animals—the HAC's primary focus is to fill this gap. We hope someday to have HAC-trained volunteers at shelters and rescues all over the world.

Our HAC program is designed to work for animals at home as well as for animals in shelters and rescues. Of course, with so many shelters and so many animals, we need a lot of help with this humongous task. In fact, we need a worldwide army of people who share our vision to help us begin to create and refine a more humane culture. It is our hope that shelters in the future will be able to better address these needs in addition to the ones they currently serve so well.

Cultivating Freedom

Freedom and choice are inseparable. To protect one, we must protect the other. And for the animals who share our lives, it's a dynamic dialogue to understand how best to support these two needs while balancing our own.

Most shelters do a wonderful job of protecting domesticated animals from the dangers of running free in a human world. They save lives by providing shelter from the elements, food and fresh water, and hopefully, excellent medical attention. Of course, many shelters suffer from a lack of resources and space. I have volunteered at many shelters in several cities and know they do the best they can with the resources they have. But that lack of resources leads to a lower quality of life, more restricted freedoms, and less socialization and play time, which results in a decline in the well-being of sheltered animals.

Beyond meeting their basic physical survival needs, we need to explore how to fulfill some of their other essential needs, such as small tastes of freedom of choice, as well as their need for connection, love, playtime, and expression of their natural behaviors. This is where the kindness of the staff and the devotion of volunteers come in. Volunteer dog walkers provide brief but essential relief from the kennel and life-affirming one-on-one interaction. In these precious moments, dogs can find some tiny morsels of freedom of choice.

When you are walking a dog, just giving them tiny moments of choice such as the speed of movement, going left or right, stopping to sniff, choosing to vocalize, or meeting someone can make a huge difference.

One way to cultivate freedom of choice is to put a treat in both fists and offer both to the dog. They will choose one. Whichever they choose first, open that fist and reward with the treat. Then they will likely nose the second fist; open it and give them the second one also. This choice of left or right may seem too simple to be meaningful, but it is the dog exercising his or her Chooser Brain and has benefit. Think of other simple choice games your animal might enjoy. Having the freedom to make even small choices is so important for the animals who share your life and for the animals you work with in shelters.

When volunteers walk and play with these dogs, call them by name, and give them treats and cuddles, they do much to save their sanity! We encourage our HAC volunteers to look for tiny moments of choice they can provide for shelter animals as they go for a walk or choose to engage in a cuddle.

Save Them All

"Save them all" is the motto of Best Friends Animal Sanctuary, which has been a leader in the movement to reduce the excessive use of euthanasia of healthy animals in shelters. In the U.S. in the 1970s, it was estimated that 23 million cats and dogs were euthanized in shelters each year. Although there is no obligation to report numbers, current reputable estimates at the time of writing this book are that 3–5 million cats and dogs are being euthanized annually. One reason for this significant reduction is that spay and neuter programs have been very effective in reducing pet overpopulation. Another reason is increased public support for adoptions and rescues. Many of today's shelters work very hard to achieve higher adoption rates instead of just euthanizing if a dog or cat has overstayed their allotted time limit.

As Sue Sternberg points out in her insightful book, *Train to Adopt – Humane Guidelines and Training Program for Dogs in Shelters*, "Now, more than ever, we need national humane guidelines, for quality-of-life issues facing dogs in shelters. Because a kennel, no matter how modern, clean, or nice, is still a stressful, unhealthy, unnatural, and destructive place to keep a dog." She points out that dogs in shelters for more than two weeks will experience mental, emotional, social, and physical deterioration. One reason is the lack of freedom of choice. She explores how shelter life in a confined space with inherent overstimulation is a setup for more aggressive behavior, which greatly reduces a dog's chances of getting adopted.

Sternberg believes that to maintain a healthy shelter environment, dogs need "twenty minutes of human touch, affection and contact daily... Two minutes of reward-based training daily...and playtime with humans and other dogs at least three times weekly." She recommends that all shelters have a *Quality-of-Life Team* to address these issues.

I would add my recommendation that we need to introduce as many small moments of freedom of choice as possible each day, such as being leash-free in a play yard for twenty minutes, so the animal can choose their own play rhythm and pace to run or walk, engaging and disengaging, the level of play energy, and whether to play or rest. These small freedoms go a long way toward maintaining their well-being. Just twenty minutes of freedom of choice will help balance shelter life.

This is another reason we encourage everyone to consider volunteering at their local rescue or shelter so they can practice these HAC methods. Animals who feel some sense of agency, the ability to make some choices for themselves, will be happier. A happy animal has the best chance of being adopted, and providing tiny moments of freedom of choice is one thing we can do to make a difference in the day of a shelter dog.

The Five Freedoms

Another significant development in the advancement of animal welfare is the codification of the Five Freedoms. The Association of Shelter Veterinarians supports the concept of the Five Freedoms, which originated in the United Kingdom in 1965 and was updated in 2009 in the form presented below. These principles, while developed to consider the welfare of horses and farm animals, are relevant and appropriate measures of welfare for any animal species. Even just using the word freedom in the context of animals in our care is important progress. The five freedoms are:

- **Freedom from Hunger and Thirst**
  By ready access to fresh water and diet to maintain health and vigor.

- **Freedom from Discomfort**
  By providing an appropriate environment, including shelter and a comfortable resting area.

- **Freedom from Pain, Injury, or Disease**
  By prevention or rapid diagnosis and treatment.

- **Freedom to Express Normal Behavior**
  By providing sufficient space, proper facilities, and the company of the animal's own kind.

- **Freedom from Fear and Distress**
  By ensuring conditions and treatment which avoid mental suffering.

I love the five freedoms! And we propose a sixth—the freedom of choice. We feel that this is the next level of consideration that animals in captivity need.

Freedom of Choice for Animals

When we are training animals, if we include the concept of "rewarding the right behavioral choice," training is much more likely to be enduring because the animal has *chosen* to do a specific behavior and then learns that it is followed by a reward. We could call this method "freedom of choice training."

There is much to be done to educate society about freedom for animals. One organization, the Animal Legal Defense Fund (ALDF), has devoted itself to educating people and defending the legal rights of animals. Their documentary *Uncaged* shows their efforts to defend the rights of animals in captivity through our legal system. This is a long fight to prove that animals have rights to freedom, as people do in a just society. One of their fights involves getting animals released from solo captivity in zoos, such as elephants, who are very social animals. They have been waging a long battle to help one elephant, Happy, who lives in a zoo in species isolation. They are trying to get her released to a sanctuary where she will have not only companionship but much more freedom of movement and autonomy.

Escape from Captivity

I had a friend who worked at the Honolulu Zoo many years ago. The morning keepers began to notice something very strange—elephant dung along the walkways, very far away from the elephant enclosures. It was a mystery; the locks on their gates were fully intact and locked. Finally, when video cameras became available, they began to record the elephants' activities. They discovered that late at night, the elephants would unlock their cages and "go on a walkabout" through the zoo and visit with other animals. Then they would return and re-lock the gates before the morning keepers arrived.

Attempts at escape from zoos and captivity happen more often than people realize. Jason Hribal's book *Fear of the Animal Planet* chronicles many stories that don't often make the news. Frequently elephants, tigers, and many primates will try to escape, as well as octopuses (which are very difficult to keep in captivity). Once caught, the escapees are often killed because zoos know they will try again. In Honolulu, an elephant escaped from the Ringling Brothers Circus during its parade through the city streets. The elephant was shot. This inhumane treatment prompted citizens to pass laws prohibiting circuses from bringing large animals for entertainment to Hawaii.

The *New York Times* published an opinion piece by Emma Marris, author of *Wild Souls: Freedom and Flourishing in the Non-Human World*. She questions the value of zoos for large animals who are often isolated from others of their kind and do not have quality of life. Zoo animals demonstrate high stress levels through compulsive behaviors, like rocking, pacing, and pulling out their hair. Many are medicated with Prozac, Xanax, and similar medications to reduce their anxiety from living in a wholly unnatural environment.

Even though stories of zoo escapes are usually kept from the public, Emma Marris tells another story about a gorilla named Evelyn at the Los Angeles Zoo who escaped seven times in twenty years. "Apes are known for picking locks and keeping a beady eye on their captors, waiting for the day someone forgets to lock the door. An orangutan at the Omaha Zoo kept a wire for lock-picking hidden in his mouth. A gorilla named Togo at the Toledo Zoo used his incredible strength to bend the bars of his cage. When the zoo replaced the bars with thick glass, he started methodically removing the putty holding it in." Clearly, these animals are making conscious choices to escape.

Marris writes, "In the 1980s, a group of orangutans escaped several times at the San Diego Zoo. In one escape, they worked together: One held a mop handle steady while her sister climbed it to freedom. Another time, one of the orangutans, Kumang, learned how to use sticks to ground the current in the electrical wire around her enclosure. She could then climb the wire without being shocked. It is impossible to read these stories without concluding that these animals *wanted out.*"

Freedom Heals

It is amazing that many animals raised in captivity as slaves to human agendas can often be rehabilitated once they are removed from these horrific situations. For example, animals who have lived all or most of their lives in research labs can heal if they are properly cared for after they are released. Once they are safe, well cared for, and receive needed medical attention, being reunited with members of their own species is enormously healing. And, as these animals get their first taste of freedom, some for the first time in their life, it is beautiful to watch them unfold like flowers. Soon, they are expressing their unique personalities, and the freedom to express their natural behaviors is a priceless tool for healing. They remind us that humans can do a lot of good when we understand the true range of animal needs.

Chimp Haven is one rescue sanctuary that has a few hundred chimps who lived their lives in research laboratories and now enjoy a tremendous balance of freedom, group living, and structure. It is a joy to watch the videos of these chimps, many of whom find a best chimp friend. Most are able to let go of fear and trauma over time and live out their lives in social units with joy and freedom. And, of course, lots of bananas!

The respect for freedom of choice for animals changes their world and ours. Keep looking for small and large ways to introduce freedom of choice into the lives of animals who share your life.

Cats choose us; we don't own them.

Kristin Cast

Journal Reflections on Freedom of Choice:

1) How important is freedom in your life? In what ways have you had the freedom you needed? In what ways did you have that freedom denied?

2) In what ways, small and large, do you need more freedom? Freedom of expression? Freedom to express your innate or natural qualities?

3) If there are animals sharing your life, in what ways do they experience freedom? How could you add more opportunities for them to express some freedom of choice?

4) What would your life be like if you had more freedom?

5) What small and large steps could you take toward living a life with more freedom?

Re-Minder: I am free.

Even though Candy, a young horse, is confined in a corral, giving her the choice of engaging or not, or how she wants to engage, and for how long is a way of showing her respect. She chose to be very close to my flute playing and to honor me with her interest and presence.

HUMAN-ANIMAL
C O N N E C T I O N

PART THREE

The Spiritual Connection

WHAT HUMANS CAN DO
TO BE OF SERVICE TO ANIMALS

*The indifference, callousness, and contempt
that so many people exhibit toward animals is evil.
First, because it results in great suffering in animals,
and second, because it results in an incalculably
great impoverishment of the human spirit.*

Albert Einstein

About Part Three of This Book:

In this section I explore the spiritual life of animals. I speak of animals having a purpose and a Soul. I imply that there is a continuity of consciousness that extends beyond death. Some readers may be enthusiastic about taking this third step in The Human-Animal Connection journey. Here we explore the potential for spiritual connections between humans and animals.

For those not wanting to adventure into these realms at this time, the first two sections of this book offer an abundance of ideas and techniques with which to play.

However, I believe it is necessary to consider animals to be spiritual beings to correct the way they are treated in our world. Now is the time in our evolution for humans to take action in the service of animals. It is time to right the wrongs and to make amends for the ways we've disregarded animals' rights. It is time to correct our misunderstandings about their inner lives, their intelligence, their emotions, their desires, and opinions, including their right to basic freedoms. We need to respect their nature and their needs and do our best to provide and support their quality of life. In the words of Albert Schweitzer, "Compassion, in which all ethics must take root, can only attain its full breadth and depth if it embraces all living creatures and does not limit itself to mankind."

We can do better for animals. And we must!

THE SOUL OF AN ANIMAL
Continuity of Consciousness

Life is as dear to a mute creature as it is to man.
Just as one wants happiness and fears pain,
just as one wants to live and not die,
So do other creatures.

The Dalai Lama

Overview

Russell Schofield, a spiritual teacher, believed that animals in the wild are directly connected to their species' Collective Group Soul. For example, a bear would be connected to the Bear Group Soul, sometimes referred to as an "Over-Soul." Wallace Black Elk, a Lakota elder and shaman, believes you can tune into this Group Soul Wisdom such as Deer Energy, Bison Spirit, Beaver Spirit, Tree Spirit, and so on.

Animals who share their lives with humans still have the potential to connect to their collective consciousness and their Group Soul, but, like humans, some may not be aware of their connection to it.

In addition to a Group Soul, I also believe animals have an Individual Soul Connection. This is their personal link to the Divine, their essential, personal spiritual nature. It is the aspect of beingness that transcends life and death and has a continuity of consciousness. Some animals are fully in tune with this spiritual dimension, others less so. When animals have experienced extreme adversity or trauma, they may greatly benefit from a little assistance in reconnecting with their Soul. Being reconnected with their innate Spiritual Nature and their personal Soul greatly accelerates healing.

Soul Retrieval for Animals

Nohea is a black shelter dog with an unusual look. She is kind of wiry and has a pointed face like an African Dingo Dog. She was recovering from many injuries and was totally shut down, terrified of everyone and everything. She would shake and cower when anyone approached, even with a treat in hand. I spent a lot of time just sitting with her in her kennel. Not only was she very afraid, but it was also as if she had given up.

I began working with her Soul. I asked her Soul to come back, to help her so she could heal. I used some shamanic methods to reintroduce Nohea to her Soul, which is like connecting her to her guardian spirit. Just as humans can connect to their Power Animals or spirit guides, animals can also. As Nohea began to slowly feel this connection, she began to have a source of comfort. It took a few weeks, but her confidence began to return. She started to accept humans and even one of the other shelter dogs. You could see her spirit return. It was joyful to watch as she became comfortable in her own skin. And soon, the perfect sensitive person came to adopt her and take her home.

Animals Have Individual Souls

What I observe is that folks who believe people have Souls are more willing to consider the possibility that animals also have individual Souls. Why would one creature have a Soul and not another? When I speak of the Soul, I am suggesting there is a continuity of consciousness past the boundary of physical death.

But don't take my word for it. I am not trying to convince anyone as I believe each person needs to experience this for themselves. However, this is a topic worthy of your exploration because doing so will deepen your connection to all animals.

For the moment, let's say that animals have Souls. Then, how does that change our relationship with them? What does it mean—in terms of practical action—to acknowledge that animals have Souls?

Many writers have written on this topic. J. Allen Boone, for example, felt he was in complete contact with and still learning from Strongheart after the dog passed. He wrote an entire book entitled *Letters to Strongheart* in which he spoke to his dog as he would to a living friend. In these conversations, Boone shared his life adventures and believed he continued to receive guidance and insight from Strongheart. This is how he starts each letter:

To
Strongheart
Eternal Playground
Out Yonder

The letter begins with the words "Dear old pal" and closes with the words "I'll be seein' you."

Reconnecting with the Soul of an Animal

I am frequently asked to work with shelter animals who are shut down due to significant trauma. One technique I use for kickstarting their desire to reengage with life is communicating with and helping them reconnect to their Soul. As I said in my story about Nohea, I felt this Soul connection work was the turning point in her healing journey. I didn't see results the first day, but when I came back the next day, something had changed. It was as if she was back in her body, and our work had given her the courage to face the world again.

If you are working with your own animals, connecting with their Soul is a wonderful way to open the two-way door of communication and gain clarity about the animal's interior life. You can then enjoy "Soul-to-Soul" communication that bypasses thought.

To begin, you want to be as peaceful and as clear of personal agendas as you can be. Then ask to speak to the Soul of the animal. It doesn't matter if you are not 100 percent convinced it's possible to speak to your animal's Soul, as long as enough of you is willing to consider it. It is all right if you don't believe it at first because you need to experience it for yourself. And, when you do, then you will know.

Be patient and stay open to learning how Soul communication works. Soul communication is very subtle. You may get your answer in a dream or through synchronous signs a few days later. (You're not likely to hear a loud booming voice from the heavens speaking in full verse.)

When I first started working with Nohea, I wasn't sure if I had gotten "through." Since then, I have learned that *just the invitation is enough to start the reconnection process*. I invite the Soul of the animal to come and help the earthbound animal, and when they feel the presence of their greater self, it is enough to begin the healing.

Soul Communication Transcends Time and Space

Soul Communication is possible across great distances. It is even possible to speak to an animal with whom you shared your life after they have passed. I speak from my own years of experience successfully communicating with deceased animals, as well as that of many other animal communicators.

Soul communication happens in its own time because there is a "rightness" of timing for the animal. How much communication are they open to sending or receiving? How quickly do they want to connect? Just like with people, there is a range of desire for conversation. For some animals, the connection is instantaneous and flows easily. For others, it could take a few sessions or a few days to settle in. This is when you want to cultivate patience and neutral acceptance because your desire for speed or any specific result may interrupt your clear understanding of the communication.

When I am in Soul communication with a client's animal, the work we do *during* the session is only a fraction of the healing experience. After a session, the animal will typically communicate with me, often at odd times of the day or night. This is always pleasant and amusing, especially if I am working with an animal with a sense of humor.

Romeo was a horse with a sense of humor. True to his name, he would "pop into" my consciousness and *flirt with me* when I was doing a communication session with another horse. He loved being able to claim my attention when I was talking to another horse, and he would also answer questions that weren't posed to him.

Soul Communication follows the path of Spirit. This means that just because you want to know something or want it now, this information may or may not be shared with you. If you are tense, afraid, or too attached to a particular answer, you will not hear clearly. It all begins with you learning how to get peaceful and calm and letting go of trying to force something specific to happen. The reward is that Soul Communication is the most tender, auspicious, enlightened, and joyous communication you will ever experience.

The Continuity of Consciousness

If you already believe that animals have a Soul, the idea of continuity of consciousness will bring you great comfort. Every animal communicator I have spoken to believes with absolute certainty that animals' specific personalities and memories continue after death. Thus, they are able to return very detailed and specific information to their people, information that only the animal and person could have known. It should also be noted that the personality continues to grow and develop after they have left the physical plane, and they generally become spiritually expansive and less and less attached to the life they left behind.

The root word for animal is *anima,* which means having breath. Like the Hawaiian word aloha, which translates as "I recognize the breath of life—or spirit—within you," anima implies Soul. Direct experience is the best teacher, so if you don't already believe animals have individual Souls, I simply see my job as asking you to *consider this possibility.* Of course, in a scientific sense, I have no proof that animals have a Soul—or that humans do, for that matter. So, until there is some method of proof, we are in the domain of experience and personal beliefs. Some would say this is a matter of faith.

Remember, there was a time when it was believed that women, Aboriginals or indigenous people, and "savages" did not have Souls. That belief seems ridiculous to us now. So, perhaps there will be a time when people will laugh if someone suggests that animals do not have Souls!

Marianne Widmalm said in the *Times of Israel,* "The Soul is a concept used primarily by people of faith. It is the part of us that continues to live eternally after death. It animates the body and is the seat of consciousness and willpower. A body cannot live without a Soul. It can also be described as energy which, according to modern physics, cannot be destroyed but can only change form."

Where does animal consciousness live? I personally don't believe that consciousness lives in the brain; however, consciousness can be experienced as flowing through the brain. And the brain can become aware of consciousness. Leslie Temple-Thurston, a spiritual teacher who works with Anna Breytenbach, believes that animal consciousness can be experienced through our unconscious mind. This is good news because it means we already have animal consciousness within us; it is not something we have to acquire. Rather it is something we can allow to emerge, to enrich our experience, and it is why communicating with animals is possible. Consider this possibility: within the deeper parts of yourself, including your biology, your animal nature is alive and well and waiting for you to connect.

Why We Can Communicate with the Souls of Animals

We are animals, so of course we can communicate with the *rest of us* once we find where the "talk" button is to allow the flow and exchange of ideas. In Principle #11, I talked about our class for high school students, Canines Teach Compassion, and one reason that it is important to teach young people about compassion is that it opens perception. Compassion means being able to see multiple perspectives. Compassion serves not only the person on the receiving end but the person on the giving side. Author of *Animal Voices*, Dawn Baumann Brunke, an animal communicator, quotes the words of her golden retriever dog, Zak, "Being kind to others means you are being kind to yourself because, in the absolute nature of things, everything you do is done to yourself. There is no other being."

Even though we find ourselves in human bodies right now, we can still communicate with animals—if we have the frame that we are all One Being. From this perspective, we are *one aspect of ourselves, communicating with another aspect of ourselves.* We are all masters at talking to "ourselves," so we can redirect that same skill to connect and talk to those who are expressing themselves in animal forms.

What Llamas Can Teach Us about Consciousness

Curious about Animal Consciousness? Ask a llama. This is what animal communicator Neda Wittels did, as quoted in *Animal Voices*. She learned that llamas have a special role in anchoring light on the planet. In a conversation with Velvet, one of her llamas, he explained that they have both individual and group consciousness. Velvet said, "A llama herd is a single unit of consciousness at one level, and a combined unit of many individual beings at another. This means that, although we are individuals, we are always connected with each other and know what every member of the herd is doing at all times. If one llama is sick or giving birth or dying or eating or whatever, we all know."

Connectedness as the Root of Spirituality

Michael Jawer, writing for the *Center for Humans and Nature*, describes sentience as "The capacity of an organism to feel—which is fundamental to being alive." In this principle, the Soul of an Animal, we are going beyond emotional states and suggesting that animals have a unique consciousness or a Soul. Jawer's perspective on the spiritual nature of animals and why we should consider that animals have a Soul is because of their *experience of connectedness* to each other and to nature.

"Animals that express gratitude, play, contemplate nature, act to save a fellow-creature, or react mournfully to the loss of family members or other close companions are all, in my view, demonstrating aspects of connectedness. Such connectedness is the root of spirituality—with the capacity to feel and emote being central.

"In the end, Soul may be a profound matter of fellow feeling. The stronger the capability of a given species for fellow feeling, the more that species can be said to exhibit soulfulness. To view things in this way offers another important step in humanity's progression toward understanding its place in creation—and to appreciate the inheritance we hold in common with other sentient beings on this increasingly small, restive, and fragile planet."

In *Pleasure: A Creative Approach to Life*, the late psychoanalyst Alexander Lowen meditated on these Soulful connections and proposed, "The soul of a man is in his body. Through his body a person is part of life and part of nature... If we are identified with our bodies, we have souls, for through our bodies we are identified with all creation." And in the same vein, Jawer adds, "As long as we are alive—and therefore feeling—we are connected to one another and to the natural world. We are, in a word, *ensouled.*"

Lecturer Kim Sheridan recounts many stories of animal communication between people and their animals who have crossed over in her book, *Animals and the Afterlife – True Stories of Our Best Friends' Journey Beyond Death.* In her book, she quotes Wernher Von Braun, who said, "Everything science has taught me—and continues to teach me—strengthens my belief in the continuity of our spiritual existence after death. Nothing disappears without a trace."

My experiences with animal communication for myself and for clients have led me to believe that there is a continuity of consciousness and that animals have a spiritual nature as well as a physical nature. I am able to converse with animals who have crossed over, and clients recognize the information given in these sessions as being authentic to their animal friends. Several authors have written of their extensive and specific experiences with connecting to the Souls of animals. And many people who have shared their lives with pets feel this to be true. The vast number of anecdotal experiences suggests the idea of a continuity of consciousness for animals is, at the very least, a possibility.

> *When I look into the eyes of an animal*
> *I do not see an animal.*
> *I see a living being.*
> *I see a friend.*
> *I feel a Soul.*
>
> *A.D. Williams*

What if there was a consensus that animals have a spiritual nature? Would that change how animals are treated in shelters, on factory farms, in zoos and laboratories? Would it change how we hunt or fish or eat animals? Does it matter that we choose to eat eggs that come from cage-free chickens? (when I crack an egg, I thank a chicken). Does it begin to shift the economy if more and more consumers choose to purchase cage-free eggs with no antibiotics, even if these eggs cost more? So many levels of society would be impacted if more people felt that animals are spiritual beings, just as we are. If the bonds of connection were strengthened, our culture would do less harm.

> *Animals share with us the privilege of having a soul.*
>
> *Pythagoras*

The Soul of Your Animal

Stepping back from these societal issues, we can focus on the question simply, *Does my dog have a Soul?* Or my cat or bird or horse? If so, what does that mean in terms of how we spend our lives together? What does it mean in terms of being able to continue to connect after death?

Lawrence Harvey, the wildlife conservationist, and author of *The Elephant Whisperer*, was a very practical and pragmatic man. I don't think he believed that animals had souls when he first started. But living and working with wild animals gave him a different understanding. He talked about how when his team needed to dart and tranquilize the rhinos in the conservatory, the rhinos always knew they were coming to do that, even before the team had left the house. He sensed the animals understood their intentions, and he forbade any of this crew to even speak the words "gun" or "dart" when they were about to head out. It was easier for him to tell his crew to avoid using those words than to tell them he believed the animals knew their intentions before they had gotten out of bed that morning. In any event, by the time they got into their jeeps on their darting mission, the rhinos were long gone.

Respecting their wisdom and listening to animals helped Harvey save an entire herd of wild elephants whose behavior would have caused them to be euthanized by authorities. When he died, many years later, these elephants traveled hundreds of miles to his new home to pay their respects. The elephants arrived the morning of the funeral.

Crossing the Rainbow Bridge

Animals have a beautiful and powerful connection to their lifeforce, another reason it is so calming and restorative to be with them. Feeling their connection to the *All That Is* rekindles our connection to the Divine. So, while they are fully engaged in living and will do everything in their power to survive, they are not afraid of dying when their time comes.

When they know it is their time to pass over the rainbow bridge, there is an attitude of acceptance. In nature, life and death live side by side. Many species are on the menu for another species to survive. From the largest possible view, there is a sense of balance in nature.

Even so, it is painful for us to witness an individual animal, such as a penguin, who is about to become lunch for a fur seal, even though we understand it is part of nature's process.

While we may understand the balance between life and death when it comes to the natural world, one of the hardest choices people must make is the decision to end the life of a sick or suffering animal they love. If an animal is suffering or not having quality of life, then euthanasia can be an act of great compassion. This choice asks us to go beyond our personal needs to keep an animal with us and assist them in moving on.

Veterinarians I have spoken to suggest that if you can manage it, it is best for the animal to have you in the room during euthanasia so that the last eyes they see are yours.

In the wild, many pack animals whose time has come will leave the pack or herd on their own to pass peacefully or at the mercy of a predator. But domesticated animals do not have these options available to them.

Many animal communicators have written on the topic of animals being peaceful and accepting of the process of death. My experience is that in almost every case where I have been asked to communicate with the animal (at the point where the human and the veterinarian are discussing euthanasia), and I ask the animal, they usually say they are ready to go. In some cases, they feel so much of the human's pain of loss that they try to hang on. Others are clear they would prefer to pass on their own.

The deaths I have witnessed have been peaceful. The animals slip out of one world and into the next with the ease of going through a doggie door. They know what is happening, and they are not afraid. If anything, they feel the weight of the human's emotions and wish for them to be at peace.

The decision to intervene in an animal's exit from this world is deeply personal; there is no one-size-fits-all-situations answer. The decision is weighted down by so many deep emotions, but it may help you to know that animals approach death with a certain neutrality. If you are faced with the decision to euthanize, do your best to listen to what the animal's needs and desires are and weigh them against your own ability to handle the process of sickness and death. In many cases, giving the animal freedom from suffering is the right thing to do. Usually, when animals pass, either on their own or with aid, they do so in peace.

Before trying to communicate with an animal that has passed, I find it is best to wait about three days, to let them settle into their new reality. Although some are available to talk immediately, I think it is respectful not to "pull them back," even in consciousness.

Once they settle in, I find many animals become excellent communicators. They are peaceful and joyous and playing in their new reality. They can become great Spirit Guides, freed from their physical form. It is important to recognize, though, that they have new worlds to explore, and we don't want to distract them unnecessarily from the magnificence that is unfolding for them.

As the English philosopher John Gray says in *Feline Philosophy – Cats and the Meaning of Life*, "Cats do not need to divert themselves from the fact that they will someday cease to exist. As a consequence, they live without the fear of time passing too quickly or too slowly."

Journal Reflections on the Soul of an Animal:

1) How do you feel about animals having an individual Soul? Have you ever felt what you would describe as a Soul connection?

2) Even if you don't believe, *could you consider it a possibility* that animals have a unique, individual Soul? How would this change your experience of living with them?

3) What would it be like if you believed that every living creature and plant has a Soul? And everyone is part of the goodness of all life? How would that change your awareness of how you relate to living creatures?

4) Would you like to communicate with the Souls of animals? Why or why not?

5) How would the idea of animal consciousness open your consciousness? How would it change human society if it was generally believed that animals have Souls?

Re-Minder: All beings have a Soul.
I connect with the Soul of (your animal).

Connecting with the Soul of an animal changes us both.

STORY

Asher: The Canine Covid Detective

Dogs serve us in so many ways. One is through their amazing sense of smell. They can be trained to detect disease and to find bombs, missing people, and contraband. During the Covid-19 pandemic, dogs in several countries were trained to detect the presence of the virus. These dogs were deployed at airports in Finland and Dubai, at sporting events in Miami, and at train stations in the U.K. Their accuracy rate was equal to the medical tests, and the results were instant. In fact, they were able to detect the presence of the virus five days before a person experienced any symptoms. This was important since about 40 percent of Covid-positive people were not experiencing any symptoms.

Asher is one notable Canine Detection Dog I want to tell you about. This brown hound with long floppy ears and soulful green eyes had been returned to the shelter seven times! "He is just—*too much dog!*" the last lady said when she tearfully handed him over. Things were not looking good for Asher. Fortunately, Dr. Claire Guest, CEO of Medical Detection Dogs in England, adopted him and trained him to become a Canine Covid Detection Dog. Asher learned to detect the presence of the Covid-19 virus by sniffing clothing samples. Not only was Asher as accurate as the medical tests, but his intense focus and drive had found the perfect outlet and structure. Now, all of Asher's natural exuberance and boundless joy have been channeled into rewarding behavior. The best thing is that he has found satisfaction—and his place and purpose.

Instead of losing his life, he is saving the lives of many people he has never met. I wish everyone could be as happy and fulfilled as Asher.

I find that many animals I work with in private consultations are aware they are living and working on many levels and share their unique sense of purpose with me. Just as we have a desire to express our *True Nature* in the world, so do they.

It's not enough to have lived.
We should be determined to live for something.

Winston S. Churchill

Principle #29

ANIMALS ON PURPOSE

Being in Truth Leads to Truth in *Doing*

Our prime purpose in this life is to help others.
And if you can't help them, at least don't hurt them.

The Dalai Lama

Overview

All animals have a purpose. Animals in natural environments are connected to their collective species' purpose. Individuals may have specific unique purposes, especially if they are interested in teaching humans.

Domesticated animals are also connected to their group Soul purpose, although their awareness of this connection may be obscured if they are deeply entwined with the human whose life they share. The Souls of some individual domesticated animals choose to have their life purpose profoundly connected with human experience. As every animal is unique, so their purpose will be unique.

When an animal is on track with their purpose, their life is richer, and they seem more fulfilled. But just like people, a domesticated animal may or may not know or be on track with their specific purpose. Thus, they may need some help to express this aspect of their nature. When I conduct an individual communication session with an animal, they often share their purpose with me, and they are often quite specific. Certain archetypal spiritual themes will be revealed as well as each animal's unique thread in the tapestry of life. When I hear this information (I don't ask; they either choose to tell or not), it is a very treasured communication. If I can help an animal be more on track with their purpose, it is one of the great joys of my work.

Ricochet's Purpose

Ricochet is a golden retriever who was being carefully trained to be a service dog. She was called a puppy prodigy because at just a few months old, she could do it all. She mastered the obedience commands, she could open doors, turn off lights, retrieve fallen objects—she was a star. And then she hit adolescence and went on strike.

Ricochet simply quit doing what she already knew how to do. And when she started chasing birds, her trainer, Judy Fridono, was about to give her up as that behavior would disqualify her for service work. Fortunately, Fridono, who had raised her from birth, noticed that Ricochet could stand up on a surfboard in a baby pool and seemed to love it.

Long story short, Fridono realized that Ricochet loved balancing on a board, so she took Ricochet to the ocean. She was a natural and became the first service or *surf-ice dog* to help injured children ride the waves. She would ride tandem on surfboards with paralyzed children and adults. Children who had never been in the water had the ride of their lives. Her videos raised awareness and many thousands of dollars for needed rehabilitation for humans. And Ricochet had found her purpose!

Living In Purpose

All of nature has a purpose. If an animal is free to express their essence, they are living in Purpose. For a human, living in Purpose means living as close as possible to your personal truth. This is not just about what you do and the actions you take but how close or connected you feel to your actual design, which is the truth of who you are. When your actions are anchored to your actual nature, you will feel a sense of purpose. If actions are untethered to your true purpose, they will feel flat and even tedious.

The Sense of Connection to Spirit and to Purpose is linked. Animals live in a sense of connection to others, to their environment, to the present moment, and many experience a sense of connection to purpose. When an animal is living in purpose, they are connected to their place in the grand scheme of life. And that is enough.

Perhaps the greatest gift an animal has to offer is a permanent reminder of who we really are.

Nick Trout

Some humans get all flummoxed when I even say the word purpose. This is because we humans have a lot of weight attached to this idea. Purpose comes with a whole pile of mental stressors and *shoulds*: "I *should* know my purpose," or "I *should* be living my purpose," or "I am lost because I have no purpose," and so on. We have the idea that if we haven't single-handedly saved the world, discovered the cure for cancer, or ended animal cruelty, then we must be failing on the *imaginary purpose scorecard*. All of these mental constructs add up to being very self-critical. This judgment is the opposite of feeling at home with your purpose.

Sometimes purpose has some grand elements, but often it is simpler. *Following your purpose is about living your life truthfully and seeing what emerges.* Living a life of purpose means being true to your essence or true nature. What if we humans understood that our purpose is to know the unity of all life? What if we sought to experience the equality of all living beings rather than to dominate others?

Animals have shared with me their sense of purpose which had to do with very subtle aspects of beingness or consciousness, as the horse named Blue showed me. Many have educational missions. Often the ones they are educating are we humans.

Three Questions about Purpose

Before we talk about the actions of purpose, first ask yourself this question:

> *"If I was living in purpose, how would I feel?"*

Second, ask yourself:

> *"Which of my actions lead to feeling more
> of the experience of living in purpose?"*

Third, explore:

> *"What is one small step I could take
> that would lead me in that direction?"*

It is very valuable to seek clarity about purpose so that more of your actions will have a clear connection to what your purpose *feels* like. This will reduce the feeling that you are very busy but spinning your wheels.

Purpose is a spectrum of experience; it is not about absolutes. You can be *Living in Purpose* a little or a lot. Your sense of purpose can shift and change with life-cycle stages. So being on purpose is a dynamic and fluid balance between the parts of yourself that are in tune with your purpose—and the parts that are busy marching to other drummers. The goal is to bend towards being more in tune and on purpose. Be gentle if you don't know what your purpose is yet. But perhaps you have a vague hunch. A soft whiff.

Nurture that. Follow its lead.

Or—Forget about Finding Your Purpose

We can get a lot of "purpose stress" if we feel it is this elusive thing, like the Holy Grail, that we vaguely (or desperately) chase but never find. Psychologist Anthony Burrow suggests that it is not about *finding* your purpose like a lost item. It is about *cultivating* your purpose. This points to a much more active perspective.

Start by recognizing *the sensation of purpose* because your mind might have one idea and your heart another. It might be a subtle *towards sensation*. Something that is drawing you in a particular direction—and it feels *good!* Once you have a sensory link, you can take small but consistent steps in the direction that feels right and replicates or amplifies this sensation.

Cultivating your purpose includes the sense of evolving and moving toward a sensory connection to your true purpose. It is not just a mental idea; it should actually feel good to you. This sense of goodness brings you the joy of aspiring instead of the obsession with achieving. So, feel into what drives you, and feel where that energy source is coming from. What is that internal quest, the motivation that makes you look forward instead of backward?

Once you connect with the good feeling of your sense of purpose, it leads you towards what actions feel meaningful. Use the sensation of what feels meaningful to help you connect with your true identity.

This sensation leads you to your purpose. Connecting in this way begins to make purposeful sense of your life.

I personally have navigated many twists and turns in understanding my sense of purpose. At each point in my journey, I was either lost or convinced I was "right on purpose." I spent over forty years in the movie business as a writer, producer, director, and editor. I loved all my titles, won awards, and was convinced there was nothing I wanted to do more.

But life has a way of disrupting our current sense of identity. Circumstances intervene, usually with a significant upheaval, resulting in intense emotional turmoil that later reveals a truer sense of purpose.

I have had periods of being asleep to my purpose with only the vaguest sense of longing as to what direction I should take or how to take the first step. I offer this personal history to make the point that it doesn't matter where you are in the journey of finding your purpose. The road to purpose is long and winding. You will get there if it is important to you.

Tracking Your Purpose

Another way to simplify this purpose conversation is to borrow the metaphor of a railroad track. The train may twist and turn, start and stop, load up people and ideas, unload others—but there is a sense of momentum and direction to the flow that, in some sense, is unstoppable. When you are on track with your purpose, you are a force to be reckoned with.

In contrast, when you don't feel you are on track, life can feel tedious, monotonous, or aimless. Like you are going through the motions as if you are being steered by agendas outside yourself. This is painful. But you are not alone.

The 2019 Welfare, Work, and Wealth Survey conducted by the CATO Institute found that 46 percent of Americans *strongly agree* with the statement, "I feel like I have purpose in my life; my life has meaning." Does 46 percent sound like a high or a low number to you? To me, it means that less than half of the people in the survey felt a strong connection to their purpose.

The survey also revealed that people with a strong connection to their sense of purpose felt less envious or resentful and had more compassion for others, had a stronger sense of personal agency in the outcomes in their lives, and strongly believed in personal responsibility for the way their lives will unfold.

This study also showed that people who had a strong sense of purpose were strongly connected to groups and activities they cared about, such as religious affiliations or social groups. Or, as we call it in Act Resilient, "Getting connected to something bigger than yourself." Finally, those who volunteered were much more likely to score high on feeling a strong sense of purpose. So, get out there and volunteer for something you really care about!

Like those railroad tracks, your sense of purpose is going to twist and turn. Ricochet's story of becoming a surfing therapy dog reminds us that this trip is rarely a straight line. You need to have a patient, long-range view of this life journey.

What Animals Can Teach Us about Purpose

Animals can help us connect with our own Purpose. They teach by example that the first step to finding or reclaiming your purpose *is to be yourself.* A sheep does not wish she was a lion, a giraffe does not wish to be a rabbit, and a goat is not trying to be a fish; they are at peace with their nature. Like our animal friends, we need to be true to ourselves and not try to conform ourselves to somebody else's mold. You need to BE yourself in order to FIND yourself. If you are struggling with feeling out of sync with your purpose, spend time with animals and notice how they are just who they are.

Being in Truth Leads to Truth in Doing

There are many ways to look at purpose. For example, do ants have a "sense of purpose"? Is it an individual or group purpose? As Virginia Morell explains, ants use the "scent receptors on their antennae, to tell if another ant is friend or foe, spread warnings of attacks, call for recruits, and pass along news of the hunt." They work together toward group goals and to solve problems, yet they do this all without a leader. By rubbing their antennae with another ant's, much information is quickly communicated, and they appear to agree on the correct next course of action. I'm sure there are many human organizations who wish they could communicate complex information to the entire group so rapidly, work efficiently as a unit, and make decisions so harmoniously.

Ant researcher Nigel Franks discovered that each ant does make choices; they are not just performing hardwired reactions. And they teach each other what the right course of action is. Each ant has their place in ant society and is motivated to build towards the collective greater good. If ants have purpose, surely all beings do.

Working with others toward a goal for the greater good is one of the ways to connect to your personal purpose.

Meeting Animals on Purpose

I have had the privilege of meeting some animals who have very subtle and profound purposes, in this earth dimension and in others. In these sacred communications, I am often in awe of how they seem to be living parallel lives. On the physical level, they are simply a horse, a cat, a dog. But they also live in another stream of awareness where they have very specific, often subtle purposes that connect them to something larger. Many times, they are dealing with themes that *help humans* and assist our understanding of the unity of all life. Such was the case with a horse named Blue.

A Horse Named Blue

The other day I visited Equinimity, a wonderful ranch, and met a huge (sixteen hands) quarter horse, who is 40 years old (which is like 120 in human years), with a black-blue roan color, named Blue. Some animals, like Blue, are working on many levels. Surrounded by his people, Blue shared with me his purpose, which had to do with his particular kind of energy healing working through geometric awareness. He was placing or linking consciousness in positive patterns and configurations. Sometimes he used his body position with another horse named Brown to anchor these energy patterns. There was a visible element in terms of the angles they were forming with their combined body positions and spacial relationships. And this was also happening in consciousness, like fourth-dimensional chess. I am doing my best to convey the images he showed me of his work that has much stabilizing benefit for the planet. I had never heard of this kind of work before, and I was in awe of his mastery. He gave me a very beautiful vision, which frankly took my consciousness to a new level of experience.

After Blue showed me his purpose, I finished the session, as I often do, by asking, "Is there anything we humans can do to make your life better?" Blue answered with two words: "More treats."

I was surprised. After opening the cosmos before my eyes, taking me to a very elevated level of vision, all he wanted was *more treats*? I asked his people if they gave him treats, and they assured me that he was given all the healthiest and best treats. As a matter of fact, Blue gets the best holistic support, energy healing, and hoof care. But when it comes to treats, just like a kid, Blue felt he should have more. This was a reminder to me that some animals function on many levels simultaneously. After taking me on a super-consciousness trip, he also made sure to remind me that he was also living life as a normal horse and wanted *more treats.*

Seeing Purpose Changes How We Perceive

Once you have had a chance to have an animal share his or her purpose with you, it is never possible to just look at them as "just" a cat, dog, horse, etc. It changes your perception of who they are. Sometimes their purpose is focused on this lifetime and on interacting with humans. But often, they speak of other lifetimes and are working on multiple levels of experience. While it may look like they are just having a snooze, sometimes they are engaged in dynamically interacting with their Greater Purpose.

Animals have much to teach us if we will be their students. J. Allen Boone discovered this when he let Strongheart teach him how to communicate with animals. He came to understand much about their Spiritual Nature and their Purpose. And if you have a desire to do the same, perhaps it is your purpose to connect with the Animal Kingdom.

> *Animals are the bridge between us*
> *and the beauty of all that is natural.*
> *They show us what's missing in our lives,*
> *and how to love ourselves*
> *more completely and unconditionally.*
> *They connect us back to who we are,*
> *and to the purpose of why we're here.*
>
> *Trisha McCagh*

Seeing that every animal species belongs in the Grand Scheme of Purpose changes how you relate to them. Just to mention a few physical manifestations of how our well-being is connected, bees are powerful pollinators that help 90 percent of wild plants and 30 percent of the world's crops thrive. Beavers reduce flooding and wildfire damage, preserve fish populations, and combat some of the effects of climate change. Llamas are great guard animals on farms, scaring off predators, and they eat invasive weed species. Squirrels help trees take root, and birds fertilize the soil. All species contribute in some way to the interwoven Purpose of All Life. We wouldn't be here without these interconnected purposes of nature.

Paul Rosalie wrote about the unity of all life in the *Huffington Post* on Earth Day:

"Without plants and animals, our lives would not be possible. Oxygen, clean water and soil, and our earliest tools, food, and clothing came from flora and fauna… Throughout our development, our oceans and rivers have provided us with fish; grasslands and forests have provided us with bushmeat; plants that we cultivated became staple fruits and vegetables; ecosystems ensured reliable weather and clean water. We domesticated some wild animals to become our livestock, providing milk, meat, and clothing. Wild canines developed over the years to become dogs, our hunting partners, and bodyguards, our most effective alarm system in the night. Throughout those early ages, just like today, our world's fruiting trees and forests were pollinated by bats and birds, squirrels, and bees… Wild animals have their own inherent value, their own reasons for existing."

Journal Reflections on Animals on Purpose:

1) How do you feel about your personal sense of purpose? Do you feel "on-track" or "off-track"?

2) Was there a time in your life when you felt more "on-track?" What was that time?

3) Would you like to feel more certainty about your purpose?

4) What are you willing to do to move your life closer to the track of your purpose?

5) If animals share your life, do you have a sense of their purpose?

Re-Minder: I am my purpose.

Ralph, a former racehorse, who was abandoned due to injuries, was rescued by Equinimity Tucson. He loves to join our healing circle in the HAC The Power of Presence workshop. He has truly found his purpose as an amazing Therapy Horse.

Principle #30

THE POWER OF NAMES
The Spirit of a Being Is Carried in the Name

Words have meaning. And names have power.

Rick Riordan

Overview

Yes, it matters what you name an animal. In the Hawaiian tradition, the spirit or *Mana* is carried in and through the name. The name expresses the essence of a being. If you believe, as I do, that animals also have spirit (Mana), it is very important to give an animal the best name to reflect their true spirit. Giving an animal the right name for them reinforces "good energy" every time you call their name. You want to give a name that expresses the best in them, their Higher Self. You can have plenty of playful nicknames but give a dog a name he or she can grow into that invites them to expand into their true nature. Introduce them to new people with their elegant full name, even if you affectionately call them something shorter when you are alone. Giving an animal the right name is one of the most basic (and I believe responsible) things you can do to support them to live into their potential.

On the Wild Horse Haven Rescue, Afton had an adopted mustang who he named Rowdy. And boy, did he live up to his name. Every day Rowdy tried to stir up some trouble with the other horses, and Afton was starting to worry that he couldn't keep him with the other horses. Afton had learned that a name has power, and he decided to change Rowdy's name to Ares, for the Greek god of courage. He felt that Ares better reflected the horse's spirit and true potential.

Ares responded immediately to this new name. "It was like he felt it suited him," Afton said. This was the only change he made. "When I started calling to him, saying, 'Ares,' he started walking more proudly as if he knew he didn't need to rumble to make his mark. The horse still has his strong spirit, but he is getting along so much better in the herd. It's as if the new name gave him some respect he didn't have before. The other horses sensed the change. He didn't have to pick fights all the time. Everybody calmed down." Yes, there is grace in finding the right name.

Call Me by My *True* Name

Perhaps the idea that a name carries energy is new to you. Naming ceremonies are significant occasions in cultures around the world, from Western Europe to many indigenous peoples.

A name is not just an inert collection of letters; it is a living force. It carries a specific sound signature, which is a literal sound vibration, like a musical note. So, when you name a being, you invoke that specific note or essence. Thus, naming a being has consequence.

Ask any child who grew up on a farm if it is easy to eat an animal you have named. Calling them by their name and having that animal recognize that name as themselves is a powerful step of connection.

It is harder to harm a being you recognize as an individual

One client came to me with a frightened and depressed rescue greyhound that she was fostering. The name he came with was Ro. When I did a communication session with Ro, he told me that was not his name. He also told me he wanted to stay with his foster, not go to the home that had been planned for him. Unfortunately, Ro was adopted away from the foster. After many months we discovered that the dog was right; his adoptive home was all wrong for him, and he was getting sick with a variety of mysterious maladies.

I encouraged my client not to give up but to see if there was any way she could adopt him. When he was returned to the rescue, she was finally able to adopt him. The first thing we did was listen for his True Name. We heard the name Raleigh. This regal name allowed him to grow into a sense of safety and confidence, and Raleigh became a wonderfully talented therapy dog and worked with disabled children. Whenever they called his name, it looked as if he smiled in response to his true name.

And of course, dogs are not the only animals who learn that their name *means them.* Crocodiles in sanctuaries can be summoned by calling their name. When they hear their name called, they know it is their turn to be fed and will surface, while the other crocodiles will wait for their names to be called.

Pigs, chickens, elephants, cats, primates, dolphins—so many species can learn that when a human calls their name, it means them and not someone else. Calling them by their right name is one of the basic acts of respect and kindness.

In the words of veterinarian Linda Bender, "In the deepest sense, to name the animals is to recognize their dignity, their individuality, their nobility, and the meaning of their lives."

In some cases, a dog's spirit can overcome the "wrong" name. However, I have seen in my practice that there are many cases where a dog's life and well-being can really improve by having the right name. This is why, when I do private sessions for clients, they will often ask me to check in with an animal to see if *he or she feels they have the right name.* The right name is one that expresses and supports their true essence and personality. I guesstimate that about twenty percent of the dogs I have worked with told me they would prefer a different name or that they have another "Spiritual Name." The reason why the Power of Names is its own principle in the HAC is that it can make such a positive difference when an animal is given a name that expresses its best nature. The stories above about Raleigh and Ares show the right name can make a difference.

Owner-surrender dogs enter the shelter with a name, but that doesn't mean it is the best name for them. When stray dogs enter shelters, their name is unknown, and they may be given a name by a busy staff person who has likely just met the dog. Commonly, they could end up with a name that doesn't serve them. One municipal shelter where I volunteer takes in 50–75 dogs a day. These stray dogs need to be named quickly to get processed and placed into the system to prepare for adoption. So, these quickly chosen names may not be the best fit for these dogs' destinies. I have often noticed that dogs with the wrong names seem to take longer to get adopted.

Dogs and other animals can absolutely learn a new name; it doesn't take long if you work with treats! There is nothing wrong with a playful name that makes everyone smile and accurately expresses the dog's unique spirit. But if you adopted a dog with a silly name, a derogatory name, or a stereotypical negative name, please consider renaming them. You are going to spend years together, and you will be using this name every day, invoking the spirit of the name, so it's best not to reinforce negative, demeaning, or trivial qualities.

There are no absolute rules about names or what the right name would be. It is not about a fancy or obscure name or a several-syllable

THE POWER OF NAMES

name. Some dogs ask for more vowels. Others ask for consonants. Generally, if they need more dynamic or confident energy, they need at least one or more consonants. If they are seeking more intuitive or gentle energy, they want more vowels. Some ask for more syllables. Some want a more refined name. Most don't like silly names like a child might give or names that make them sound like bad dogs. Finding the right name is a deeply intuitive process. When I hear a possible new name, I always let it settle for some time before making a change to make sure it is the right one and that I have heard correctly. This is not a science, so be both humble and confident when a new name comes to you. See how the animal reacts by using this name multiple times and watching their reaction.

The Naming Ceremony

Many indigenous cultures embark on the process of naming a child with great reverence because they know the power of a name. A name invokes the spirit or essence of a being. The name holds and shapes energy. In the Hawaiian tradition, the child is not officially named until their first birthday. The family members will have "listened for" the baby's name; it may come in dreams to the grandparents. Some mothers will be given the name in a dream before the baby is born. The Baby Luau is the celebration where the baby is formally given their name, and the entire extended family, friends, and neighbors attend. In the Hawaiian tradition, naming a child is never a slap-dash task (although there may be nicknames). You have probably heard those very long Hawaiian names that might include ancestors' names in the middle. A name is given with reverence to achieve great spiritual clarity so the person can live into—and live up to—their name.

When I have adopted shelter pets myself, I ask for guidance from the Soul of the Animal to hear the right name. And I listen carefully, usually over several days or weeks. When I think I have heard it, I test it with the animal's response. While I take my time to make sure the name is right, I can usually get it down to two choices, and the final one "feels right."

I only make suggestions when asked, but when clients ask for this service, I will check very carefully to see if their dog has the best name. Usually, I send the person on their own mission to hear the name as this is part of the spiritual connection between them and the animal. When people find the best *mana* or spirit carrier for their dog, their relationship always improves, and the animal seems to be proud and more confident.

At the beginning of her career, the brilliant Jane Goodall was attacked by colleagues with a viciousness that equaled the violence she observed in the wild. The old guard was incensed that she referred to the wild chimps she was studying at Gombe as "he" or "she" instead of "it." At the time, animals were given numbers by researchers instead of names. Jane dared to give them names, like Greybeard the older male, and the first one to engage with her; and Flo, who became the dominant matriarch; and Frodo, the bully. Giving them names helped her to connect by acknowledging their unique personality and individuality. The wild chimps responded to her use of their names and knew who she was calling to. This did not sit well with those academics who wanted to view chimps as "things" you put in cages and experiment upon. Once you name an animal, he or she is now an individual, and you notice their specific nature.

Jane Goodall was very wise to name the animals she was observing because it created a bridge between her and the chimps, allowing for very close observation and astute understanding of the uniqueness of each one. There are those who believe we shouldn't interact with the animals we are observing. But because Jane Goodall did not let those academic prejudices stifle her, she was able to open the lives of wild chimpanzees to the world. And it all started with giving them meaningful names.

Anna Breytenbach, a very gifted animal communicator, speaks about the importance of naming an animal. She tells a story about working with Diablo, a black jaguar in a rescue sanctuary. Diablo would not come out of his inside enclosure. His attendants were afraid of his angry displays. Anna spoke to Diablo, and he said many things, one of which was he no longer wanted the name Diablo. Working with him, she discovered that he preferred the name Spirit. When they made this one change at the sanctuary, his behavior changed. He came out of his shell and began to interact peacefully with staff. This resulted in the staff *changing their attitude.* They were less afraid of him, and he felt this shift in their energy. As their energy changed, he was able to see himself differently. As they called him Spirit, he was able to move into this new persona. It all started with him telling Anna he wanted a new name. His entire life at the sanctuary changed. Thank you, Spirit, for showing us this wonderful example of the power of finding your right name.

Signature "Peeps"

Karl Berg, the parrotlet researcher working in Venezuela, found that birds call each other by their "name." He has shown that these birds' "peeping" sounds are quite complex and include sounds that the human ear can't detect. Using sound analysis equipment, he discovered that parrotlet birds call to each other by unique "name signatures" that they recognize.

The ability to be known by a unique name has significant survival implications. For example, a "wife" will only pick her head up from the nest if she recognizes the call of her "husband" returning with food. To pick her head up for just any parrot could be deadly, as wives can be captured. Many other species also assign names to each individual, such as dolphins who learn their names at a few months old and have "signature whistles" that are understood by the others.

What is also fascinating about Berg's study of mated pairs is that in addition to using their sounds to call each other's names, he has identified about fifteen basic calls that indicate the birds are delivering important information to each other about the environment, events, even gossip about their neighbors. Most importantly, Berg's works reveal that the parrotlets are having true conversations. That is, what is "said" by one bird influences another bird's response.

Remember the story of the man who lived with several cats discussed earlier in this book? He would call the name of one cat, and, even if that cat didn't choose to respond, the other cats would turn to look at the cat whose name had been called.

Names carry meaning. If you have named your dog, and you love the name, and you believe your dog loves his or her name, that is fine. I never argue about this. I don't offer my opinion unless asked or unless the animal tells me they are unhappy with the name they have been saddled with. One client I worked with had two dogs named by her young children; one was called Frank, and the other was called Beans. Beans didn't mind his name, but Frank let me know that his name did not express his elevated spirit.

Names don't have to be fancy. They can be ordinary; they just need to reflect the true nature of the animal. At Jacob's Ridge Animal Sanctuary in Spain, a donkey named Steve has a worldwide following on social media.

Here are some names of the animals I have adopted—whose names I changed:

1) Seymour – a guinea pig – original name was Doink
2) Madeline – a kitten, shelter name – Lou (turned out to be a female)

3) Wolfie – (Wolfgang Amadeus Mozart), a stray – name unknown

4) Seraphina – cat – shelter name was Fluffy

5) Oscar – dog – shelter name was Hoover

6) Sophia – dog – shelter name was Allyson

When I did some animal communication sessions at one horse rescue, the horses just asked for minor variations. Betsy asked to become *Miss Betsy*. Dixie asked to be called *Princess Dixie*. Fire (a formerly violent horse) asked to be called *Sweet Fire*. In every case, being called by their new names resulted in much-improved behavior and gentleness. For me, finding the right name allowed me to connect with their essential nature. This allowed them to move past some of the limiting judgments humans had imposed on their behavior.

If you have already named an animal and don't want to change it, that is okay. I am simply offering the concept of the power of names. If you are adopting a new animal into your life, make sure you listen and really feel into the name. Is this a name that conveys the animal's true spirit? Is this the name that helps the animal fulfill their purpose and destiny?

Journal Reflections on the Power of Names:

1) How do you feel about your name? Do you feel it expresses your essence? Does your name support who you are?

2) If not, what name would you like to be called? It doesn't necessarily mean you have to have a legal name change. However, it can be valuable to be called by the name of your choice by loved ones, or even just keep this name as a private "spirit guide" name. Talk to this new name in your meditations, and you will find great power in this connection.

3) How do you feel about the names of animals in your life? If an animal shares his or her life with you, do you feel they have the right name?

4) How do you feel about changing the name of your animal? If it doesn't feel right to change, *don't do it*. The Power of Names Principle is intended to inspire you to be in a process of exploration. Only do what feels right to you.

5) If an animal were to come to you in the future, imagine what his or her name would be.

Re-Minder: I am who I am.

When I adopted Sophia, her shelter name was Allyson. It is not a bad name; it just didn't express her essence. Finding her true name helped her Soul blossom, and she went from being an intense feral dog who scared grown men to becoming a wonderful therapy dog.

Principle #31

POWER ANIMALS
AND SPIRIT GUIDES
You Do Not Walk Alone

Overview

In Polynesian, Native American, African, and every indigenous culture I have explored, there is the principle that animals and the natural world speak to us. Their presence is a reminder that we do not walk alone. The animals offer wisdom and unique healing medicine. As Black Elk, a Lakota elder from South Dakota, has stated, there was a time when communication between the various natural kingdoms was always an open channel. While shamans (wise men and women who are healers) are still able to connect to the animals and nature, the average person has lost easy access. But that is something that can be restored. Our relationship with nature is not just physical; it is spiritual as well. We can open ourselves through pure intention to receive wisdom from our personal animal guides as well as from the entire realm of nature.

*We are always connected to the earth and it to us. Everything
we do repercusses upon it, and everything within it
repercusses on us. Unfortunately, most choose to ignore it
or are unable to recognize it. The saddest part is that when
we fail to reverence any aspect of nature and our intimate
connection to it, we are failing to reverence intimate aspects
of our own self.*

Ted Andrews

Talking to Clouds

In the Hawaiian tradition, there are signs everywhere. These are communications that can be read in the patterns of waves, clouds in the sky, flowers that cross your path, and in the movement of animals (especially from your Aumakua, your protective spirit animal). This simple but powerful awareness of the presence of communication and signs from the natural world opens the door to deeper connection. You will feel the unity between you and the sky, you and the mountain, you and the daisy, you and the fly.

I had one friend in Hawaii, Leilani, who would often stop right in the middle of a conversation and look up at the clouds in the sky. I came to understand that she was reading signs in the shape and movement of clouds. She would "see" animals in the clouds that had specific meanings in terms of qualities that she needed or were answers to questions she had asked in her morning meditation. Although I could rarely see what she was seeing, I saw how this moment of stopping and "listening" to the clouds gave her wisdom for her life and for those of her friends and family. I was once struggling with a decision and asked her to "read" the clouds for me. Her answer saved me a lot of heartache. I pay much more attention to clouds now.

Native Connection to Animal Wisdom

For the last 50,000 years or so, human life and the natural world have been entwined, although the level of respect for animals has varied greatly. While many cultures treated animals as mere tools of survival, shamans of various indigenous cultures have traditionally revered animals. These wise ones speak of mythical times when journeying between the world of animals and humans was commonplace. In the last few centuries, however, we who live in modern times have become very alienated from our animal nature. This disconnection leaves us feeling incomplete and vaguely lost. The good news is that we can restore our natural instincts, our Sense of Connection to the All That Is.

Many people have experienced the rejuvenation of spending even a brief time in nature, which is why there are many programs for veterans that involve immersion in the wild. This is a powerful way to restore the human spirit. But even if you are not able to leave civilization behind, nature is in the air you breathe and everywhere you look. Wherever there is a tree, a weed, a bird, a bug, an animal, a view of the sun, the moon, or the sky—that is your chance to switch your focus to the sustaining power of All Life. Take a moment to say "Hello," either silently or out loud. If some creature-being has crossed your path or entered your field of view, consider this a moment to develop your Animal Connection and Communication. What if this passing encounter wasn't something to ignore but a delivery of meaningful information or a sign of connection? What if it was an opportunity to take a breath and allow the connection? What if there was something to be shared between you two?

Getting yourself peaceful and calm in the presence of another life form is healing for both of you. Feeling gratitude or expressing positive energy changes you both. This does not require an elaborate ceremony (although you are welcome to do one). It can be as simple as breathing in the awareness that another being is here—as are you.

Talking to Daisies

Getting reconnected is simpler than you might think. It starts with a basic but powerful awareness of the presence of yourself and another being. You can open your heart to feel the unity and connection between you and the rest of nature. Once you invite this connection, nature begins to communicate with you. Rather, it has been communicating all along, but now you are choosing to listen.

My dog, Sophia, and I have chosen to listen to daisies. We have established a communication "sign" from little yellow daisy-like wildflowers. When we see one, it is a message to tune in and connect to higher wisdom. Sometimes Sophia will stop to pee near one, which allows me to notice this tiny flower. Once, in Patagonia, Arizona, in the middle of a huge barren field, she found the one daisy in a huge expanse of desert dust. It was an invitation to communicate, and I took the moment to listen for the message. These subtle but awesome experiences help me to stay connected to nature in a deeper way. Tiny experiences of accepting and receiving connection opens the communication door wider.

Native Americans, Polynesians, Aboriginals, Tibetans, and so many other cultures have a belief that each person has an Animal Spirit Guide, sometimes several. As mentioned earlier in this book, in Hawaii, these guides are called your *Aumakua*. These helpers protect us—if we listen to their warnings. They guide us—if we ask for help. They comfort us and give us strength—if we are open to their presence. Our *Aumakua* may have been with us since birth (or earlier), and others may join us later in the journey of life when we are ready for more power and wisdom. We can learn a lot from these gentle guides, but they will never intervene without our request and acceptance of their help.

Say Hello to Your *Aumakua*

Several Hawaiians I know have a shark as their *Aumakua*. Others have turtles, birds, butterflies—every species you can name. These animals were seen as wise guides who could provide wisdom when asked.

It is very likely that you have one or more animal guides who have been with you as a witness to all that has unfolded on your life's journey. If you know who your Aumakua is, say hello (often) to keep the lines of communication flowing. (You don't have to be in the physical presence of your animal guides to communicate with them.) Having a strong connection to your animal guides and a two-way flow of communication can help you feel less alone and help steer you in more glorious directions. Sometimes a new animal guide will "appear" to teach you something specific or to connect you to a needed inner resource for a particular healing.

Ted Andrews recommends cultivating a relationship with your animal guides and speaking to them as you would to a person. He says in *Animal Speak*, "The animal world has much to teach us. Some animals are experts at survival and adaptation. There are times when we can use those same skills. Some animals have great immunity. Wouldn't it be wonderful to learn their secrets? Some are great nurturers and protectors. Some have great fertility, and others have great gentleness. Some embody strength and courage, while others can teach playfulness. The animal world shows us the potentials we can unfold. But to learn from them, we must first learn to speak with them."

These vast learning opportunities are just one reason we want to encourage you to open your Animal Communication ability, as we do all our HAC students. James French, creator of the Trust Technique, offers a wonderful online course in Animal Communication.

Animal Communication is an essential skill for those working with animals in shelters and of course, those animals who share their lives with humans. It is also possible to speak to wild animals, and you can tune into a specific species to connect with their unique wisdom.

Each animal spirit brings unique and specific wisdom, as well as warnings if you are out of balance in some area. To give one example, if you wish to have more ability to manifest abundance through the right action and wisdom, you can work with the spirit of the Bison. The Bison Spirit reminds us to align our desires with our True Divine Plan.

However, the Bison can be unpredictable and dangerous if threatened. As Andrews states, "This can serve as a warning about keeping yourself well-grounded as you begin to work toward greater abundance in some area of your life. It is a four-footed animal and thus implies groundedness."

If you are drawn to Bison and begin seeing images of them, or they appear in your dreams, it means that there is support for your abundance as long as you are in alignment with nature.

The Praying Mantis and the Power of Stillness

Much has been written about Power Animals and the meanings of various Animal Guides. Read as much as you can from different authors to get a variety of perspectives and insights. Some teachers may have different viewpoints about the symbology of individual species, so have an open, curious mind. But in the end, listen to your own intuition; that is more important than what any expert says. Use the work of various teachers on the subject as a springboard for your own explorations, and don't treat others' opinions as gospel.

If Power Animals are new to you, I will just mention a few more examples to tickle your curiosity. Ted Andrews speaks about the Praying Mantis, an insect who represents the power of stillness. Some Chinese martial arts systems evolved around the observation of the activities of various animals. The Praying Mantis has also shown up in the mythology of various cultures. According to Andrews, "Most prominent are the tales of the Praying Mantis in African lore and to the Kalahari Bushmen… Whenever Mantis got himself into trouble, he would go off and hide. The Bushman would apply this wisdom by going off to sleep and dream of a solution to his problem. This epitomizes the keynote for this insect—the power of stillness…It is this ability for stillness that makes the mantis a great hunter and enables it to survive. It will wait motionless, blending into its surroundings. Then at the most opportune time, it will suddenly grasp its prey in its long forelegs, which fold over its victim and close like a jackknife upon it… Through learning to still the outer mind and go within, we can draw upon greater power—physical, emotional, mental, or spiritual…This is part of what the Praying Mantis teaches. It teaches how to still the outer so that when it is time to act, it is done with surety, accuracy, and great power."

If you are dealing with a situation where you face an opponent or opposition, and you want to make sure you choose the right response, the energy or spirit of the Praying Mantis will help you slow down and wait until you have come to understand the best strategy for a response. It is important not to take outer action until you turn inward, listen, and gain certainty about the *right* action. Meditating and asking for guidance from the Praying Mantis will help you strengthen your internal power of stillness and listening.

Many Native American cultures speak of connecting to various animals as a form of healing. For example, one can invoke *Swan Medicine*. According to Andrews, Swan Medicine relates to the power of awakening the healing principles of "True Beauty and Power of the Self, or Personal Power." Andrews says, "Swans are powerful birds… They are also devoted parents, and they mate for life, and some live as long as 80 years. They reflect the power and longevity that is possible as we awaken to the beauty and power within ourselves."

For those who are looking for a lifetime romantic partner, Swan energy-medicine can be beneficial, but only if one feels full of confidence in one's inner beauty and power. If you are feeling empty or ugly inside, you may thwart attraction to the right partner. The first level of swan energy is to fully accept one's own inner beauty and power. Then, with that foundation solidly in place, seek companionship.

Discover Your Power Animal

I hope you will be inspired to explore the possibility of connecting to your power animals, even if it starts as a simple curiosity about the mythology of the inner nature of various animals. Consider this a lifelong sacred journey of exploration. Take a moment to express gratitude, even if you are uncertain about the details of your animal spirit guides. Gratitude strengthens the bond and the communication, whether these are for spirit animals who have been with you your whole life or those who come and go to give you guidance and join you on your journey for various twists and turns.

In our high school class, Canines Teach Compassion, and for other classes, we at the HAC offer a meditation whose purpose is to help you open the door to meet your Power Animal. Have the attitude that connecting with your power animal is a relationship, an ongoing process. Our meditation is not meant to be a "quick stop to the Power Animal Convenience store." It is an inner focus and a lifelong learning adventure.

When I did this meditation with a woman who has been blind since birth, an animal came into her *inner vision*. Although she couldn't name this animal, we could both *see* and *feel* him, and each time we did this meditation, the same furry creature came to the session.

Also, remember that this is sacred work. It is not a good idea to discuss your power animals in casual conversation. Most Native

Americans will be secretive, at least about their primary power animal (as there is much lore about those who would use this information to attempt to steal the person's power). So, outside of a learning context or guided meditation or with a life partner, we recommend you keep this work and your evolving relationship with your power animal to yourself.

I will end this chapter with some more words from *Animal Speak* by Ted Andrews:

When we learn to speak with the animals, to listen with animal ears and to see through animal eyes, we experience the phenomena, the power, and the potential of the human essence, and it is then that the animals are no longer our subordinates. They become our teachers, our friends, and our companions. They show us the true majesty of life itself. They restore our forgotten childlike wonder at the world, and they reawaken our lost belief in magic, dreams, and possibilities.

Journal Reflections on Power Animals:

1) What is awakened in you in reading this chapter?

2) Do you feel you know who your power animal is? What experiences have you had that led you to know this one?

3) Would you like to open your heart and mind to discover your power animal? You can have more than one.

4) What would you like to learn or discover in connecting with your power animal?

5) Can you imagine being able to connect, talk, and receive guidance from your power animal?

Re-Minder: I am connected to my Animal Guides.

In our Canines Teach Compassion class, hearts and minds are opened through loving connection. When you connect with your animal guides, your life becomes much sweeter.

Principle #32

ETHICAL CONNECTIONS

Behaving As If We All Belong

Until we stop harming all other living beings,
we are still savages.

Thomas Jefferson

Overview

Metaphorically speaking, if there is a *Great Scorecard in the Sky,* we are flunking when it comes to how humans have treated the animal kingdom. As a species, we are dangerous! We have not only viewed ourselves as separate from animals but as superior to them. This attitude allowed humans to believe they should dominate animals and disregard their rights. We can't undo the past, but we can educate ourselves and do better in the future. It is time for humanity to change the course we have been on and become better stewards to our brothers and sisters in the wild and with those animals who share our lives.

A Bovine's Sophie's Choice

A cow had recently delivered a calf, and was thus expected to produce 12 gallons of milk twice a day. She would go out to pasture each morning on the dairy farm in upstate New York where she lived, but when she returned each evening, she produced no milk. The farmer called the veterinarian, Holly Cheever. Soon after he discovered that the cow had delivered twins. She had brought only one to the farmer, and had kept one hidden in the woods at the edge of the pasture. Every day and every night she stayed with her baby and fed her. Dr. Cheever examined her, and described this story in an article in Best Friends Magazine. The cow understood that bringing a new calf to the barn resulted in never seeing her baby again. She formulated a plan, keeping one calf hidden in the woods, and took care of her. She also seemed to understand that hiding both would have aroused the farmer's suspicion, so chose to keep only one for herself. "I cannot tell you how she knew to do this," Dr. Cheever writes. "All I know is this: There is a lot more going on behind those beautiful eyes than we humans give them credit for."

> *If you talk to the animals, they will talk with you,*
> *and you will know each other.*
> *If you do not talk to them,*
> *You will not know them,*
> *And what you do not know, you will fear.*
> *What one fears, one destroys.*
>
> *Chief Dan George*
> *Tsleil-Waututh Nation, Canada*

We Belong Together

Brother David Steindal-Rast defined ethics this way: "Ethics is how we behave when we decide that we belong together." I love this quote because it points to a culture of unity for all beings. If we truly believe that all life is interconnected, we won't ignore the plight of other animals. But because humans have put their own interests above other forms of life, we have destroyed many animal habitats, and now many species are facing extinction. And we have to face the facts that billions of animals are raised in cruel industrial farming, sometimes without the ability to even move. Is there any hope for doing better? Yes!

If you agree that a mind shift towards viewing all life with reverence is needed, there are actions we can take to turn the tide. One person can't fix it all, but if enough of us work for change, it will happen.

One way to start your contribution to change is by identifying the area that you would like to focus on. Maybe you want to help a specific species or type of habitat. Your interests may be close to home or across the world. You are sure to find many good groups doing great work on land, in the sea, in the air—everywhere. Research beyond the fundraising PR on their mailings or websites and look at the actions they take. When you find those organizations that match your vision and who are doing great sustainable work, support them. Volunteer if you are nearby, send money if you can, and spread the word!

You Can Save the Butterflies

Just one way we can impact our environment and help other species is to protect butterflies. According to the Environmental Defense Fund, (EDF), the beautiful orange and black monarch butterfly "makes a multi-generational 3,000-mile migration, traveling south to Mexico each fall and back up to Canada in the spring. West of the Rockies, the western population migrates to central and southern California each fall." The EDF reports that 90 percent of the monarch butterflies have disappeared within the last twenty years.

But you can help in your community by planting milkweed plants, which is what the caterpillar needs to survive. The National Wildlife Federation is one group that is working to restore the Monarch's habitat by "engaging communities in recovery efforts and empowering people to grow native plants like milkweed in the places where they live, work, learn, play, and worship."

Sacred Activism

A spiritual teacher, Brad Laughlin of CoreLight, believes that the first step to changing the world is to change yourself—your words, thoughts, and actions. He speaks of sacred activism, meaning that if you want to create change in the outer world, you want to make sure you are doing it from a pure heart. If you are in an angry or fearful place, you are not going to be as effective in communicating with others or in getting them to accept the changes you are proposing. While he sees the value in outer action, too, he suggests that the more peaceful and loving you are in your words and actions, the more effective you will be in changing mindsets about helping animals and the more impact you will have.

Anna Breytenbach, a wild-animal communicator, suggests that while we can have great compassion for animals, we do not need to see them as victims and ourselves as their great saviors. (This does not mean we shouldn't take certain actions to support their well-being, but rather we need to first attend to our own motivations.) She talks about how the animals often understand more than we think they do about how they are being treated. Elephants are in danger of extinction from a lack of natural habitat and from those who kill them to sell their ivory tusks. She offers a glimmer of hope when she mentions that in Mozambique, in Central Africa, a group of baby elephants is being born without tusks. She believes that this is a DNA adaptation to the situation in which they find themselves.

Solitary Confinement

In many laboratory experiments, such as in the cosmetics industry, social animals are kept in separate cages. This isolation just adds another unacceptable level of cruelty, as primates and many others gain a sense of well-being from connection and proximity to their species. The Kyoto University Primate Research Institute in Japan balances the rigors of scientific research with the social needs of primates. The chimps in their laboratories are allowed to spend time together and choose when they want to participate in the testing research. Giving social animals the option to engage with others of their species (at least some of the time) in more laboratories would make a huge difference in the ethical treatment of animals. Just restoring some elements of choice for animals in captivity leads to greater well-being, as we spoke of in Principle #27, "Freedom of Choice."

The opinion that animals are empty inside and just instinctual beasts of burden leads to animals being very mistreated. But if animals have emotions, if they feel pain, if they have a sense of self—if they have sentience—then we must do better. It is time to step away from savagery and make the world a safer place for all animals.

As Linda Bender, DVM, explains, "All the creatures of the earth have lives of meaning and purpose, aside from the values we place on them. Now more than ever, the nonhuman beings that share the earth with us have been entrusted to our care. How we value all life forms and how we treat them are true measures of our humanity."

In the Human-Animal Connection, our mission is focused on healing and education. So, we believe that every time we open people to the possibilities of animal sentience and consciousness, we are part of the solution.

Obviously, there are serious problems everywhere you look—on land, on factory farms, in the oceans. Ezra Klein writes in the *New York Times* about the unprecedented level of cruelty of factory farming in which the United Nations Food and Agriculture Organization estimates about 80 billion land animals are slaughtered each year for food, and between 50–160 billion farmed fish live and die in terrible conditions.

The massive nature of these problems can feel overwhelming. That is why even though all the issues are important, we suggest you get started by picking one cause or species you want to help: wolves, elephants, rhinos, animals on factory farms, the stray cats in your neighborhood, or any specific issue that calls to your heart.

One group I support, even though they are far away, is *Animals Asia,* as they are rescuing and saving bears from the East Asian bile trade. Earlier in this book I mentioned that lovely, peaceful moon bears are kept in tiny cages their entire lives, so their bile can be extracted to make men more virile, which is a destructive superstition. These animals get no veterinary aid, are in pain their whole lives, get no exercise, and have no contact with members of their own species. Animals Asia has rescued hundreds of moon bears and has done much to educate the public, which has led to laws that aim to end this practice and protect these gentle animals.

On their website, you can see videos of how these bears are able to overcome a lifetime of trauma with the right medical attention, good nutrition, and the support of members of their own species. Getting involved in a cause you really care about will lift your spirits, and it will make a difference.

Although Temple Grandin's understanding of the importance of reducing fear as animals head to slaughter has greatly helped, much more needs to be done to improve the quality of life for farm animals. So much about life for industrial farm animals is beyond horrific. (If you are brave, read Peter Singer's classic book *Animal Liberation*.) I couldn't possibly address all the issues where animals need our help, so I thought I would focus on one area for this chapter: animals being used in research labs. It is not that this is the only problem or even the worst. I just find that many people I speak to do not realize the scope of this abuse and the importance of speaking up to protect animals trapped in research labs.

Animal Experimentation

In 1929, the National Anti-Vivisection Society (NAVS) was formed to end cruel and outdated research methods. Their definition of vivisection is "the practice of cutting into or using invasive techniques on live animals." To be clear, NAVS is very much pro-science. Their position is that science needs to be updated with new knowledge and needs to include an ethical perspective. Animals are not just disposable things. Here is NAVS's mission statement:

"NAVS promotes greater compassion, respect, and justice for animals through educational and advocacy programs based on respected ethical, scientific, and legal theory. Supported by extensive documentation of the cruelty and waste of vivisection, NAVS works to increase public awareness about animal experimentation, to promote positive solutions that advance humane science, to support the development of alternatives to the use of animals, and in cooperation with like-minded individuals and groups, to effect changes which help to end the unnecessary suffering of animals."

There is a movement to rescue laboratory animals after they are no longer valued as research subjects and send them to special sanctuaries who are prepared for their healing. Many labs just euthanize when they are finished with the animals. One rescue group, ChimpHaven, gives primates a final chance to have a happy life through their impressive rehabilitation process. (In the HAC, we invite students to watch videos of these chimps who manage to let go of their past. The chimps are role models for humans to understand that resilience is our nature.)

Many different animals end up as research subjects. Dogs, often beagles (because they are sweet and trusting), as well as pigs, mice and rats, rabbits, kittens, and primates, are just some of the animals used in research labs. I am all for scientific progress, but the issue NAVS points out is that *95 percent of the products tested on animals (and appear to be safe for animals) turn out not to be safe in human trials.* The moral of the story is that:

*Animal research for human medicine is highly **ineffective**.*

One example from a 2013 report found that around 100 different vaccines had been shown to prevent HIV in animals, and yet not a single one had any effect on humans. Thus, many animals were sacrificed for no good reason.

Ekaterina Breous-Nystrom, PhD, Head Investigative Safety-Toxicology at Roche, said, "Roughly three out of five drugs fail clinical trials based on safety issues. This is despite all tested drugs currently having undergone safety testing in multiple animal species. The limitation of predictability of human safety in animal models is often due to subtle contextual differences which can only be understood after failure in man."

NAVS gives grants to promising researchers who are devising more accurate methods of testing that do not involve animal research. These new technologies and methodologies using human cells and computer models are much more cost-effective and potentially much more accurate when it comes to how these experimental drugs and procedures will work with humans.

Much military animal research is done in secrecy (funded by taxpayers), so we don't know how many animals are euthanized in these labs. We do know that the animals in these military studies are often not protected by the Animal Welfare Act. NAVS estimates that 90 percent of the animals in these military labs have no protection at all. They live like prisoners without any comfort and are not given a chance to be adopted afterward.

It is difficult to know how many animals die in labs each year as there is no proper accounting, but NAVS cites a 2021 statistic of 111.5 million mice and rats exterminated in labs. And each year in the U.S, at least 44.5 million mice and rats are estimated to be used in painful or distressful experiments. NAVS makes the point that "Current selection of a specific animal model (for experimentation) seems to be based on tradition rather than its potential predictive value (for humans) in clinical outcome."

Alternatives to Frog Murder

Frog dissection in schools results in 6–10 million frogs being captured and then killed to be sent to classrooms each year. Many ethical-minded students are traumatized by this dissection process, as I was. Students who refuse, as I did, are often given harsh grades. Today, in about eighteen states in the U.S., students cannot be penalized if they opt out of dissection. NAVS has been working to create computer-simulated dissection models that are cheaper and more humane. Even though there are better learning alternatives, many educational institutions defend old practices simply because they have always been done that way. These dissection experiences turn off many compassionate students, and NAVS fights for their rights to opt out of these outdated learning models.

Only a few states in the U.S. currently have laws that prohibit the use of animals for product testing when alternatives are available. Perhaps you have seen the horrific experiments done by Volkswagen that put monkeys in glass cages, watching cartoons, to test carbon emission, and gassed them until they died.

Animal testing for cosmetics is still allowed in 80 percent of the countries in the world and results in millions of animals dying each year. The experiments on rabbits, guinea pigs, and mice often involve barbaric methods, yet according to the US Humane Society, the Federal Food, Drug, and Cosmetic Act, regulated by the FDA, "*does not require that animal tests be conducted to demonstrate that the cosmetics are safe.*" Yet, they are still being done—even though they are not scientifically justified—because these animal studies do not effectively prove their safety in humans.

Do *Something!*

What can you do about these overwhelming ethical issues? Start small. Or start large. Get involved with the animal welfare issues that matter the most to you. Lobby your elected officials and support organizations that are doing good work. Find others who share your passion. We can do better for the animals who have given their lives; it is time to stop this unscientific and brutal practice.

Virginia Morell ends her book *Animal Wise* with these important questions: "What do the minds of animals tell us about ourselves? That, like us, they think and feel and experience the world. That they have moments of anger, and sorrow, and love. Their animal minds tell us that they are our kin. Now that we know this, will our relationship with them change?"

Please. Do what you can to help!

> "*The greatness of a nation and its moral progress can be judged by the way its animals are treated.*"
>
> *Mahatma Gandhi*

Journal Reflections on Ethical Connections:

1) What emotions arise in you from reading this chapter?

2) What are you most passionate about relating to ethical connections with animals?

3) Are you ready to connect with others who share your passion and commitment to help?

4) What actions most draw you to participate in to help animals?

5) What scale of action do you feel drawn to? Local actions? National or international?

Re-Minder: It is time for humanity to have a more ethical relationship with animals. And humanity starts with me.

In our Canines Teach Compassion course we practice loving animals and being loved in return. This is the growing ground of compassion.

Principle #33

DIVINE CONNECTIONS

Loving an Animal Awakens the Soul to Divinity

If having a soul means being able to feel
love and loyalty and gratitude,
then animals are better off than a lot of humans.

James Herriot, DVM

Overview

Readers of this book are ready to move beyond the framework of pet ownership to one of spiritual partnership with animals as we embrace the divine connection between all life. We accept that animals have rich inner lives, emotions, desires, and they have a right to express their true nature. We are all animals and understanding that we are more alike than we are different helps us to see the fundamental unity of all life. As we invite the profound connection that we have with animals, much healing occurs. And we get to experience joy and sweet, pure love.

A Monk Becomes a Parrot

"In my last life I was an enlightened Tibetan monk." These were the words of Jing, an African Gray parrot that animal communicator Dawn Baumann Brunke had extensive conversations with. According to Jing, one hundred years ago, he had lived a peaceful, deeply spiritual life high in the mountains of Tibet, but after he passed, he chose to come back as a parrot to further express his divine purpose of teaching humans. In her book *Animal Voices – Telepathic Communication in the Web of Life*, she recounts Jing's description of why he chose to come back as a bird: "My mission is to bring awareness and awaken humanity by teaching reverence for all life, including animals."

Pope Francis took a stand on the question of dogs going to heaven and told a little boy who had lost his dog that "Paradise is open to all creatures." Author James Thurber said, "If I have any beliefs about immortality, it is that the dogs I have known will go to heaven, and very, very few persons." If you are fortunate enough to have loved an animal and been loved in return, you have tasted divinity.

Summary: What We Believe

The Human-Animal Connection philosophy begins with a basic belief in good. This good exists in both animals and humans. And while there are certainly examples of *un*-good, the perspective that goodness exists and potentially exists across all species can change how we relate to all life. In other words, the belief in and cultivation of goodness is a force for change.

We believe that embracing our animal nature helps to undermine the false edifice of separation between humans and animals, which has caused so much harm. As we come to know the unity of all life, we evolve as a species.

For humans, the path to an authentic life involves embracing the sensory intelligence that animals demonstrate so clearly. This perspective allows us to recognize the inner lives of animals and their emotions, desires, and opinions. Once we see any being as a sentient individual, it is harder to deprive them of basic freedoms, including the freedom to express their true nature and the ultimate freedom: the protection of life itself.

When we respect the wisdom of animals, we become wise. And as we *come to our senses,* our lives become more truthful and meaningful.

Animals Guide Us to Compassion

The Human-Animal Connection Therapy Dog program, *Canines Teach Compassion,* has shown over a 50 percent decrease in reported stress levels. This is the power of loving connection in action. Our research with students using HeartMath technology, which measures heart rate variability and other indicators of stress shows that interacting with animals creates a calm, safe, stress-free state called coherence. And when we bring this sense of safety to humans and animals, the body's natural healing resources are best activated. Both humans and animals can experience trauma, but just as importantly, by increasing a visceral sense of safety, trauma can be healed.

Healing between people and animals goes both ways. Helping animals heal benefits people. And therapy and companion animals benefit us in ways that are beyond words.

Humans Can Be of Service to Animals

As humans, we can do better to make the world a happier and safer place for animals. With the animals that share our lives, we can become more attuned to who they are, give them a name that expresses their spirit, and listen to what they really want. When we attune to their divine nature, our intuition opens, and communication easily follows. It is possible and very natural to communicate with animals. It takes time, practice, and some understanding of the way in which they communicate, but if this is a true heart desire, you can learn to do it. Animals are communicating all the time; we just need to receive the messages.

There is much to be done to right the wrongs of civilization when it comes to the treatment of animals. Most spiritual thinkers reject the notion of separation between other animals and us, which leads to the idea that humans should have dominion over animals. As minister and author Cesar Bujosa says, "In the practice of non-Duality humans and animals are equally and inextricably connected to God, therefore the notion of hierarchy is false."

When we cultivate reverence for animals and choose love over other impulses, we are elevated in consciousness. If you are yearning to make lives better for animals, take the actions that call to you, that move your heart, that feel good as you think about doing them. You don't have to solve every problem. If you adopt one animal and give them a life filled with love and kindness, you have changed the world for that one animal. If you can do more, please do.

Please spread the word about this work to those who are interested in making the world a better place for all life. And join us in the mission of loving connections between people and animals.

Some Pig

In E.B. White's book *Charlotte's Web*, a spider saves the life of Wilbur, the pig, by writing the words "Some pig" in her web, and then the farmer thinks twice about having Wilbur for dinner. You never know what it is that will wake people up to the plight of animals, so keep looking for the right message. One film, a remarkable documentary made in 2020 by Viktor Kossakovsky called *Gunda*, is the story of a mother pig and her fate on the farm. It is told entirely in the style of neutral observation. The film is in black and white, and there are no actors, no dialogue, no narration or music, and only natural sounds. It is a story of Gunda, a pig, told from her point of view.

It is a powerful cinematic experience that will change you as there is no mistaking the emotional life of Gunda and her life on the farm. We have to do better than this for farm animals! Kossakovsky said in an interview after the film, "If you have a Soul, an animal has a Soul."

To Re-Be or Not to Re-Be

If there are no dogs in heaven,
I want to go where they went.

Will Rogers

Do we reincarnate? Do animals reincarnate? Or do we just get one shot at life? Many people believe in reincarnation. Some believe that a human may have once had a life as an animal. Some believe animals and humans go back and forth in the reincarnation cycle, meaning you could come back as an animal after living life as a human. The story of Jing, the African gray parrot who was able to recount details of his previous life as a Tibetan monk, is one example of a human choosing to come back as a bird. Occasionally I have met animals who seem to be very, *very* human. And I've had more than one client tell me they would like to come back as my dog! But others believe that once you incarnate as a human, you don't reincarnate again as a nonhuman animal.

What do you believe? Do animals have Souls? Do they have more than one lifetime here on Earth? Will you see them again after they pass? One very good reason to learn to communicate with animals is that they love to tell you about their experiences with life beyond this one.

Once you open the door to communicating with animals, your world and theirs expand. Animal truth is always surprising and sublime. Welcome to the wonderful world of authentic communication. It is a journey of connection and joy.

Journal Reflections on Divine Connections:

1) How have animals contributed to your life? Emotionally, mentally, physically, spiritually, and for companionship?

2) What have you learned from this book that you wish you had known earlier in your life about animals?

3) What is one thing you would like to change in your interactions with animals?

4) How does the perspective that our relationship with animals is a Divine Connection change how you live together?

5) What is one small action step you are willing to commit to that would strengthen your Divine Connection with animals?

Reminder: I have a Divine Connection with all Animals

Sophia taught me that teachers
come in all shapes, sizes, and
colors.

AFTERWORD

Three Steps to Make a Better World for Humans and Animals:

1) Add more love
2) Apply the principles in this book
3) Add *more* love

APPENDIX

WORKBOOK
Practice Exercises for the Principles in This Book

Part One:
HOW TO BE A BETTER HUMAN FOR YOUR ANIMAL

Principle #1
GOOD MEDICINE

Practice Lessons and Training Tips – For Becoming a Good Human:

1) Practice saying "Good (doggie)" to another being. The tone of voice matters, as it reflects the truth of how you feel. Say it tenderly. Or softly, or enthusiastically, or while giggling or sweetly touching another. Notice how you feel. Notice the receiving energy from the other being.

2) Practice saying, "I am good." You may feel silly at first. You may not believe it. Your mind may produce a series of reasons why this is not true. Saying these words may trigger an eruption of objections, a laundry list of your perceived faults. "I can't say I'm good because I know I am an awful, selfish, horrible person." Just say to yourself, "Thank you for sharing

that." And politely go back to saying, "*And I am still a good person.*" If you are wondering why all the negative thoughts burst through when we open the door of goodness, it is a natural quality of the mind to see duality and contrast. For example, you know cold because you know hot. You know on because you know off. You know day because you know night.

3) Mentally holding the feeling of goodness builds your goodness muscle. Over time you can train yourself to orient toward good. Do not let the "bad" thoughts win. You may be undoing a lifetime of "bad programming," so be patient and persistent, as these are the same qualities you will need if you are training an animal. This is how you heal your relationship with yourself. And this is how you improve the quality of all your relationships.

4) Now expand your experience of goodness. After you have some comfort with these exercises and have proven to yourself the benefit to well-being, then expand this silent process to all living beings. Say *good tree.* Or *good cloud, good bird, good world,* or *good* (anything you want to add). You may do this while moving or sitting still. Try it while you are walking, brushing your teeth, grooming an animal, doing the dishes, taking a shower—any time you have a bit of privacy and can have some inward focus. See if you can speak these words for a few seconds at first, then work up to sustaining it for a few minutes.

5) Enjoy this powerful *Good Medicine.* Animals convey this energy when you connect with them deeply. This experience helps you transcend the duality of good and evil and moves you into the higher realms of goodness as the natural state of life. If this exercise is challenging, it is because we have so much false programming that has made us believe we are

bad and unworthy of the experience of good. So, if this is hard, you are stretching and doing it right. It means you are hungry to remember your own innocence. Claiming your good-ness will heal your Soul.

Re-Minder Affirmation: I am good.

Principle #2
CONNECTING TO YOUR ANIMAL NATURE

Practice Lessons and Training Tips – For Welcoming Your Human-*Animal* Nature:

1) Spend a day with your full attention on each of your senses as an animal might sense them. Imagine hearing with a horse's sensitive, swiveling ears. Touch various textures as if with a cat's soft paw. See your world as a bird might see it. If you like, make notes in your sensory journal. Returning to read these impressions will be good medicine.

2) Without judging, simply and neutrally observe animals—in the wild, in captivity, in your life, and around you. The goal is to just observe with as little thinking as possible. How is what you are observing in animals true for you also? What does it show you about your animal nature?

3) Think about the times when you "just knew." Did you follow your intuition or gut sense? Or did you ignore it? What

were the consequences of listening or not listening? Make a choice to connect with your sense of your True North. See what happens as you make this commitment to pay attention to your inner compass.

4) Embrace your animal nature. Trust this part of yourself. As you do this, it takes you on a very personal journey of discovery. It is exciting to find your animal-self anew.

5) Find a place where you can howl. Howl long. Even in your bathroom or bedroom, or car. Even if you must do it quietly, feel the flow of connection that comes with giving yourself this little dose of freedom.

Re-Minder: I am a human-animal.

Principle #3
COME TO YOUR SENSES

Practice Lessons and Training Tips – For Coming to Your Senses:

1) As mentioned in this chapter, take a moment each day to fully experience life and the world around you, wherever you are, through your senses. One day for each sense. Notice what you see around you, what you hear, what your hands can feel, and what smells and tastes. Deliberately put your attention on opening one of the sensory systems that you use the least.

2) Trust your senses and let them lead you where they want to go. Follow what feels good. Try that for a day or an afternoon hike.

3) If possible, spend a few minutes each day with your body or bare feet in contact with the ground, the earth, and see if you can feel the sense of rejuvenation this provides.

4) Observe what an animal is observing and observe with them. If you are working with a cat, and you can't see what they see, just turn your attention towards what they are looking at. Use your imaginary "cat eyes" and pretend you can see as they might be seeing.

5) The sense of smell opens access to your primal brain and is connected to memory. Pay particular attention to awakening your sense of smell. You might work with some pure essential oils, such as pure orange, pine, or lavender. Find a scent you delight in and take "scent breaks" during your day; simply inhale the fragrance and let it open your senses. You can also enjoy scents you have around the kitchen like natural vanilla, cinnamon, coffee, or dark chocolate. Principle #23 explores more deeply how sniffing is so good for all animals and helps them reset their nervous system. It has just as many benefits for humans.

Re-Minder: I come to my senses.

Principle #4
SENSE-SATIONAL AWARENESS

Practice Lessons and Training Tips for Sense-Sational Awareness:

1) Spend some time each day being in *the embrace of the present* by using your senses to be here now.

2) Do one thing each day that brings pleasure to one or more of your senses.

3) Really look at your personal environment. What is one thing that pleases you? What is one change you can make that would make it even more pleasurable?

4) What is one routine thing that you have to do that doesn't please you? It could be the dishes or brushing your teeth. What if you put all your focus on one of the senses as you do it? Notice how this changes the experience.

5) Do our "Feel-Safe-Breathing" exercise. Breathe in to the bottom of your belly. As you exhale, feel the sensation as you silently say the words, "I am safe now."

Re-Minder: I sense what I need to know.

Principle #5
ANIMAL PRESENCE

Practice Lessons and Training Tips for Animal Presence:

1) If you share your life with an animal, take time each day to just be present with that animal. The purpose of this exercise is to experience how presence affects each of you.

2) Observe, without judgment, how present animals are. Use as many of your senses as possible to experience their presence. Avoid having a specific agenda or an idea about what you think should happen.

3) When you pass a dog on the street, take a second to just acknowledge their presence without approaching. See what happens. Notice if the animal can receive this silent greeting.

4) Spend some time in the presence of wild birds or other wild creatures. Notice how still you have to be inside and outside for them to accept your presence. If you live in a city, practice with pigeons; offer breadcrumbs. We have greatly underestimated the intelligence of pigeons and have given them far too little respect.

5) Notice how you feel when you take even a moment to simply be here now. Get present, be still, focus on your senses. Compare this sensation of presence to the clutter you feel when you are being swept away by your mind's chatter.

Re-Minder: My presence is my power.

Principle #6
LOVE BEYOND WORDS

Practice Lessons and Training Tips for Love Beyond Words:

1) Think of an animal you love or have loved. Express your love and gratitude to them, not through words but silently. Then express the same feelings out loud through words and through a loving tone of voice. Compare how these two styles of communication feel to you. Do you observe any differences in how the animal receives them?

2) If there is an animal in your presence, how can you express your love through touch? What other ways can you connect without physical touch?

3) Spend some time with an animal. Focus your thoughts and emotions on the feeling of love. Notice how the feeling of love changes you and also the animal's behavior.

4) After you do step three above, focus on opening your own heart to feel *the return* of love. Let go of any preconceived ideas of what that should look like or feel like. Just allow yourself to be open to receiving. Notice how you feel and what you come to understand.

5) What area of your life or your body needs healing? Focus on that area and then mentally send the feeling of love to that place. Notice how love can be delivered with or without words. Notice what happens when you send yourself love.

Re-Minder: Loving animals heals us both.

Principle #7
THE LANGUAGE OF TOUCH AND CONNECTION

Practice Lessons and Training Tips for Touch and Connection:

1) Be grateful for your hands and for the sensations your feel. Spend the week paying attention to touch and texture. Really feel the objects you touch, the various surfaces and textures in your environment. Add some squishy things to your life because they awaken the touch sensation. Squeeze different things, like stress balls, or things with different "hand feels." Massage your own hands to activate their sensitivity.

2) Give a massage to an animal who would enjoy it. Let go of any concept you might have about what an animal massage should be, and just let your intuition be your guide. Vary your method and style and observe the animal's response to specific touches. Occasionally stop touching or leave your hand still on their body and see if they nudge you to continue. Be aware of when enough is enough. Stop if or when the animal walks away. It doesn't mean your massage wasn't enjoyed; it means they have had enough for that moment. Especially if you are giving a massage to a cat, a little goes a long way. Accept a short session with appreciation and try again another day.

3) Make an honest assessment of how you feel about touch. How has the experience of touch been in your life in the past? Did you get your touch needs met or not? What was touch like at different times of your life?

4) If you had touch that was unwanted or inappropriate, how does that impact your current desire or willingness to be touched now?

5) What are your needs for touch? Can you initiate more positive touch? Can animals provide some of the touch that you need? How can you add more pleasant touch in your life? Find more ways to interact with animals that enjoy your touch.

Re-Minder: I am willing to be touched.

Principle #8
THE HEALING POWER OF PLAY

Practice Lessons and Training Tips for the Power of Play:

1) Imagine giving yourself more permission to play. What would that look like? Take one step in that direction and actually play.

2) Spend some time daydreaming about play. What would your life be like with more play in it? Who else could be part of this play?

3) Watch animals playing. If this is not possible in real life, watch some animals playing on social media. Find your favorites and keep a "play file" so that whenever you see them, you giggle.

4) If you share your life with an animal or have a friend who does, spend some time discovering what playtime is like for them. Don't assume that you know—not all dogs fetch, for example. This is a process of discovery. Find out what is fun for the animal.

5) Make a new decision to include more play in your life. It can be a tiny step or a big step. But take action, even if that action is just researching HOW you could play in this way.

Re-Minder: I allow myself to play.

Principle #9
THE POWER OF FOCUS

Practice Lessons and Training Tips for Focus to Master Your Emotions:

1) Practice one or more of the focus exercises mentioned in this chapter. If focus is very challenging for you, be patient, and don't give up. Aim for seven seconds of absolute focus on something good. Do this "short-burst" focus exercise until it feels easy, then increase with the goal being to get to thirty seconds to a minute. Very gradually increase until you feel a certain mastery with the shorter time intervals. Remember, focus is like a muscle. The more you use it, the stronger it gets.

2) Alternate between short-focus bursts, turning your head to the left (and really looking) and turning your head to the right (and really looking). Stretch, yawn, or move your body in between the focus bursts. You are looking to achieve stillness in the focus portion, followed by movement and head turns in between the focus bursts. The head turns are significant for switching focus, which helps reset the brain.

3) Focus your imagination. In your mind, build a sanctuary for peace. This will be your personal Perfect Place of Peace. This can be a real place you have been to or an entirely fictitious place. Either way, imagine every detail—what you see, hear, feel, smell, and touch. Is there a physical structure, like a sacred building, or is it all in nature? Are there animals in your Place of Peace? Other beings or spirit guides? Water? Trees and flowers? Mountains? Valleys? Vistas? This place can become your sanctuary, your personal cathedral, a mental workshop where you go in your mind to resolve issues. Continue to build and refine this mental environment until it is perfect, comfortable, and peaceful. It can change as you see fit.

Spend some time in your Place of Peace each day, perhaps before you fall asleep or as you are just awakening. The more time you spend there, the more solid this becomes as a mental, emotional, and spiritual resource. It is a great tool for those who wish to do animal communication work.

4) When you are doing routine, "mindless" activities that don't require a lot of conscious direction, such as doing the dishes, taking a shower, brushing your teeth, and vacuuming, instead of just allowing your mind to chatter away, direct your focus to something good. Dedicate these opportunities to be focused on goodness, such as "I love my dog." Keep it simple, but keep your senses focused on something good. This is not an activity you would do while driving, but rather in your home environment.

5) Spend just a few minutes focusing on a positive future outcome, something you want for yourself. Imagine it as real and vividly as possible. Then notice how you feel after just a few minutes of focusing on your positive future.

Re-Minder: What you focus on is what you get more of.

Principle #10
ANIMALS HAVE OPINIONS

Exercises and Training Tips for Working with Animals' Opinions:

1) Spend the day (week, month, year, life) accepting the fact that animals have opinions. For this first step, you don't have to *do anything* more than just recognize this as an operating principle. Notice what that acceptance does to open your own awareness and consciousness.

2) Listen and observe at least one opinion of an animal who shares your life, something you hadn't noticed before.

3) How does awareness of this opinion change the dynamic between you two? What is one small thing you could do differently to accommodate this opinion, at least some of the time?

4) Consider how willing you are to become aware of your animal's opinion.

5) Cultivate a practice of becoming aware of your animal's opinions, at least sometimes. Nobody is perfect in their willingness to listen or adjust. But every now and then, let your animal lead you.

Re-Minder: Animals have opinions.

Principle #11
CANINES TEACH COMPASSION

Practice Lessons and Training Tips for Cultivating Compassion and Empathy:

1) You are an empathetic person, or you wouldn't be reading this book. If you would like to increase your personal empathy skills, begin with nonjudgmental observation of people and animals. As discussed, neutral observation means that you seek to understand an animal's behavior without judgment or assume you know what the animal is feeling. Just watch without making assumptions, such as *he's happy now* or *she's mad now*. Just observe behavior without labeling the emotion. Spend a few minutes each day in neutral observation of an animal. Focus on the fine details of body movement or stillness, the direction of movement (toward or away from other animals or people), eye contact, or avoidance behaviors. Is the animal seeking closeness or distance? Notice whether their body position is soft and fluid or staccato or still.

2) Spend a few minutes or more each day observing people. Focus on specific details of nonverbal communication and body language. Really pay attention to the nuances of facial expression, posture, tone of voice, and eye movement.

   When observing animals, focus on the fine details of the tail and ear position, movement or stillness, the direction of movement (such as toward and away from other people or animals), eye contact, or avoidance behaviors. Is the animal seeking closeness or distance? Notice whether body position is soft and fluid, or staccato or still.

3) Practice a deliberate act of kindness, an act of compassion to an animal or a human, or both. Make sure you consider what THEY would consider an act of kindness, not just what you would like to do.

4) Practice the Golden Rule (do unto others as you wish them to treat you) with a stranger as well as with someone you know, such as a kind action. It could be as simple as holding open a door, letting someone go ahead, a smile, or kind word. Next, also do this invisibly, an act of energy, or positive *intentional thought*. In other words, send a human or animal being a silent *good thought*. Notice if there is any reaction from the receiver.

5) Mentally review your day before you go to sleep and recount your moment(s) of empathy, either giving *or receiving* compassion.

Re-Minder: Compassionate connections
make the world a better place.

Principle #12
RELATIONSHIP TRAINING METHODS

Practice Lessons and Training Tips on Relationship Training:

1) Do you have a specific training goal with your animal? Is it something you can teach by yourself? Or do you need to find a specialist trainer? Research methods for achieving this goal.

2) If you have specific training goals such as "I want my dog to be a therapy dog" or "a service dog," make sure these are realistic goals for this specific dog. The HAC has an online course – *Could My Dog Be a Great Therapy Dog*. Or you could hire a professional for a consultation and objective assessment, not someone who is trying to sell you a package of lessons and makes a lot of claims for transformation. Instead, hire an expert for *an evaluation*, especially if you are not sure if your goals match your dog's Soul Purpose.

3) Set a specific training goal and work towards it. At home, spend just a few minutes (five to ten minutes) each day, once or twice a day. Keep these sessions short, fun, and positive. If you need help, work with someone you respect—someone who respects you and your animal.

4) In what way do YOU need training? Do you need more discipline, focus, consistency, positivity, patience, and persistence? More gentleness? More clarity? More precision of your verbal or hand signals? More clear intentions? A more consistent tone of voice or speed of rewards?

5) Choose one small thing that you would like to train YOURSELF to do. Notice what issues come up as you decide to change or train yourself into new behavior. What motivates you to stay with the program? What causes resistance? What

habits are you willing to give up to make room for the new behavior? This is not an exercise in self-judgment. This is about understanding your own motivation strategy. Do you move TOWARD what you want or AWAY from what you don't want? Understanding the most effective ways to train yourself will make you a better trainer with another being.

Re-Minder: My relationship with (your animal's name) is precious.

Principle #13
HONORING ANIMAL WISDOM

Practice Lessons and Training Tips for Honoring Animal Wisdom:

1) Spend some time in the presence of wild birds or pigeons. You can offer food treats or be as still as you can and just observe. Let go of any expectations. Simply receive sensations and perceptions from them.

2) Treat every encounter with an animal as a sacred encounter. Even passing a dog you don't know on the street, silently honor their true beingness. How does it change YOU to see them in this sacred light?

3) If there is an animal you share your life with, spend some time in complete silence and stillness with this animal. See if you can feel their *Divine Nature*.

4) Before you go to sleep, say a prayer for individual animals. And for all the animals.

5) If you wake up in the middle of the night and can't go back to sleep, apologize to all the animals throughout history on the part of humanity for our lack of understanding and compassion. Even though it is not your fault, send the apology into the ethers.

Re-Minder: I connect with my Animal Wisdom.

Part Two:
WHAT ANIMALS CAN TEACH US
ABOUT BEING A HAPPIER HUMAN

Principle #14
OPENING THE DOOR TO ANIMAL COMMUNICATION

Practice Lessons and Training Tips for Opening the Door to Animal Communication:

1) The first step is to have an open mind about animal communication. It is okay to have doubts that you can do it—or do it well. But it is essential to at least be open to the possibility of animal communication. Just consider the possibility that communication is possible; consider the number of stories about people who are successfully communicating with animals. Also consider the possibility that with pure intention, patience, and practice, you can learn to do it too.

2) Begin practicing by talking out loud to your animals, just as if they were people. Do not worry about whether or not they can understand. Just "act as if they can." Notice how they respond to your words, your intentions, mood, energy, your body language. How do they seem to react to your conversation?

3) Next, begin communicating silently with the animals with whom you share your life. Do not worry about whether it is working or not; just trust and send a message. Be as truthful, simple, and clear as you can be. You can talk about your feelings or even make requests for new behavior. If this is a new thing between you and your animal, it may take a little while for the animal to realize you are talking to them. Just notice if anything changes between you and the animal.

4) Read one or more books written about animal communication. Every book is different, so you may have to find an author you trust. One of my favorites is *How Animals Talk* by William Long. This book was written over a hundred years ago, so the language is a little archaic, but it is profound and inspiring. Ruppert Sheldrake called this book "the classic book on animal telepathy."

5) Sometimes it is harder to practice with your own animals when you are first learning because you know them so well, and you might think you are making up the answers. It can be a good way to start by practicing with a friend's animals. You can both ask some simple questions, write down your answers (write everything you hear, don't edit!), and then have your friend give you feedback on the accuracy of the answers you receive. Make sure you choose someone who is open to this type of exploration. Otherwise, their negative attitude could interfere with clear communication.

Have fun with this! Be gentle, be patient, be persistent. Take a course in Animal Communication if you learn well in that way.

Re-Minder: I can communicate with animals.

Principle #15
ENTERING THE LANGUAGE OF SILENCE

Practice Exercises and Training Tips for Entering the Language of Silence:

1) Take some time to set a clear intention about entering the language of silence. What do you want to do, and why do you want to do it? The clarity of your intention is the rocket fuel that will launch you into a realm of richness. If you are not clear yet about what you want and why you want it, you may confuse the animals you are working with. They can feel a mixed message and may choose not to engage.

2) You will need a practice that will help you become peaceful, still, calm, and mentally quiet. Choose a method that will allow you to get peaceful because animals prefer to talk to people who are peaceful. If you are too busy mentally, animals may not converse with you until you are calmer. Meditation, walking in nature, and simply being still, are practices that will help you to experience peacefulness.

3) Develop a discipline of silence. Psalm 46:10 reminds us: "Be still and know that I am God." Silence and stillness are powerful tools for well-being for you and for animals. Animals are much better at silence than we are, but we can learn. This doesn't mean you must maintain silence for hours, months, or years. Even just a few minutes of deep and profound silence each day will lower your stress levels, open your Animality Senses, and help you access your intuitive knowing. Spend some time with animals in silence, without petting, just being together. Petting is a beautiful thing, but for this exercise, you are just practicing being still together. Don't worry if the animal is moving. You

are developing your own capacity for stillness. At first, you may only be able to be mentally still for a few seconds. Take breaks. Then go back to stillness. Aim to work toward a period of ten to twenty minutes of stillness practice each day.

4) Whenever possible, spend time in nature. Even if you live in a city, find a tree. Feed some pigeons. Whatever you can manage. But make spending some time outdoors a priority. As you walk, hike, or sit outside, think of opening your inner senses and allowing yourself to receive messages from nature. Don't worry about whether you are making it up. With practice and time, you will be able to tell the difference between thoughts that you are generating that *come from* your mind and impressions you receive that *come into* your awareness.

5) Practice listening to the sound of silence. Ask Silence to speak to you. Then listen. The Universe wants to communicate with you. Animals will recognize this sublime channel of communication.

Re-Minder: In silence, all answers can be heard.

Principle #16
ANIMALS: OUR PARTNERS IN HEALING

Practice Exercises and Training Tips for Animals as Partners in Healing:

1) If you have an animal in your life that you are considering for therapy work, ask the animal how they feel about doing this kind of work. If you are new at communicating with animals, ask for a sign that shows you this activity is a match for your animal's purpose.

2) Find a situation that is a close match to the kind of work you are interested in and do a "test visit." In other words, if you want to work with children, bring your animal to a situation where you can observe them interacting with children or bring the children to the animal. Observe how the animal responds to your target participants. You might want to test out different people or in different circumstances and observe how the animal responds. Does the animal seem to enjoy the experience or find it stressful?

3) The HAC has on online class called *Could My Dog Be a Great Therapy Dog* that helps you evaluate if your animal is right for therapy work. Research the organizations in your area that are doing this work and learn their testing criteria. If possible, seek an independent evaluator (not someone who is trying to sell you lessons) to evaluate whether your dog or animal is a good candidate for therapy work.

4) If there is an organization of therapy dogs nearby, ask to be an observer and go on a visit in the context of the work you would like to do. Observe two or three handlers, as everyone and every animal brings something unique to the experience.

5) Look for a partner who wants to train in therapy dog work and join up to support each other through the process of training and certification and finally to visits.

Re-Minder: Dogs are healers.

Principle #17
HEALING FROM TRAUMA

Practice Lessons and Training Tips on Healing from Trauma:

1) Remember that every being heals in their own time. Respecting the timing of other beings is an excellent way to support them. They may not transform in the timing that you would like, but know that they can and will change, no matter how they appear today.

2) Recall a circumstance in your life that you consider an adverse experience. Look at that circumstance with this perspective: All you have experienced in life has led you to this moment of healing, so it was purposeful. Then practice being patient with another being who may be experiencing the effects of adversity.

3) If you don't have much or any experience with a pit bull, make friends with one, either a neighbor's or a friend's. Spend some time with a pitty at a shelter or foster one. If you love a pitty, they will teach you everything you need to know about healing and resilience.

4) Consider that adversity is one path to resilience. We can all learn from Cherry, the pit bull whose story I told in this principle, who was forced to be a "bait dog" in a dogfighting ring. It is inspiring how Cherry has moved beyond his past. Forgiveness opened his future to great love from a family, and he is able to receive and give so much more. Watch his story in the documentary *The Champions*.

5) Read *The Act Resilient Method* for tips on ways humans can heal from trauma. Break the trigger-response cycle in your own life. When faced with situations that could cause suffering, choose to move *towards* joy. (Yes, you can do this!)

Re-Minder: My past does not dictate my future.

Principle #18
REBUILDING A SENSE OF SAFETY

Practice Lessons and Training Tips to Develop a Sense of Safety:

1) Consider that one aspect of resilience in people and animals is the degree to which their Safety Tanks feel full. What is it that causes you and your animals to have a reduced sense of safety? What can you do to increase the sense of safety for both of you?

2) Notice each day where you are on your Safety Tank gauge. Notice when you wake up—check your Safety Tank level.

Notice as you go about your day and interact with people. What causes you to feel more or less safe?

3) Take a moment each day to *breathe in safety*. You are safe at this moment, no matter what stresses are playing out in your life. Step outside of the stress, at least a few minutes each day, to refill your Safety Tank. Do this in the presence of the animals who share your life and include them mentally in your process. Notice how just a few minutes of deliberate acceptance and gratitude for your core safety can raise your spirits and help you see possible solutions more clearly.

4) Make sure your own Safety Tank is as full as it can be before you try to help others. If you are drowning, it is hard to help others. Put your mask on first, as the saying goes. Make cultivating a sense of safety part of your daily mental hygiene routine.

5) The Sense of Safety gets stronger with use. It will become more reliable the more you make a habit of it. That way, when a crisis comes, you will have more inner resources to weather the storm. Make a firm commitment to yourself to begin feeding your Safety Tank.

Re-Minder: I am safe.

Principle #19
TRUST: THE FOUNDATION OF HEALING

Practice Lessons and Training Tips on Trust – The Foundation of Healing:

1) Choose a time frame that works for you (one hour, one day, one week) and put your focus on the mantra "All events are neutral." Be aware that initially, *un-peace* may emerge (such as disagreements and arguments with this idea). However, if you just keep repeating it, something magical and healing will begin to happen.

2) Say to an animal, "I trust you." Say it out loud and say it silently. See how it feels to think or say these words. Notice what happens for them if you truly mean it.

3) Practice Meister Eckhart's advice: loosely translated over the centuries as, "Let it Be, Let it Go…and you will be free."

4) Watch videos about the Trust Technique on their website.

5) Say to a person, "I trust you." This exercise is not about whether they are trustworthy. This exercise is about two things: First, notice how you feel when you say those words. And second, notice how it changes something in the relationship. Maybe they will decide to live up to your trust. If not, then you have given them a chance, and it is time to trust the evidence before you.

Re-Minder: I trust what is.

Principle #20
CONNECTIVITY AND BELONGING

Practice Lessons and Training Tips for Connectivity and Belonging:

1) Considering your answers to the journal reflections for this principle, what is one step you could take to improve social connections in your life?

2) If there was a "perfect group" for you to belong to, what would it be called? Who would be in it? What would this group do?

3) Research and see if a group that is somewhat similar to your perfect group exists.

4) Try joining an existing group. If you don't like it, try another one. Challenge yourself to get out of your un-belonging comfort zone. If your "perfect group" does not exist, could you start one? Or on social media?

5) Do your animals get their needs met for social connection with other people or animals? What could you do to explore more variety and experience for them?

Re-Minder: I belong.

Principle #21
TOWARDS & AWAY

Exercises and Training Tips for *Towards & Away*:

1) Practice paying attention to your sense of desire to move *Towards or Away*. Experiment with making minor choices and seeing how each choice feels as you move *Towards* as well as *Away*. Which feels better in each moment?

2) As you gain more confidence in your *Towards & Away* impulses, you begin to open access to your intuition. In time you will trust yourself with issues that you don't already know the answer to because your senses will tune you either toward or away from a person or situation. Continue working with minor issues until you feel absolute trust in the process of connecting with your inner wisdom about moving *Towards & Away*.

3) Pick a day (or week, month, year) during which you will put your full attention to your *Towards & Away* desires. Even if you can't always act on these intuitions, just recognizing that they are there will help make you feel less conflicted. You have a right to feel what you feel. How you choose to act is another matter.

4) Observe *Towards & Away* behaviors in wild animals, at a zoo, at a dog park, with pigeons, or whoever you can observe. Notice how they read each other's signals and how clear they are. No apology needed, no hurt feelings. They are just being truthful.

5) Test your *Towards & Away* feelings about something big in your life as an exercise in imagination. You do not have to take action if you don't feel ready to do so, but just experiment with a wild dream idea you would like to explore. Notice how your body feels as you allow this *flight of fancy*. Does it

scare you? Do you move away in your mind? Or do you feel a surge of energy as you consider moving toward it? Remember, you don't have to take any action you are not ready to take. But this exercise will set something in motion as you allow yourself the freedom—at least in your mind—to explore a new adventure.

Welcome to the new adventure of getting in sync with your *Towards & Away Guidance System*!

Re-Minder: I choose to move toward—
and I choose to move away.

Principle #22
SHAKING WISDOM

Practice Exercises and Training Tips for Shaking:

1) Try shaking for yourself. Move slow. Move fast. Move any way that feels good to you. Let your body lead you.

2) Follow some of the suggestions in the Journal section for how to get started. There is no wrong way to shake. If it feels good, it is good!

3) Be gentle at first. This is like learning a new language, a moving language without words, but it will take you to places you haven't been before. Consider it an adventure. It is a process of seeing what unfolds.

4) Let go of any ideas you have—any preconceptions, good or bad. Let go of any expectations or assumptions you might have about how it should look or feel. Allow yourself to have this pleasurable experience.

5) Welcome to the freedom and ecstasy of shaking! You are joining an ancient club. Invite your Power Animals to join you and guide you on your healing, shaking journey.

Re-Minder: I can shake it off.

Principle #23
THE ORDER OF THE SENSES

Practice and Training Tips for The Order of the Senses:

1) If you share your life with an animal, let some part of your daily walk be in honor of the Art of Sniffing.

2) Let the animal lead you for some walks or a portion of the walks. Letting them choose the direction, pace, etc., and follow their choice. Letting them lead will allow your senses and the animal's to come into balance.

3) If the animal stops to sniff, honor that by giving a loose leash and staying still while you focus on your breathing and your senses. This is your moment too. Use a favorite sense to reorient and reset. What do you see, hear, smell, or what touch is compelling, such as a leaf or tree bark? This deliberate

Art of Slowing Down develops a more flexible relationship to time (Principle #24).

4) Honor the Wisdom of the Sniff. Recognize that this is your dog being true to their dog nature. Release your habit of impatience or thinking there is someplace more important to be or that you are "losing time."

5) Spend a few moments each day really focusing on one sense at a time to tune up your vagus nerve.

Re-Minder: My senses will lead me where I need to be.

Principle #24
CHANGING YOUR RELATIONSHIP TO TIME

Practice Tips and Training Tools for Changing Your Relationship to Time:

1) Identify your "default" time style, that which you naturally gravitate to most of the time.

2) While you want to celebrate your strong suit, you also want to develop the ability to switch to the opposite style for a more balanced life. Choose a day or a few times during a day when you deliberately switch to your weaker style.

3) Observe how animals are in *Now Time*—or not. Just be a student in their presence. What can they teach you about being more deeply in *Now Time*?

4) Spend time in nature or with animals completely in *Now Time*. Even twenty minutes can rejuvenate you. More is good, but any time spent in *Now Time* recharges the system.

5) When you are in nature or with an animal, use your senses to become aware of whatever is happening in the moment to bring you more fully into *Now Time*. It is okay if linear thoughts emerge and try to steal your attention. Just gently notice them and get back to the experience of being in the present. Then open your "*Now-Time Perception*" and listen, see, or feel. Let go of the *Linear Time* idea that anything specific is supposed to happen. Just allow what IS to be experienced.

Re-Minder: I have all the time in the world.

Principle #25
RHYTHM, TIMING, AND DISTANCE

Practice Lessons and Training Tips for Rhythm, Timing, and Distance:

1) Find some musical rhythms that you like or drum songs. Let your whole body "hear" them and see how that makes you feel, how it makes you move or shake.

2) Pick one area where you would like a more disciplined cycle— perhaps with sleep, eating, walking, being creative, engaging (or not) with others, solo time, contemplation time—and

create a schedule that makes you feel empowered when you think about doing it. Then stick to it for thirty days. You can adjust it if needed and then stick to the adjustment.

3) Consider how your "timing" is going in your life and how that affects your sense of personal rhythm. Are you rushed too often? Can you find a slower rhythm? How could you benefit by balancing speed with some slowness? For example, taking five minutes at dusk or dawn to look at the sky and just watch the clouds? Watching clouds, moving or stationary ones, is a great way to re-tune yourself to a natural rhythm. What could you do to add more variety to your timing, more rhythms that follow your natural cycle?

4) Spend a day (or longer) really paying attention to how you feel when strangers move into and out of *your space* while you go about your daily activities. How do you feel standing in line at the bank, post office, or grocery store? How do you feel when people follow your car too closely?

5) Spend some time with animals, gently observing how they manage space. How do they react to others coming close? Do they signal each other when they need more space? Do they move Toward or Away? Feel in your body what they are feeling as you watch them navigate spacial relationships. This will help open your animal communication skills.

Re-Minder: I have perfect timing.

Principle #26
THE SECRET OF BALANCE

Practice Lessons and Training Tips on Balance:

1) What is your first priority as you look at the need for more balance in your life? What is one baby step you could take to bring more of the pleasure of balance to your life?

2) What about for your animals? How could more balance serve them? What baby step can you take toward that?

3) Can you imagine a life with more balance? What would that look like? What is one small step you could take to bring more balance into your life? Where can you implement the Goldilocks Principle into your daily life?

4) What is a larger step you might be willing to make? What new habits do you need to cultivate?

5) If some of these changes scare you, can you be as gentle with yourself as you would be with a shy dog?

Re-Minder: I can balance my world.

Principle #27
FREEDOM OF CHOICE

Practice Lessons and Training Tips for Freedom of Choice:

1) Decide to take one small step toward greater personal freedom in your own life.

2) Decide to experiment with creating some more freedom of natural expression for your animals.

3) Spend time or volunteer at a local rescue or shelter. Notice how your expanded awareness of freedom can help you provide enrichment to the animals you work with.

4) Consider a field trip to a zoo or a visionary rescue that you admire. Observe, learn, and if you are an HAC student, practice the distance healing and nonphysical touch techniques you are learning.

5) Make a commitment to supporting freedom in your own life and in the lives of other beings. It could be through donating, volunteering, or lobbying elected officials. The Humane Society Legislative Fund rates individual lawmakers on their records of animal welfare issues. Learn who supports animal well-being and vote for them! Whatever action you choose to take will support the freedom and respect for all life.

Re-Minder: I am free.

Part Three:
THE SPIRITUAL CONNECTION –
HOW HUMANS CAN BE OF SERVICE TO ANIMALS

Principle #28
THE SOUL OF AN ANIMAL

Practice Lessons and Training Tips on the Soul of an Animal:

1) If you have had an animal in your life who has passed, would you consider connecting with that Soul? Even if you don't feel you know how, just set your intention to connect and see what happens. It may not happen immediately. Be alert for signs from a variety of sources.

2) Have a conversation with an animal that is currently in your life. Say to this animal, "Do you have a Soul? Can you give me a sign to help me understand?" Ask to receive guidance about the presence of Animal Souls. Remember that this guidance can come in a variety of ways and times, and the answer may not come immediately. Be on the lookout for a sign from your Animal's Soul. Ask the Soul for information about something that you would like more clarity about.

3) Consider the possibility that your Soul has been present with you your whole life—and possibly longer. How does that make you feel?

4) Have you ever felt that your Soul and your animal's Soul are connected? How does that feel? Would you like to have more experiences with this connection?

5) If you work with rescue or shelter animals, when you are with them, just think about unifying or connecting with their Soul. Ask their Soul to come in more fully and for the animal to

feel this supportive presence. Ask the Soul to protect them and help them to feel worthy and safe.

Re-Minder: All beings have a Soul.
I connect with the Soul of (your animal).

Principle #29
ANIMALS ON PURPOSE

Practice Lessons and Training Tips for Animals on Purpose:

1) Spend some time in nature and with animals. Get as calm as you can and ask them to show you something about your True Purpose. They may or may not "speak" to you at the moment you ask, but your answers may come in dreams or in synchronistic encounters you weren't expecting that shed light on your unique purpose.

2) If you are comfortable and confident with animal communication, talk to your animals about their sense of purpose. And ask about yours.

3) If you are struggling with your sense of purpose, be gentle and light about this process. You can play a game like "My purpose is NOT..." and add all the things you know it isn't. This will help you begin to find the ballpark, such as "I want to improve the lives of animals," or "I want to learn to cross the communication bridge between people and animals," and so on.

4) If you have a sense of what your purpose might be, decide to take one small step towards that. Get on your Purpose Train!

5) Trust that your purpose will be known when you are ready. Relax. Listen. Spend more time with animals and nature. Listen to the Language of Silence.

Re-Minder: I am my purpose.

Principle #30
THE POWER OF NAMES

Practice Lessons and Training Tips for the Power of Names:

1) Look through baby names online or in a baby name book. Find out the meaning of the names. Make a list of the names you love. Feel into the quality or *Mana* of each name you feel drawn to.

2) If you rescued an animal with an inherited name, would you like to "listen in" for a better name? Don't rush. Take your time to hear; let it come in dreams or through moments of synchronicity. You may be *coincidentally* introduced to a person who has the right name for your animal, or you come across a name in a book or on television. Ask your animal guides to send you the perfect name or give you a sign.

3) Imagine what your life would have been like if you were given your "Ideal Name."

4) Is it a leap for you to consider that names actually carry energy or meaning? Learn about the numerology or meaning of the sacred vibrations of your name.

5) Imagine a name that best carries or expresses your Mana. How do you feel when you say that name aloud or in your mind?

Re-Minder: I am who I am.

Principle #31
POWER ANIMALS AND SPIRIT GUIDE WISDOM

Practice Lessons and Training Tips on Connecting to Your Power Animal:

1) Spend some time getting clear about your goals, your intentions. Why do you want to connect with your power animal?

2) Get peaceful in your mind by going to your imaginary Place of Peace. Or if you can, go to a wonderful, peaceful place in nature. Express gratitude for your power animal, who may have been watching over you your whole life.

3) Ask your power animal to reveal himself or herself to you more fully in your mind. Spend some time in silence in the presence of this animal in your mind.

4) Ask the animal to reveal himself/herself in unexpected ways. Begin to notice these symbolic or subtle messages. For example, if your power animal is a tiger, begin to notice images

of tigers in places you weren't expecting. Consider this an affirmation or confirmation of connection. Acknowledge and thank the animal for giving you a sign. Be patient; this will happen over time. But whenever it happens, thank the animal for directing your awareness to its image.

5) In your quiet meditations, when you go to your Place of Peace, set your intention to meet the animal. When he or she appears, begin to talk. Ask simple questions. You may or may not hear the answer immediately. The answer may come as you are in the shower, exercising, or dreaming. Always thank the animal for communicating with you, as this gratitude strengthens the connection. Enjoy! This is sacred work.

Re-Minder: I am connected to my Animal Guides.

Principle #32
ETHICAL CONNECTIONS

Practice Lessons and Training Tips for Ethical Connections:

1) Do a ceremony (whatever that means to you) where you apologize to the animals. Not for what you have done, but for what humanity has done. In some of the HAC workshops, we do a Hawaiian *Ho'Oponopono* meditation where we apologize to all animals throughout all time. We ask for their forgiveness, and we tell them how much we love them.

This is a very powerful experience that you can do yourself or with like-minded friends.

2) Are there any animals in your past that you wish you had treated better or more ethically? Do a ceremony for each one, even if they are no longer living.

3) Research the organizations that are doing good work in the areas that you are most passionate about.

4) Develop a plan of action for how you can get involved in the issues of animal welfare, whether at a small scale, at one rescue, or with a larger organization.

5) While it never works to preach to people, when you see opportunities to educate people about animal issues, please gently do so. And make sure your elected officials know how you feel about these issues. As mentioned in Principle #32, the U.S. Humane Society Legislative Fund keeps a running total of how elected officials are doing relative to animal welfare legislation. Vote for those whose records show they care.

Re-Minder: It is time for humanity to have a more ethical relationship with animals. And humanity starts with me.

Principle #33
DIVINE CONNECTIONS

Practice Lessons and Training Tips for Divine Connections with Animals:

1) Focus on your heart. Breathe in the feeling of good. As you exhale, let this good energy expand. Allow for expanding good to unfold in your life.

2) Treat any encounter with an animal as an opportunity to recognize their divinity and yours.

3) Ask an animal to share their opinion on something you want to know about. Listen. And know that the answer may or may not come at the moment you ask.

4) Practice with insects or animals you don't feel as connected to. In their presence, send them love and see what happens.

5) The next time you are confused about an animal's behavior, ask yourself, "How can I make this situation more comfortable or safe for you?"

Re-Minder: I have a divine connection with all animals.

Thank you for practicing with the Human-Animal Connection and for your dedication to improving the quality of life for all animals. Make sure to join our free newsletter and let us know how you are doing with your connections with animals.

Visit TheHumanAnimalConnection.org

ACKNOWLEDGMENTS

Mahalo and an endless thank you to all the animals I have had the privilege of knowing. You have taught me so much by your presence, your willingness to share heart-space. Eternal gratitude to the beings who shared my life, Seymour, Madeline, Wolfie, Sushi, Seraphina, Oscar, and Sophia. And to all the animals in rescues, shelters, and barns and ranches I have worked with—especially the Hawaiian Humane Society, the Humane Society of Southern Arizona, Wild Horse Haven Rescue, Sol Dog Lodge, Equinimity Tucson, and Pima Animal Care Center. And to all the staff and volunteers who give endlessly to make the lives of animals just a little better. To Alliance of Therapy Dogs and everyone who volunteers with a therapy animal to bring comfort and smiles to strangers. To everyone who has adopted an animal and given them a loving home. And thank you to the clients who have trusted me with the tender lives of animals who share their world. To James French and Shelley Slingo of the Trust Technique, which has brought so much peace to so many animals and informs my practice every day.

A deep, deep special thanks and gratitude to my cousins, Neena Lurvey and veterinarian Joel Locketz, for the contribution of the initial investment to launch the Human-Animal Connection from the Jeffrey David Locketz Trust Fund.

To our initial board members of The Human-Animal Connection who have helped shape and guide our journey: Tom Crowley, Caleb

Files, Nathan Bush, and Dr. Trisha Billard. A special thanks to Caleb, whose contributions to every aspect of the HAC are beyond measure. And to psychologist Chantal Boshuizen who gathered and analyzed our stress data in Canines Teach Compassion class, and to Andy Mahon for videotaping and bringing his sweet therapy dog, Zora.

And of course, a book doesn't come to life without a lot of expert help from many experts - developmental editor Bonnie McDermid, publishing coach Susie Schaefer, business coach Shelby Long-Hammond, illustrator Elisabeth Geel, layout and publishing support Chris O'Byrne, and Everett O'Keefe for introducing me to Bonnie. To Kristin Overn, Executive Director of The PAGE International Screenwriting Awards for offering her opinion so many times. To all my students in The Human-Animal Connection, high school students in Canines Teach Compassion, and the 4,000 service members and veterans of all branches of the U.S. military who transformed before my eyes.

And thank you from the top of my heart to anyone who has donated to the Human-Animal Connection or given me a moment of support and good words of encouragement. And, most of all, thank you to the entire patient Animal Kingdom—we humans have so much to learn.

Photo Credit

(page 172 Ch 13) Photo: Ben Allwein
(page 401 Ch 28) Photo: ThatGirlProductions.com

ABOUT GENIE JOSEPH, Ph.D

Genie Joseph, Ph.D., is an Emmy Award-winning filmmaker, creator of The Act Resilient Method, and author of a book by the same name. Her Act Resilient program facilitates PTSD recovery for U.S. military service members through guided interactions with therapy animals, improvisational comedy, and expressive arts. Act Resilient has been successfully utilized by over 4,000 service members and their families. In recognition of this life-changing work, President Barack Obama honored Ms. Joseph with the President's Volunteer Service Award. In addition, her Act Resilient team at Tripler Army Medical Center received a National Award for Workplace Resilience from the American Psychological Association.

As the founder and Executive Director of The Human-Animal Connection (HAC), a nonprofit organization, Ms. Joseph serves the greater community through the HAC's dedication to creating joy, health, and healing through profoundly enhanced connections between people and animals. The HAC staff conducts therapy dog and resilience training for high school students, healthcare providers, and the general public. Ms. Joseph is an innovative dog trainer and a Certified Trust Technique Practitioner who works with scared and traumatized shelter animals to help them get adopted, and train those whose purpose is to become therapy dogs. The HAC provides free live and online classes for veterans and active-duty military to train their dogs to become Morale Dogs for their unit. Ms. Joseph also volunteers her time at animal shelters and shares her life with Sophia, her rescue therapy dog, who brings smiles and healing to many humans.

Thank you, thank you, thank you... to all the animals who have graced me with their presence. They have taught me everything I present to you.

Sign up for our free newsletter.

We have over 100 blog articles, videos, and offer live,
and online training classes on a variety of subjects related to
The Human-Animal Connection.

We are a 501c3 nonprofit and appreciate donations
of any amount to help us continue our work.

Please visit our website

TheHumanAnimalConnection.org